EXPLORING SCIENCE

INTERNATIONAL 11-14

BIOLOGY

Mark Levesley, Sue Kearsey

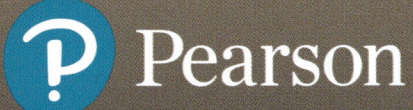

CONTENTS

	How to use this book	4

7A Cells, tissues, organs and systems

7Aa	Doctors past and present	5
7Aa	Life processes	6
7Ab	Organs	8
7Ab	Medical doctors (STEM)	10
7Ac	Tissues	12
7Ac	Microscopes (WS)	14
7Ad	Cells	16
7Ae	Organ systems	18
7Ae	Transplants	20

7B Sexual reproduction in animals

7Ba	Escaped zoo animals	21
7Ba	The scientific method (WS)	22
7Ba	Animal sexual reproduction	24
7Bb	Reproductive organs	26
7Bc	Becoming pregnant	28
7Bd	Gestation and birth	30
7Bd	Endangered species (STEM)	32
7Be	Growing up	34
7Be	The work of zoos	36

7C Muscles and bones

7Ca	Fitness	37
7Ca	Muscles and breathing	38
7Cb	Muscles and blood	40
7Cb	Scientific questions (WS)	42
7Cc	The skeleton	44
7Cd	Muscles and moving	46
7Cd	Artificial limbs (STEM)	48
7Ce	Drugs	50
7Ce	Drugs and sport	52

7D Ecosystems

7Da	Exploring the world	53
7Da	Variation	54
7Da	Charts and graphs (WS)	56
7Db	Adaptations	58
7Dc	Effects of the environment	60
7Dd	Effects on the environment	62
7Dd	Greener cities (STEM)	64
7De	Transfers in food chains	66
7De	Nomads	68

8A Food and nutrition

8Aa	Food and advertising	69
8Aa	Nutrients	70
8Ab	Uses of nutrients	72
8Ac	Balanced diets	74
8Ac	Making new foods (STEM)	76
8Ad	Digestion	78
8Ae	Surface area (WS)	80
8Ae	Absorption	82
8Ae	Packaging and the law	84

8B Plants and their reproduction

8Ba	Useful plants	85
8Ba	Classification and biodiversity	86
8Ba	Accuracy and estimates (WS)	88
8Bb	Types of reproduction	90
8Bc	Pollination	92
8Bc	Air quality (STEM)	94
8Bd	Fertilisation and dispersal	96
8Be	Germination and growth	98
8Be	Animals using plants	100

8C Breathing and respiration

8Ca	Water sports and breathing	101
8Ca	Aerobic respiration	102
8Cb	Gas exchange system	104
8Cb	Means and ranges (WS)	106
8Cc	Getting oxygen	108
8Cc	Epidemiology (STEM)	110
8Cd	Comparing gas exchange	112
8Ce	Anaerobic respiration	114
8Ce	Fitness training	116

8D Unicellular organisms

8Da	The Black Death	117
8Da	Unicellular or multicellular	118
8Da	Tackling diseases (STEM)	120
8Db	Microscopic fungi	122
8Dc	Bacteria	124
8Dc	Pie charts (WS)	126
8Dd	Protoctists	128
8De	Decomposers and carbon	130
8De	Black Death hypotheses	132

9A Genetics and evolution

9Aa	Monsters and myth	133
9Aa	Environmental variation	134
9Ab	Inherited variation	136
9Ab	Probability (WS)	138
9Ac	DNA	140
9Ac	Genetic counselling (STEM)	142
9Ad	Genes and extinction	144
9Ae	Natural selection	146
9Ae	Recreating animals	148

9B Plant growth

9Ba	On a farm	149
9Ba	Reactions in plants	150
9Bb	Plant adaptations	152
9Bc	Plant products	154
9Bd	Growing crops	156
9Bd	Protecting wild plants (STEM)	158
9Be	Farming problems	160
9Be	Bias and validity (WS)	162
9Be	Organic farming	164

9C Transition to further study

9Ca	Threat from disease	165
9Ca	Diseases	166
9Ca	Veterinary science (STEM)	168
9Cb	Control systems	170
9Cc	Treating diseases	172
9Cc	Median and quartiles (WS)	174
9Cd	Ecology	176
9Ce	In and out	178
9Ce	Combatting pandemics	180

9D STEM projects

9D	Clear writing	181
9D1	Project 1: Animal smuggling	182
9D2	Project 2: Enzyme investigation	183
9D3	Project 3: Teeth	184

Glossary	185
STEM skills	195
Index	197
Acknowledgements	199

HOW TO USE THIS BOOK

UK NC, iLS, CEE

9Aa ENVIRONMENTAL VARIATION

WHAT CAUSES ENVIRONMENTAL VARIATION?

The monster pumpkins in photo A did not get that big by chance. The plants were carefully looked after and given all the **resources** they needed, including additional light, water, warmth and mineral salts.

An organism's surroundings are its **environment**. In all environments there are **environmental factors** that can change the organism. There are **abiotic factors** or **physical environmental** factors (e.g. temperature, the amount of light). There are also **biotic factors**, which are the activities of other organisms (e.g. competition, predation, infectious disease).

A | The pumpkins in this growing competition did not break any records – the world's heaviest pumpkin had a mass of 1190 kg.

1 Suggest what abiotic factors allowed the pumpkins in photo A to grow so big.

2 a| Describe two physical environmental factors in your environment at the moment.
   b| Apart from physical factors, what other environmental factors are in your environment?

FACT
In 2008, some Japanese cherry tree seeds spent 6 months in space. When planted back on Earth the trees flowered 6 years early. Scientists are still trying to work out why.

The features of an organism are its **characteristics**. The differences between the characteristics of organisms are known as variation. **Environmental variation** is variation caused by an organism's environment.

In humans, examples of environmental variation include scars and hairstyles. Scars are made by physical environmental factors, such as fire or sharp objects. Hairstyles follow fashion, which is an environmental factor caused by other people in your environment.

3 a| Describe the environmental variation shown in photos B, C and D.
   b| Suggest what environmental factor has caused the variation in each case.

  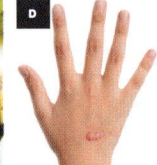

134

> You should be able to answer the question at the top of the page by the time you have finished the page.

> **Fact boxes** contain fascinating facts for you to think about.

> The **Key words** for the page are in bold. You can look up the meaning of these words in the **Glossary**, on pages 185–194.

> If you are having trouble finding information about something, use the **Index**, on pages 197–198.

> **Questions** are spread throughout the page so you can answer them as you go along.

> **I can …** boxes help you to reflect on what you have learned. Consider each statement carefully and think about how well this applies to you.

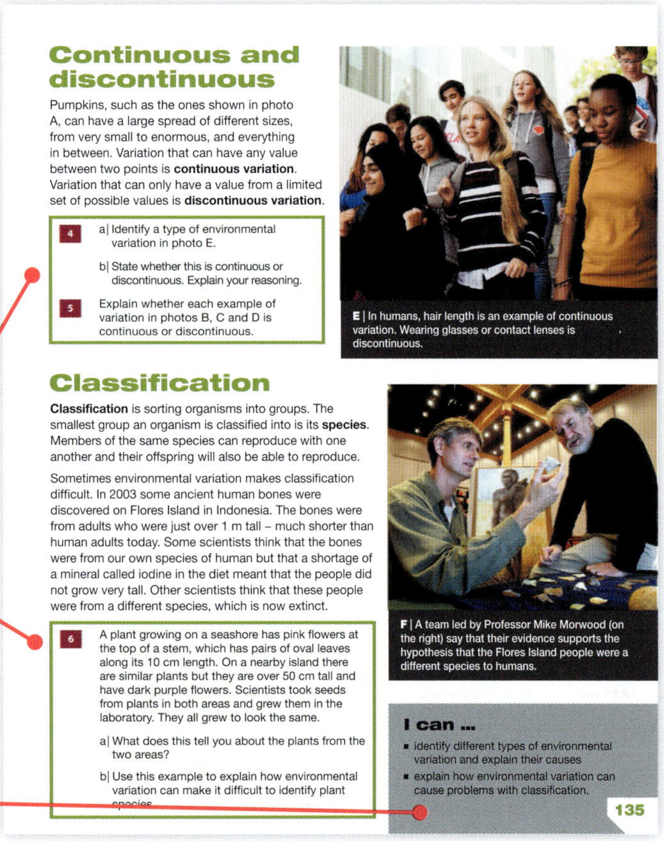

Continuous and discontinuous

Pumpkins, such as the ones shown in photo A, can have a large spread of different sizes, from very small to enormous, and everything in between. Variation that can have any value between two points is **continuous variation**. Variation that can only have a value from a limited set of possible values is **discontinuous variation**.

4 a| Identify a type of environmental variation in photo E.
   b| State whether this is continuous or discontinuous. Explain your reasoning.

5 Explain whether each example of variation in photos B, C and D is continuous or discontinuous.

E | In humans, hair length is an example of continuous variation. Wearing glasses or contact lenses is discontinuous.

Classification

Classification is sorting organisms into groups. The smallest group an organism is classified into is its **species**. Members of the same species can reproduce with one another and their offspring will also be able to reproduce.

Sometimes environmental variation makes classification difficult. In 2003 some ancient human bones were discovered on Flores Island in Indonesia. The bones were from adults who were just over 1 m tall – much shorter than human adults today. Some scientists think that the bones were from our own species of human but that a shortage of a mineral called iodine in the diet meant that the people did not grow very tall. Other scientists think that these people were from a different species, which is now extinct.

6 A plant growing on a seashore has pink flowers at the top of a stem, which has pairs of oval leaves along its 10 cm length. On a nearby island there are similar plants but they are over 50 cm tall and have dark purple flowers. Scientists took seeds from plants in both areas and grew them in the laboratory. They all grew to look the same.
   a| What does this tell you about the plants from the two areas?
   b| Use this example to explain how environmental variation can make it difficult to identify plant species.

F | A team led by Professor Mike Morwood (on the right) say that their evidence supports the hypothesis that the Flores Island people were a different species to humans.

I can …
- identify different types of environmental variation and explain their causes
- explain how environmental variation can cause problems with classification

135

4

7Aa DOCTORS PAST AND PRESENT

For thousands of years people have gone to see doctors when they feel unwell. Some of the ways in which doctors examine patients have not changed! For example, 3000 years ago, Ancient Egyptian doctors knew that if a person's **heart** was not beating as well as usual that person could be ill.

Today, doctors still find out how well your heart is beating. They may also measure temperature and do blood and urine tests to see if there are changes in your body compared to normal. These changes are called **symptoms**. Different problems cause different symptoms. The symptoms of a cold include a sore throat and runny nose.

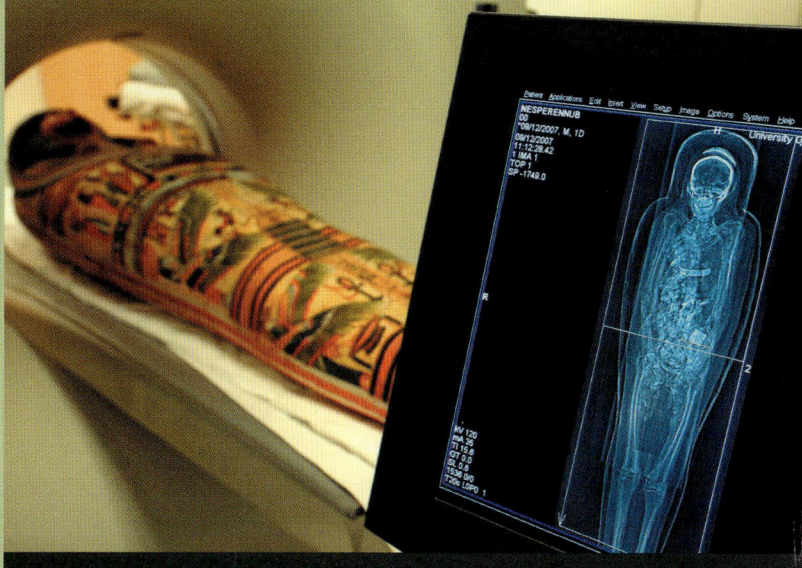

A | Modern equipment can see **organs** inside our bodies. Scientists have used this technology on Egyptian mummies and found that many had heart problems.

B | Doctors have written instructions for how to treat problems for thousands of years. This Ancient Egyptian carving records the range of instruments and medicines that a doctor used to treat patients. Many of the instruments still look familiar!

A doctor sees if there is a match between a patient's symptoms and a known problem. If there is a match, the symptoms are **evidence** that the person has a certain illness.

Luckily, if you need a **medicine** today it will not contain a favourite ingredient of Ancient Egyptian medicine – animal dung!

1 a| A patient has a high temperature, a headache and a stuffy nose. Which word in bold on this page best describes these findings?

b| Suggest what illness the patient has.

2 A doctor tells a patient that they have acne. Suggest what evidence the doctor has found to make them think this.

3 a| Which of the following best describes the heart:

A| an organ   B| a cell
C| a tissue   D| a system?

b| State one job that the heart does.

5

UK NC, iLS, CEE

7Aa LIFE PROCESSES

WHAT DO ALL LIVING THINGS DO?

The Ancient Egyptians believed they had cures for death, including one made from onions. It is doubtful that this worked! When they died, the bodies of important people were treated to stop them rotting – they were mummified. This was done because Ancient Egyptians believed that living things contained a 'life force' called *ka*, which needed somewhere to live.

Today, we have different ideas about what it means to be alive. We look at what things do. If something can do the following **life processes**, it is a 'living thing' or **organism**:

- move
- reproduce
- sense things
- grow
- respire
- excrete waste
- need nutrition.

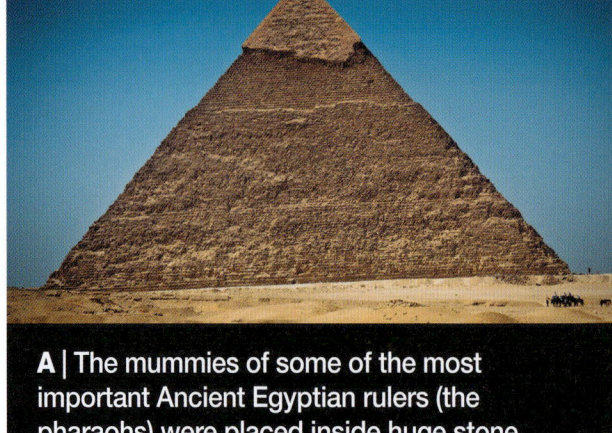

A | The mummies of some of the most important Ancient Egyptian rulers (the pharaohs) were placed inside huge stone pyramids.

> **1** Copy and complete the table below with the items in the list.
> car, chair, coal, cow, daffodil, goldfish, mouse, octopus, robot, rock, snake, Sun
>
> | Organism | Not an organism |
> |----------|-----------------|
> | | |
>
> **2** A **mnemonic** is a word or phrase that helps you remember a list. It is usually made using the first letters of the words in a list. What mnemonic is spelled out by the first letters of the life processes?

Movement

All living things can either **move** from place to place or move parts of themselves.

B | Arctic poppies move parts of themselves. Their flowers turn to follow the Sun during the day.

> **3** Suggest one difference between how most animals move and how most plants move.

Reproduction

Organisms can make more living things like themselves. We say that they can **reproduce**.

C | Offspring are the result of reproduction.

> **4** Suggest one thing that many plants do to reproduce but animals do not do.

Sensitivity

Organisms **sense** and react to things around them.

D | This sensitive plant closes its leaves if it senses something touching them.

Growth

Living things increase in size. We say that they **grow**.

E | Some types of bamboo can grow 4 cm taller in an hour.

Respiration

Living things use a process called **respiration** to release energy for them to use.

F | Humans, like many living things, need **oxygen** and food in order to respire.

Excretion

Organisms produce waste materials. When they get rid of these waste materials we say that they **excrete** them.

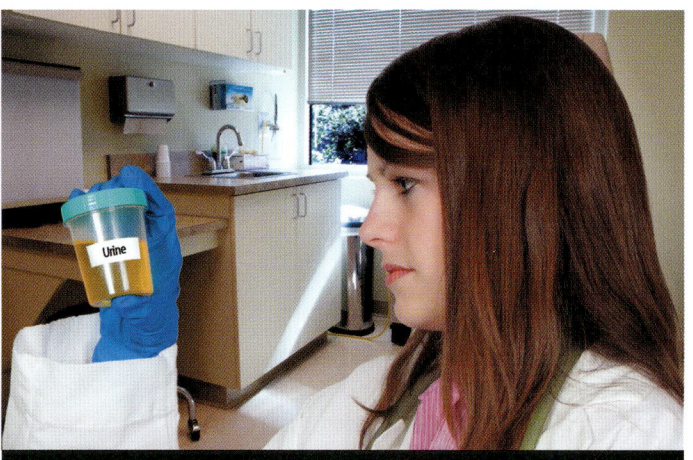

G | Waste materials include liquids (urine).

Nutrition

Living things require various substances to help carry out other life processes. We say that they need **nutrition**.

H | Animals eat food but plants make their own food. However, even plants need small amounts of substances from the soil to help them grow well.

5	Describe two ways in which you show sensitivity.
6	Suggest one difference between how trees grow and how humans grow.
7	Suggest one difference between how fish and humans get their oxygen.
8	a| In what ways is a car like an organism? b| Why is a car not an organism?

I can ...

- recall and describe the life processes
- explain the differences between organisms and non-living things.

7

UK NC, iLS, CEE

7Ab ORGANS

WHAT DO ORGANS DO?

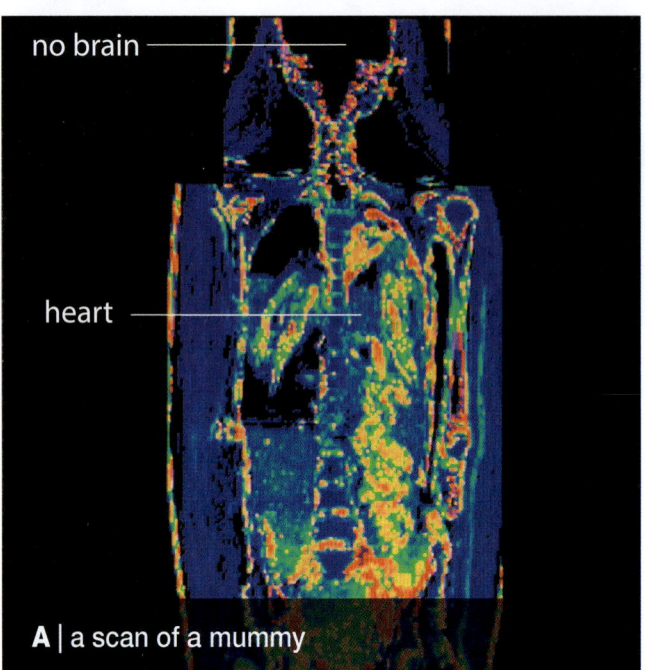

A | a scan of a mummy

In Ancient Egypt, the heart was thought to be the most important part of a person. When people were mummified, the organs in their bodies were removed but the heart was left in place. The stomach, intestines, lungs and liver were thought to be useful on the person's journey in the afterlife and these organs were preserved. They did not think the **brain** was important and so it was often thrown away.

Human organs

The heart, stomach, intestines, lungs and liver are **organs**. Every organ has an important **function** (job). We now know that the brain is also an organ and has the very important function of controlling the body!

Your body's biggest organ is on the outside. It's your **skin**. Skin is used for protection and sensing things.

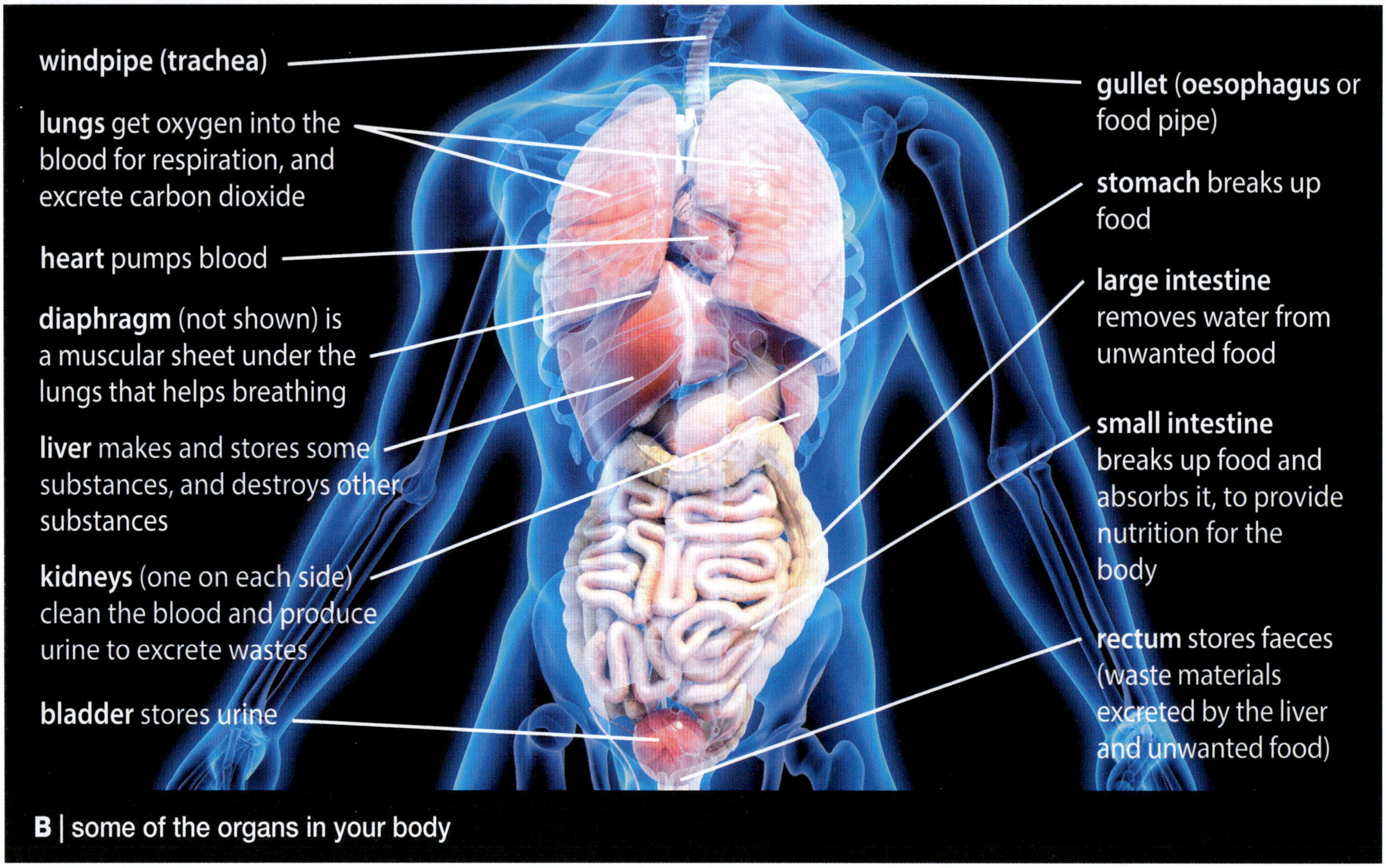

- **windpipe (trachea)**
- **lungs** get oxygen into the blood for respiration, and excrete carbon dioxide
- **heart** pumps blood
- **diaphragm** (not shown) is a muscular sheet under the lungs that helps breathing
- **liver** makes and stores some substances, and destroys other substances
- **kidneys** (one on each side) clean the blood and produce urine to excrete wastes
- **bladder** stores urine
- **gullet** (**oesophagus** or food pipe)
- **stomach** breaks up food
- **large intestine** removes water from unwanted food
- **small intestine** breaks up food and absorbs it, to provide nutrition for the body
- **rectum** stores faeces (waste materials excreted by the liver and unwanted food)

B | some of the organs in your body

1	Draw a table to show the functions of five different organs in your body.
2	Which organ gets bigger as it fills with air?
3	List the organs that help to get nutrition into the body.
4	List the organs that excrete waste materials.
5	List two organs that store solid or liquid wastes.

Plant organs

Photo D shows some of the main organs in plants.

Leaves are plant organs that are designed to collect sunlight. Plants that live in shady areas often have very large leaves. The leaves of the giant water lily can be up to 3 m in diameter.

leaf traps sunlight to make food for the plant

stem carries substances around the plant and supports the leaves and flowers

root holds the plant in place. Roots also take water and small amounts of other substances from the soil.

D | the organs found in most plants

Plants make their own food using a process called **photosynthesis**. This process occurs in the leaves when there is light. Photosynthesis needs **carbon dioxide** from the air, and water. Some plants also have **storage organs**, which they use to store some of the food that they make. Potatoes and carrots are storage organs.

E | Many plants have underground storage organs, which they use to store some of the food that they make. Humans often eat these.

6	Which organ is the main organ of nutrition in a plant?
7	a| What process produces the food stored in plant storage organs?
	b| Why won't a potato grow if the potato plant does not get much light?
8	Which human organ is most similar to a leaf? Explain your reasoning.

I can ...

- identify and locate important plant and animal organs
- describe the functions of important plant and animal organs
- describe what happens in photosynthesis.

7Ab MEDICAL DOCTORS

HOW DO MEDICAL DOCTORS USE STEM SKILLS?

STEM stands for sceince, technology, engineering and maths. There are many interesting jobs open to people with skills in these subjects. These include careers in communications, farming, fashion, films, finance, health, sport and video gaming.

All STEM subjects are linked:

- similar skills are needed for each one
- changes or advances in one subject may change the way the others are done.

STEM skills

An important STEM skill is problem-solving. This is often done by thinking up ideas and then testing them. Results from the tests are used as **evidence** (information used to decide if an idea is correct or incorrect). A decision made using evidence is called a **conclusion**.

Doctors think up ideas about what might be wrong with a patient. They then perform tests. They use the test results and their knowledge of the human body to make a conclusion (called a 'medical diagnosis').

> **1** List the STEM subjects.

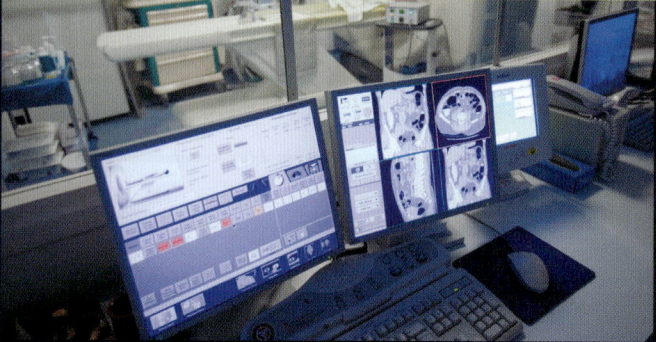

A | X-ray technology was invented in 1895 and allowed doctors to see the bones inside people. Advances in the technology have produced scanners (like this one) that show the organs inside our bodies. Engineers also use X-ray technology to check joins between pieces of metal.

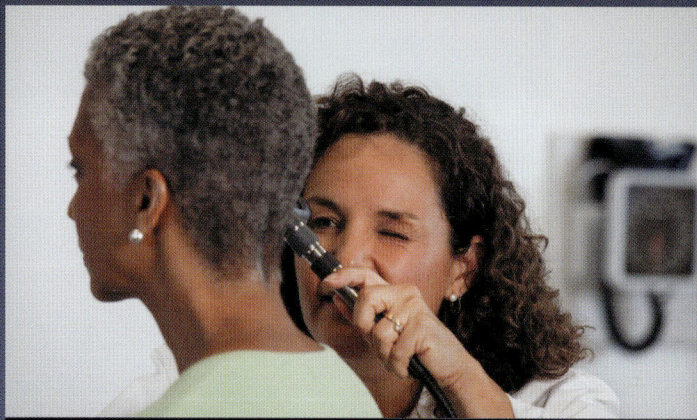

B | a doctor performing a test

> **2** a | When a girl broke her leg, it was put in plaster for 2 months. Suggest how a doctor might check to see if the two ends of the broken bone have now joined together?
> b | A doctor thinks that a patient has a heart problem. Suggest why the patient is put in an X-ray scanner.
>
> **3** Look at photo B. What organ is the doctor testing?
>
> **4** A man has been getting pains in his chest. His doctor thinks the man may have a heart problem.
> a | What does the heart do?
> b | Suggest two tests the doctor uses to discover if the man's heart is working properly.
>
> **5** A patient has yellow skin. The doctor thinks the patient's liver has a problem and is releasing a substance called bilirubin into the blood. A test finds bilirubin in the patient's urine. The doctor says that the patient has liver disease.
> a | What does the liver do?
> b | What is the doctor's diagnosis?
> c | What evidence does the doctor use?
> d | Which organ produces urine?
> e | Which organ stores urine?

STEM

STEM careers

Many other interesting jobs need a knowledge of the human body and its organs. Pathologists use their knowledge of the body and problem-solving skills to reach conclusions about how someone has died.

C | physiotherapists at work

Physiotherapists help people to recover from muscle and bone injuries. Physiotherapists are an important part of your country's sporting teams.

> **6** Explain why a country's athletics team includes many physiotherapists.

To develop their skills and knowledge, people who want to become physiotherapists, nurses or doctors do more training after they leave school. Doctors, for example, usually train at a university for six or seven years. Some doctors then do even more training to specialise in a certain area of the body or to become surgeons or pathologists.

> **7** Find out what a cardiologist is.

ACTIVITY

Work with others in your group to think about the different jobs that need a knowledge of the human body and its organs. Write down as many jobs as you can think of. For each job, give a reason why a knowledge of the human body is useful.

PRACTICAL

A doctor uses a stethoscope to listen to a person's heart beating and their breathing. The first stethoscope was a rolled-up tube of paper. In your group, make a range of different stethoscopes using paper, different types of tubing, funnels and sticky tape. Test them out and decide which one works best.

D | a modern stethoscope

11

UK NC, iLS, CEE

7Ac TISSUES

WHY ARE TISSUES IMPORTANT?

Many good detective stories have a 'pathologist', who inspects a dead body to look for evidence to help to solve a murder. Pathologists have a long history; dead bodies were examined in Ancient Egypt, Ancient Greece and in Roman times.

Pathologists are fully trained doctors. Some pathologists examine dead bodies to try to work out causes of death. Others examine small pieces taken from living people to try to identify diseases.

A | Pathologists use microscopes, which magnify things. This allows pieces taken from a body to be examined in great detail.

1. What does a microscope do?
2. Look at photo B. Describe what a heart looks like.

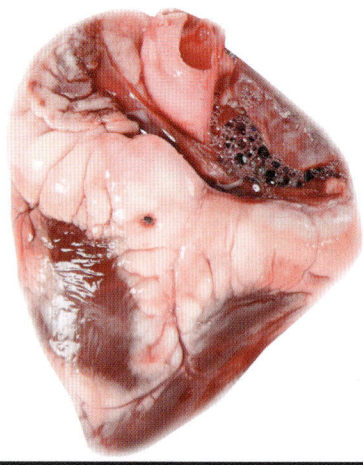

B | a human heart

A pathologist will look at a heart in detail because it is such an important organ and damage to it often causes death. Its function is to pump blood around the body. The blood carries oxygen and nutrients (from food) for all the different parts of the body to use.

The heart has different parts. In photo B, the whiter parts are fat and the reddish parts are muscle. These are **tissues**. All organs are made up of different tissues.

Each tissue in an organ has a certain function. For example, the **muscle tissue** in the heart is the part that moves, to pump blood. The **fat tissue** helps to protect the heart.

FACT

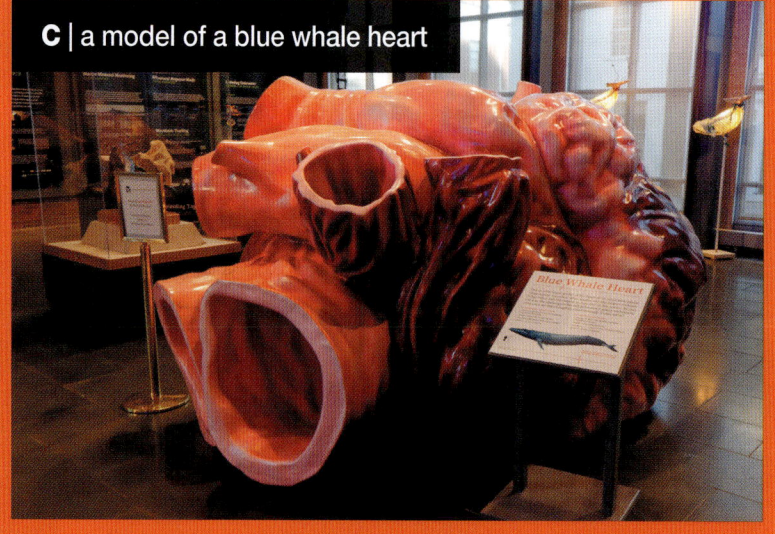

C | a model of a blue whale heart

About 20 per cent of the mass of a mammal heart is fat. For an adult human, that is about 60 g of fat. For an adult blue whale that is about 120 kg of fat; a blue whale heart can have a mass up to about 600 kg!

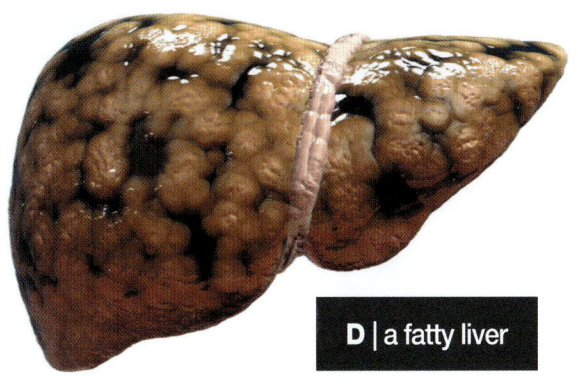

D | a fatty liver

> 3 a| Name two tissues found in the heart.
>   b| What does each of these tissues do?
>
> 4 A pathologist says that the liver in photo D comes from someone with 'fatty liver disease'. Compare it with the healthy liver in diagram B on page 8. What evidence supports the pathologist's conclusion?
>
> 5 Your intestines move, so that food is pushed along. What tissue would you expect to find in intestines?

Plant tissues

Plants also have organs made out of tissues. Many roots, like the one shown in photo E, have hairs on the outside. This is **root hair tissue** and it helps the root to take water out of the soil quickly.

If you cut open a plant organ, you can see more tissues. Photo F shows that a carrot contains different tissues. The tissue in the middle of the carrot is called **xylem tissue** (pronounced '*zy-lem*'). Xylem tissue carries water. In a carrot, the xylem tissue carries water up from the roots, through the carrot and on into the rest of the plant.

F | Carrots contain different tissues.

G | a carrot plant

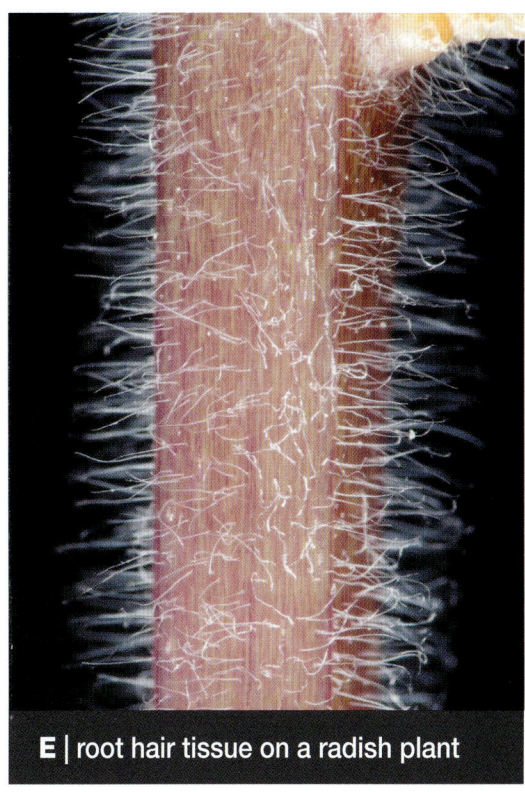

E | root hair tissue on a radish plant

> 6 a| What sort of organ is a carrot?
>   b| How many tissues does a carrot contain? Explain your reasoning.
>
> 7 a| Name two tissues you would expect to find in a radish plant root.
>   b| What does each of these tissues do?
>
> 8 Name a plant organ that is above ground and contains xylem tissue.
>
> 9 Which life process does xylem tissue help with?

I can ...
- identify and recall named tissues in human and plant organs
- describe the functions of different tissues in an organ.

UK NC, iLS, CEE

7Ac MICROSCOPES

HOW IS A LIGHT MICROSCOPE USED TO EXAMINE A SPECIMEN?

To find out what is wrong with an organ, doctors do tests. Some tests involve taking a small piece of tissue (a biopsy) from an organ and looking at it under a light microscope. Microscopes make things appear bigger; they magnify things. The Method below shows how to use a light microscope.

Method

A | Place the smallest **objective lens** (the lowest **magnification**) over the hole in the stage. Turn the **coarse focusing wheel** to make the gap between the objective lens and the stage as small as possible.

B | Place the **slide** under the clips on the **stage**. The slide contains the **specimen** (the thing you want to look at). Then adjust the light source so that light goes up through the hole.

C | Look through the **eyepiece lens**. Turn the coarse focusing wheel slowly until what you see is in focus (clear and sharp).

D | To see a bigger **image**, place the next largest objective lens over your specimen.

E | Use the **fine focusing wheel** to get your image in focus again. Do not use the coarse focusing wheel since you can break the slide and damage the objective lens. If you cannot see your specimen clearly go back to a lower magnification.

! Never point a microscope mirror at the Sun. This can permanently damage your eyesight.

1	How many types of lenses are found in a light microscope?
2	Write down some rules of your own for: a| using a microscope safely b| taking care of a microscope.
3	What part of a microscope makes the image clearer?
4	What is a specimen?

14

WORKING SCIENTIFICALLY

Both of the lenses in a light microscope do some magnifying. How much a lens magnifies is written on its side (e.g. ×10). To work out the total magnification of both lenses working together, we use this formula:

> **5** A microscope has a ×10 eyepiece lens and a ×15 objective lens. What is its total magnification?

total magnification = magnification of eyepiece lens × magnification of objective lens

Preparing a specimen

The specimen on a microscope slide needs to be thin so that light can pass through it. A thin, glass **coverslip** is put on the specimen to keep it flat, hold it in place and stop it drying out. The Method below shows how to prepare a slide of onion tissue.

Method

A | Take a slide and place a drop of water in the centre. The water may contain a **stain** to make the specimen show up better.

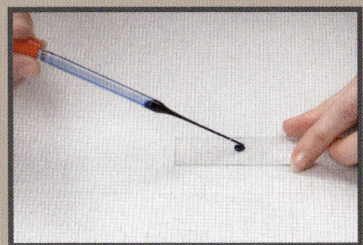

B | Use some forceps to peel off the inside layer of a piece of onion.

C | Place a small piece of onion skin onto the drop of water on your slide.

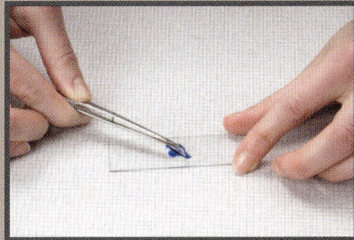

D | Use some forceps to lower a coverslip onto your specimen. If you do this carefully and slowly you will not get air bubbles trapped under the coverslip.

 **Wear eye protection when carrying out this method. Slides and coverslips are made of thin glass. Be very careful when using them.**

6 Why does a specimen need to be thin?

7 Why do we use coverslips?

8 Suggest the names of two plant and two animal tissues you could examine using a light microscope.

9 Plan an investigation to examine rhubarb stem tissue in detail.

10 Jake sets up a microscope but only sees darkness when looking into the eyepiece lens. What might be wrong? Write down as many things as you can think of.

I can ...

- describe how to prepare a microscope slide
- describe how to use a light microscope to examine a specimen.

UK NC, iLS, CEE

7Ad CELLS

HOW ARE PLANT AND ANIMAL CELLS SIMILAR AND DIFFERENT?

Mummification preserves tissues. In 1825, Dr Augustus Granville tried to work out how a 2500-year-old Egyptian 'mummy' had died. His study included using a microscope to examine tissues. His conclusion was 'cancer'. Technology has now advanced and another examination of the same mummy in 2009 concluded that the person died from a lung disease called tuberculosis (TB).

FACT
Today's most powerful microscopes are called electron microscopes. One of them can show things that are one ten-millionth of a millimetre wide.

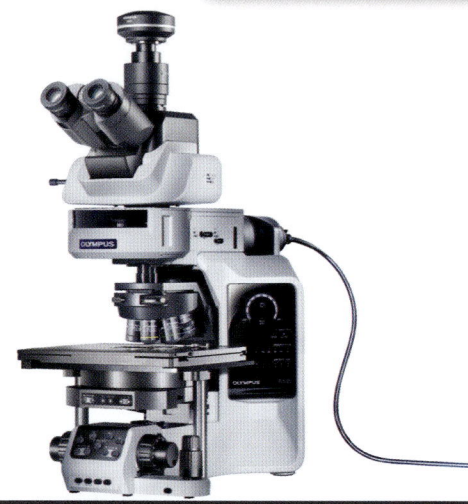

A | Hooke's microscope (far left) had a total magnification of about ×30. Early 19th-century microscopes magnified to about ×200. Modern light microscopes go up to about ×1500.

Robert Hooke was the first person to study tissues with a microscope. In 1665, he examined the bark of a cork oak tree and saw little box shapes. He thought that they looked like the **cells** (small rooms) in a monastery and so that's what he called them.

Today we know that cells are the basic units from which all tissues and all living things are made. A tissue is a group of cells of the same type working together.

1. What is a cell?
2. Granville was able to see much more in the mummy tissues than Hooke saw in the cork tissue. Why was this?
3. What do organisms always have that things that have never been alive do not?

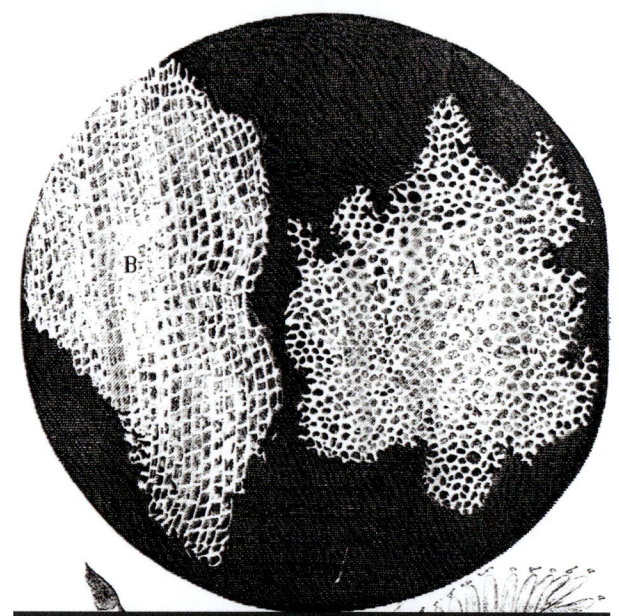

B | Hooke's drawing of cork cells, published in his book *Micrographia*

16

Animal cells

Photo C shows a cell from someone's cheek, viewed using a modern microscope. The photograph has a magnification of ×600, which means that it is 600 times bigger in the photo than in real life. The different parts of the cell are labelled.

All animal cells have the same basic parts, but cells from different tissues have different shapes, sizes and functions to help them do their jobs. The cells are **specialised**.

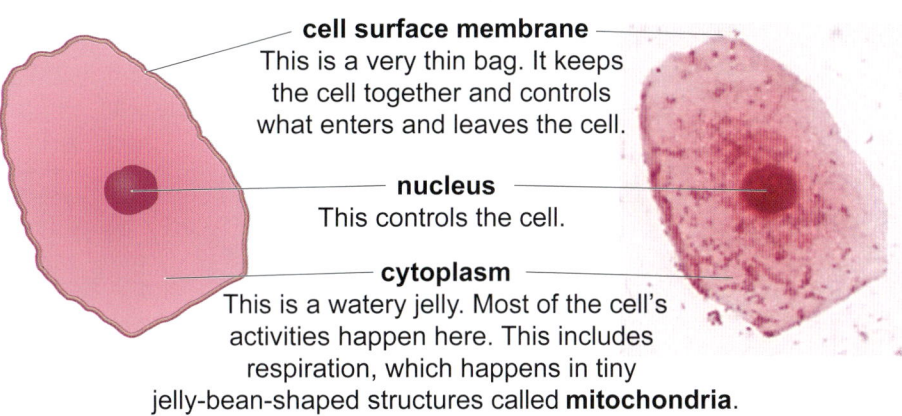

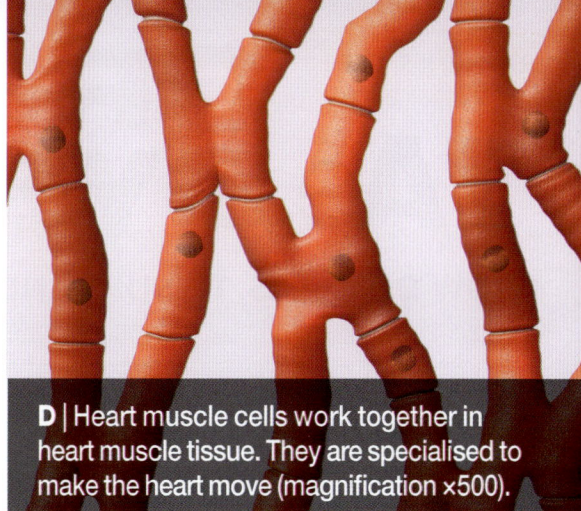

D | Heart muscle cells work together in heart muscle tissue. They are specialised to make the heart move (magnification ×500).

C | a drawing and microscope image of a cheek cell showing its parts (magnification ×600)

Labels on C:
- **cell surface membrane** – This is a very thin bag. It keeps the cell together and controls what enters and leaves the cell.
- **nucleus** – This controls the cell.
- **cytoplasm** – This is a watery jelly. Most of the cell's activities happen here. This includes respiration, which happens in tiny jelly-bean-shaped structures called **mitochondria**.

Plant cells

Plant cells have thick **cell walls** and may have some other features that are not found in animal cells.

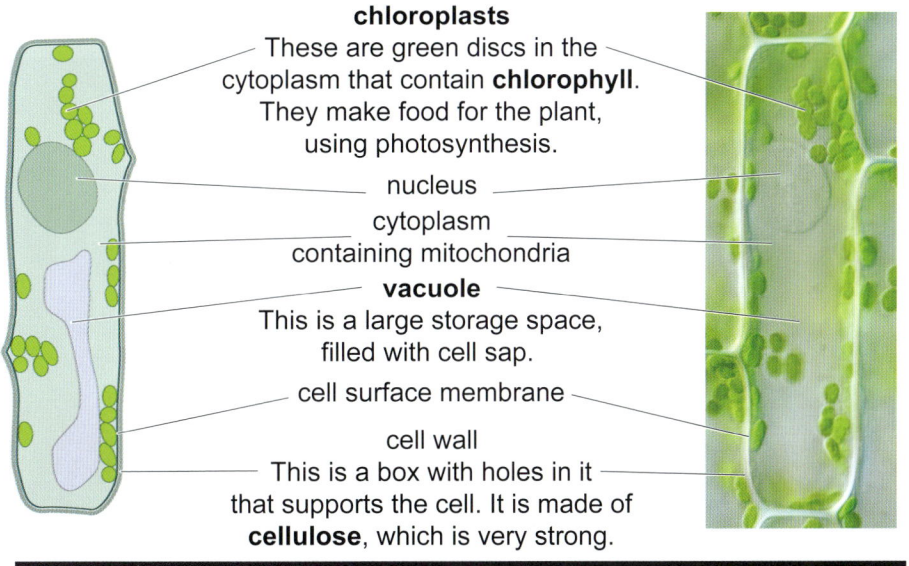

E | a drawing and microscope image of a leaf cell showing its parts (magnification ×275)

Labels on E:
- **chloroplasts** – These are green discs in the cytoplasm that contain **chlorophyll**. They make food for the plant, using photosynthesis.
- **nucleus**
- **cytoplasm** containing mitochondria
- **vacuole** – This is a large storage space, filled with cell sap.
- **cell surface membrane**
- **cell wall** – This is a box with holes in it that supports the cell. It is made of **cellulose**, which is very strong.

4
a| Look at photo D. What are the dark blobs?
b| What do these structures do?
c| What other parts would you find in a heart muscle cell?
d| What do these parts do?

5
a| Measure the widest part of the animal cell in photo C. Work out its real width.
b| Measure the length of the plant cell in photo E. Work out its real length.

6 Draw a table to compare the parts that can be found in animal cells and plant cells.

7
a| What makes some plant cells green?
b| Which are bigger, chloroplasts or mitochondria? Explain your evidence.

8 Draw and label a root hair cell.

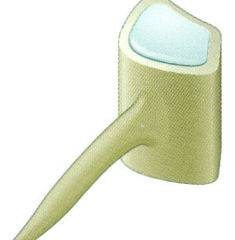

F | Root hair cells are specialised to take water from the soil (magnification ×30).

I can ...

- identify the main parts of animal cells and plant cells and describe their functions.

17

UK NC, iLS, CEE

7Ae ORGAN SYSTEMS

HOW DO CELLS, TISSUES AND ORGANS WORK TOGETHER?

When cells of the same type are grouped together they form a tissue. Different tissues are found grouped together in an organ.

> **1** Name three tissues found in the heart.

Doctors in Ancient Egypt could see that organs were connected but did not understand how or why. For example, they thought that you breathed air into your lungs and your heart, and all the tubes going to and from your heart. They could only examine the heart and its tubes in dead bodies when these organs were full of air, and so they thought that they always contained air.

Today we know that the heart and its tubes carry blood around the body. The tubes are called **blood vessels** and work with the heart to form an **organ system** called the **circulatory system**.

An organ system is a group of organs that work together. Other organ systems in humans include the **locomotor** (muscles and bones), **digestive**, **urinary**, **nervous** and **breathing systems**. (The last of these is also called the **respiratory system**.)

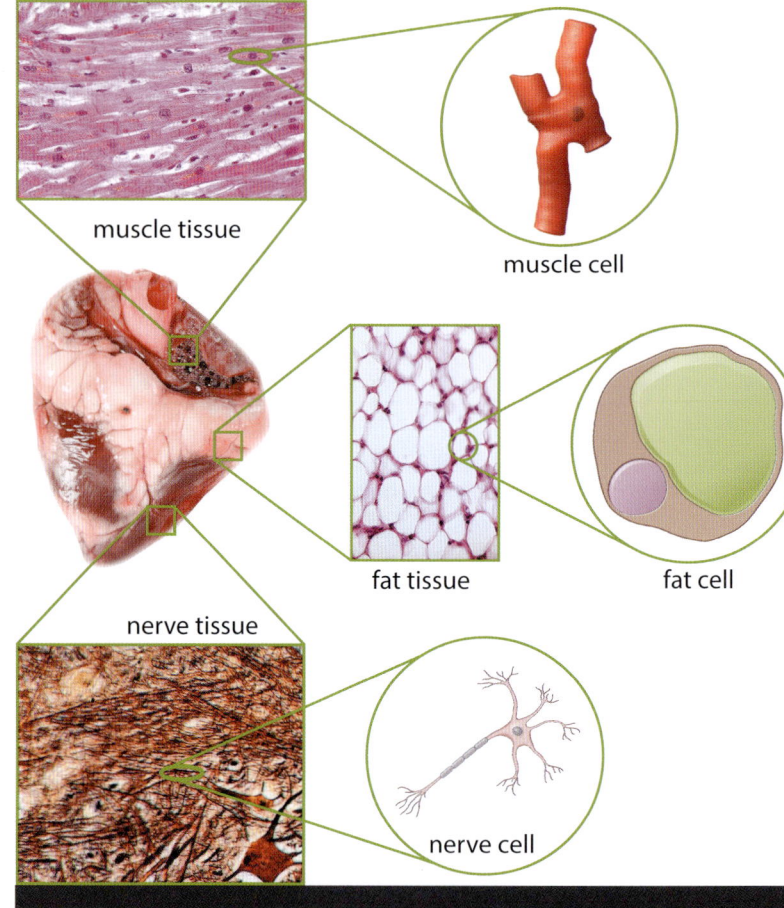

A | Organs, such as the heart, are made of many tissues.

> **2** a| Why did Ancient Egyptians think that blood vessels contained air?
> b| Suggest a piece of evidence that we have today that shows this is not correct.
>
> **3** What is an organ system?

FACT
An adult's circulatory system contains over 100 000 km of blood vessels. That is four times around the Earth!

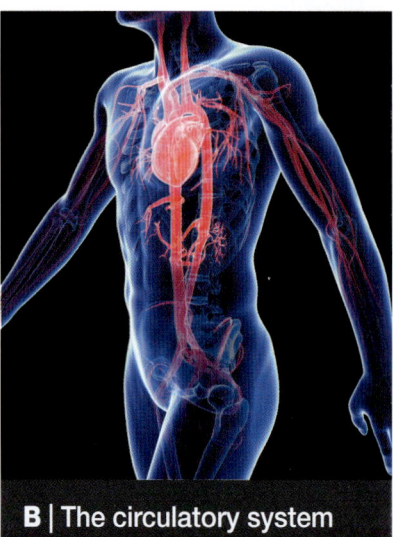

B | The circulatory system carries oxygen and nutrients (from food) around the body.

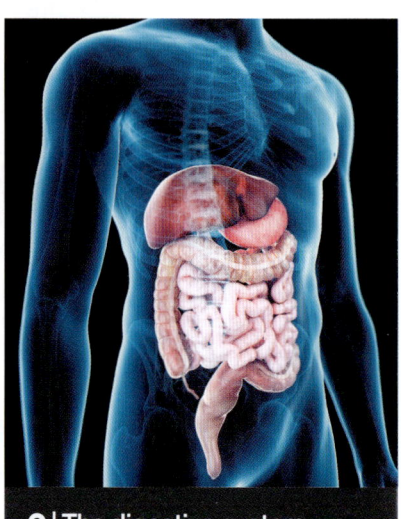

C | The digestive system breaks down food and takes nutrients from it into the blood.

4 What organs are found in the breathing system? (*Hint:* You may find page 8 helpful.)

5 Draw a table to show the organs found in each human organ system mentioned on pages 18–19. (*Hint:* You may find page 8 helpful.)

6 Which life processes do the organ systems in diagrams C, D and E help with?

FACT

In your urinary system, your kidneys clean all of your blood every 40 minutes.

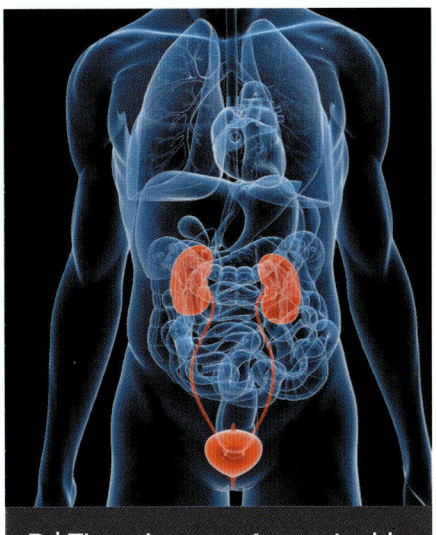

D | The urinary system gets rid of waste materials produced in the body.

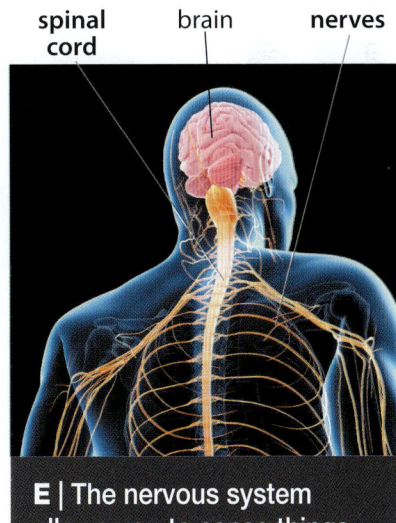

E | The nervous system allows you to sense things.

Organ systems in plants

Plants also have organs made up of tissues.

Plant organs work together in organ systems too. For example, the water transport system takes water from the ground up to the leaves. Water is always flowing through this organ system because leaves constantly lose water (by **evaporation**).

F | the water transport system in a plant

G | A plant root is made up of different tissues.

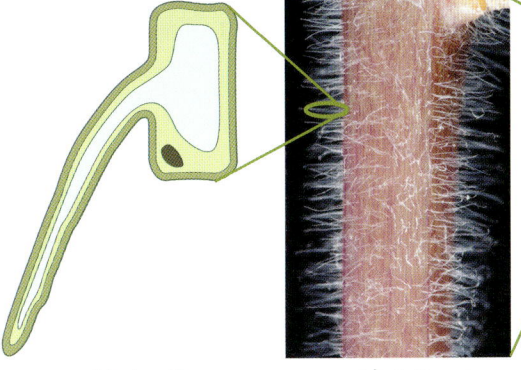

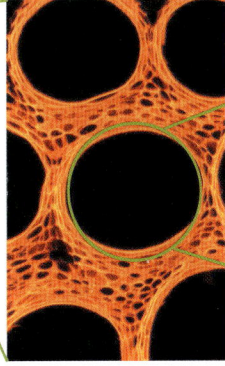

root hair cell   root hair tissue   root   xylem tissue   xylem cell

7 a| What are the organs in a plant's water transport system?

b| Name one tissue you would expect to find in all these organs.

8 Leaves lose water through small holes. How would you examine a leaf to find out whether more water is lost from its upper or under side? Plan an investigation.

I can ...

- identify and recall the main organs in the plant water transport system
- identify and recall the main organs in the human locomotor, digestive, circulatory, breathing, urinary and nervous systems.

7Ae TRANSPLANTS

WHAT IS AN ORGAN TRANSPLANT?

Doctors today know a lot about cells, tissues and organs. They also have microscopes and other tools to help investigate problems with our bodies.

If a doctor thinks there is something wrong with an organ, a biopsy (piece of tissue) might be taken from the organ and examined. This can help to identify the problem and a doctor can plan a treatment.

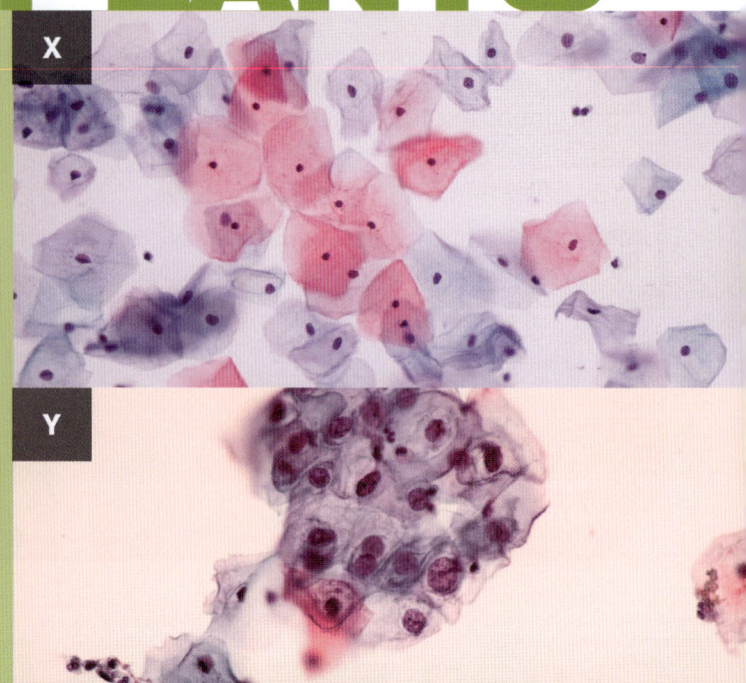

A | biopsy samples under a microscope

Sometimes an organ cannot be treated and doctors may consider doing an **organ transplant**. This is when an unhealthy organ is replaced with a healthy organ (usually from a person who has recently died).

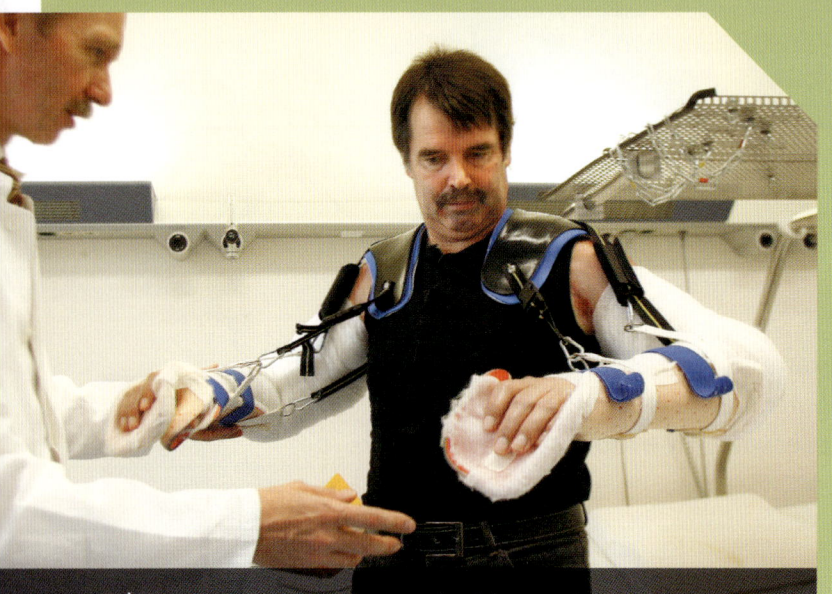

B | This farmer was given a double arm transplant.

The idea of replacing damaged tissues and organs goes back at least 2700 years to an Indian doctor, called Sushruta. He successfully replaced skin on a part of someone's body using nearby skin from the same person. Today doctors can transplant hearts, lungs, livers, kidneys and even faces, arms and legs between different people.

C | Some people want their organs to be used for transplants if they die. They may carry a card to show this.

1
a| Draw one cell from biopsy sample X. Label its parts and their functions.
b| In some cancer cells the nuclei become very large. Which biopsy sample (X or Y) shows cancerous tissue?

2 Draw a diagram to show how organ systems, organs, tissues and cells are linked. In your diagram use one example from plants and one from humans.

HAVE YOUR SAY

'People should carry cards only if they do not want to donate their organs – the opposite of donor cards.' What you do you think of this idea?

7Ba ESCAPED ZOO ANIMALS

There are reports of big cats, such as panthers and leopards, living wild in the United Kingdom. One idea is that these cats have escaped from zoos, which often keep rare animals such as large cats to breed them and for visitors to learn about them.

Most of the reports are unlikely to be true because people are mistaken about the sizes of the cats they see. However, there is a little **evidence** that big cats could be living in the UK. The Canadian lynx in photo B was discovered in 1903 in Devon. This is the only big cat that has ever been found in the UK, dead or alive.

There is good evidence that other animals have escaped from zoos and live in the wild. In the 1970s, a pair of wallabies escaped from Curraghs Wildlife Park on the Isle of Man and now there are about 100 of them living on the island.

A | Is this a panther on Bodmin Moor (in Cornwall in the UK)?

B | This Canadian lynx died in 1903, in countryside in the UK.

C | Wallabies are originally from Australia. This photo was taken on the Isle of Man.

1. Why are there now about 100 wallabies on the Isle of Man if only two escaped?
2. Why do you think there are not large numbers of Canadian lynx in Devon, even though one escaped?
3. What evidence supports the conclusion that there are wallabies on the Isle of Man?
4. Suggest why most sightings of big cats in the UK are probably cases of mistaken identity.
5. Wallabies and cats are both mammals. Suggest two ways in which you would expect their reproduction to be similar.

UK NC, CEE

THE SCIENTIFIC METHOD

7Ba

A | Socorro doves hatched at Edinburgh Zoo. The birds became extinct in the wild in the 1970s.

1. What life process do organisms use to increase their numbers?

2. Suggest why people used to think that rotting rubbish produced rats.

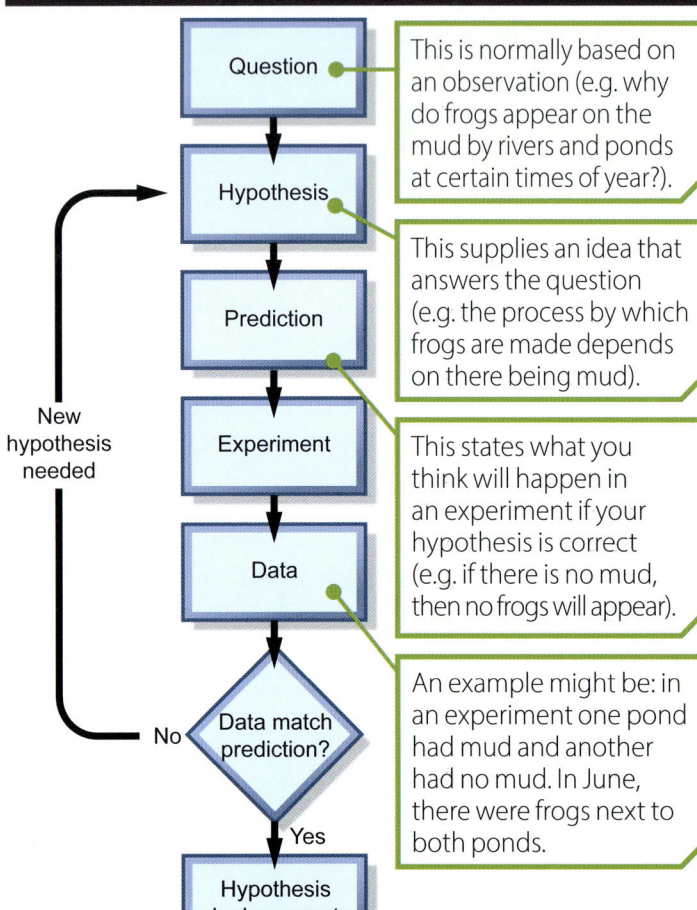

B | a common way in which the scientific method is done

WHAT IS THE SCIENTIFIC METHOD AND WHY IS IT USEFUL?

All **organisms** must **reproduce** to increase their numbers and make sure that their type of organism does not die out (become **extinct**). Reproduction is obvious in some animals. Mammals (such as humans) give birth to babies and many other animals hatch from large eggs.

People did not always know how new animals were made! This was especially true for smaller animals whose reproduction could not be seen easily. For example, when some rivers flood in spring they leave areas of mud, which attract lots of frogs. So, people thought that frogs were produced by mud.

Until a few hundred years ago many people thought that rotting rubbish produced rats, that old fruit produced flies and that meat produced maggots.

FACT

People in the 17th-century believed this was a recipe for mice: Place some sweaty underwear in a jar with some wheat. Wait 21 days. The sweat will turn the wheat into mice.

These sorts of ideas were not scientific. People observed maggots in old meat and so they thought that the meat produced maggots, but they did not test this idea. Today, scientists test their ideas using 'the **scientific method**'. The scientific method is any way of testing that involves collecting information in order to show whether an idea is right or wrong. Diagram B shows how it is often done.

First, you use an **observation** to think up a question that can be answered using experiments. Then you think of an idea to answer your question, which can be tested using experiments. This is called a **hypothesis**.

Next, you say what will happen in a certain experiment if the hypothesis is right. This is called 'making a **prediction**'. The results from an experiment are called **data**. If the data matches the prediction, this is evidence that the hypothesis is correct.

WORKING SCIENTIFICALLY

3 Look at diagram B.
   a| What is a hypothesis?
   b| What prediction has been made?
   c| Do the results match the prediction?
   d| What would the scientist do next?

4 Decide whether each of these statements is a hypothesis, a prediction or a result.
   A| The seeds at the warmer temperature sprouted first.
   B| The ability of animals to reproduce depends on there being males and females.
   C| If people lack vitamin C in their food, then they will get a disease called scurvy.

The following experiment tests the hypothesis that rotten banana peel produces flies.

Method

A | Peel a brown banana and place half of the peel in each of two jars.

B | Immediately place a piece of gauze over one jar and secure it with an elastic band.

C | Stand the jars outside. Small flies will be able to enter the jar that has no gauze covering. After a few hours, cover that jar with gauze as you did for the first jar.

D | Bring the jars inside and observe for 2 weeks.

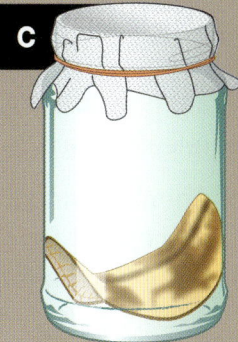

Redi's experiment

In 1668, the Italian scientist Francesco Redi (1626–1697) had an idea that maggots were caused by flies laying tiny eggs on meat. He tested this hypothesis by putting meat into a set of jars. He sealed some of the jars, put gauze over the tops of others and left others open. He put all the jars in an area where there were flies. Maggots were only found in the open jars. This was evidence that his hypothesis was correct.

5
   a| In the banana peel experiment, what question has been asked?
   b| What hypothesis is being tested?
   c| Make a prediction.

D | Redi's experiment

6
   a| What was Redi's hypothesis?
   b| Suggest a prediction that Redi might have made.
   c| Explain how Redi's results provide evidence to support his hypothesis.

I can ...

- state the purpose of and the common steps in the scientific method.

23

UK NC, CEE

7Ba ANIMAL SEXUAL REPRODUCTION

HOW DO DIFFERENT ANIMALS REPRODUCE SEXUALLY?

Endangered animals are those that are in danger of becoming extinct because there are very few left. Many zoos try to stop endangered animals becoming extinct by breeding the animals. It is hoped that the **offspring** can be released back into the wild.

Animals living in zoos do not always mate successfully and sometimes their offspring die for unknown reasons. So it is important that scientists study **sexual reproduction** in different animals to work out how to help them breed.

A | In 1945, there were only 31 Przewalski's horses left and only in zoos. Thanks to a breeding programme, there are now hundreds of Przewalski's horses living wild in their natural habitat in Mongolia.

1 What are human 'offspring' called?

FACT

Scientists from all over the world work together at the International Union for the Conservation of Nature and Natural Resources (IUCN) to publish a list of endangered organisms. It is called the 'Red List'. There are over 13 000 animals on this list.

B | a human egg cell or **ovum** (left) and a human sperm cell photographed using a light microscope (magnification ×600)

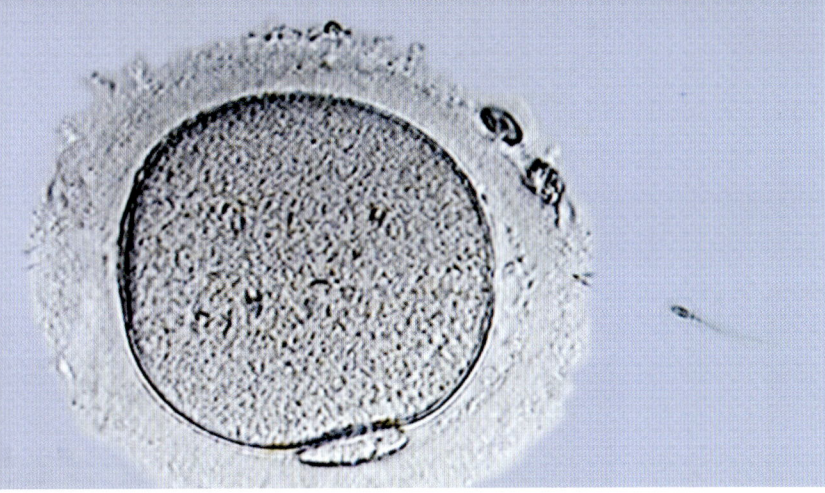

Gametes

Sexual reproduction requires two individuals to produce new organisms of the same type. Usually, two types of **specialised** cells are used. These are called **sex cells** or **gametes**. Males make gametes called **sperm cells** and females make **egg cells** (or **ova**).

During **fertilisation**, a sperm cell enters an egg cell and the two cell nuclei **fuse** (become one). A single **fertilised egg cell** or **zygote** is formed, which can grow into a new organism.

2 What type of reproduction needs males and females?

3 a| Which are bigger in real life, sperm cells or egg cells?

b| Use a ruler and photo B to calculate the actual sizes of sperm cells and egg cells.

4 a| In animals, what is the male gamete?

b| What happens to this cell during fertilisation?

For fertilisation to happen, the sperm cells must reach the egg cells. **External fertilisation** is when this happens outside the bodies of the animals (e.g. in fish). This usually occurs in water. Other animals use **internal fertilisation**, in which the male **parent** places sperm cells inside the female.

In external fertilisation, some egg cells do not get fertilised because the sperm cells are washed away. Many animals that use external fertilisation do not protect their fertilised egg cells, so a lot of cells are eaten by other animals. Animals that use external fertilisation must produce huge numbers of egg cells to ensure that some of them get fertilised and survive.

C | These snapper fish use external fertilisation. The male and female fish swim together and release their gametes.

> **5**
> a| Name an animal that uses external fertilisation.
> b| Give two reasons why the females of the animal you chose produce many egg cells.

Birds and mammals use internal fertilisation. They produce fewer egg cells because sperm cells are more likely to reach the egg cells. These animals also usually care for their fertilised egg cells and offspring. Birds lay their fertilised eggs in nests and protect them. In mammals, the offspring grow inside the mother. Birds and mammals protect their new offspring until they are able to survive on their own.

D | Birds, like this stone curlew, use internal fertilisation but their offspring develop outside the mother (externally). Numbers of stone curlews in the UK have fallen by over 80 per cent since 1940.

E | Black rhinoceroses, which are hunted for their horns, use internal fertilisation. The offspring develop inside the mother (internally).

> **6**
> a| Name an animal that uses internal fertilisation.
> b| Give two reasons why the females of the animal you chose produce only a few egg cells.
>
> **7** Why is external fertilisation unusual for animals that live away from water?
>
> **8** A female mouthbrooder fish sucks her fertilised eggs into her mouth, where they hatch. Would you expect mouthbrooder females to produce more or fewer egg cells than other fish of the same size? Explain your reasoning.

I can ...
- describe how egg cells (ova) are fertilised in animal sexual reproduction
- compare fertilisation and offspring care in fish, birds and mammals.

25

7Bb REPRODUCTIVE ORGANS

UK NC, CEE

WHAT ARE HUMAN REPRODUCTIVE ORGANS LIKE?

Scientists are trying to stop some animals from becoming **extinct**, including helping them to reproduce in zoos and game parks. Methods include artificial insemination, in which male gametes (sperm cells) are placed into a female using a thin tube.

Gametes are produced in **reproductive organs**, which form an organ system called the **reproductive system**.

In mammals, the male gametes are made in the **testes**. The testes hang outside the body in a bag of skin called the **scrotum**. Their position helps to keep the sperm cells at the correct temperature to develop properly. After **puberty**, males produce sperm cells for the rest of their lives (up to 100 million every day). A sperm cell has certain features to help it do its job. It is **adapted** to its **function**.

When sperm cells are released from the testes, they travel through **sperm ducts**, where fluids are added from **glands**. The fluids provide a source of **energy** for the sperm cells. The mixture of sperm cells and fluids is called **semen**, and it leaves the body through the **urethra** (which is inside the **penis**). This tube also carries urine from the **bladder**, but never at the same time as semen.

The head of the penis is sensitive and is protected by a covering of skin (the **foreskin**). This can be removed in a process called **circumcision**.

A | These lion cubs, born in 2018, were the first big cats to be bred using artificial insemination.

B | a sperm cell (drawn at a magnification of ×2000)

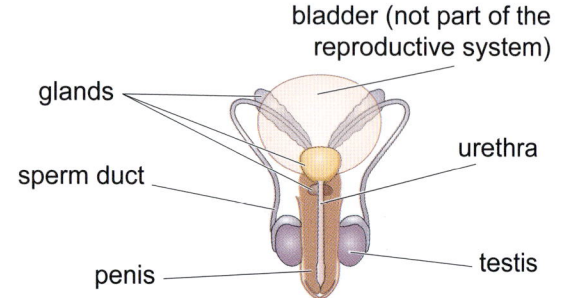

C | the male reproductive system

1. Which organ is in both the male urinary *and* the reproductive systems?

2. a| Where are sperm cells made?

   b| Do you think sperm cells need to be warmer or cooler than the body to develop? Explain your reasoning.

3. Explain how a sperm cell is adapted for swimming.

4. The prostate gland (in yellow on diagram C) controls the flow of semen and urine. It sometimes swells up. Suggest a problem this may cause and explain your reasoning.

The female reproductive system

In females, each **ovary** contains small, undeveloped egg cells (ova). After puberty, egg cells start to develop and one is usually released from an ovary every 28–32 days. A woman's ovaries stop releasing egg cells at about the age of 45–55 years – a time known as the **menopause**. Like sperm cells, egg cells are adapted to their function (as shown in photo E).

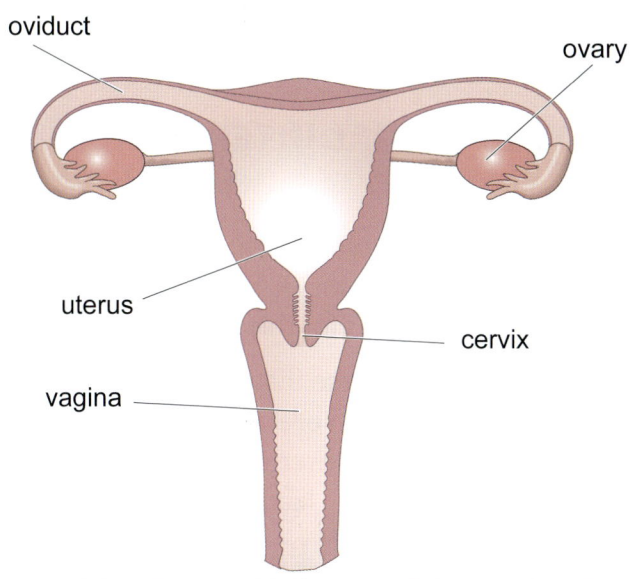

D | the female reproductive system

> **5** A woman releases an egg cell every 28 days for 35 years. How many egg cells does she release in total? Show your working.
>
> **6** Which organ makes and releases female gametes?

FACT

Girls are born with about 100 000 undeveloped egg cells in each ovary.

After leaving an ovary, an egg cell enters an **oviduct** (or **fallopian tube**). The oviducts are lined with hairs, called **cilia**, and these sweep egg cells towards the **uterus**. The uterus is where a baby will develop. It has strong, muscular walls and a soft lining.

The lower end of the uterus is made of a ring of muscle called the **cervix**. The cervix holds the baby in place during pregnancy. The cervix opens into the **vagina**.

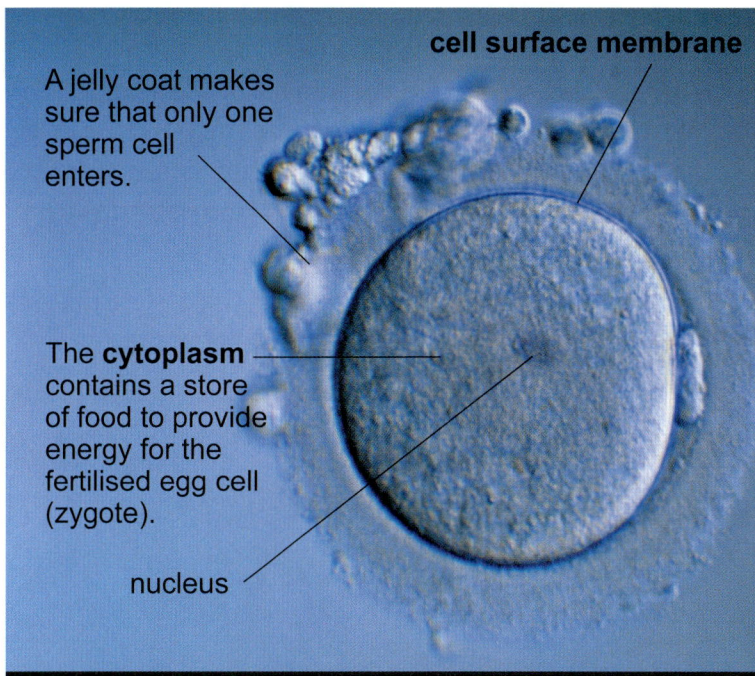

E | An egg cell is a specialised cell that is adapted to its function (magnification ×625).

> **7** Which female reproductive organs contain muscles?
>
> **8** How does an egg cell reach the uterus?
>
> **9** Explain how a developing fertilised egg cell has a supply of energy.
>
> **10** Suggest reasons why a certain woman's ovaries are not releasing egg cells. Think of as many reasons as you can.

I can ...

- name the parts of the male and female reproductive systems, and their jobs
- explain how sperm and egg cells are adapted to their functions
- state what happens at the menopause.

27

7Bc BECOMING PREGNANT

UK NC, CEE

HOW DOES SEXUAL INTERCOURSE LEAD TO A GROWING FOETUS?

In animals that use internal fertilisation, the male must place sperm cells inside the female. Male mammals have penises for this purpose.

Before **sexual intercourse** the man's penis fills with blood, making it hard (an **erection**). During sexual intercourse, the penis is inserted into the vagina. The penis is stimulated, which leads to **ejaculation** (in which semen is left at the top of the vagina).

> **1** What is semen?

The semen is sucked up through the cervix. Small movements of the uterus wall carry it to the oviducts. From here the sperm cells swim along the oviducts. If a sperm cell meets an egg cell, the sperm cell can enter the egg cell and fertilise it. During fertilisation, the nuclei of the cells fuse. Each nucleus contains half the instructions for a new human and so the baby will have features from both its mother and its father.

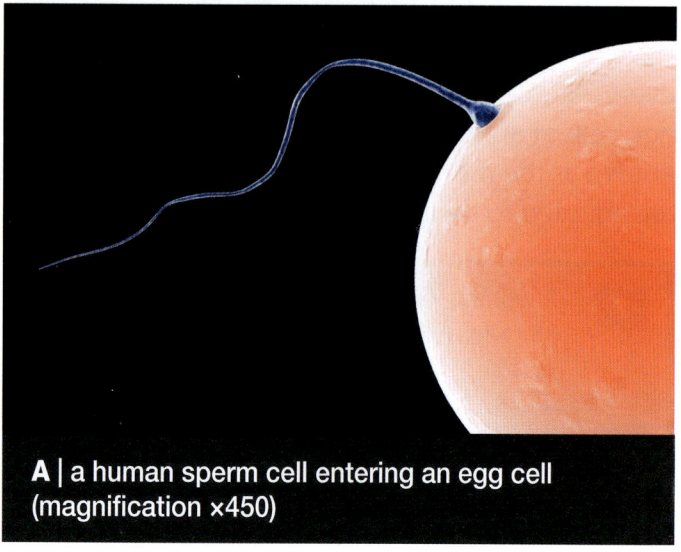

A | a human sperm cell entering an egg cell (magnification ×450)

> **2** Where does fertilisation occur?
>
> **3** How is a sperm cell adapted to enter an egg cell? (*Hint:* Look back at page 26.)

The fertilised egg cell divides into two. Each of these cells then divides into two again. The cells carry on dividing and form a ball of cells as they travel towards the uterus. In the uterus, the ball of cells (called an **embryo**) sinks into the soft lining. This is called **implantation**. The woman is now **pregnant**.

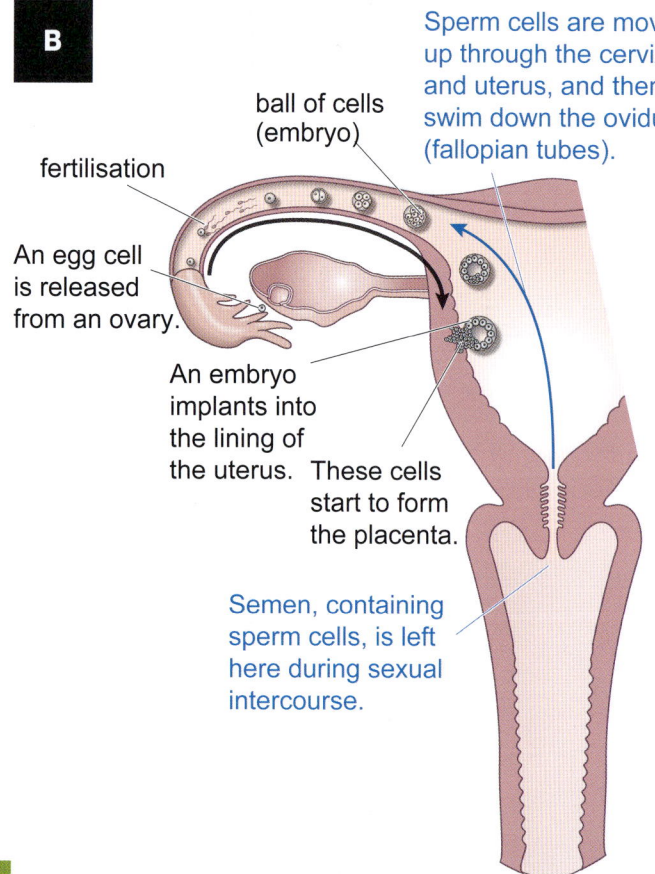

B

- fertilisation
- ball of cells (embryo)
- An egg cell is released from an ovary.
- An embryo implants into the lining of the uterus.
- These cells start to form the placenta.
- Sperm cells are moved up through the cervix and uterus, and then swim down the oviducts (fallopian tubes).
- Semen, containing sperm cells, is left here during sexual intercourse.

> **4** In diagram B, the 'ball of cells' is the result of cells dividing a total of four times. How many cells does it contain? Explain your reasoning.

FACT

When a fertilised egg cell divides into two, the cells can separate. They may both grow into new embryos and form identical twins. However, if these cells do not fully separate, the twins can be born sharing parts of their body. They are joined together or 'conjoined'.

C | triplets (three children born at the same time)

Each of a woman's ovaries might release an egg at the same time. If both are fertilised, twins are produced. These twins will not be identical. Sometimes, when a fertilised egg cell divides in two, the two new cells get separated. Both of these cells can grow into embryos and produce identical twins. Having more than one baby is called a multiple birth and most types of animal have multiple births.

5 a| Which children in photo C are identical?

b| Explain what happened in the mother's body to produce these triplets.

Pregnancy

After implantation, the embryo continues to grow and becomes surrounded by watery **amniotic fluid**, to protect it. The fluid is contained within a bag called the **amnion**.

A **placenta** also grows. This is a plate-shaped organ that is attached to the uterus lining. Inside the placenta, **oxygen**, water and food from the mother's blood go into the embryo's blood. Waste materials (like **carbon dioxide**) go from the embryo's blood into the mother's blood. The **umbilical cord** carries the embryo's blood to and from the placenta.

The mother's blood does not mix with the embryo's blood. This is because the mother's blood is pumped around her body under a lot of **pressure**, which would damage the **blood vessels** of the delicate embryo.

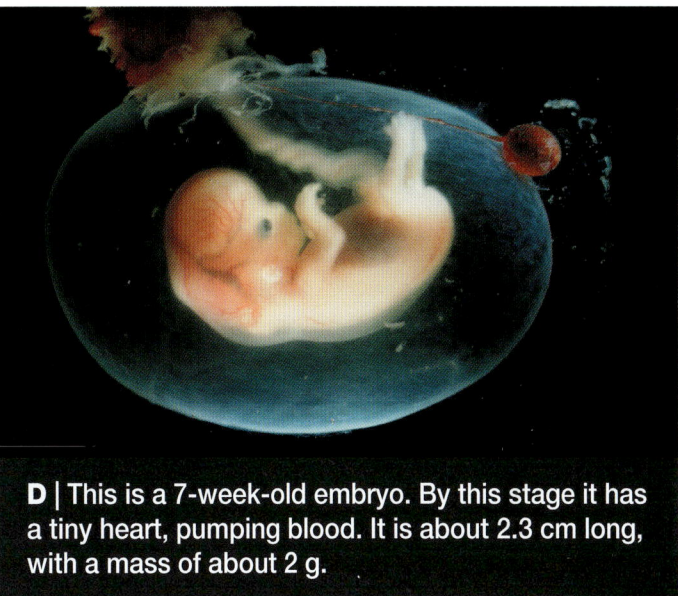

D | This is a 7-week-old embryo. By this stage it has a tiny heart, pumping blood. It is about 2.3 cm long, with a mass of about 2 g.

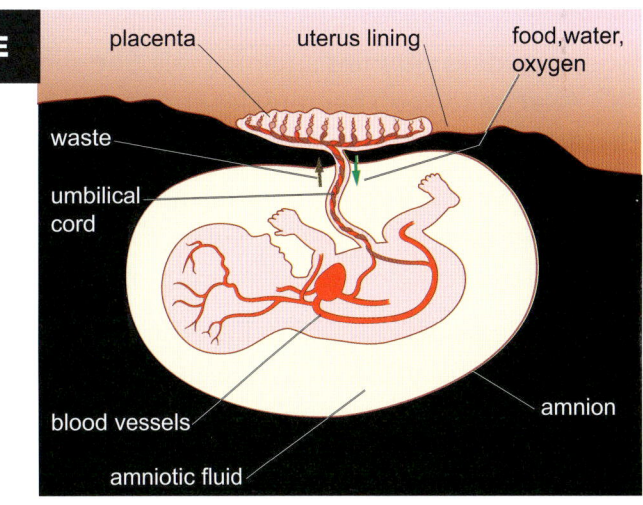

6 a| List three substances the embryo needs to grow.

b| Name one substance the embryo excretes.

7 Is the placenta made by the embryo or the mother?

8 What is the function of:

a| the placenta b| the umbilical cord
c| amniotic fluid?

9 As an embryo grows, its cells become specialised. Suggest one type of specialised cell that would be in the embryo in photo D and one type that would not.

I can ...
- describe how sexual intercourse can lead to the implantation of an embryo
- describe how an embryo is protected and cared for in the uterus.

29

7Bd GESTATION AND BIRTH

UK NC, CEE

WHAT HAPPENS DURING THE GESTATION PERIOD AND BIRTH?

The **gestation period** is the time from fertilisation until birth. It lasts about 9 months (40 weeks) in humans. The gestation period is very long in some animals, which can make breeding them in zoos difficult.

Once an embryo has developed a full set of **organs** it is called a **foetus** (pronounced '*fee-tus*'). This takes about 8 weeks in humans.

> **FACT**
> The endangered black rhino has a gestation period of 16 months.

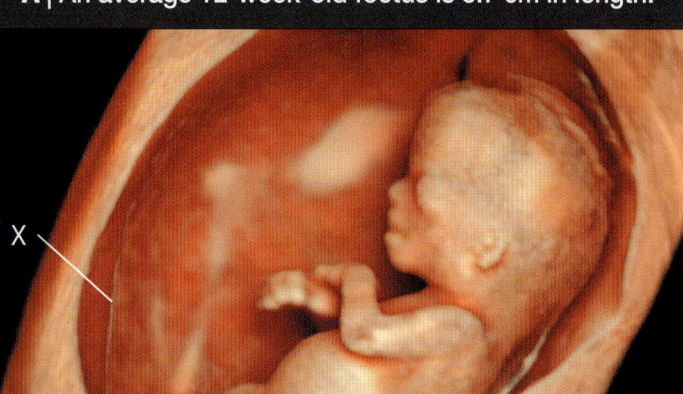

A | An average 12-week-old foetus is 8.7 cm in length.

1 About how long does a human spend as a foetus?

2 a| What are the parts labelled X and Y on photo A?
b| Explain the importance of these parts for the developing foetus.

A pregnant woman needs a healthy diet because she provides the growing and developing foetus with food, including vitamins and minerals. She should also exercise to keep her muscles strong and her **circulatory system** working well.

Most pregnant women go for **ultrasound scans**, which produce **images** of the foetus. Doctors use scans to check the stage of development and for any problems.

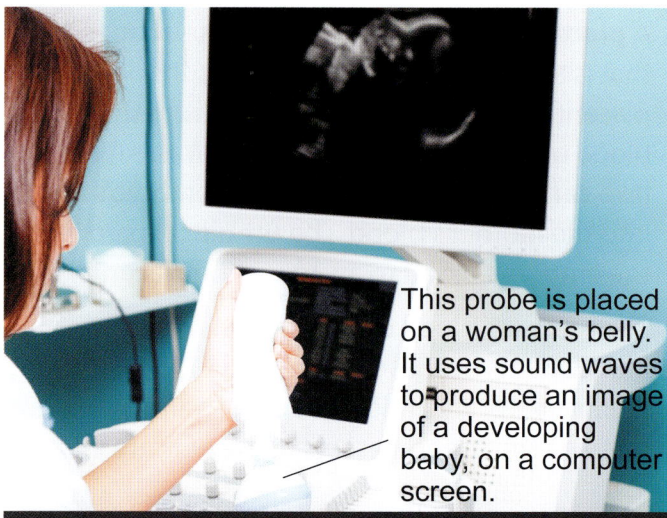

This probe is placed on a woman's belly. It uses sound waves to produce an image of a developing baby, on a computer screen.

B | Ultrasound scanners usually produce basic black and white images but some can produce detailed colour images (such as photo A).

Alcohol, illegal **drugs** (such as **heroin**), nicotine from cigarette smoke and some viruses can go through the placenta and harm the foetus (particularly its brain). Doctors also need to be careful about what medicines they give to pregnant women.

3 a| A scan shows a foetus is 7 cm long. What can you say about its age? Explain your reasoning.
b| Suggest two advantages of having ultrasound scans during pregnancy.

> **FACT**
> In the 1950s, a drug called thalidomide was given to pregnant women to help them stop feeling sick. It caused many babies to be born with very short arms and legs.

The blood of a woman who smokes carries less oxygen than it should, which means that the foetus may not get enough oxygen. A foetus like this is more likely to be **premature** (born small and early).

Viruses are tiny microorganisms that can cause diseases. The virus that causes rubella can cause a foetus to become deformed. Girls are often vaccinated against rubella.

> **4** Describe how a foetus can be harmed by substances in cigarette smoke.

C | Premature babies often need help to breathe and keep warm.

Birth

When a baby is ready to be born, the uterus begins to contract (squeeze). This is the start of **labour**. The **contractions** start gently but become more powerful and more frequent. The muscles of the cervix then slowly relax, making it wider. At some stage, the amnion breaks and the amniotic fluid flows out of the vagina.

Once the cervix is about 10 cm wide, the strong contractions of the uterus push the baby through it, usually head first. This is painful and the woman may be given medicine to ease the pain.

When the baby is out, its umbilical cord is cut, leaving a short stump. This falls off after about a week and leaves a scar called the **navel** (or 'belly button').

Within 30 minutes after birth, the placenta detaches and passes out through the vagina. This is called the **afterbirth** and is the end of labour.

A new baby is fed on milk from **mammary glands** in the breasts. This contains nutrients to give the baby energy and help it grow. It also contains **antibodies** – substances that help to prevent diseases caused by microorganisms. After a few months the baby can start eating semi-solid food.

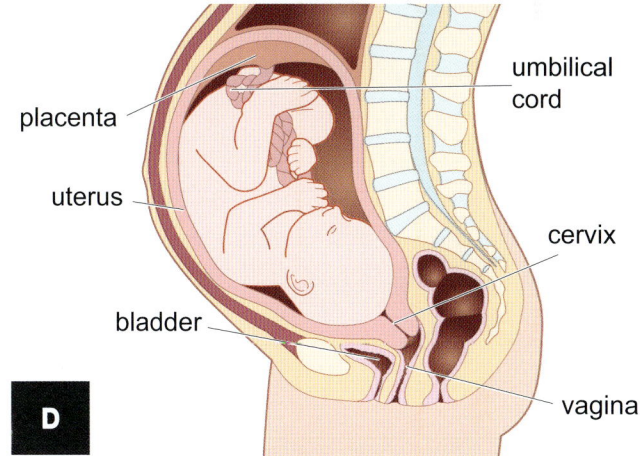

D

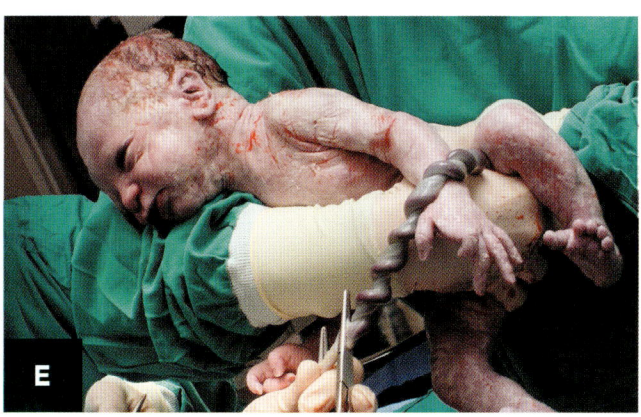

E

> **5** List the main stages of labour.
> **6** Write a caption for photo E.
> **7** Why does the cervix need to open after contractions start?
> **8** Explain the actions that a woman can take to care for her foetus. Make notes, perhaps using a table of actions and reasons, before writing a paragraph.

I can …

- explain how a pregnant woman should care for her foetus
- recall the stages of birth and how a newborn baby is looked after.

7Bd ENDANGERED SPECIES

HOW DO ZOOLOGISTS TRY TO STOP EXTINCTION?

About 27 000 **species** (types) of organism are **endangered**, which means they may soon be **extinct**. Scientists count organisms to find out how endangered they are. Technology, such as satellites and drones, helps to do this.

In the 1960s, the numbers of Arabian oryx became very low, due to hunting. So, scientists decided to set up a breeding programme. To start, they captured three oryx from the Arabian Desert. Many others wanted to help the project and found other oryx to give to the programme, including the King of Saudi Arabia, the Emir of Kuwait and London Zoo. It was decided to fly the oryx to Phoenix Zoo in the USA, because it had plenty of space and desert conditions similar to the natural **habitat** where the oryx lived.

A | Warm animals show up on thermal images. This image was taken in a zoo while training a computer to recognise animals from thermal images. A drone carries the thermal camera and sends images to the computer.

The last wild Arabian oryx died in 1972, but the oryx in the zoo had bred and their numbers were increasing. Now, some of these oryx have been put back into the wild in Oman, Saudi Arabia, the UAE and Jordan. The scientists saved the Arabian oryx from extinction and local conservation organisations in these countries ensure that the species continues to survive and grow in numbers.

B | an Arabian oryx

1
a | Name the animal in photo A.
b | Suggest why it is difficult to count these animals in areas covered with large bushes.
c | Explain how drone technology could make it easier to count the animals.

2 State why Arabian oryx became extinct in the wild.

3 The gestation period of an Arabian oryx is 8 months. What does this mean?

STEM

Careers in zoology

Scientists who study animals are zoologists. Some zoologists study animals in their natural habitats (e.g. forests, deserts, the Arctic). Other zoologists help to breed endangered species in zoos.

Zoologists need a university degree and must be good at applying knowledge to new situations. For example, at a zoo they need to know about the conditions in an animal's habitat and then apply that knowledge to create similar conditions in the zoo. They start by listing the natural conditions and the zoo conditions (e.g. amount of rain, temperature). They then compare them. This identifies the conditions that may need changing at the zoo.

C | This tiger enclosure at a zoo in Spain tries to match the conditions of the natural tiger habitat in India.

Zoologists also apply their knowledge of human reproduction to animals. For example, doctors have invented ways to help some people have children, such as by placing sperm cells directly into oviducts to increase the chances of fertilisation. Zoologists compare the reproductive organs of humans and animals, so they can adapt processes such as this for endangered animals. Now, sperm cells from a male animal can be transported to a zoo instead of a whole animal.

4 Suggest an advantage of transporting sperm cells to a zoo rather than a whole animal.

5 Using your knowledge of humans, suggest how a zoo could check the health of an unborn baby animal.

ACTIVITY

D | This giant panda cub was the result of sperm cells being placed directly into his mother.

Red pandas are endangered. They live up in the trees in mountain forests in Bhutan, India, Myanmar and China. The temperature range is usually 10–25 °C but their thick fur means that the pandas can survive periods of snow.

A zoo in your country wants to turn an open, grassy area into a home for red pandas. Work in a group to design an enclosure. Present your ideas as a diagram and write a report to show all the steps in your design process.

E | Red pandas mainly eat bamboo leaves.

33

7Be GROWING UP

WHAT HAPPENS DURING PUBERTY AND ADOLESCENCE?

A newborn animal needs to grow and go through **puberty** before it can reproduce. Puberty is a process in which big changes happen in its body, including fast growth and development of the reproductive system.

Puberty in humans usually starts between the ages of 10 and 15 years, with girls often starting before boys. During puberty, the testes begin making sperm cells and the ovaries begin releasing egg cells. Puberty is usually finished by the age of 18.

A | Obvious changes happen to male mandrills during puberty, starting when they are about 6 years old and ending when they are about 9.

Puberty is started by **sex hormones**, which are substances released by the brain, ovaries and testes. Sex hormones also cause spots (**acne**) and emotional changes, including becoming more aware of others. The time when all these emotional and physical changes occur is called **adolescence**.

Changes in boys during puberty	Changes in girls during puberty
shoulders get wider	hips get wider
hair grows on arms, face and chest	underarm hair grows
stronger body smell	stronger body smell
pubic hair grows	pubic hair grows
testes start to make sperm cells	ovaries start releasing egg cells (ova)
voice deepens (or 'breaks')	
testes and penis get bigger	

B

1. a| What is puberty?
   b| What chemicals control puberty?
   c| Where are these chemicals produced in girls?
2. What is adolescence?
3. Suggest three ways in which the changes during puberty are similar for boys and girls.
4. Describe the changes that happen to a male mandrill during puberty.
5. Imagine you write a magazine advice column. Somebody asks why they have suddenly got acne. Write a response.

FACT

Sex hormones cause skin pores to make more of a substance called sebum, which bacteria feed on. As the body kills the bacteria, the skin around a pore becomes red and a white pus may form. This is acne.

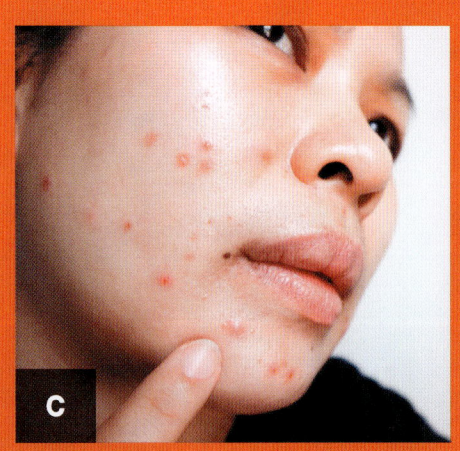

C

The menstrual cycle

The **menstrual cycle** is a series of events that occur in the female reproductive system. It starts soon after puberty begins and stops at the menopause. Each cycle takes about 28 days and is controlled by sex hormones.

D About 14 days after ovulation, if the egg cell has not been fertilised, the lining of the uterus breaks apart again and the cycle restarts with another period. If the woman becomes pregnant the cycle stops and the thick uterus lining continues to grow to provide the placenta with a good supply of nutrients and oxygen.

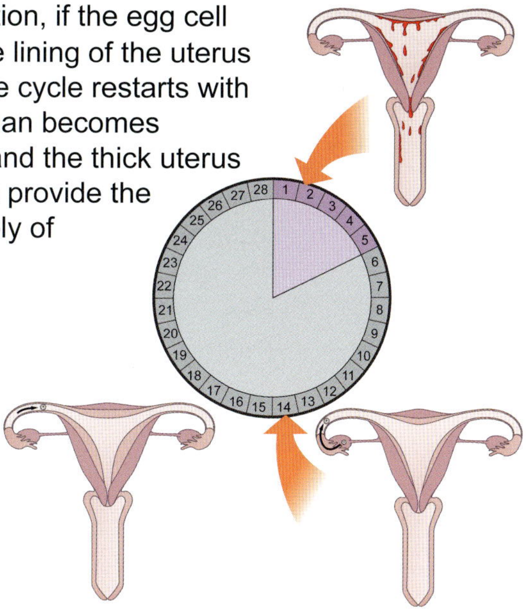

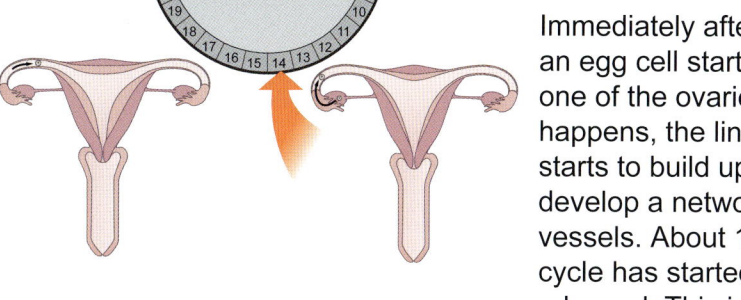

Menstruation ('having a period') is when the soft lining of the uterus breaks apart. It passes out of the vagina along with a little blood and an unfertilised egg cell. A period usually lasts for 3–7 days.

Cilia sweep the egg cell along the oviduct towards the uterus. If it meets a sperm cell it can be fertilised. The lining of the uterus helps to support, feed and protect an embryo, so it is replaced every cycle with fresh material to make sure it is in as good a condition as possible. It continues to thicken for about a week after ovulation.

Immediately after menstruation, an egg cell starts to develop in one of the ovaries. While this happens, the lining of the uterus starts to build up again, and to develop a network of blood vessels. About 14 days after the cycle has started, the egg cell is released. This is **ovulation**.

E | sanitary products

6	How long does one complete menstrual cycle usually take?
7	Describe what happens about 14 days after menstruation starts.
8	How might a woman tell that she is pregnant?
9	Why does the lining of the uterus have to become thick?

Periods usually occur once every 28–32 days, but this can vary a lot, especially when periods first start. Sanitary towels or tampons are used to absorb the blood.

Life cycles

The changes in an organism from birth until it can have offspring are called its **life cycle**. Humans have a long life cycle – it takes a long time for offspring to be able to reproduce. Mice have short life cycles – baby mice can reproduce in 5 weeks.

10	Draw out a human life cycle. Label it with information about what happens at the different stages.

I can ...

- describe and explain what happens during adolescence
- describe and explain what happens in the menstrual cycle.

7Be THE WORK OF ZOOS

HOW CAN STUDYING REPRODUCTION HELP ENDANGERED SPECIES?

Animals with short life cycles often produce many offspring, which are quickly able to reproduce. This can make it reasonably easy to breed these animals in captivity.

On the other hand, animals with long life cycles can be difficult to save from extinction because they take so long to reproduce and only produce small numbers of offspring. For example, a female Sumatran rhinoceros takes 7 years to become sexually mature. She has one calf at a time with a gestation period of 16 months.

Scientists in zoos try to help endangered animals like the Sumatran rhinoceros reproduce. They care for the animals and their offspring, and help them reproduce successfully by using technology that has been developed for humans.

A | The Panamanian golden frog was last seen in the wild in 2007. A successful breeding programme has produced nearly 2000 of them.

B | There may only be 150 Sumatran rhinoceroses left.

Things do not always go to plan. In the 1980s and 1990s, 40 Sumatran rhinoceroses were caught and sent to zoos. By 1997, 36 had died and no live calves had been born. The difficulty was that zoos did not know enough about their diet or reproduction. A solution was found in 2000 and the first calf was born in the USA in 2001, helped by sex hormone treatments. Since then other calves have been born in captivity.

1. Explain why many frogs produce a lot of offspring.
2. What is meant by 'gestation period'?
3. Suggest one technology developed for humans that is used to help endangered animals breed. Explain how this technology helps.
4. Draw a life cycle for the Sumatran rhinoceros. Label it with as much detail as you can.

HAVE YOUR SAY

Some people think we should get rid of zoos and only try to stop animals becoming extinct by protecting the areas in which they live. What do you think of this idea?

7Ca FITNESS

Being 'fit' means that your body is able to do the activities that your lifestyle demands. This includes things like being able to run upstairs without getting out of breath or being strong enough to lift things.

Fitness therefore means different things to different people, but we can think of fitness being made up of four S-factors: 'suppleness', 'strength', 'speed' and 'stamina'. A dancer needs to be supple to be able to turn their bodies and wave their arms smoothly, a wheelchair athlete needs speed, a bike rider needs stamina to go a long way without getting tired and in judo you need strength.

Just being able to do everyday things does not give you any idea of *how* fit you are. Scientists use **criteria** (standards) to work out how fit someone is. For example, how far you can run could be used as a criterion to judge fitness.

People exercise to develop different S-factors and keep their **organs** and **organ systems** working properly.

A | All these people are fit.

- **windpipe (trachea)**
- **lungs** get oxygen into the blood for respiration and excrete carbon dioxide
- **heart** pumps blood
- **diaphragm** helps breathing
- **liver** makes and stores some substances, and destroys other substances
- **kidneys** (one on each side) clean the blood and produce urine to excrete wastes
- **bladder** stores urine
- **oesophagus (gullet)**
- **stomach** breaks up food
- **small intestine** breaks up food and absorbs it to produce nutrition for the body
- **large intestine** removes water from unwanted food
- **rectum** stores faeces (waste materials excreted by the liver and unwanted food)

B | Physical exercise helps to keep many different organs working properly.

1. Look at the photos above. For each activity write down which S-factor you think is the most important. Explain your reasoning in each case.

2. Arrange this list in order of size, starting with the smallest: cell, organ, organ system, tissue.

3. The breathing (or gas exchange) system is important for athletes. Name three parts of this system.

4. What organ system do each of the organs in photo B belong to? Use a table to show your answers.

5. A long-distance runner is training to increase her stamina. Suggest a criterion she could use to judge whether her training programme is working.

37

7Ca MUSCLES AND BREATHING

HOW DO MUSCLES HELP WITH GAS EXCHANGE?

About one-fifth or 20 per cent of the air is **oxygen**. The athlete in photo A is **breathing** 100 per cent oxygen. The idea is that this makes sure all his **cells** get all the oxygen they need, to help him recover quickly from an injury.

You need oxygen for your cells to respire and release **energy**. Energy is needed for everything your body does. Cells get the oxygen they need from your blood. Oxygen enters your blood in your lungs.

Respiration in cells produces **carbon dioxide** gas, which enters your blood. In your lungs, a lot of carbon dioxide leaves your blood and is removed from your body when you breathe out. The carbon dioxide is **excreted**.

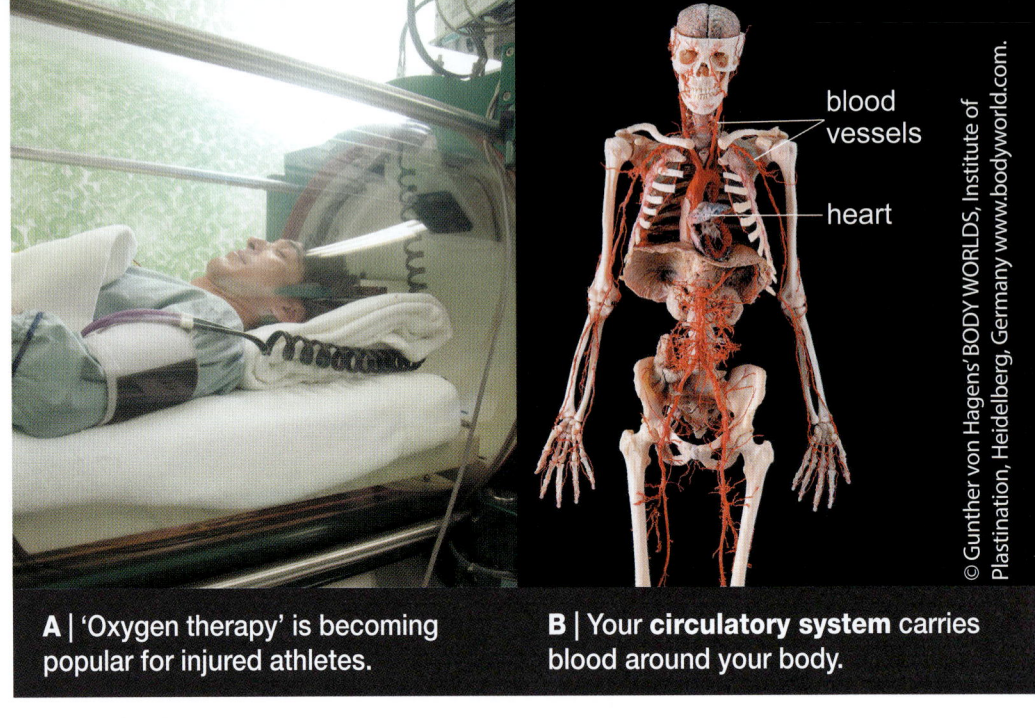

A | 'Oxygen therapy' is becoming popular for injured athletes.

B | Your **circulatory system** carries blood around your body.

FACT
There is a lot of tubing in the lungs. There are about 2400 km of tubes carrying air and another 1600 km of tubes carrying blood!

The gas exchange system

In your lungs, oxygen goes into the blood and carbon dioxide leaves the blood. One gas is exchanged for the other and so this is called **gas exchange**. The organs that help with gas exchange form the **breathing** or **gas exchange system**.

- trachea (windpipe) channels air into and out of the lungs
- lungs, where gas exchange occurs
- ribs
- diaphragm helps you to breathe
- **intercostal muscles** attached to ribs (mostly between the ribs) help you to breathe

C | some organs in the gas exchange system

1. What does your body need oxygen for?
2. List two organs in the circulatory system.
3. a | List two gases that are carried around your body.
   b | How are these gases carried?
   c | What happens to each of these gases in the lungs?

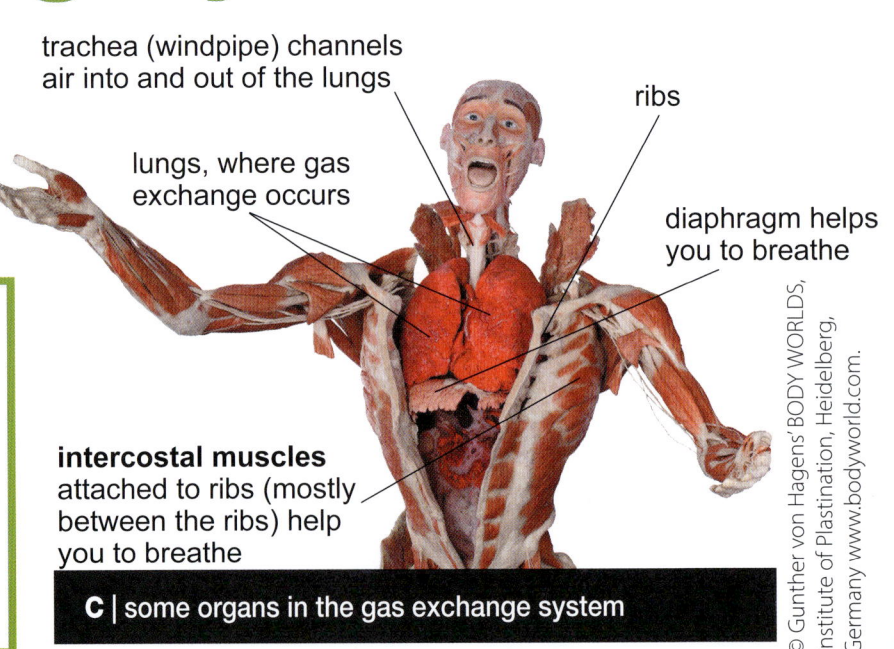

Breathing

Breathing is when muscles between the ribs and in the diaphragm change the size of the lungs. **Muscles** contain different types of **tissue**, including nerve tissue and **muscle tissue**. Muscle tissue is made of muscle cells, which can change shape.

A muscle cell gets short and fat as it **contracts**. When it goes back to its original shape and size, it **relaxes**.

Cells in a tissue all work together. So, all the muscle cells in muscle tissue contract and relax together, which means that the whole muscle contracts and relaxes.

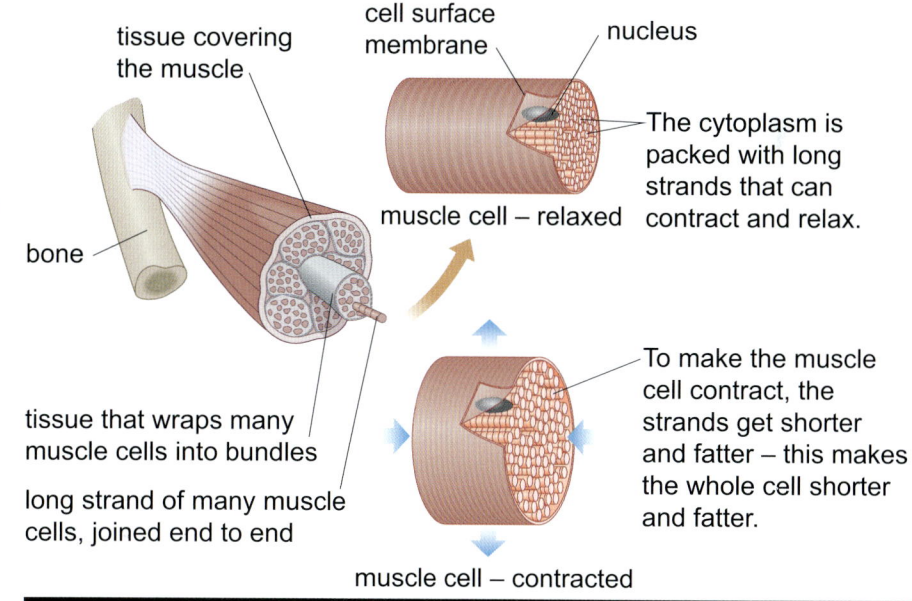

D | Muscle cells are **adapted** to their **function** – they can change shape. These muscle cells are not branched (unlike those in the heart).

Labels: tissue covering the muscle; bone; tissue that wraps many muscle cells into bundles; long strand of many muscle cells, joined end to end; cell surface membrane; nucleus; muscle cell – relaxed; The cytoplasm is packed with long strands that can contract and relax. muscle cell – contracted; To make the muscle cell contract, the strands get shorter and fatter – this makes the whole cell shorter and fatter.

4 Why is a muscle an organ?

5 a| What is the function of muscle cells?
b| How are muscle cells adapted to their function?

When the intercostal muscles between your ribs contract, they pull them outwards and upwards. When the muscles in your diaphragm contract, the diaphragm moves downwards and flattens out. These actions happen together and allow your lungs to increase in size. As they increase in size, air flows into them – you **inhale**.

When the rib and diaphragm muscles relax, the opposite happens. Air flows out of your lungs – you **exhale**. The movement of air into and out of your lungs is called **ventilation**. The number of times you inhale and exhale in one minute is your **breathing rate**.

E

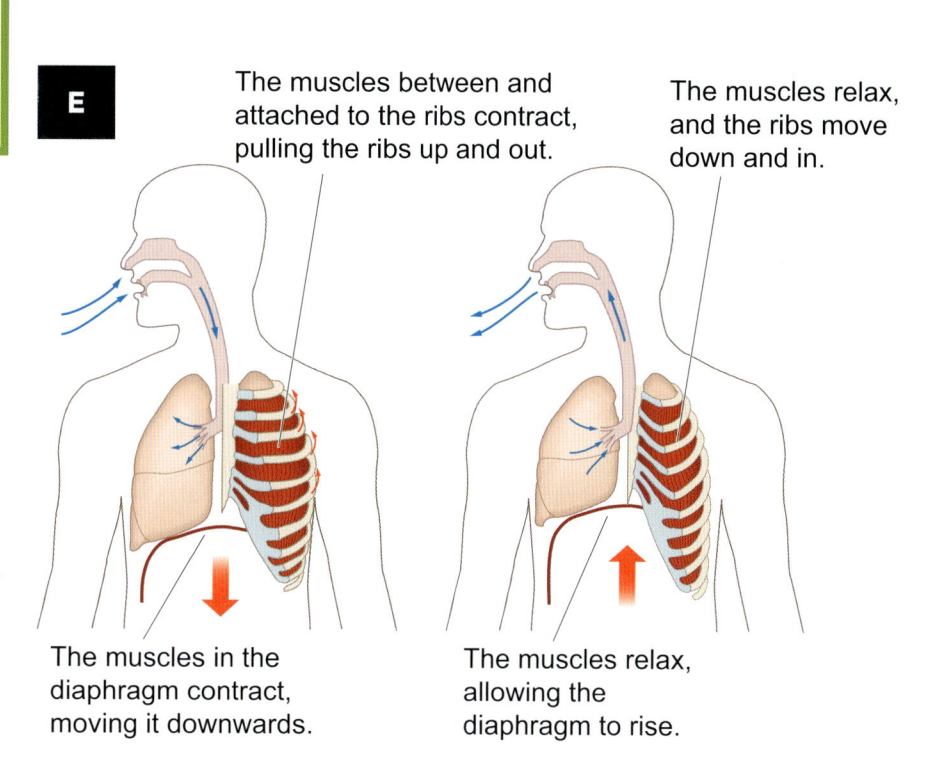

The muscles between and attached to the ribs contract, pulling the ribs up and out.

The muscles in the diaphragm contract, moving it downwards.

inhalation or inspiration (breathing in)

The muscles relax, and the ribs move down and in.

The muscles relax, allowing the diaphragm to rise.

exhalation or expiration (breathing out)

6 Omar breathes in and out seven times in 30 seconds. What is his breathing rate?

7 Guillain-Barré syndrome is a disease in which muscles become weak.
a| Explain why someone with this disease may find it difficult to breathe.
b| Explain why people with this disease may not get enough oxygen in their blood.
c| Suggest how a person with this condition might be helped.

8 The gas exchange system is also called the breathing, respiratory or ventilation system. Which of these terms do you think is the least good? Explain your reasoning.

I can ...

- describe how muscles in the gas exchange system allow ventilation
- describe what happens during gas exchange in the lungs.

7Cb MUSCLES AND BLOOD

HOW DO MUSCLES HELP WITH THE CIRCULATION OF BLOOD CELLS?

Sports scientists use machines to measure how well an athlete's body copes with exercise. The machines record things like breathing rate and **pulse rate**. The **data** helps the scientists to see if training programmes are working.

Each time your heart pumps blood, it causes a **pulse** that you can feel in places like your wrist. Your pulse rate is the number of pulse beats you can feel in a minute.

Inside the heart there are **chambers** that fill with blood. When the chambers are full, the muscle tissue in the wall of the heart contracts. This makes the chambers smaller, pumping the blood out of them.

A | a sports scientist at work

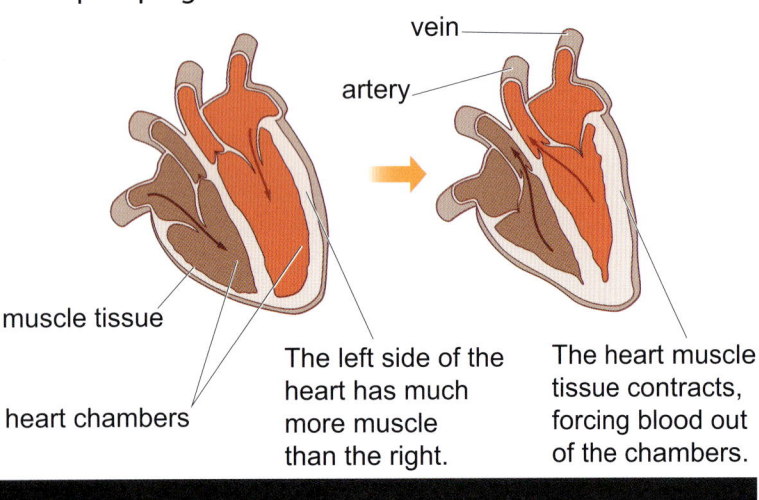

B | Muscle tissue in the heart contracts to push blood through the heart and into blood vessels called arteries.

Labels: vein, artery, muscle tissue, heart chambers, The left side of the heart has much more muscle than the right., The heart muscle tissue contracts, forcing blood out of the chambers.

1. Suggest two measurements that are being taken from the athlete in photo A.
2. a) What is a pulse caused by?
   b) Hattie counts 16 pulses in her wrist in 15 seconds. What is her pulse rate?
3. After blood has left the heart, what must the muscle tissue do so that the chambers can fill with blood again?

FACT
Fitter people have lower pulse rates than unfit people when resting. Most people have a pulse rate of 60–100 beats per minute. Athletes' pulse rates are often below 50 beats per minute.

Blood vessels

The heart pumps blood into **blood vessels** called **arteries**. The walls are thick and strong to withstand the high pressure of the blood from the heart. Arteries lead into tiny blood vessels called **capillaries**. Capillaries have very thin walls so that nutrients and oxygen can leave the blood and get to the cells in all the tissues in the body. Cells use these substances for respiration and to produce new materials for growth and repair.

The blood also picks up waste materials from cells as it travels through capillaries. It then flows into **veins**, which are wider, thin-walled tubes carrying blood back to the heart. Since veins are wider and have more flexible walls than arteries, the blood is under less pressure in veins and so flows more slowly.

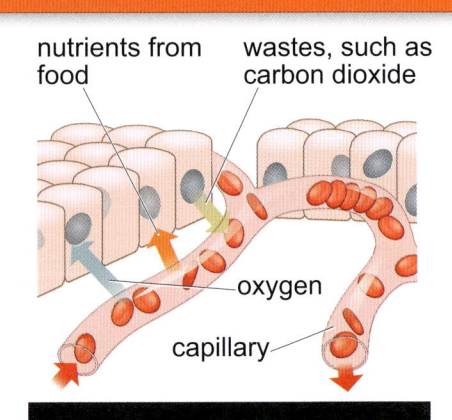

C | Substances can move into and out of capillaries.

Labels: nutrients from food, wastes, such as carbon dioxide, oxygen, capillary

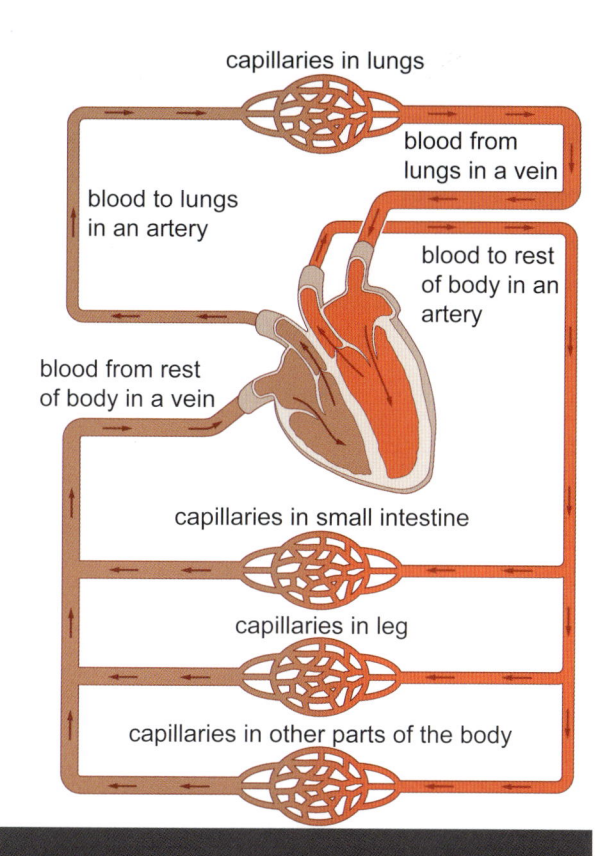

capillaries in lungs

blood to lungs in an artery

blood from lungs in a vein

blood to rest of body in an artery

blood from rest of body in a vein

capillaries in small intestine

capillaries in leg

capillaries in other parts of the body

D | The bright red blood is carrying more oxygen than the dark red blood. A circulatory system with two main loops is a **double circulatory system**, and blood goes through the heart twice. If there is only one loop it is a **single circulatory system**.

4	Name one waste produced by cells.
5	a| What are the functions of arteries, capillaries and veins? b| How are capillaries adapted to their function?
6	Look carefully at diagrams B and D. Suggest why the left-hand side of the heart has more muscle tissue.

Blood

Blood is mainly a liquid called **plasma**. Nutrients and waste materials are carried by blood dissolved in the plasma.

Oxygen is carried in cells called **red blood cells**. These cells lack **nuclei**, which allows the **cytoplasm** to be packed full of a substance called **haemoglobin** (*hee-mow-glow-bin*). The haemoglobin carries the oxygen. The cells have a curved disc shape, which gives them a large **surface area**. This means that oxygen can quickly get into and out of the cells.

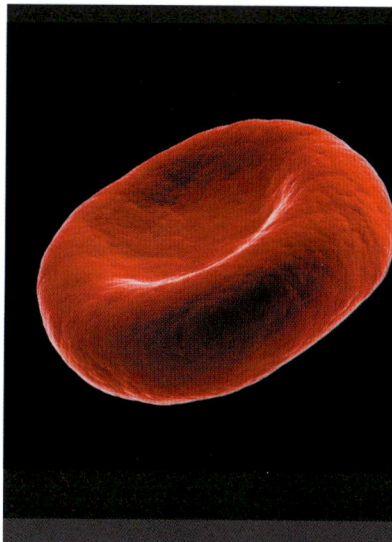

E | a red blood cell (magnification ×6000)

Red blood cells are made inside your bones, in a tissue called **bone marrow**. Blood contains other cells too. **White blood cells**, which are used to fight infections and keep you healthy, are also made in bone marrow.

FACT

A red blood cell only lasts for about 120 days. We need so many of them that an adult produces about 200 000 000 000 (200 billion) red blood cells every day.

bone marrow tissue

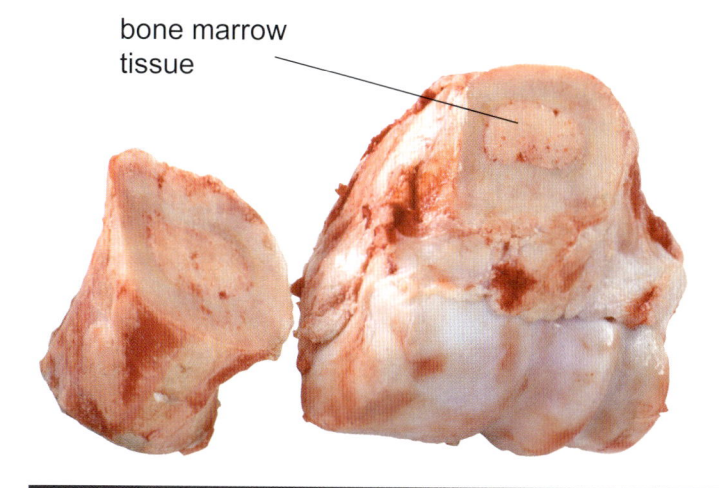

F | cross-section through a bone

7	Explain the differences in pressure between blood going away from the heart and returning to the heart.
8	a| List three main parts of the blood. b| What does each part do? c| Where are blood cells made? d| How are red blood cells adapted to their function?
9	A chicken has a double circulatory system. Explain what this means.

I can ...

- describe the functions of the different parts of the human double circulatory system
- describe the functions of the different parts of blood, and where the cells are made.

7Cb SCIENTIFIC QUESTIONS

UK NC, iLS, CEE

WHAT ARE SCIENTIFIC QUESTIONS?

A Roman doctor called Galen (129–200 CE) said that the liver looked like blood and so blood must be made in the liver. He also thought that the body used up blood and that the heart had to beat in order to 'attract' blood into it. Blood in the heart then mixed with oxygen from the lungs and formed a different type of blood that travelled to all the parts of the body, where it was used up. Galen did not know about capillaries because they are too small to see without magnifying them. Galen was so famous that people believed him for another 1500 years! Believing what someone says is one way to gain knowledge but it is not how modern scientists work.

Scientists often use the **scientific method** to gain knowledge (see pages 22–23). They ask questions and come up with ideas (**hypotheses**). They keep testing those hypotheses to see if they are correct or whether they need changing.

Scientists often start by thinking up questions about **observations** they have made. Galen observed hearts moving and asked 'Why do hearts beat?'

William Harvey (1578–1657) asked the same question but he thought that the heart was a pump. Unlike Galen, he tested his idea. For example, he squashed an animal heart with his hand and made it move some water. This showed that the heart could act as a pump, and that it only pumped liquids in one direction. He then did a famous calculation, shown in the Method opposite.

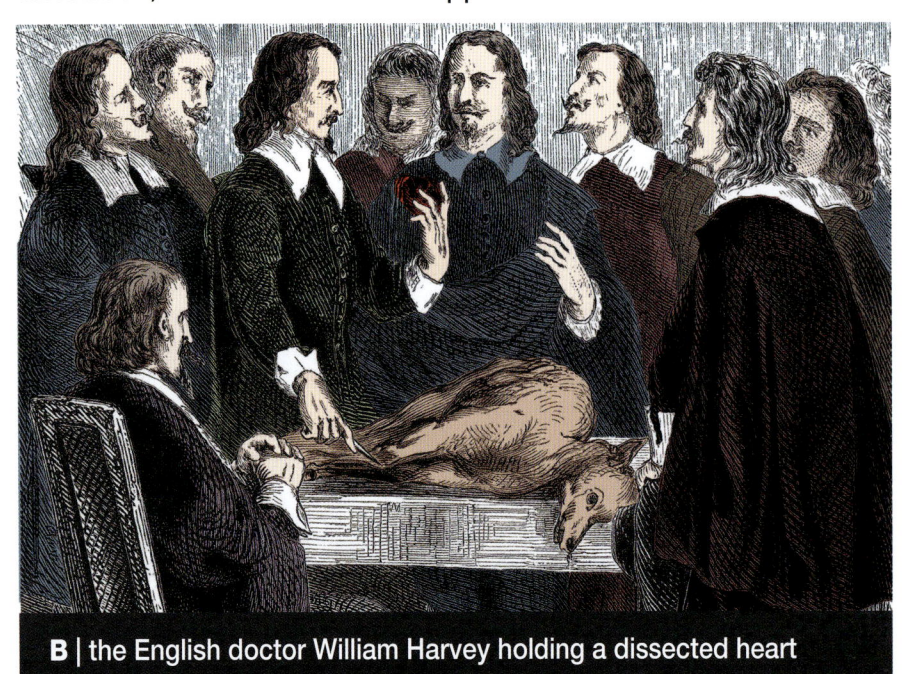

A | Galen's ideas

Harvey calculated that so much blood comes out of the heart each day that it would be impossible for the liver to make it all. Harvey's work led him to the **theory** that blood was not used up but flowed away from the heart in arteries and then back towards it in veins. This theory of blood circulation predicted the existence of other tubes connecting arteries to veins. Capillaries were later discovered in 1661 by Marcello Malpighi (1628–1694).

B | the English doctor William Harvey holding a dissected heart

1 Where are blood cells actually made?

WORKING SCIENTIFICALLY

Method

A | Hold two fingers firmly on your wrist, as shown in photo C. You should feel your pulse.

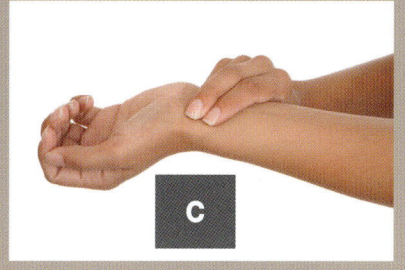

B | Count the pulse beats you feel in 15 seconds. Multiply this by four and this gives you your pulse rate in beats per minute.

C | Harvey measured the volume of the big left-hand chamber of the heart in dead bodies. The volume of this chamber in you is about 130 cm^3. This volume falls to about half that when your heart muscle contracts. Use this information to work out the volume of blood your heart pumps each minute.

D | Now work out the volume of blood your heart pumps each day.

Types of question

The question 'Why do hearts beat?' is a scientific question. However, of the two doctors mentioned here, only Harvey answered it in a scientific way. A scientific question is one that can be answered again and again using information from experiments and investigations.

Some scientific questions have not been answered because we do not yet have the right technology or because we have not done enough experiments. For example, 'What do the newly discovered MSC cells do in the heart?'

Other questions are not scientific because they cannot be answered using investigations or experiments. These include **ethical questions**, which are questions about what people think is fair or right or wrong.

D | different types of questions

Should we treat this patient?

Would we look better wearing a darker blue colour?

Why is this patient's pulse rate so high?

Why is this patient's blood pressure so high?

2 Arwa's pulse rate is 65 beats per minute. Using the information in step C in the Method above, work out the volume of blood her heart pumps each hour. Show your working.

3 What prediction did Harvey make using his theory about circulation?

4 In what way did Harvey act more scientifically than Galen?

5 Think up a scientific question about the liver.

6 Say whether each of these questions is a scientific, non-scientific and/or an ethical question.

A| Are parts of a taxi driver's brain bigger than average?

B| Should William Harvey have killed animals to use for his experiments?

C| Do older people generally have lower pulse rates than younger people?

D| Do roses smell nicer than freesia flowers?

E| Does exercise affect your pulse rate?

I can ...

- describe the role of scientific questions in the scientific method
- identify scientific, non-scientific and ethical questions.

7Cc THE SKELETON

WHAT ARE THE FUNCTIONS OF THE SKELETON?

People who do sport for a living need to get treatment quickly if they are injured. Big football clubs spend millions on building specialist treatment centres to ensure their players get the best possible treatment.

Bones

Many people think that bones are not living, but bones *are* living organs. They grow as you grow and repair themselves if they **fracture** (break). Bones are hard and strong so that they can stand up to hard knocks and **pressure**. They are also light so they can be moved easily.

circles of bone produced by bone-making cells called osteoblasts

cartilage tissue

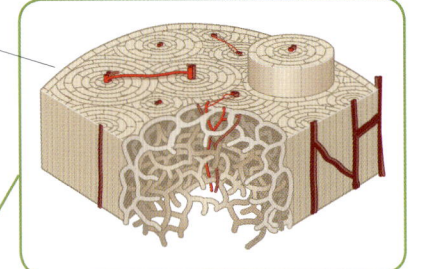

Spongy bone material has many spaces in it to keep the whole bone light.

Compact bone material is very hard and strong, but is also heavy. It is used to form a tube shape, which is a very strong shape.

The inside of a bone is filled with bone marrow tissue. This helps to reduce the mass of the bone (and the bone marrow makes blood cells).

B | Bone-making cells (osteoblasts) can produce bone material in different ways, forming compact bone and spongy bone.

FACT
Babies have about 270 bones but some of them fuse together as they grow. An adult has 206 bones.

A | Common footballing injuries include broken bones and damage to cartilage, tendons and ligaments.

1. a| State two things that osteoblasts need to stay alive.
   b| What process do osteoblasts need these things for?
2. Explain why a large bone can be both strong and light.
3. How can you tell that the bone in diagram B is an organ?

Support

The bones in your body form your **skeleton**, shown in photo C. Your skeleton makes sure that your body keeps its shape and also supports your body. The **backbone** is made up of smaller bones called **vertebrae** and is the human body's main support.

Some bones help to support organs. For example, your lungs would collapse without your ribs.

4. What do your ribs and sternum form?
5. Give one function of the backbone.

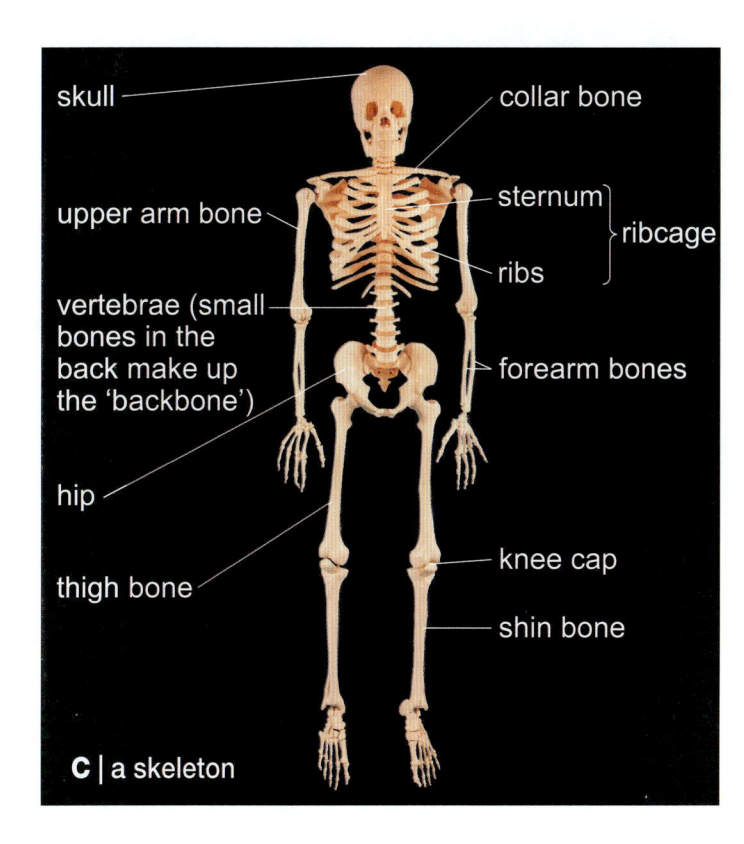

C | a skeleton

Labels: skull, collar bone, upper arm bone, sternum, ribs, ribcage, vertebrae (small bones in the back make up the 'backbone'), forearm bones, hip, knee cap, thigh bone, shin bone

Protection

Some bones protect organs in the body. For example, the **skull** protects the **brain**. The skull is actually made of 22 bones that are connected by **fixed joints**.

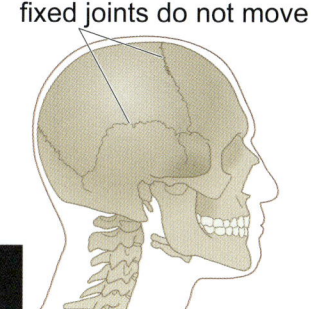

D — fixed joints do not move

> **6** The nervous system includes the brain and the spinal cord. Your spinal cord is a large bundle of important nerves that runs down your back. Which bones protect:
> a| your brain   b| your spinal cord?
>
> **7** Which organs are protected by your ribcage?

FACT
The smallest bone in the body is the stapes or stirrup bone in the ear. It is about the size of a grain of rice, and its function is to transfer **sound waves** into the inner ear.

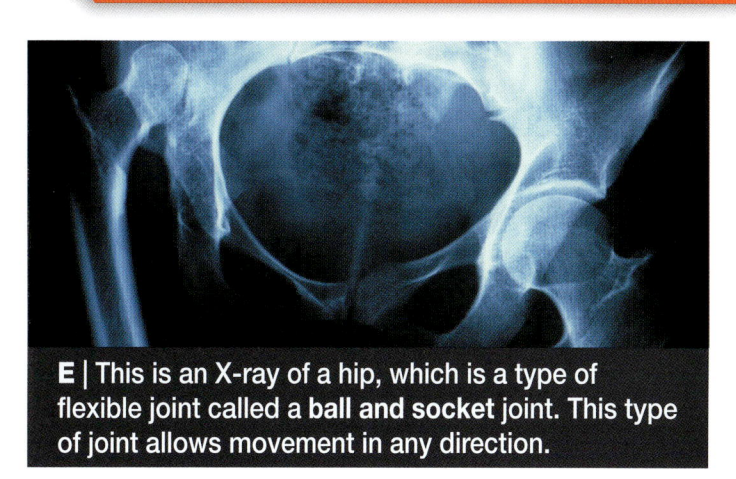

E | This is an X-ray of a hip, which is a type of flexible joint called a **ball and socket** joint. This type of joint allows movement in any direction.

Movement

Two bones next to each other can form a **flexible joint**. The bones in a flexible joint are moved by muscles, which are attached to the bones by **tendons**. **Ligaments** hold the bones in a flexible joint together. The ends of bones in a flexible joint are often covered in a slippery tissue called **cartilage**, which helps them slide past each other.

Flexible joints can be damaged when playing sports. A sprain occurs when a ligament stretches or tears. Sprains can cause dislocations, in which bones in a joint move out of line so that the joint does not work. When people 'pull muscles', either a muscle or the tendon that connects the muscle to a bone gets a small tear in it.

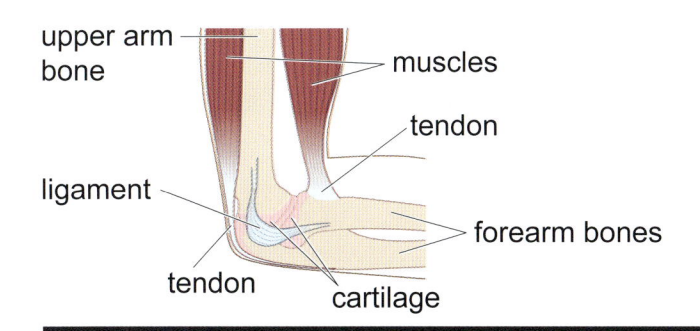

Labels: upper arm bone, muscles, tendon, ligament, tendon, cartilage, forearm bones

F | The elbow is a type of flexible joint called a **hinge joint**, which only allows back and forth movement.

> **8**
> a| List three different types of joint.
> b| Which joint allows the most movement?
> c| What causes the bones to move?
>
> **9** Describe the different functions of bones.
>
> **10**
> a| In X-ray E, what bone forms the 'ball' in this joint?
> b| The joint on the right of the X-ray is normal. What has happened to the joint on the left?
> c| Suggest how this has occurred.

I can ...
- describe the functions of different bones in the skeleton
- describe some different types of joint.

7Cd MUSCLES AND MOVING

HOW ARE MUSCLES USED IN THE LOCOMOTOR SYSTEM?

Skeletons are always changing, and athletes' training programmes are designed to change both their muscles and their bones. These changes help the athletes become better at their particular sports. This does not just apply to athletes, though. People who do a lot of manual work develop thicker arm bones than people who work in offices. The thicker bones are needed to support bigger muscles.

The muscles and bones in your body form an organ system called the **locomotor system**. It is this system that allows you to move all the parts of your body. The study of how muscles and bones work together is called **biomechanics**.

A | When people train, they change both their muscles and their bones.

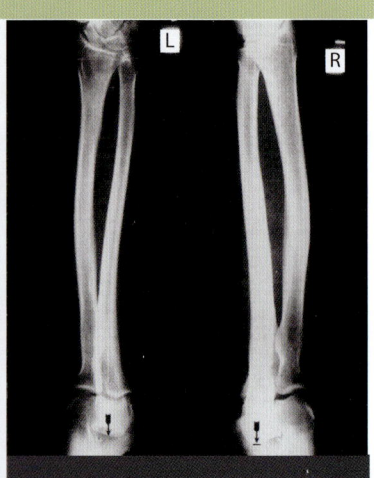

B | an X-ray of the forearm bones of a professional tennis player showing that playing tennis has changed the bones

1. A boxer fights in the lightweight class (59–61.2 kg). After a few years of training he then fights in the light welterweight class (61.3–63.5 kg). Suggest why his mass has increased.
2. Look at photo B. In which hand do you think the tennis player holds the tennis racquet? Explain your reasoning.
3. Make a fist and tighten your fingers.
   a | Where are the muscles that let you tighten your fingers?
   b | What happens to them when you tighten your fingers?

C | The force from a muscle or a group of muscles can be measured in newtons using a type of force meter.

Antagonistic muscles

Muscles are organs that can contract. When they contract they get shorter and fatter. So, if a muscle is attached to a bone, it will pull on the bone when it contracts. The muscle will generate a **force** that can be measured, in **newtons (N)**.

FACT

The smallest muscle in your body is attached to the smallest bone. The stapedius muscle is attached to the stapes bone in the ear. The muscle is about 1 mm long.

4 Name two organs in the locomotor system.

When a muscle stops contracting, it relaxes. This means that it returns to its original size and shape. Muscles do not generate a force when they relax, which means that muscles cannot push on bones – they can only pull them.

For a bone in a joint to be moved in two different directions, it needs to be pulled by two different muscles. Pairs of muscles like this are called **antagonistic pairs**. The **biceps** and **triceps** are an antagonistic pair of muscles in the upper arm, shown in diagram E.

When you lift your arm, the biceps muscle contracts.

When you put your arm down, the biceps muscle is stretched.

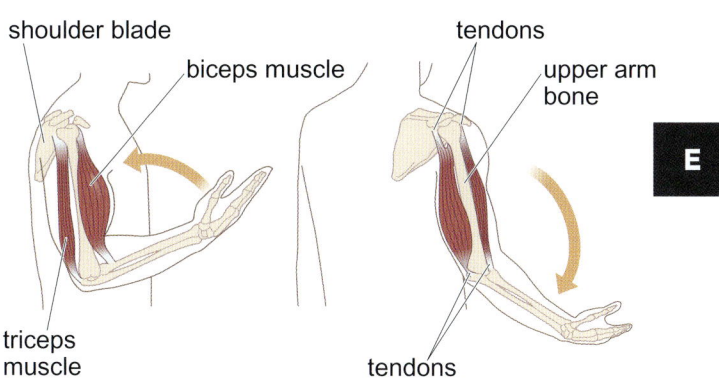

When you lift your arm, the triceps muscle is stretched.

When you put your arm down, the triceps muscle contracts.

E

5 When the biceps muscle contracts, what happens to the triceps muscle?

6 Why do muscles work in antagonistic pairs?

7 Look at drawing F. It shows some muscles in the body. You do not need to remember all their names!

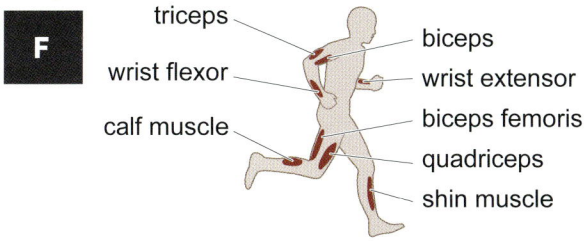

F triceps, wrist flexor, calf muscle, biceps, wrist extensor, biceps femoris, quadriceps, shin muscle

a| Write down all the antagonistic pairs you can see.
b| If you point your toes to the ground, which muscle contracts?
c| If you raise your toes, which muscle contracts?
d| Describe fully what happens just before and during contraction of the biceps femoris muscle.

D | the bite force of an alligator being measured

FACT

The human muscle that can exert the most force is the masseter or jaw muscle. The maximum force of a human bite is about 2500 N. In dogs it is about 6900 N. Alligators have 9 500 N of bite force.

Muscle control

To make a muscle contract, the brain sends electrical messages down the **spinal cord** into **nerves** attached to the muscle. These electrical messages are called **impulses**.

Energy needs

Muscles have to work hard and so their cells need a lot of energy. Respiration releases energy and occurs in tiny structures in cells called **mitochondria**. So, it is no surprise to find that muscle cells usually contain more mitochondria than other cells do.

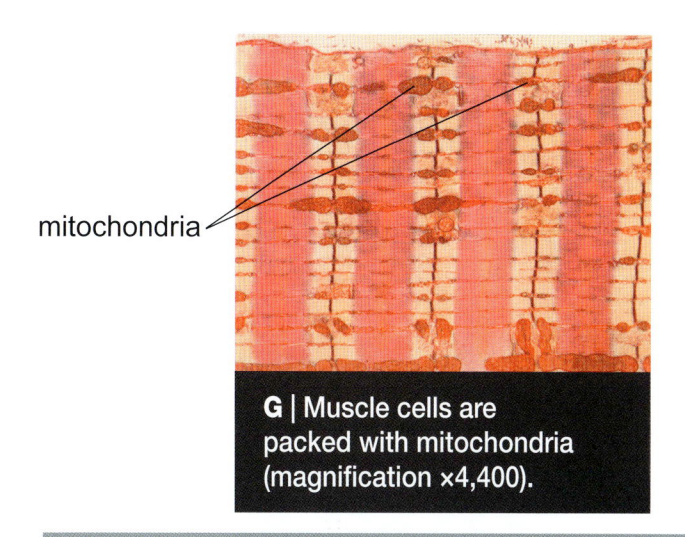

G | Muscle cells are packed with mitochondria (magnification ×4,400).

I can ...

- explain how antagonistic pairs of muscles operate and are controlled, to allow movement.

47

7Cd ARTIFICIAL LIMBS

HOW DO WE HELP PEOPLE WHO NEED REPLACEMENT LIMBS?

An artificial part to replace something in your body is called a prosthesis (*pros-thee-sis*). The wooden toe in photo A is an ancient example.

Today, common prostheses include arms and legs. These must be comfortable, strong and light, and allow the person to move parts of their body again.

Each prosthesis is designed and adapted to fit a specific person, and many adjustments may be needed. New technology (such as 3D printing) is speeding up the process.

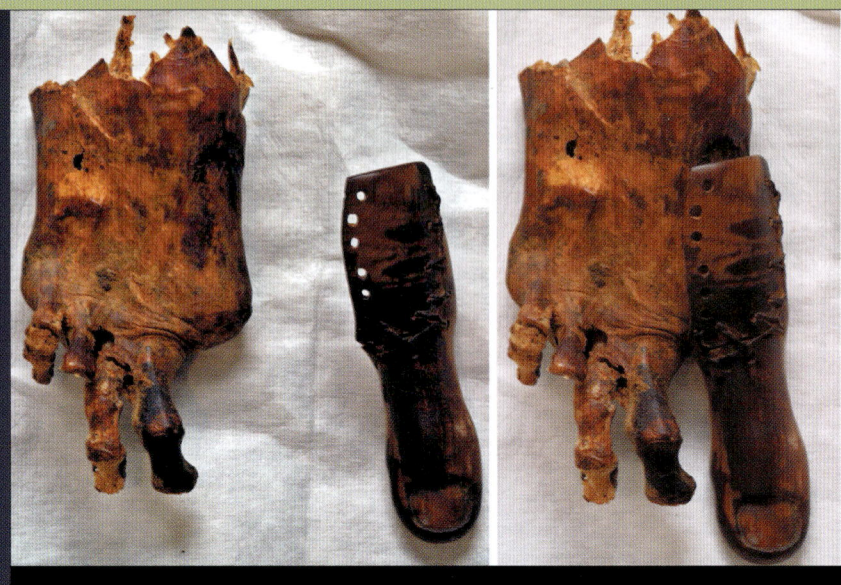

A | a toe prosthesis found on a 3000-year-old skeleton in Egypt

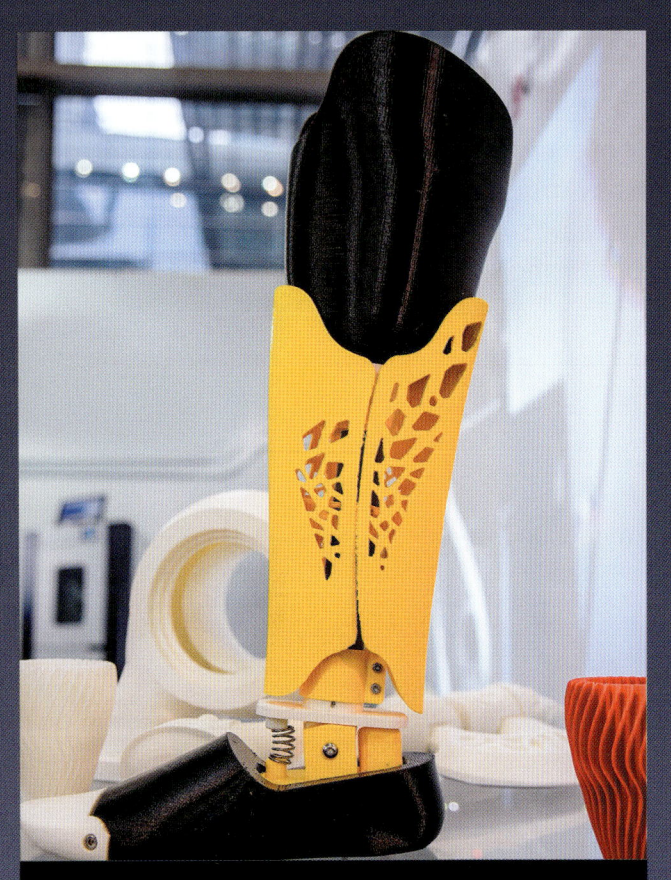

Arms with gripping attachments, as in photo C, were invented over 100 years ago but are still common. A spring holds the gripper shut. The wearer moves their shoulder backwards to open the gripper. Plastics can make the attachment look more like a hand. Adding electrical switches or computer control can give a larger range of movements.

Advances in our understanding of the nervous system allow some artificial limbs to be controlled by thoughts in a person's brain. Scientists are also developing artificial limbs that let people feel again.

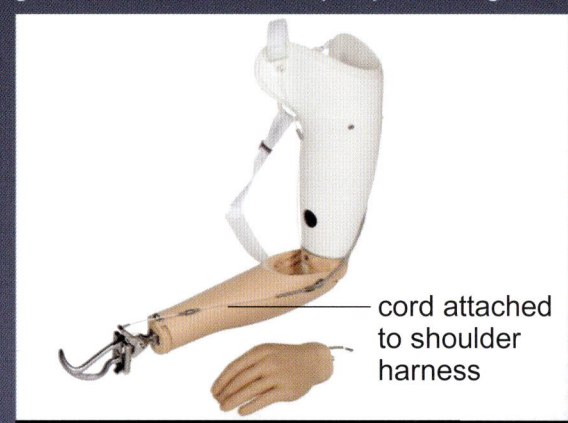

B | 3D printing is making it easier for people to get artificial limbs that fit well.

C | artificial arm — cord attached to shoulder harness

STEM

Designing prosthetics

A prosthetist designs and makes prosthetics. A patient says what they need to do and the prosthetist chooses the best type of prosthetic. After taking measurements (often using a scanner), the prosthetist makes a full-size model.

The prosthetist and patient work out how well the model does its job – they **evaluate** it. To do this, they score the model points for things it should do (e.g. be comfortable, allow movement). These things are called **criteria**. The model is then changed and evaluated again. Once the model is correct, the prosthetic can be made. The prosthetic is also evaluated and further adjustments may be needed.

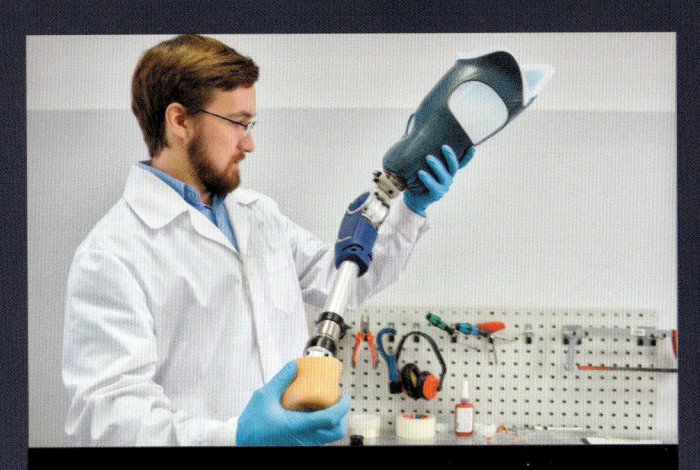

1 Suggest one way in which a person's life is affected if they lose a thumb.

2 a | Suggest one way in which a big toe prosthesis helps someone without a big toe.
b | Suggest why the toe in photo A was adjusted several times during the person's life.

3 List four features of a good artificial leg.

4 Explain how the gripper on the arm in photo C is opened and closed.

D | a prosthetist at work

A prosthetist often works in a hospital, along with physiotherapists (who design exercises for patients) and occupational therapists (who help patients to find ways to do certain actions). To become a prosthetist you need good levels of maths, physics and biology when you leave school. You then go to university or a teaching hospital to study for a degree in prosthetics.

5 a | Why must the materials used to make a prosthetic leg be strong?
b | Give two more criteria you would use to work out if a material was suitable for a leg.

PRACTICAL

A patient has had their left leg removed just above the knee. They want to be able to stand and walk slowly.

a In a group, design and build a model prosthesis. Your teacher will give you some materials to choose from.

b Evaluate your model, using a copy of the chart.

c List improvements for your model and explain why you would make each improvement.

E

Criteria	How easy is it on a scale of 0–4? (0 = not possible, 4 = very easy)
able to stand still	
comfortable when standing still	
feel steady when standing still	
able to walk slowly	
comfortable when walking slowly	
feel steady when walking slowly	

UK NC, CEE

7Ce DRUGS

HOW DO DRUGS AFFECT OUR BODIES?

Many professional athletes avoid certain substances because of the effects that they have on their bodies.

A **drug** is a substance that affects the way your body works. Caffeine, nicotine and alcohol are all drugs. Some drugs are **medicines**, which help people recover from illness or injury. For example:

- paracetamol reduces pain
- ibuprofen reduces pain and swelling
- decongestants in medicines for colds help you breathe more easily.

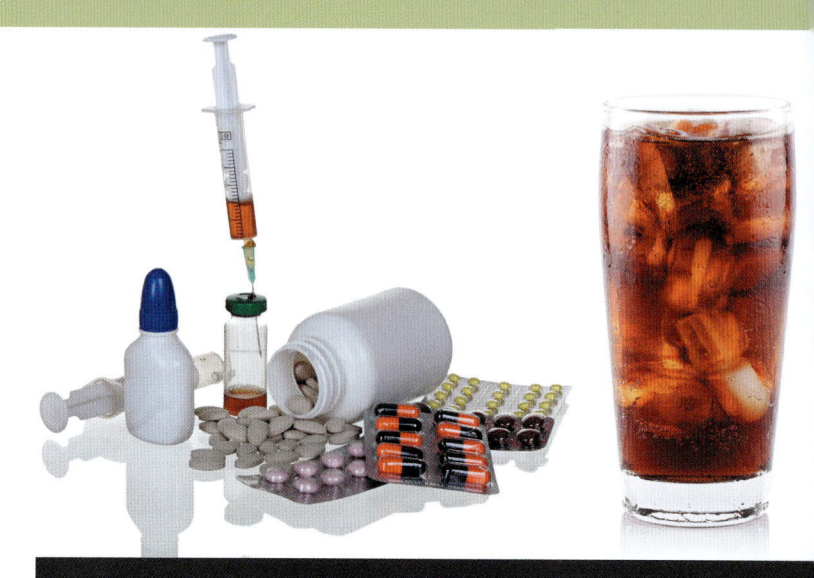

During an asthma attack, the muscles surrounding the tubes carrying air contract hard. This makes it difficult to breathe, but a medicine can make the muscles relax.

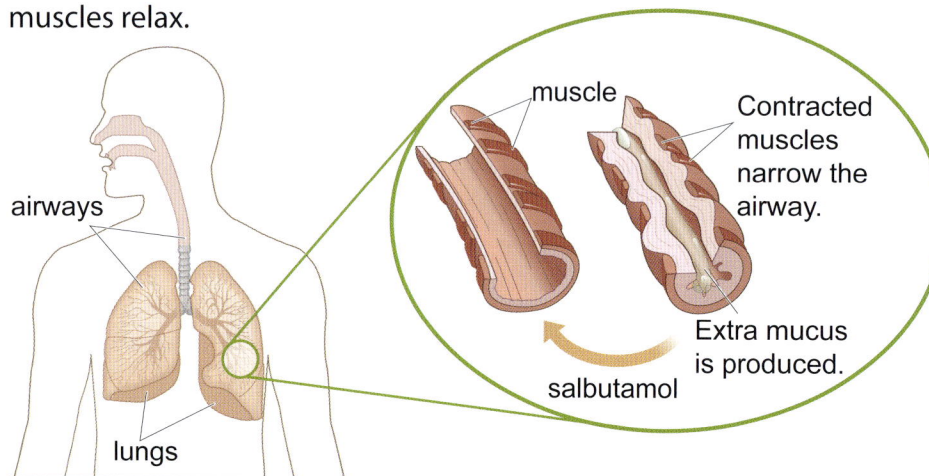

A | Medicines and everyday items like cola contain drugs.

B | Medicines like salbutamol are used to treat asthma attacks.

1 a| Suggest a sports injury that you might take medicine(s) for.
b| What medicine(s) would you take and why?

2 In an asthma attack, why is it hard to breathe?

Although many drugs are useful, they can have harmful or unpleasant **side-effects**. For example, paracetamol can damage the liver. Drugs often damage the liver because this organ breaks drugs down.

3 a| What is the useful effect of paracetamol?
b| What is its side-effect?

Substance misuse

Some drugs (such as **nicotine**) can become **addictive**, which means that people feel they cannot manage without them. Addicts often continue using a drug even though they can see the damage it is causing. The harmful use of any substance is called **substance abuse** (or **substance misuse**), and often causes brain and liver damage.

Recreational drugs

Recreational drugs are drugs taken for pleasure. **Caffeine** is a legal recreational drug. Others are illegal because of their side-effects. **Cannabis** can cause memory loss and mental illness. **Ecstasy** can cause mental illness, kidney problems, and even death. **Cocaine** can cause blocked arteries. **Heroin** can cause collapsed veins, vomiting and severe headaches.

Stimulants

Drugs often affect the **nervous system**, which controls your body using electrical signals called impulses. Drugs that cause the nervous system to carry impulses faster are **stimulants**. They can decrease your **reaction time**, which is the time it takes you to respond to things happening around you. Caffeine, cocaine and ecstasy are all stimulants.

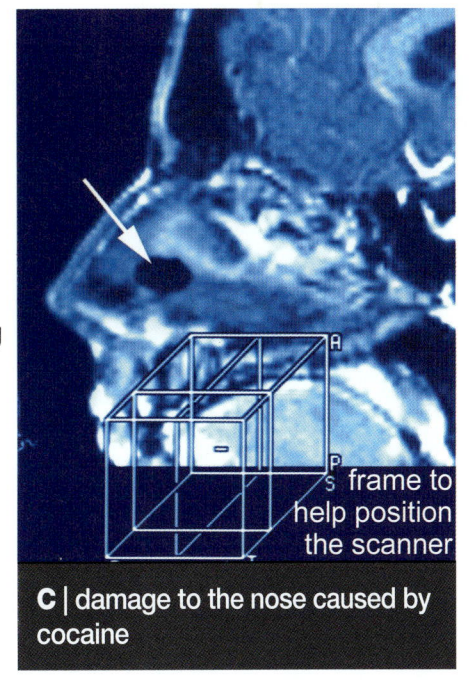

C | damage to the nose caused by cocaine

D | The man in this advert had his legs removed because of a disease caused by smoking.

4 Why do people continue to abuse cocaine even when they see it harming them?

5 Give the name of one recreational drug in photo A.

Depressants

Drugs that cause the nervous system to carry impulses more slowly are **depressants**. Heroin and the **solvents** found in glues and paints are dangerous depressants. Solvents can stop the heart and lungs working and cause severe brain damage.

Alcohol is a depressant and can change a person's behaviour. Drinking alcohol may make people become loud and aggressive because this drug stops parts of the brain from working. Alcohol may also cause vomiting, and can even cause death, because it stops the brain from sending impulses to the breathing muscles and so breathing stops.

6 Explain why some people feel more awake after drinking coffee.

7 Complete a table to describe four drugs of your choice. Use the headings 'Name of drug', 'Stimulant or depressant?' and 'Side-effects'.

8 a| Where are the muscles for breathing found?
b| Explain how alcohol can stop these muscles working.

FACT

In the 1890s, in some countries, heroin was a major ingredient in a cough syrup.

I can ...

- recall how different drugs affect the body.

7Ce DRUGS AND SPORT

HOW DO SOME ATHLETES TRY TO IMPROVE THEIR CHANCES OF WINNING?

Sports competitors are regularly tested for drugs to try to stop the use of drugs to improve performance. It can, though, be difficult to decide what is cheating and what is not.

In 1964, the Finnish cross-country skier Eero Mäntyranta won two Olympic gold medals. He could ski faster than other competitors because he had more red blood cells than them. His body naturally produced more of a chemical, nicknamed EPO, which causes red blood cell production. In 1989, a drugs company started making artificial EPO to help people for medical reasons, but some athletes were soon using it.

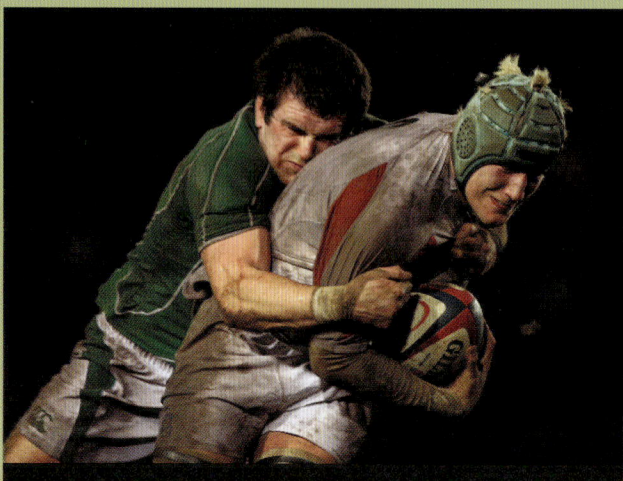

A | Frankie Sheahan (on the left) got a two-year ban from rugby after salbutamol was found in his body. The ban was lifted after he proved he needed the drug for asthma.

B | The gymnast Andreea Răducan lost her Olympic gold medal when a drugs test found a decongestant in her body. She said she had only taken two tablets for a cold.

Some athletes take steroids, such as testosterone, to increase muscle growth. Testosterone is a steroid **sex hormone** made in the **testes** and **ovaries**. Some people naturally produce more than others but it can also be made artificially. A side-effect is increased aggression (so-called 'roid rage').

C | Lance Armstrong won the Tour de France seven times. His medals were taken away from him when it was found he had used EPO and testosterone.

1. a| Why are steroids classified as drugs?
   b| Suggest a disadvantage of developing new steroid medicines.
2. Suggest why salbutamol is a banned drug in sports competitions.
3. Why would using EPO give an athlete an advantage?
4. Bones can develop 'stress fractures' during exercise. Why are athletes who misuse testosterone more likely to get stress fractures?

HAVE YOUR SAY

Should *all* drugs be banned in sport?

7Da EXPLORING THE WORLD

There are many reasons why people explore our world. Some explorers want to find oil or valuable minerals. Some are interested in searching for undiscovered **organisms**. Other explorers want to make contact with people to find out about how they live and about their languages.

David Good is a biologist and explorer. Unlike most explorers, when he set off in July 2011, to go deep into the Amazon jungle in Venezuela, it was to find his mother.

A | This mammal, called an olinguito, was discovered in 2013 in Ecuador.

B | These people were discovered living in the Amazon jungle in 2008, near the border between Peru and Brazil. They have probably never had any contact with the outside world.

David's father was an American scientist, who travelled to visit the Yanomami people in the Amazon in the 1970s. He was interested in what the people ate. He married a Yanomami woman called Yarima, and they had three children. The family then moved to America, but Yarima was unhappy and returned to the jungle without her children. That was when David was 5 years old. When he returned he was 19.

1. Yanomami people hunt deer for food. The deer eat forest plants. Draw a food chain to show this.
2. Apart from food, suggest something else that animals need to get from the places in which they live.
3. Apart from clothing, jewellery and hairstyles, suggest two things that are often different between humans from different parts of the world.
4. a| Suggest one reason why exploration of our planet is a good idea.
   b| Suggest a problem that might be caused by explorers.

C | David's expedition was a success and he was reunited with his mother.

7Da VARIATION

WHAT IS VARIATION?

The place where an organism lives is called a **habitat**. The Yanomami people live in a jungle habitat.

Each habitat has many different types or **species** of organisms living in it. **Variation** is the word used to describe the differences between organisms. There is often a lot of variation between different species (**inter-specific** variation) and less variation between members of the same species (**intra-specific** variation).

A | desert habitat

B | Arctic habitat

C | grass plains (savanna) habitat

D | Humans all belong to the same species but there is some variation between us.

1. What habitat do you live in?

2. Suggest two habitats in which you might find fish.

3. Describe two features that all the animals in photos A, B and C share, and two ways in which they all differ.

4. The zebras in photo C are all the same species. Describe the intra-specific variation.

Continuous and discontinuous

Humans vary in height. If you measure the heights of people in your class, you will find that very few people are exactly the same height. This variation is described as **continuous**, and it means that your measurements can have any value (within limits).

Some people can roll their tongues and others cannot. This variation is described as being **discontinuous**. This means that there is *not* a continuous range of measurements that can be made and measurements must fall into certain categories.

A good way to think about the difference between continuous and discontinuous variation is to consider foot length and shoe size. The actual length of your foot (measured in centimetres) is an example of continuous variation. Your shoe size is discontinuous because shoes only come in certain sizes.

E | Blood groups are discontinuous. Your blood is one of four main 'blood groups' (A, B, AB or O).

5. How can you tell if a certain type of variation is continuous?

6. Copy the list of features below and say whether each variation is continuous or discontinuous.

   natural eye colour   natural hair colour
   length of hair   having a cold
   having a scar   blood group
   height   having naturally curly hair

F | Tongue rolling is discontinuous.

Species

A species is a group of organisms that can **reproduce** with one another to produce **offspring** that can also reproduce.

Usually members of two different species cannot reproduce but in rare cases it can happen. The offspring are called **hybrids** but they cannot reproduce. For example, horses and zebras can produce zebroids but the hybrids cannot reproduce.

FACT

Yanomami are quite short people. Yanomami men have an average height of about 153 cm, 20 cm shorter than men living in the capital of Venezuela.

7. Olinguitos (see photo A, page 53) had been discovered before 2013 but people thought they were animals called olingos. One olinguito, called Ringerl, lived in a zoo in the 1970s with olingos. The zoo keepers thought that Ringerl would reproduce but this never happened.

   a| Why do you think olingos and olinguitos were thought to be the same? Use the term 'variation' in your answer.

   b| Why did Ringerl not reproduce?

8. Ligers are hybrids produced by lions and tigers. Ligers cannot reproduce. What does this tell you about lions and tigers?

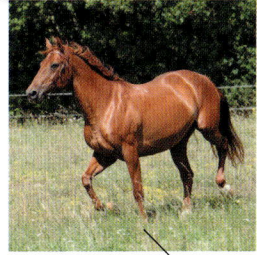

zebra   horse   zebroid

G | Horses and zebras are different species.

I can ...

- recall what a species is
- describe variation as continuous or discontinuous.

7Da CHARTS AND GRAPHS

UK NC, iLS, CEE

HOW ARE BAR CHARTS AND SCATTER GRAPHS USED?

Variation is the term for the differences between organisms. When we make measurements of variation (such as human height), what we measure is a **variable**. A variable is anything that can change and be measured. You will meet variables in all parts of science.

In an investigation, you choose the values of the **independent variable**. You then measure the **dependent variable**. The values of the dependent variable depend on those of the independent variable.

On a chart or a graph, the independent variable goes on the horizontal (x) axis and the dependent variable goes on the vertical (y) axis.

Chart A is a **bar chart** but it is also a **frequency diagram** because the dependent variable is a number of things that have been counted up (a frequency).

Grouped data

If the dependent variable is *continuous*, we can split the **data** into groups. We then count up the numbers that are in each group, and plot a bar chart but without leaving gaps between the bars.

On bar charts of grouped data, the bars often form a 'bell shape'. This is the pattern we expect to find when the y-axis shows a number of things that have been counted up. So we call this shape **normal distribution**.

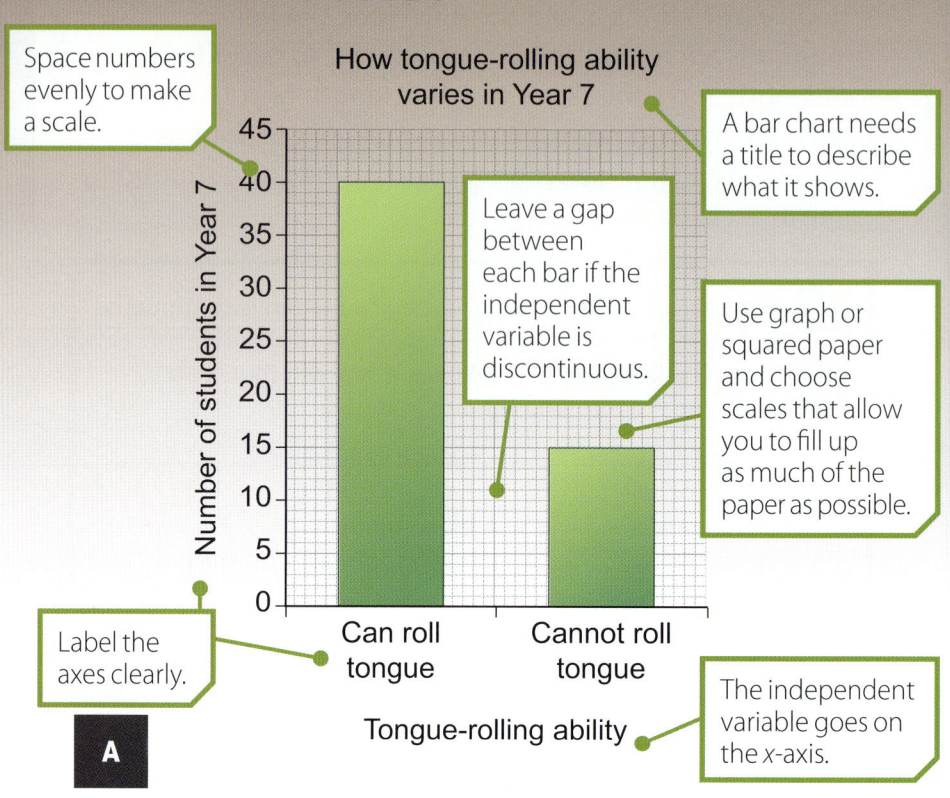

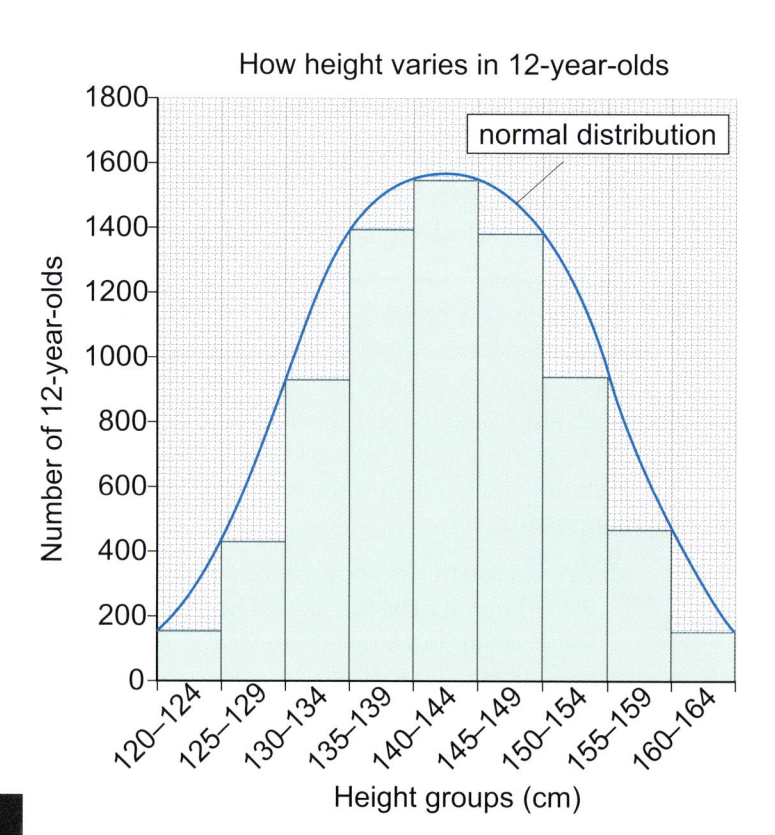

A — How tongue-rolling ability varies in Year 7

- Space numbers evenly to make a scale.
- A bar chart needs a title to describe what it shows.
- Leave a gap between each bar if the independent variable is discontinuous.
- Use graph or squared paper and choose scales that allow you to fill up as much of the paper as possible.
- Label the axes clearly.
- The independent variable goes on the x-axis.

B — How height varies in 12-year-olds (normal distribution); Height groups (cm): 120–124, 125–129, 130–134, 135–139, 140–144, 145–149, 150–154, 155–159, 160–164.

WORKING SCIENTIFICALLY

Scatter graphs

Sometimes we want to know if there is a **relationship** (link) between two variables. In this case we draw a **scatter graph**.

In graph C we can clearly see that there is a pattern in the points. As the width of the top of a tree increases, so does the **mass** of its leaves. A **line of best fit** is often drawn through the points, and it can help to make a relationship look more obvious.

If there is no link between two variables, then there will be no clear pattern of points (see graph F).

How the mass of leaves depends on the width of the top of an oak tree

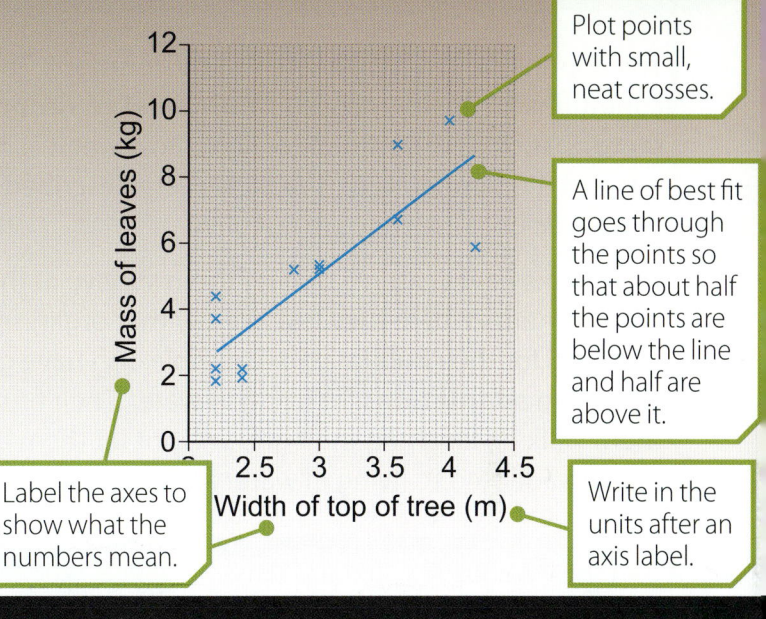

- Plot points with small, neat crosses.
- A line of best fit goes through the points so that about half the points are below the line and half are above it.
- Label the axes to show what the numbers mean.
- Write in the units after an axis label.

C | A scatter graph is used to see if there is a link between two variables.

1 What are the dependent and independent variables in chart A?

2 Present the data in table E as a bar chart.

E	Blood group	Number of students in class 7K
	A	17
	B	8
	AB	2
	O	2

3 Table F shows the lengths (L) and widths (W) of some leaves from rose plants.

a| Divide the data into groups, using either the widths or the lengths of the leaves.

b| Draw a bar chart for the data you have selected in part a.

F | Lengths and widths of some rose leaves (mm)

L	W	L	W	L	W	L	W	L	W
26	20	41	32	54	42	50	36	69	53
42	31	39	30	51	38	62	47	71	54
47	37	55	40	56	44	59	45	73	56
48	37	35	27	79	61	76	58	56	43
82	62	31	22	65	50	80	64	57	44

4 Use the data in table F to find out if there is a relationship between rose leaf length and width. Use length as the independent variable.

How the mass of leaves depends on the height of an oak tree

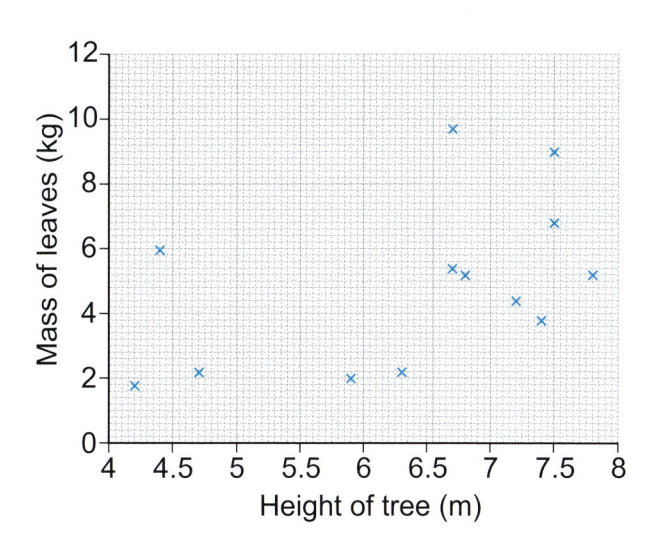

D | There is no relationship between these two variables (for the same trees as in graph C).

I can ...

- present information as bar charts and scatter graphs
- identify relationships using scatter graphs.

57

UK NC, iLS, CEE

7Db ADAPTATIONS

WHY IS THERE VARIATION BETWEEN AND WITHIN SPECIES?

The conditions in a habitat are its **environment**. The conditions are mainly caused by **physical environmental factors**, such as the amount of light, how wet it is, how windy it is and the temperature. The factors are described as 'physical' or **abiotic** because they are not alive.

Organisms have features that let them survive in the environments where they live. We say that organisms are **adapted** for their habitats. For example, fish have gills and fins, which are **adaptations** for living in water. Their fins will not let them walk on land and their gills will not let them breathe air. Fish are adapted to living in watery habitats but not on land.

1 Which of the following are physical environmental (abiotic) factors:

ant   bird   frog   fungus
light   temperature   tree   wind?

2 Describe the environment in each habitat in photos A, B and C on page 54.

3 Describe your environment at the moment.

A | polar bear adaptations

- white fur for camouflage – useful for creeping up on seals without being seen
- smalls ears to stop it losing too much heat
- thick fur to help keep it warm
- rough soles to grip the ice
- large feet to spread out its weight and stop it from sinking in the snow – also good for swimming

B | cactus adaptations

- no leaves, which means that the cactus loses less water than a plant with leaves
- Roots cover a large area to absorb as much water as possible when it rains. This saguaro cactus can absorb a tonne of water a day, after a storm.
- spines
- stem stores water

C | jack rabbit adaptations

- large ears to allow heat to escape and improve hearing
- does not drink and gets all its water from its food
- large hind legs to run away quickly (at up to 70 km/h) from animals that might eat it

4 How are polar bears adapted to the cold?

5 Why do cacti have spines whereas most other plants have leaves?

6 Suggest the names of the habitats in which polar bears, cacti and jack rabbits live.

7 Look back at page 54. How do you think the length of hair on meerkats and wolverines helps them survive in their habitats?

FACT

Many organisms are adapted to their habitats by both their features and their behaviour (what they do). Vultures in deserts urinate on their legs! The urine evaporates, which cools the birds down.

All the animals and plants that live in a habitat make up a **community**. Members of communities may have similar adaptations to cope with the problems of living in a particular habitat. For example, many organisms that live in fast-flowing rivers have suckers to allow them to attach to rocks and stop them being swept away.

The community of organisms and all the physical environmental factors in a habitat form an **ecosystem**.

> 8 Draw a design for a plant that could live in the same habitat as a hogsucker fish.
>
> 9 Describe the Arctic ecosystem.

D | Hogsucker fish live in fast-flowing water.
flexible, streamlined body
sucker to attach to rocks

Inherited variation

Many of an organism's features come from its parents. These features are **inherited**.

Variation between these features is **inherited variation**. There is a great deal of inherited variation between different species, such as polar bears and meerkats.

There is also inherited variation between members of the same species (intra-specific variation) because of what happens in **sexual reproduction**. All **gametes** contain slightly different instructions for features. These instructions are carried on **genes** inside the nucleus. A different **sperm cell** and **egg cell** are used to produce each offspring, and so each inherits a slightly different mix of features. The exception to this is identical twins, who both develop from the same **fertilised egg cell** (or **zygote**).

E | David Good with his parents and younger sister. The children inherited features from both parents.

F | Children inherit features from both parents.

> 10 Name three features you have inherited.
>
> 11 Look at photo F, which shows a family group. There are four adult women in the picture. Who are their children? Use the labels to identify them.
>
> 12 Kim's mother has blue eyes and blond hair. Kim's father has brown eyes and brown hair. Kim has blue eyes and brown hair. Her brother, Harry, has brown eyes and brown hair.
>
> a| From which parent has Kim inherited blue eyes?
>
> b| Why are Kim and Harry's features slightly different?

I can ...

- identify and describe some adaptations for different habitats
- describe how inherited variation is caused.

7Dc EFFECTS OF THE ENVIRONMENT

UK NC, iLS, CEE

HOW DO ENVIRONMENTS AFFECT ORGANISMS?

In 1534, the French explorer Jacques Cartier sailed to what is now Canada to find gold and look for a way to China. Nearing land, he saw native people and wrote: 'They wear their hair tied up on the top of their heads like a handful of twisted hay ....'

Cartier was describing an **environmental variation** of the people. Environmental variation is caused by environmental factors. Hairstyles are caused by an environmental factor called fashion!

All organisms show inherited variation *and* environmental variation. The beech leaves in photo B inherited their leaf shape, but not all the leaves are the same size. The leaves that get more sunlight are smaller than the shaded leaves. The environmental factor is light and this causes an environmental variation in leaf size.

A | Jacques Cartier (1491–1557) and a tribesman from Hochelaga (present-day Montreal).

B | environmental variation in beech leaves

FACT
Hydrangea plants are blue in acidic soils and pink in soils of a higher pH.

1. List three examples of environmental variation in drawing A.

2. For sentences A–C below, identify:
   a| the environmental variation
   b| the environmental factor causing the variation.

   A| Bilal found that the cress seedlings he grew in a dark cupboard were yellow.
   B| Jayesh discovered that there were very few leaves on the apple tree after the storm.
   C| Tanya put fertiliser on one sunflower plant. It grew 20 cm taller than the others.

3. In what type of soil are the hydrangeas in photo C growing?

Environmental factors affect organisms in other ways too. Organisms inherit features that allow them to change when environmental factors change. Changes during a day are known as **daily changes**, and changes during a year are **seasonal changes**. Organisms are adapted to these changes.

Daily changes

Many animals are adapted to changes in light during a day (24 hours). **Nocturnal** animals are only active at night and have adaptations for this. Many mice are nocturnal and have excellent eyesight. Nocturnal owls have superb hearing and eyesight, and fly silently so they can catch nocturnal animals.

> **4** What change causes dormice to become active?

Seashore organisms are adapted to tides. Sea anemones use tentacles to feed but when the tide goes out they pull in their tentacles to stop them drying out.

D

E | a sea anemone feeding and (inset) when the tide is out

Seasonal changes

In winter, **deciduous** (des-*id*-U-us) trees lose their leaves because there is not much light for **photosynthesis** and their leaves lose water (which cannot be replaced when the ground is frozen). **Evergreen** trees have tougher leaves that do not lose much water, so they keep their leaves all year round.

Some plants, such as poppies, die completely in the winter. Their **seeds** grow into new plants in the spring. In other plants, such as bluebells, only the parts above ground die. They leave **bulbs** underground that will grow again in the spring.

Animals are also adapted to seasonal changes. Rabbits grow longer fur to help them keep warm in colder months. A ptarmigan's feathers change colour with the seasons.

Some animals, such as hedgehogs, become inactive when it is cold in winter so that they do not need food when there is less food available. This is **hibernation**. Many birds fly to warmer places for the winter to find food. This is **migration**. Paddyfield warblers migrate to the rice fields in India in October and return to Russia in April.

F | a ptarmigan in summer and (inset) in winter

> **5** Describe one difference in the community of an Indian rice field habitat between July and December.
>
> **6** Suggest why a ptarmigan's feathers change colour with the seasons.
>
> **7** Explain how these organisms are adapted to surviving winter:
> a| hedgehog   b| oak tree
> c| paddyfield warbler   d| poppy.

I can ...

- identify causes of environmental variation
- describe adaptations to daily and seasonal changes.

7Dd EFFECTS ON THE ENVIRONMENT

HOW DO ORGANISMS AFFECT THEIR HABITATS?

To survive and grow, organisms need **resources** from a habitat. Animals need resources such as **oxygen**, space, shelter, food, water and mates. Plants need light, air, water, warmth, mineral salts and space. If any of these are missing, the numbers of an organism (its **population**) will go down.

> **1** State three resources scientists would need to take into a desert habitat.

Island problems

Easter Island in the Pacific Ocean was named by the Dutch explorer Jacob Roggeveen. He described it as a land with huge standing statues but no trees.

Scientists have found evidence that the island was once covered in trees. Over hundreds of years, the people cut down trees for building materials, to make fires and to build fishing boats. By about 1600, all the trees were gone and the people started to starve. Birds also disappeared from the island at this time.

The islanders affected their habitat, which caused many populations to decrease. The Easter Island palm tree died out altogether – it became **extinct**.

Competition

We can see what eats what in a habitat by looking at a **food chain** like this:

grass → hare → lynx

Organisms compete with one another for resources. There is **competition** between organisms of the same species (**intra-specific competition**) and between different species (**inter-specific competition**). The organisms with the best adaptations to get the resources are more likely to survive and reproduce. The others may move away or die.

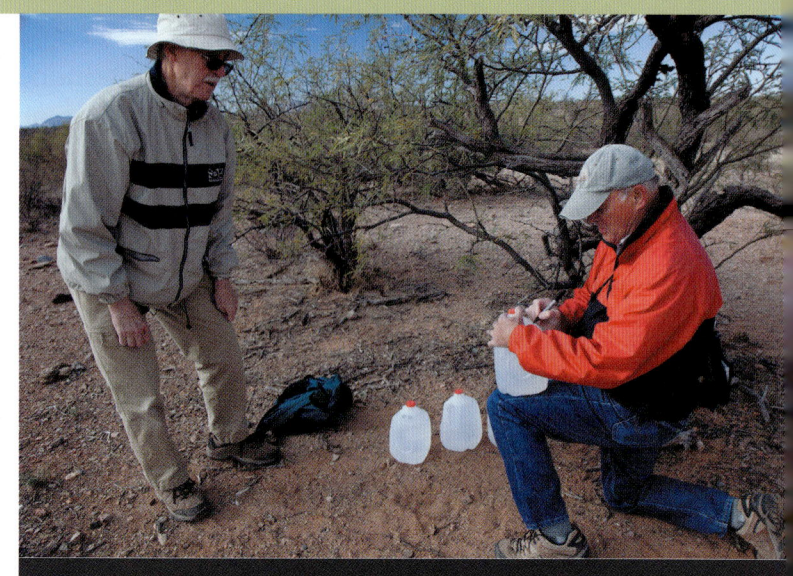

A | These men are leaving water for people who may become lost in the desert (where there are few natural resources for humans).

B | Easter Island

> **2** Suggest why fewer plants grow in a desert habitat compared with a jungle habitat.
>
> **3** What organism caused the Easter Island palm to become extinct?
>
> **4** a| Why did the human population decrease on Easter Island?
> b| Suggest two reasons why birds died out on the island.

Food chains can be joined together to form **food webs**, which show how different animals compete for the same food (inter-specific competition). In food web C, you can see that goshawks compete with lynxes for hares. If the goshawks get a disease and die, there will be more hares. The population of lynxes may then increase.

The organisms in an ecosystem all depend on one another for many things, not just food. We say that they are **interdependent**. For example, birds use trees for shelter and plants use animal waste to help them grow (the waste contains mineral salts).

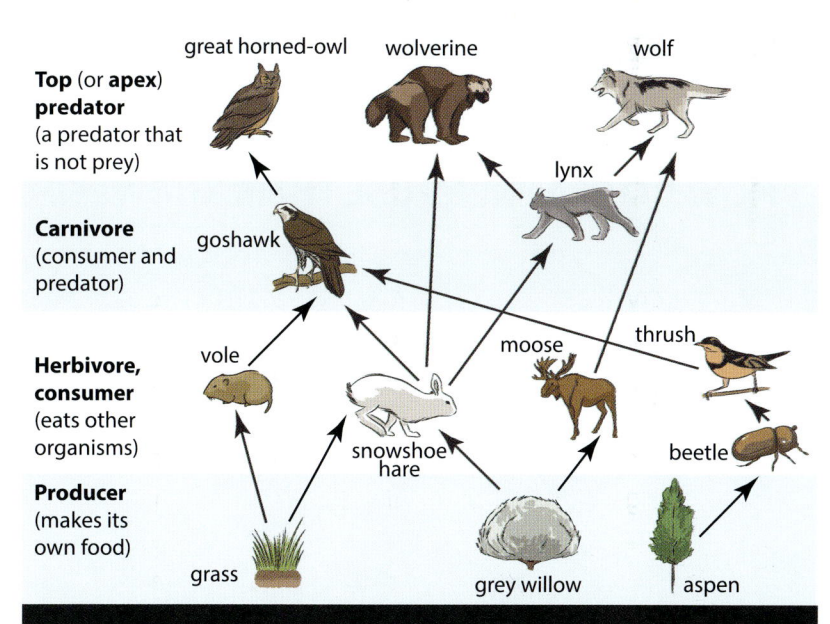

> **5**
> a| Write out the longest food chain in food web C.
> b| Choose one or more of these words for each organism in your food chain: carnivore, consumer, herbivore, omnivore, producer, top predator. Explain your choices.
>
> **6** Why are goshawks and wolverines in competition with each other?
>
> **7** Use food web C to predict what would happen to the vole population if:
> a| the snowshoe hares all died
> b| there was no rain for a long time.

Populations

Populations change depending on how much food is available. In northern Canada, the lynx is a **predator**. Its main **prey** is the snowshoe hare. When there are a lot of hares, the lynxes have lots to eat. They reproduce successfully and their population goes up. When there are fewer hares, the lynx population decreases – some starve (including newborn offspring) and others move to a different area. An activity of an organism that affects another organism (such as competition or **predation**) is called a **biotic factor**.

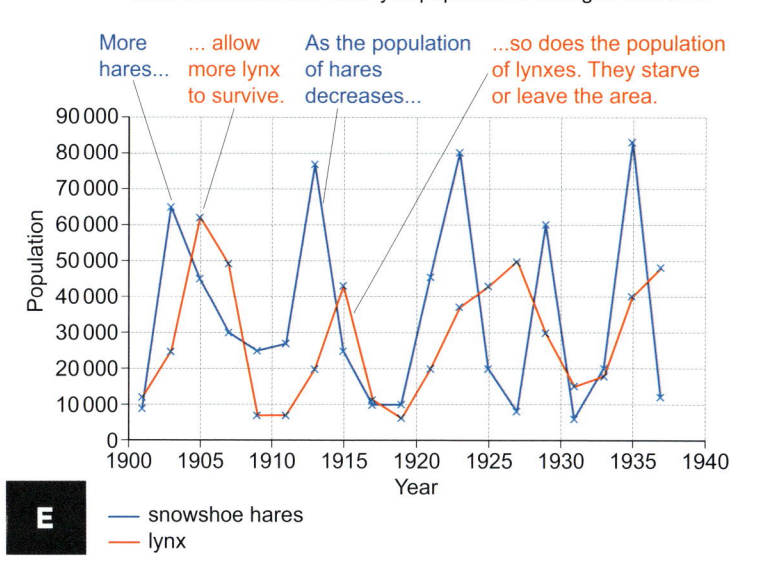

> **8** Look at graph E.
> a| Which animal is the predator and which is the prey?
> b| Suggest one reason why the hare population might increase.
> c| Suggest two biotic factors that could cause the lynx population to decrease.

C | a food web in northern Canada

D

How snowshoe hare and lynx populations changed with time

More hares... ... allow more lynx to survive. As the population of hares decreases... ...so does the population of lynxes. They starve or leave the area.

E
— snowshoe hares
— lynx

I can ...

- describe ways in which organisms affect their habitats and communities
- describe intra- and inter-specific competition
- use a food web to make predictions.

63

7Dd GREENER CITIES

HOW DO PLANNERS USE THEIR KNOWLEDGE TO BUILD GREENER CITIES?

Building cities and roads uses land that is home to many plants and animals. If we do not plan greener cities that include many plants and animals, they will not be able to get the resources they need and so may die out. Greener cities help people too, by keeping the air cooler, reducing pollution and making people feel happier.

When new city buildings and roads are designed by architects and engineers, environmental planners advise on the resources that plants and animals need. They may suggest changes to a building's design or the use of technology. For example, sensors might detect when soil is getting too dry for plants, and so turn on a watering system. Engineers then work out how to construct the buildings and supply resources for humans and other organisms.

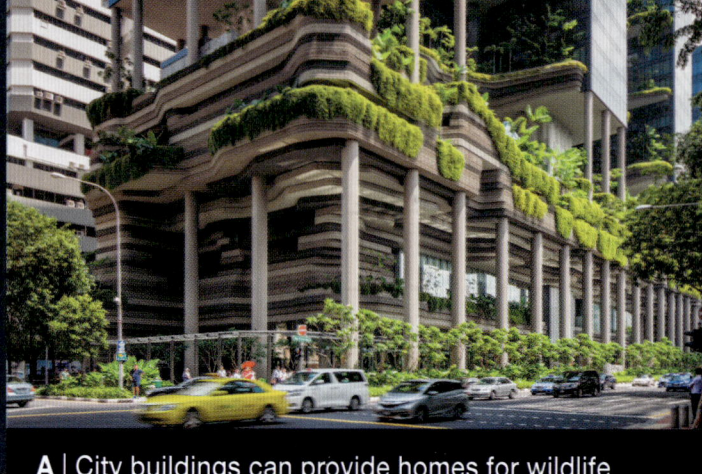

A | City buildings can provide homes for wildlife as well as people.

B | When people live in skyscrapers, there is more space in cities for plants and animals to share.

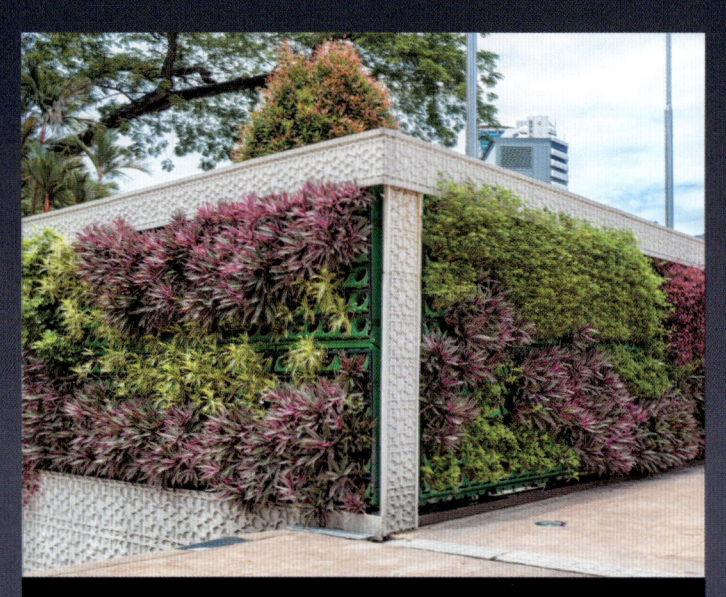

C | Plants growing on a 'green wall' need something to support their roots. Pipes in the wall continually supply the plants with the right amount of water and nutrients.

1 State what you think the term 'greener city' means.

2 State two resources that plants need to grow well.

3 Explain why increasing the number of different plants in a city can lead to an increase in the number of different animals living there.

Environmental planners

An environmental planner may have a degree in planning, or in a related subject such as environmental science or geography. They then do further study, to learn more about the environment and planning before they start work.

Environmental planners may work in a team to exchange ideas about what knowledge could be used to help make city buildings greener. This may include sharing knowledge about the resources that different organisms need. They may also use and develop **models**, such as food chains to see how organisms rely on one another for food.

They then select the most useful knowledge for a particular project. For example, they will think about where a building is to be built and how much space there will be for plants. They then select and apply only the most relevant knowledge to the project and come up with suggestions for changes. By only using relevant knowledge, the reasoning for their suggestions is very clear to the architects.

> What do we need to think about so we can include plants and animals in this new apartment block?

> How much light will each side of the building get? How much water will the trees on the building need?

> Which plants and animals are most likely to be displaced by the building? Does thinking about food chains help?

D | identifying useful knowledge for a new project

ACTIVITY

Your team of environmental planners are tasked with making a city in your country greener.

Work as a group to do the following:

- Make a list of all the knowledge you could use, such as the different plants and animals living in or near that city, resources that plants and animals need, and the climate in the city.
- Identify the most useful knowledge for a greener 18-storey apartment block in this city.
- Draw a design for the tower block. Label it to explain each of your 'green' suggestions.

4 Suggest what knowledge the other planner in photo D could offer that might be useful.

5 Write down all the knowledge that you think an environmental planner might use to decide which plants and trees should be planted on buildings in a particular city.

6 Carry out research to find examples of changes designed to encourage more plants and animals to live in your area.

65

7De TRANSFERS IN FOOD CHAINS

UK NC, iLS, CEE

HOW DO ENERGY AND POISONS MOVE THROUGH FOOD CHAINS?

Organisms contain **energy** stored in the substances that make up their bodies. The arrows in food chains and webs show how this energy passes from organism to organism. Normally there are fewer organisms as you go along a food chain because energy is lost at each stage.

A | The arrows in a food chain show energy flow.

A lot of energy stored in food is released by respiration to let animals move and keep warm.

Only some of the energy in food becomes stored in new substances in an animal. Only the energy stored inside the rabbit can be passed on to the fox.

A lot of energy is stored in undigested foods, which pass out of animals.

Pyramids of numbers

Energy losses at each stage of the food chain mean that hundreds of lettuce plants feed a much smaller number of rabbits. These rabbits feed an even smaller number of foxes. The numbers of different organisms at each stage (**trophic level**) of a food chain can be shown using a **pyramid of numbers**.

fox ——— secondary consumer
rabbits ——— primary consumer
lettuce plants ——— producer

B | This pyramid of numbers also shows the trophic level names.

Pyramids of numbers do not look like pyramids if the organisms have very different sizes. For example, many aphids feed on one rose bush.

ladybirds
aphids
rose bush

C

1. Why do organisms respire?

2. a| What does the red arrow on the left of diagram A show?
   b| Why does the fox not get all the energy that was in the lettuces eaten by the rabbit?

3. Look at food web C on page 63.
   a| Draw a food chain from the food web, starting with grass.
   b| Sketch a pyramid of numbers for this food chain.

4. Look at the food chain below.
   grass → grasshopper → frog → grass snake
   100 000   500   5   1
   a| Draw a table to show the top predator, the consumers, the producer, the herbivore and the carnivores.
   b| Sketch a pyramid of numbers for this food chain.

5. Explain why diagram D is not shaped like a pyramid.

fleas
rabbit
lettuce plants

D

Poisons

Pesticides are poisons that kill **pests** (organisms that cause problems). However, these poisons can kill other organisms as well.

In 1810, Australian explorer Frederick Hasselborough discovered Macquarie Island, which is halfway between New Zealand and Antarctica. It soon became a base for fishermen, who brought in cats, rats and rabbits. The cats ate young birds, the rats ate bird eggs and the rabbits destroyed nesting sites. Various species of bird became extinct.

In 2000, scientists removed the last cat but removing cats caused a big increase in the populations of rats and rabbits. In 2010, poison was put down for rats and rabbits, but it killed many birds, including **endangered** species. The poisoning was stopped and a virus disease was introduced to kill most of the rabbits. This meant that less poison needed to be spread over the island in 2011. Now the island is clear of these pests.

Some poisons kill organisms they are not intended for because the poisons are not broken down in nature (they are **persistent**). This means that they can be passed along food chains. DDT is a persistent pesticide used to kill insects. It was used a lot in the USA and Europe in the 1950s and 1960s but it caused the shells of apex (top) predator birds to be weak and break easily. DDT was banned in many countries in the 1980s.

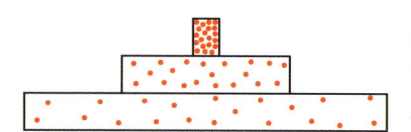

E | Poison on Macquarie Island killed giant petrels. The wingspans of these birds can be over two metres.

FACT
Around the world, 2.5 billion kg of pesticides are used each year.

6 a| What effect did removing cats from Macquarie Island have?
b| Why did it have this effect?

7 Suggest what has happened to the populations of birds on Macquarie Island since 2011. Explain your reasoning.

8 Look at food web C on page 63. Beetles can kill aspen trees. To save the aspens in an area it has been suggested that the beetles be poisoned.
a| Suggest a problem with using poison.
b| Predict the effects of the poison on the thrush and aspen populations.

9 Explain why the peregrine falcon population in the UK decreased in the 1970s.

earthworm → blackbird → peregrine falcon

peregrine falcon
blackbird
earthworm

F | Each dot represents a dose of DDT. The poison gets more concentrated further along the food chain.

I can ...
- use pyramids of numbers to describe how energy is lost in a food chain
- explain why pesticides need to be used carefully.

7De NOMADS

HOW DO SOME HUMANS COMPETE WITH ONE ANOTHER?

Nomadic people move from place to place. In Bhutan, the Brokpa people herd yaks. In summer they build camps up in the mountains where the yaks eat grass and shrubs. They protect the yaks from animals like snow leopards. In the winter they move down to warmer areas, selling their products in villages.

Nomads in Mongolia herd sheep and goats to high mountain grasslands in summer and then move their animals down to the valleys for the winter, into areas protected from the harsh winds. However, copper has now been found in the mountains and mines are being built. These provide employment and money for this very poor country, but the nomads worry that the mines will use up the scarce water supplies.

A | Brokpa yak herders

Some Amazon rainforest people were traditionally nomads, moving to new areas as resources started to run out. Today this may not happen because farmers move in and clear land to grow grass for cattle. There are also problems with illegal logging and mining. The outsiders bring diseases, like colds and measles, which kill the local people. They also destroy the habitats of animals that local people rely on for food.

B | a winter encampment in Mongolia

C | A huge area of rainforest in Brazil has been destroyed to make way for farmland.

1. Give the name of one predator on this page, and its prey.

2. a| Describe how seasonal changes affect the Brokpa.
   b| How is this similar to the effect on some birds, such as paddyfield warblers?

3. Is having measles an example of continuous or discontinuous variation? Explain your reasoning.

4. Explain one adaptation of yaks to their their habitat.

5. a| Sketch a pyramid of numbers that links three organisms mentioned on this page.
   b| Label your pyramid of numbers with the names of the trophic levels.

HAVE YOUR SAY

Should exploration in certain areas of the world be banned?

8Aa FOOD AND ADVERTISING

You would not see adverts like the ones on this page today! There are now much stricter rules on the **claims** that a food advert can make. A claim is a statement that is supposed to be true. Adverts often contain claims to convince you to buy a product. Many countries now have laws that say that all health claims must be supported by scientific evidence.

We also know much more about the effects of food on the body today. Scientists think that foods that are high in fat and sugar can cause people to put on too much weight. For this reason, these types of foods cannot be advertised on children's TV.

A | This advert is from 1952.

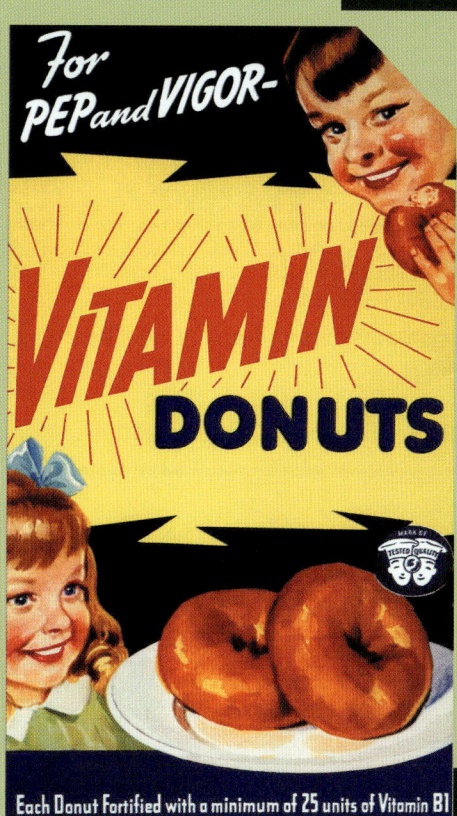

B | This doughnut advert is from 1942.

1. Why do we need to eat food?

2. Look at advert A.
   a| What claim is being made?
   b| Suggest why a company would not be able to make this claim today.

3. Look at the advert for doughnuts (B).
   a| Explain why these doughnuts are supposed to be good for you.
   b| Suggest what is wrong with eating too many doughnuts.

4. a| In what organ system is food broken down and taken into the blood?
   b| Name two parts of this organ system.
   c| Describe the functions of these parts.

5. Suggest one thing people should do in order to eat healthily.

UK NC, iLS, CEE

8Aa NUTRIENTS

WHAT DOES OUR FOOD CONTAIN?

In science, the word **diet** means what you eat. Your diet provides **raw materials** for your body, which are needed for energy (to move, keep warm, make new materials), growth and repair, and health.

Food substances that provide raw materials are called **nutrients**. These include **carbohydrates**, **fats**, **proteins**, **vitamins** and **minerals**.

The main carbohydrates in food are insoluble **starch** and soluble **sugars**. There are many different sugars, including **sucrose** (table sugar) and **glucose**.

There are many different sorts of fats. Some are solid and some are liquid at room temperature. We call liquid fats **oils**. Fats and oils are sometimes called **lipids**.

We also need to eat **fibre**. This is made of plant cell walls and is not used by the body, but it keeps us healthy by helping food move through the intestines and stopping them getting blocked (**constipation**). Wholegrain cereals and breads contain a lot of fibre.

Water is also very important since about 65 per cent of you is water! Water:

- acts as a lubricant
- dissolves substances so that they can be carried around the body
- fills up cells so that they hold their shape
- cools you down, when you sweat.

> **1** What do scientists mean by diet?
>
> **2** a| What is a nutrient?
>
>   b| What does your body use nutrients for?

A

> **3** How are water and fibre helpful for preventing constipation?
>
> **4** FullBran is a new cereal that contains a lot of fibre. Write a health claim for use in a FullBran advert.
>
> **5** Explain why you should drink plenty of water in hot weather.

Food labelling

Nutrition information labels show the amounts of different nutrients in a food. You can compare the nutrients in different foods using the 'per 100 gram (g) of food' values. You cannot compare foods using 'per serving of food', since servings of different foods are different sizes.

B

Nutrition labels also show the amount of fibre and the amount of energy stored in the food.

Food labels have a list of ingredients and highlight substances that people may be allergic to (e.g. nuts, eggs). Labels also show warnings about substances that can cause problems. For example, in Europe, if a drink contains a lot of caffeine, the label will state: 'Not suitable for children, pregnant women and persons sensitive to caffeine'.

Testing foods

In many countries, government scientists test food to make sure that labels are correct. Photos C, D and E shows tests for starch, protein and fats.

> **6** List the names of the nutrients on label B.
>
> **7** Suggest why a breakfast cereal box states: 'May contain traces of nuts'.
>
> **8** The food referred to in label B contains two carbohydrates: starch and sugars. How much of each is there in one serving?

FACT

In 2013, tests in Europe discovered that many products that claimed to be 100 per cent beef actually contained horse meat.

C | Test for starch: add two drops of iodine solution. If there is starch you will see a blue-black colour.

D | Test for protein: place a food sample in a test tube to a depth of about 1 cm. Add five drops of Biuret solution. If there is protein you will see a purple colour within a few minutes.

E | Test for fats: rub a small dry food sample on some white paper. Hold the paper up to the light. Fats leave a greasy mark.

> **9** Gita tested butter and bread with iodine solution. Which nutrient was she testing for?
>
> **10** 100 g of a milk powder contains 27 g of fat, 38 g of carbohydrate and 26 g of protein.
> a| Describe how you would test for the nutrients in milk powder and what results you would expect.
> b| Why do the totals of the nutrients not add up to 100 g?

I can ...

- recall the nutrients we need in our diets
- interpret nutrition information labels
- recall the tests used to detect some nutrients.

71

UK NC, iLS, CEE

8Ab USES OF NUTRIENTS

WHY DO WE NEED THE DIFFERENT NUTRIENTS?

Different nutrients are used for different things in your body.

For energy

When you eat food, you gain mass. When doing everyday activities, the **fuel** in your food is used up and so you lose mass. To make sure your mass does not change, the amount of fuel you use should be balanced by the amount you eat.

Your body's main source of energy is carbohydrates. There is a lot of starch in foods like bread and potatoes, and sugars are found in sweet foods. Another source of energy comes from fats. There are a lot of fats in dairy products and fried foods.

Fats are stored in your body so that there is always a source of energy. A lot of this stored fat comes from the fats that you eat. However, if the carbohydrates you eat are not all used up, they can be turned into fat. Some fat is stored under your skin to insulate your body and help you stay warm.

| 1 | List all the different types of nutrient in food. |

You gain mass when you eat.

You lose mass doing everyday things.

A | The amount of energy stored in your food should balance the amount of energy that you need.

2	Gareth's mass has increased. Suggest why.
3	Why do you need starch in your diet?
4	What does your body use fat for?

B | Hard exercise uses up to 4 g of carbohydrate per minute. Long-distance athletes often drink liquids and eat foods containing sugars during races.

Energy transfers

Different foods contain different amounts of energy, which is measured in **kilojoules (kJ)**. **Respiration** in your cells releases the energy. As your cells respire, the energy is **transferred** (moved) from the nutrients, making it available for you to grow, move, think and keep warm.

The amount of energy your body needs to transfer depends on your age, whether you are male or female and how active you are.

C

Activity	Energy required per hour (kJ/h)
Sleeping	180
Watching TV	250
Walking slowly	470
Cycling slowly	660
Cycling quickly	1090
Running fast	1700

D How daily energy requirements change with age

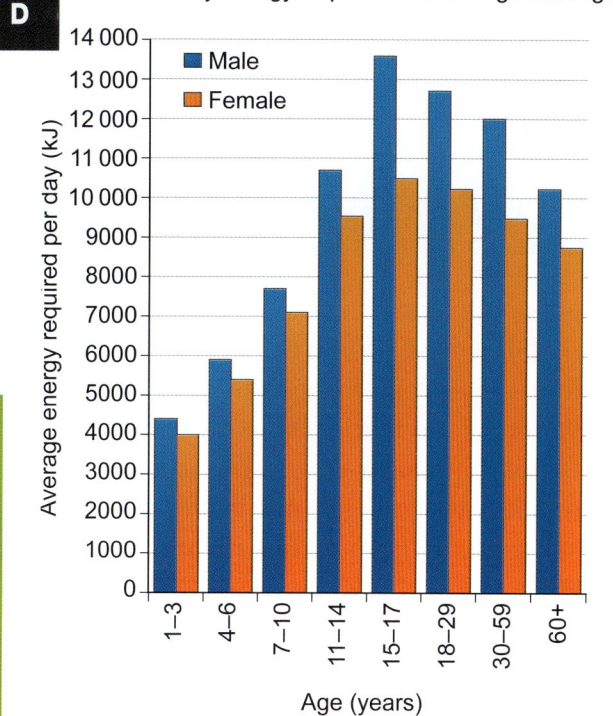

Bar chart showing average energy required per day (kJ) by age group (1–3, 4–6, 7–10, 11–14, 15–17, 18–29, 30–59, 60+) for Male and Female.

5
a| Look at label B on page 70. How much energy is in 100 g of the food?
b| How much of this food would provide the energy needed by someone of your age and sex for one day?
c| How much of the food would provide the energy for 2 hours of slow walking?

6
a| Between which ages do people need most energy?
b| Suggest a reason for this.

7
a| Ravi is a fitness trainer. His wife is the same age and works at a call centre. Who will need more energy per day?
b| Explain why this is.

8 Jasmine eats more carbohydrates than she needs for energy. Explain why her mass will change.

Growth and repair

Proteins are very important for making new cells to help us to grow and repair our bodies. Proteins are found in foods like meat, fish, eggs, beans and milk.

For health

All nutrients are important for health, and these include tiny quantities of vitamins and mineral salts (usually just called minerals). For example, vitamin A is needed for healthy skin and eyes, and vitamin C helps cells in tissues to stick together properly. Vitamin D and calcium are needed to make bones, and iron is used to make red blood cells.

FACT

In many countries, insects provide a good source of protein.

E

F | Food packaging and adverts often point out the vitamins and minerals the foods contain.

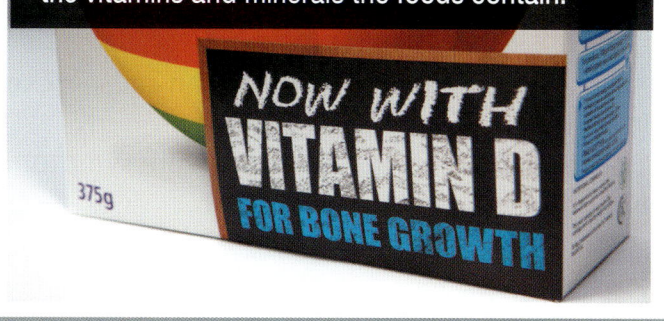

9 Give three important reasons for eating food.

10
a| State two good sources of each type of nutrient found in food.
b| Why do our bodies need each type of nutrient? Present your answer as a table.

11 Suggest one effect of a lack of iron on your body. Explain your reasoning.

I can ...

- recall good sources of different nutrients
- describe how factors change the amount of energy we need
- describe what each nutrient does in the body.

UK NC, iLS, CEE

8Ac BALANCED DIETS

WHY IS A BALANCED DIET IMPORTANT?

No single food contains all the substances that you need, so you must eat many different foods. If you eat the right amounts of a wide variety of foods you have a **balanced diet**. People who have a problem caused by too much or too little of a nutrient in their diets are said to suffer from **malnutrition**.

> **1** What is a balanced diet?
>
> **2** Why is someone who is very overweight suffering from malnutrition?

Deficiency diseases

People who lack a nutrient for a long time can suffer from a **deficiency disease**.

A lack of protein can cause **kwashiorkor** (pronounced '*kwash-ee-or-ker*'). One symptom is a large belly, caused by fluid collecting around the intestines and muscles that become too weak to hold the stomach and intestines in place.

A lack of vitamin A causes **night blindness** (not being able to see well in low light). **Scurvy** is caused by a lack of vitamin C, and causes painful joints and bleeding gums.

A lack of calcium and vitamin D can cause **rickets**, in which weak bones do not form properly. Tiredness and shortness of breath are symptoms of **anaemia**, caused by a lack of iron.

It is recommended that you eat five portions of fruits and vegetables per day. They are rich in fibre and many vitamins and minerals.

Bread, rice, potatoes and pasta contain lots of starch.

Meat, fish, beans, eggs and nuts contain lots of protein. Beef and eggs are good sources of iron.

Foods and drinks high in fat and/or sugar. You should only have these as an occasional treat.

Milk and dairy foods (things made from milk) are good sources of fat and calcium.

Public Health England in association with the Welsh Government, the Scottish Government and the Food Standards Agency in Northern Ireland

A | The Eatwell Guide helps people to eat a balanced diet. It shows how much you should eat from different food groups.

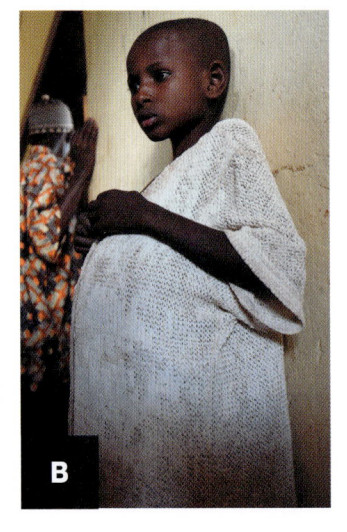

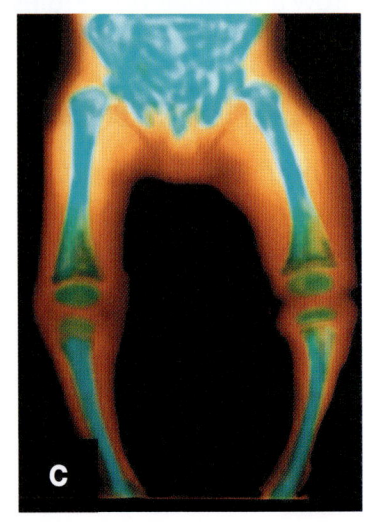

> **3** a| What diseases are shown in photos B and C. Explain your reasoning.
>
> b| Suggest a change that someone could make to their lifestyle to cure scurvy.

FACT

Too much of a vitamin or mineral can also cause problems. Children have died from eating iron tablets that they thought were sweets. Polar bear and husky dog livers contain so much vitamin A that they are poisonous if eaten by humans. In 1913, the Antarctic explorer Xavier Mertz died from eating his sledge dogs' livers.

Starvation

The worst form of malnutrition is **starvation**, in which people lack nearly all the nutrients they need. People who are starving get thinner and thinner.

Obesity

People whose food contains more energy than they need may become overweight. This can cause **heart disease**, when fat clogs the arteries and stops enough blood reaching the heart muscle tissue. If very little blood reaches the heart muscle, it can start to die (a **heart attack**), which causes a painful squeezing feeling in the chest.

People who are overweight are more likely to have high blood pressure, which can damage the heart or kidneys or cause blood vessels to burst.

People who are very overweight are said to be obese. **Obesity** is increasing in many countries, so some scientists want to stop adverts for fatty or sugary foods.

> **4** How will a balanced diet stop people becoming overweight?
>
> **5** a| What condition is the man in photo E suffering from?
> b| Suggest why he has developed this condition.
> c| What health problems is he more likely to develop?

Help with your diet

Many nutrition information labels give people an idea about how much of each nutrient can be eaten in a day. These **Reference Intakes** (or **RIs**) are usually shown for adults.

Note: 1 mg (milligram) = 0.001 g;
1 µg (microgram) = 0.000 001 g.

	Reference Intake (RI)	100 g of wholemeal bread contains	100 g of oranges contains	100 g of butter contains
energy	8400 kJ	920 kJ	150 kJ	3000 kJ
carbohydrate	260 g	38.4 g	8.5 g	0 g
protein	50 g	10.3 g	0.8 g	0.5 g
fat	70 g	2.5 g	0 g	81 g
fibre	24 g	6.5 g	2.1 g	0 g
vitamin A	800 µg	0 µg	5 µg	887 µg
vitamin C	60 mg	0 mg	50 mg	0 mg
calcium	800 mg	28 mg	41 mg	15 mg
iron	14 mg	3 mg	0.3 mg	0.2 mg

F

D | Starving people in Leningrad in Russia during World War II had to eat 'famine bread' made using leaves, grass and clay.

E | Obesity is a form of malnutrition.

> **6** a| How much wholemeal bread would an adult need to eat for it to provide all their energy needs for a day? Give your answer to the nearest 100 g.
> b| Suggest why only eating wholemeal bread would be a bad idea.
> c| In what way would putting butter on the bread be good?

I can ...

- describe the benefits of a balanced diet
- explain the causes and effects of some different types of malnutrition.

8Ac MAKING NEW FOODS

HOW AND WHY ARE NEW FOODS INVENTED?

People have been inventing new foods for thousands of years, often to solve the problem of foods going bad. Yoghurt, for example, was probably discovered by accident about 7000 years ago in the Middle East. Bacteria got into some stored milk and caused it to thicken and go sour. People liked the taste and the food lasted longer.

Food technologists are still inventing new foods that last longer, taste better, look better or are healthier.

> 1 Give one advantage of canned foods.
>
> 2 Give two reasons why food technologists invent new foods today.

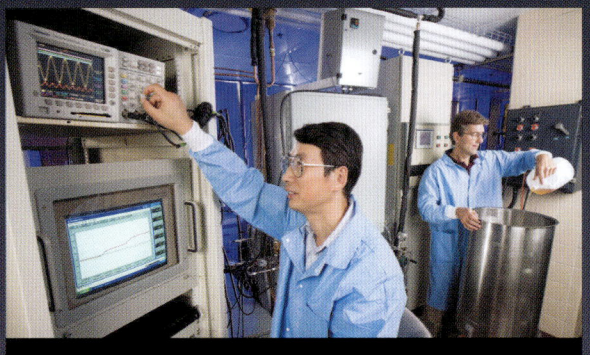

A | Canning, salting, jamming, pickling and drying are ways of changing foods to make them last longer.

B | investigating the use of electricity to destroy harmful microorganisms in foods

Careers in food technology

Not all food technologists develop new foods. Some of them test foods to ensure that they contain the right ingredients and are safe to eat. Others improve food production, making it faster or cheaper. This often involves engineering and new technology. The researchers in photo B, for example, are passing electricity through liquid foods (such as milk) to destroy microorganisms. They hope to use this technology to make the foods safe without heating them (which changes their flavour).

Most food technologists leave school with a good knowledge of chemistry, biology and maths and go to university to get a degree in food technology. It may also be possible to leave school and join a company that will train you as a food technologist while you work for them.

C | The production of many foods is automated in huge factories. This involves a lot of engineering.

> 3 Suggest two advantages of killing microorganisms in foods using electricity rather than heat.
>
> 4 A food packet claims that the food contains starch. Explain how a food technologist would test this claim.

STEM

Inventing new foods

Food technologists who develop foods need to be inventive. They first identify something that people want (e.g. a snack bar with less sugar). They then think up different ideas to do this. They try out each idea and find the best one.

To come up with ideas, food technologists think about whether they can:

- substitute something (e.g. take an ingredient away and replace it with something else)
- combine something new (e.g. add an extra ingredient to a food)
- adapt ideas from other products (e.g. use ideas about how one food is made to make another)
- modify the product (e.g. change the amounts of the different ingredients).

> **5** Suggest two ways to make a snack bar with less sugar.
>
> **6** Explain one new food product that you would like to see for sale.

D | Food technologists tasting different versions of the same food.

ACTIVITY

People have asked a pizza company to use healthier pizza bases. The nutrition information for the existing pizza base is shown.

1. State some ways in which the pizza base could be made healthier.
2. Choose one way and explain two ideas for changing the pizza base in this way.
3. Choose one idea and design a delivery box to advertise your new pizza base.

Pizza base	
Ingredients	
Bleached white flour, water, glucose, sucrose, salt, hydrogenated vegetable oil (to add stretchiness), xanthan gum (to add stretchiness)	
Nutrition Information	
Typical values	per 100 g	per serving (¼ base)
Energy	1059 kJ	585 kJ
Protein	9 g	5 g
Carbohydrate	62 g	34 g
of which sugars	14 g	8 g
Fat	5 g	2.5 g
Fibre	0.2 g	0.1 g
Allergy advice Product contains gluten	

UK NC, iLS

8Ad DIGESTION

WHAT DO THE PARTS OF THE DIGESTIVE SYSTEM DO?

Proteins, fats and most carbohydrates are too big for your body to use and need to be broken down into smaller pieces. **Digestion** turns large **insoluble** molecules into smaller **soluble** ones. Digestion occurs as your food passes through your **gut** (a tube made up of different organs). The gut and some other organs that help digestion (such as the **salivary glands**, **liver** and **pancreas**) form the **digestive system**.

1
a| What does the digestive system do?
b| Why do we need to digest food?

1. Putting food in your mouth is **ingestion**. Your teeth grind food into small pieces and mix it with **saliva**, which is produced by your **salivary glands**. Saliva is an example of a **digestive juice** – it helps digest food. It also makes food easier to swallow.

tongue
salivary glands
pancreas

4. In the **small intestine**, more digestive juices are added (including from the pancreas). The liver adds a substance to help digest fats. Small molecules of digested food are then **absorbed** (taken into the body) here.

liver
anus

2. When you swallow, food enters the **oesophagus** (or **gullet**). Muscles in the oesophagus contract to make the tube above the food narrower, and this pushes food towards the stomach. Food is moved through the whole gut in the same way.

3. In the **stomach**, food is churned up with acid (pH 1–2) and more digestive juices are added.

5. Food that we cannot digest (e.g. fibre) goes into the **large intestine**, where water is removed. This forms a more solid material called **faeces** (pronounced '*fee-sees*').

6. The **rectum** stores faeces, which are then pushed out of the **anus** in a process called **defaecation** or **egestion**. It takes about 24–48 hours for food to go through the gut. (Note that *defaecation* is getting rid of undigested food. *Excretion* is getting rid of wastes produced by your cells.)

A

FACT

The appendix is a small tube that helps some animals to digest grass. In humans it helps the immune system but can get infected (appendicitis). If this happens it is removed.

2 Draw a flow chart to show what happens in each organ of the gut.

3 What are ingestion and egestion?

4 Describe how food is pushed through the gut.

78

Gut bacteria

Bacteria are **microorganisms** (organisms you need a microscope to see). Although they are tiny, your intestines contain about 1 kilogram (kg) of them! Some of these bacteria are useful, but other types are harmful.

The bacteria in your gut feed on your food and can digest some foods that your body cannot. The bacteria grow and reproduce using some of these digested molecules, but the rest of the molecules can be absorbed into your body.

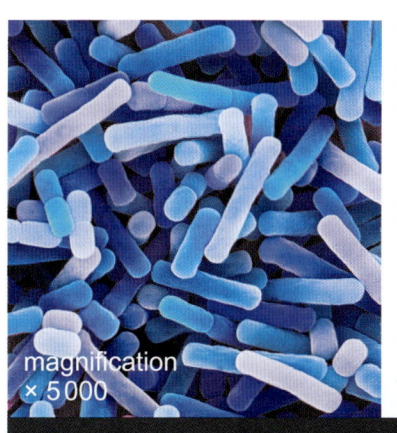

B | This yoghurt drink contains bacteria that may help control harmful gut bacteria.

FACT

Some gut bacteria produce gases as they feed, causing flatulence. Bacteria in cattle make them burp a lot and produce a great deal of flatulence, making some scientists think that cattle farming is affecting the atmosphere. This cow is having its gases collected as part of research into this hypothesis.

C

Enzymes

Enzymes are substances that speed up the breaking down of large molecules into smaller ones. Substances that speed up reactions (without being changed themselves) are called **catalysts**. Enzymes are biological catalysts.

Most of the enzymes needed for digestion are produced by your body and are found in the various digestive juices that are added to food as it travels through the gut.

A **model** that helps us think about how enzymes work compares them to scissors. The enzymes help to cut through the connections that hold the molecule together.

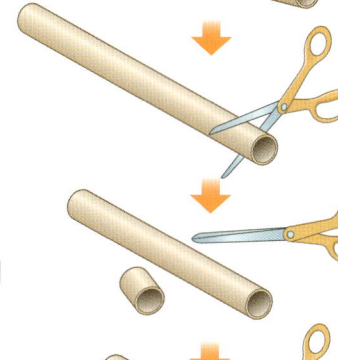

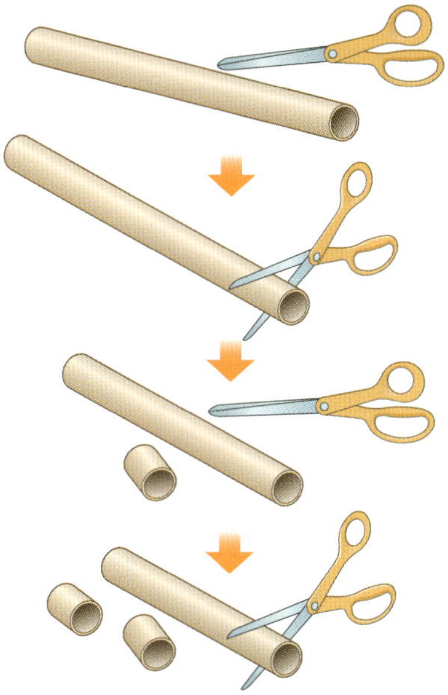

D | the scissors model of enzyme action

---

5 Give one benefit and one disadvantage of having bacteria in your gut.

6 a| How do digestive juices help with digestion?
b| Use the scissors model to explain how enzymes work.

I can ...

- recall the parts of the digestive system and their functions
- explain why enzymes and bacteria are useful for digestion.

8Ae SURFACE AREA

HOW ARE SURFACE AREAS CALCULATED?

The area of a rectangle is worked out using this formula:

area of a rectangle = length × width

Area is measured in square units, like metres squared (m^2), centimetres squared (cm^2), millimetres squared (mm^2). So, if the length and width are in metres (m), the area is in m^2.

A tennis court is a rectangle 23.78 m long and 10.97 m wide:

area = 23.78 × 10.97
     = 260.87 m^2

1 What is the area of a soccer pitch that is 100 m long and 45 m wide? Show your working.

A

The total area of all the surfaces on a three-dimensional shape is called the **surface area**. It is important because it can affect the speed at which things happen.

Radiators and air conditioning evaporators have folds or fins on them to increase their surface areas. This means that more energy can be transferred from them in a certain length of time.

Calculating surface areas

A cube has six faces. To find the surface area of a cube you find the area of each face and add them all together. Some cells are roughly cuboid, so we can estimate the total surface area by finding the total of the areas of a cell's six rectangular faces.

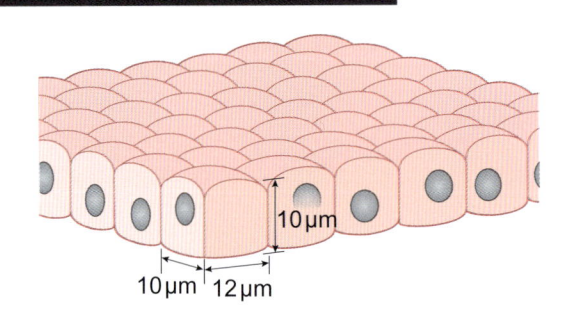

B | Air conditioning evaporators have large surface areas.

top area = 12×10
        = 120 µm^2

front area = 12×10
          = 120 µm^2

end area = 10×10
        = 100 µm^2

C

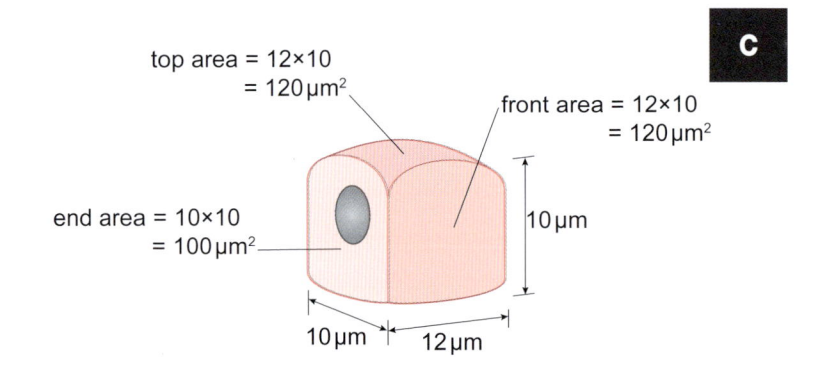

WORKING SCIENTIFICALLY

In diagram C, the top face of the cell is the same size as the bottom face, so:

Area of top and bottom = 120 + 120 = 240 µm²

Area of front and back = 120 + 120 = 240 µm²

Area of both ends = 100 + 100 = 200 µm²

Surface area of the cuboid = 240 + 240 + 200 = 680 µm²

2 Estimate the surface area of an approximately cuboid cell, with length 10 µm, width 15 µm and height 20 µm. Show your working.

If food is given a greater surface area, there is more room for enzymes to get to work and break down the food. This is why, for example, teeth are important for grinding up food.

Surface area is also important for the small intestine; the larger its surface area the faster it can absorb digested food.

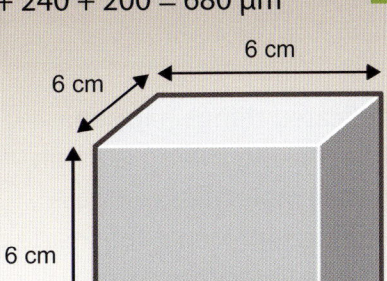

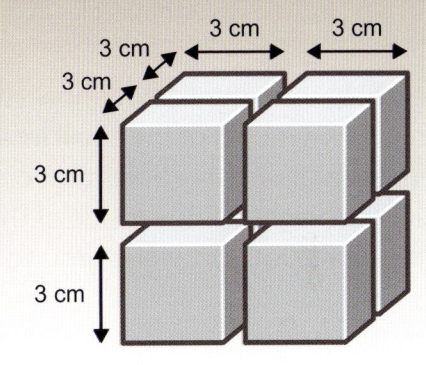

surface area of large cube:

6 × (6 × 6) = 216 cm²

if the large cube is split into eight smaller cubes:

surface area of one smaller cube = 6 × (3 × 3) = 54 cm²

there are eight smaller cubes, so total surface area = 54 × 8 = 432 cm²

3 A cuboid measures 8 cm long, 4 cm wide and 6 cm tall.
   a| Calculate its surface area.
   b| The cuboid is cut in half along its longest edge. Calculate its new surface area.

D | If the big cube is broken down into many smaller cubes, there is a big increase in surface area.

4 Explain why a sugar cube dissolves more slowly in a cup of coffee than the same amount of loose sugar granules.

5 Explain why the same amount of food is digested faster when it is in small pieces compared with large pieces.

6 Look at diagram D. Calculate the surface area : volume ratio of:
   a| the large cube
   b| one of the small cubes.
   Show your working.

Surface area : volume ratio

The **surface area : volume ratio** is the surface area divided by the volume, or $\frac{\text{surface area}}{\text{volume}}$

The bigger the surface area : volume ratio, the more surface area something has per unit volume. Cells need large surface area : volume ratios to be able to take enough of the substances they need from their surroundings.

I can ...

- calculate areas of rectangles and cuboids
- explain the importance of surface area in science, including surface area : volume ratios.

8Ae ABSORPTION

HOW DOES DIGESTED FOOD GET INTO THE BLOOD?

Enzymes break up large molecules into smaller, soluble ones. The small molecules can then be absorbed by the small intestine.

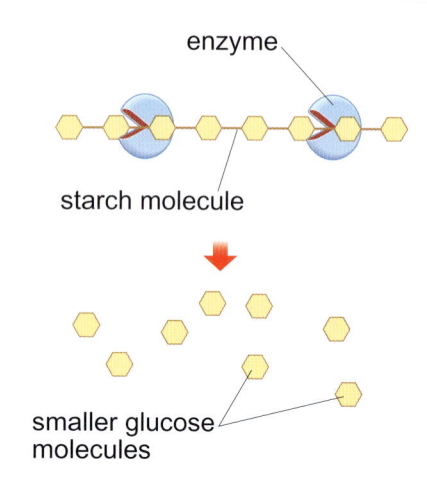

> **1**
> a| Where is digested food absorbed?
> b| Explain which molecules in diagram A can be absorbed.

Models help us to think about how complicated things happen. Diagram B is a model of the small intestine. Visking tubing is a thin material containing tiny holes that only small molecules can pass through. In diagram B the inside of the tubing represents the inside of the small intestine. The water around the tubing represents the blood.

A | Starch is digested into smaller sugars, such as glucose, by enzymes.

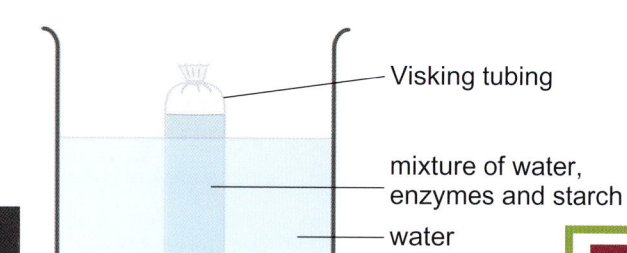

B | model small intestine

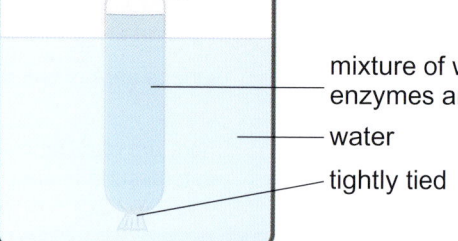

> **2** What would you expect to find in the water at the end of the experiment shown in diagram B that was not there at the start? Explain your reasoning.
>
> **3**
> a| Why do your cells need to respire?
> b| Which parts of the blood carry the substances needed for respiration?

Once absorbed, digested nutrients are dissolved in the blood **plasma** (the liquid part). Blood carries the nutrients around the body for cells to use. For example, all your cells need glucose in order to release energy (using respiration).

All particles naturally spread out. This is called **diffusion**. If there are more particles of a substance in one area than another, eventually the particles become evenly spaced due to diffusion. After a meal, there are many more digested nutrient molecules inside the small intestine than in the blood. This causes an overall movement of these molecules into the blood, by diffusion.

Particles move randomly in all directions. So some molecules of glucose will move from the blood into the small intestine, but many more go the other way. There is an *overall* movement of glucose molecules in one direction.

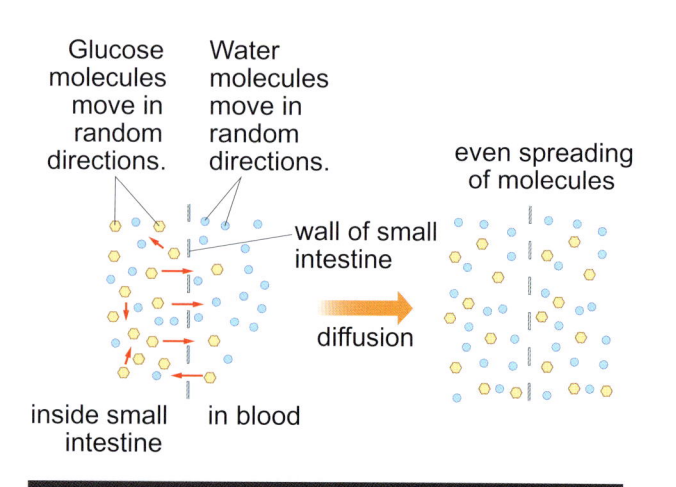

C | diffusion in the small intestine

4	What is diffusion?
5	Why do some glucose molecules move out of the blood and others move into it?
6	Explain how diffusion allows the small intestine to absorb soluble molecules but not insoluble ones.

FACT

The surface area of the small intestine is about the area of a tennis court (about 260 m^2).

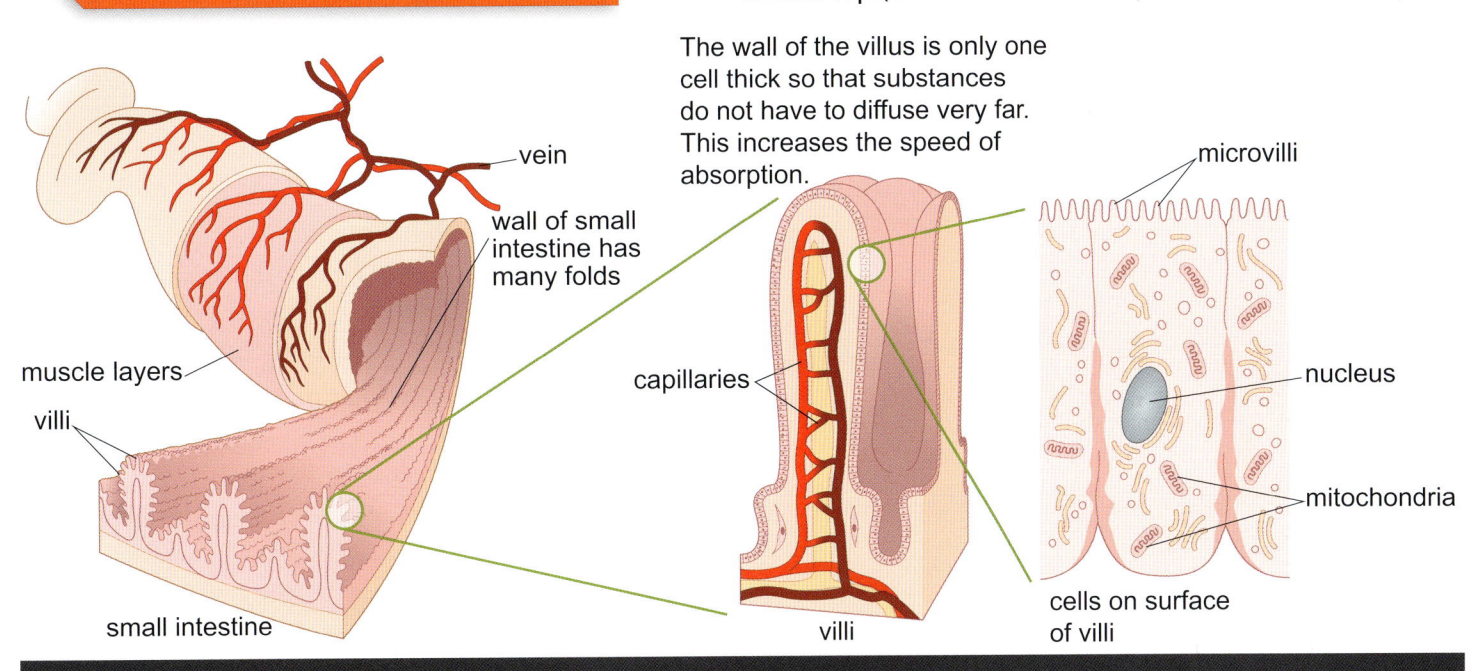

Small intestine adaptations

The greater the surface area, the more room there is for molecules to pass between the inside of the small intestine and the blood. So, a greater surface area allows more diffusion of molecules. This allows more glucose to be absorbed more quickly.

To increase its surface area, the wall of the small intestine is folded. It also contains lots of little finger-shaped villi (one is called a **villus**).

To further increase surface area, each villus cell has a folded top (that forms microvilli, one is a **microvillus**).

The wall of the villus is only one cell thick so that substances do not have to diffuse very far. This increases the speed of absorption.

D | The small intestine is adapted to its function.

7	How is the small intestine adapted to absorbing digested nutrients quickly?
8	a| Give one short-term effect of drinking alcohol on the digestive system. b| Explain why this may cause fewer nutrients to get into the blood. c| Explain why someone who drinks alcohol may suffer from malnutrition.
9	You can think of the human small intestine as a tube which is about 6.5 m long and has a diameter of 2.5 cm. A tube of these dimensions has a surface area of about 0.51 m^2. Why is this different from the area given in the fact box?

Alcohol

When alcohol is drunk, fewer digestive enzymes are released into the small intestine. Drinking alcohol can damage the villi and cause them to become shorter.

I can ...

- explain how diffusion enables absorption by the small intestine
- explain how the small intestine is adapted to its function.

8Ae PACKAGING AND THE LAW

Most food companies put nutrition information labels on food packaging. Many companies also add traffic lights. Red means high, orange means medium and green means that a food is low in a certain nutrient. The more green the better. The percentage of the Reference Intake in a serving may also be shown.

Companies must show ingredients on packaging and most foods must be dated. A 'best before' date tells you how long a food's taste will be at its best. A food is usually safe to eat after this date but does not taste as good. Foods with a 'use by' date may cause harm after this date, often because harmful bacteria grow in them.

A | Food traffic lights: some fats (saturates) increase the risk of heart disease more than other fats. Salt helps our nerves to work, but too much can cause high blood pressure.

B

In some countries there are strict rules on some words found on food packaging. For example, in the EU foods labelled 'organic' must be produced without the use of artificial fertilisers and pesticides. A low fat food must contain less than 3 g of fats per 100 g of food. A reduced fat, light or 'lite' food must contain 30 per cent less fat or energy than another food of the same type.

However, many other words have no rules, including 'traditional style', 'finest' and 'handmade'.

1
a | Suggest why food producers use words like 'finest' on their foods.
b | Suggest why food producers advertise some foods as 'light'.

2
a | List the different types of nutrients in photo A.
b | What does each nutrient do?
c | Suggest why only certain nutrients appear on food traffic lights.

3 Describe how bacteria can be both useful and harmful in the digestive system.

4 Draw a flow chart to show how cells get a fuel for respiration after you have eaten starch.

C

HAVE YOUR SAY

Some people think that putting nutritional information labels on all foods should be made law. What do you think of this idea?

8Ba USEFUL PLANTS

It is estimated that we use products from over 100 different plants every day, and only some of these are for food.

Many fabrics and dyes come from plants. Linen, for making tea towels and sheets, comes from flax plant stems. We make cotton from the fruits of a plant called *Gossypium hirsutum*. The original blue dye for jeans came from indigo plant leaves.

We use plant scents in perfumes, soaps and shampoos. An example is the scent produced by lavender plants to attract bees, which pollinate them.

Many medicines originally came from plants. The compound that aspirin was developed from came from willow tree bark and the heart medicine digitalis came from foxglove plants.

Many musical instruments are made from plants, and so are some pieces of sports equipment, such as cricket bats.

We use wood for buildings and furniture. Oils from rape seeds and sunflower seeds are used for biodiesel. Tyres are made from a liquid extracted from rubber trees. The list goes on and on!

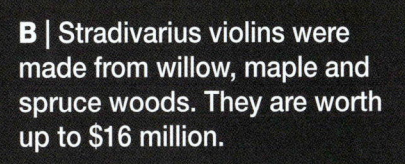

A | These denim (cotton) jeans are dyed using natural indigo.

B | Stradivarius violins were made from willow, maple and spruce woods. They are worth up to $16 million.

1. All plants are in the plant kingdom. Name one other kingdom.

2. Look at the first sentence on this page. What is an estimate?

3.
   a| What happens when bees pollinate flowers?
   b| Suggest two ways plants attract insects for pollination.
   c| Fertilisation follows pollination. What happens in fertilisation?
   d| Suggest one way in which plants spread their seeds.

4. Many organisms have a common name and a scientific name. Identify an example of each of these on this page.

UK NC, CEE

8Ba CLASSIFICATION AND BIODIVERSITY

HOW IS CLASSIFICATION USEFUL?

We use the different **characteristics** of organisms to **classify** them into groups. The five largest groups are the **kingdoms**. Each kingdom can be split into smaller groups.

Animals
- no cell walls
- multicellular (many cells)
- feed on other organisms

Fungi
- cell walls contain chitin ('**ky-tin**')
- mostly multicellular
- live on dead organisms

Protoctists
- mostly unicellular (made of one cell)

Plants
- cell walls made of cellulose
- multicellular
- make their own food

Prokaryotes (mainly bacteria)
- cells have no nucleus
- unicellular

1
a| What characteristics of animals are different from those of plants?
b| What are the other three kingdoms?

2 How are flowering plants and conifers:
a| similar
b| different?

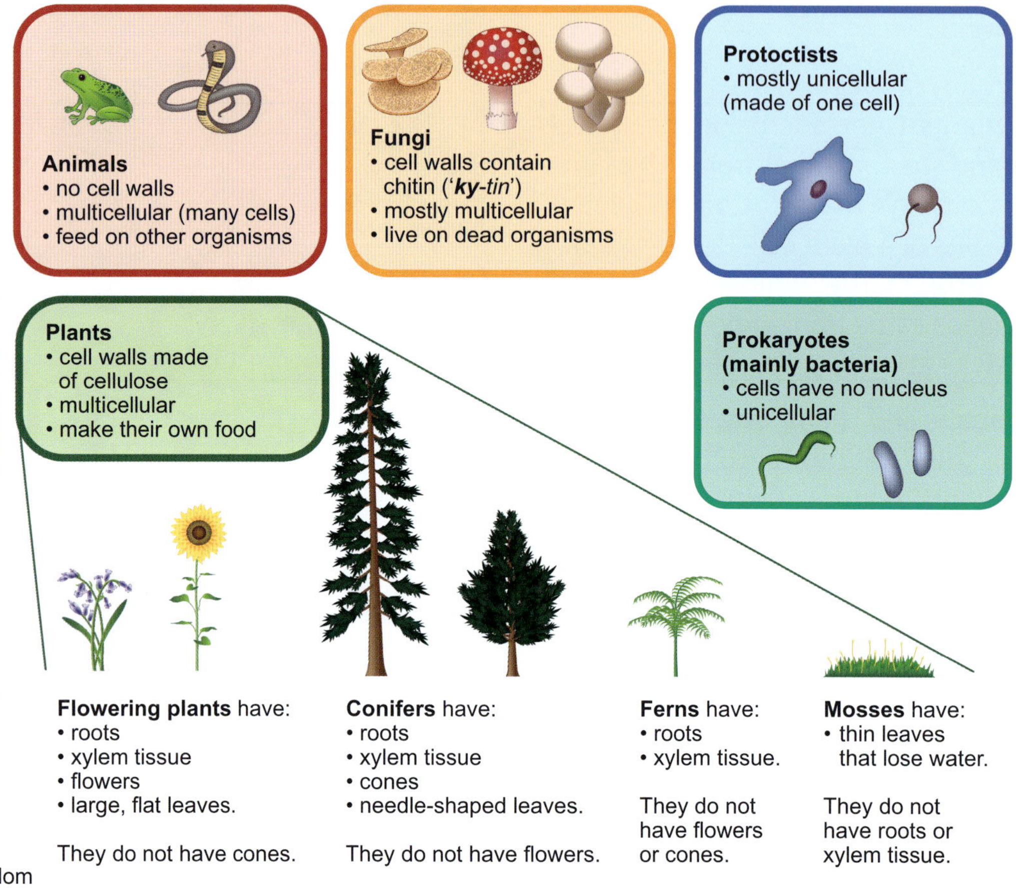

Flowering plants have:
- roots
- xylem tissue
- flowers
- large, flat leaves.

They do not have cones.

Conifers have:
- roots
- xylem tissue
- cones
- needle-shaped leaves.

They do not have flowers.

Ferns have:
- roots
- xylem tissue.

They do not have flowers or cones.

Mosses have:
- thin leaves that lose water.

They do not have roots or xylem tissue.

A | the five kingdoms

The five kingdoms are split into smaller groups based on their characteristics. Plants are split into flowering plants, conifers, ferns and mosses. Each smaller group is divided into even smaller groups, as shown in diagram B. The characteristics of organisms in a group get more and more similar as the groups get smaller.

The last group contains only one type of organism. We give this organism a scientific name using the names of the two last groups (the **genus** and the **species**). Although scientific names are in Latin and look complicated, they are less confusing than common names. One species can have different common names and some different species all have the same common name.

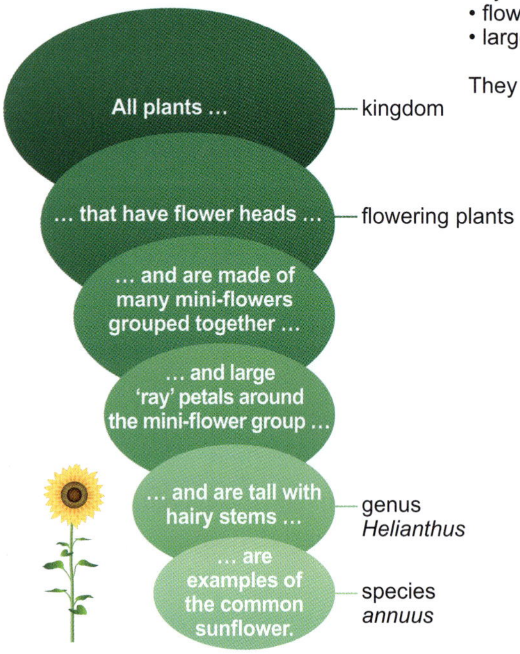

- All plants … — kingdom
- … that have flower heads … — flowering plants
- … and are made of many mini-flowers grouped together …
- … and large 'ray' petals around the mini-flower group …
- … and are tall with hairy stems … — genus *Helianthus*
- … are examples of the common sunflower. — species *annuus*

B | These groups are used to classify sunflowers – an important crop for biodiesel, cooking oils and spreads.

3 Give two differences between fungi and plants.

4 What is the scientific name for a common sunflower?

86

Diagram C shows some of the important groups in the animal kingdom.

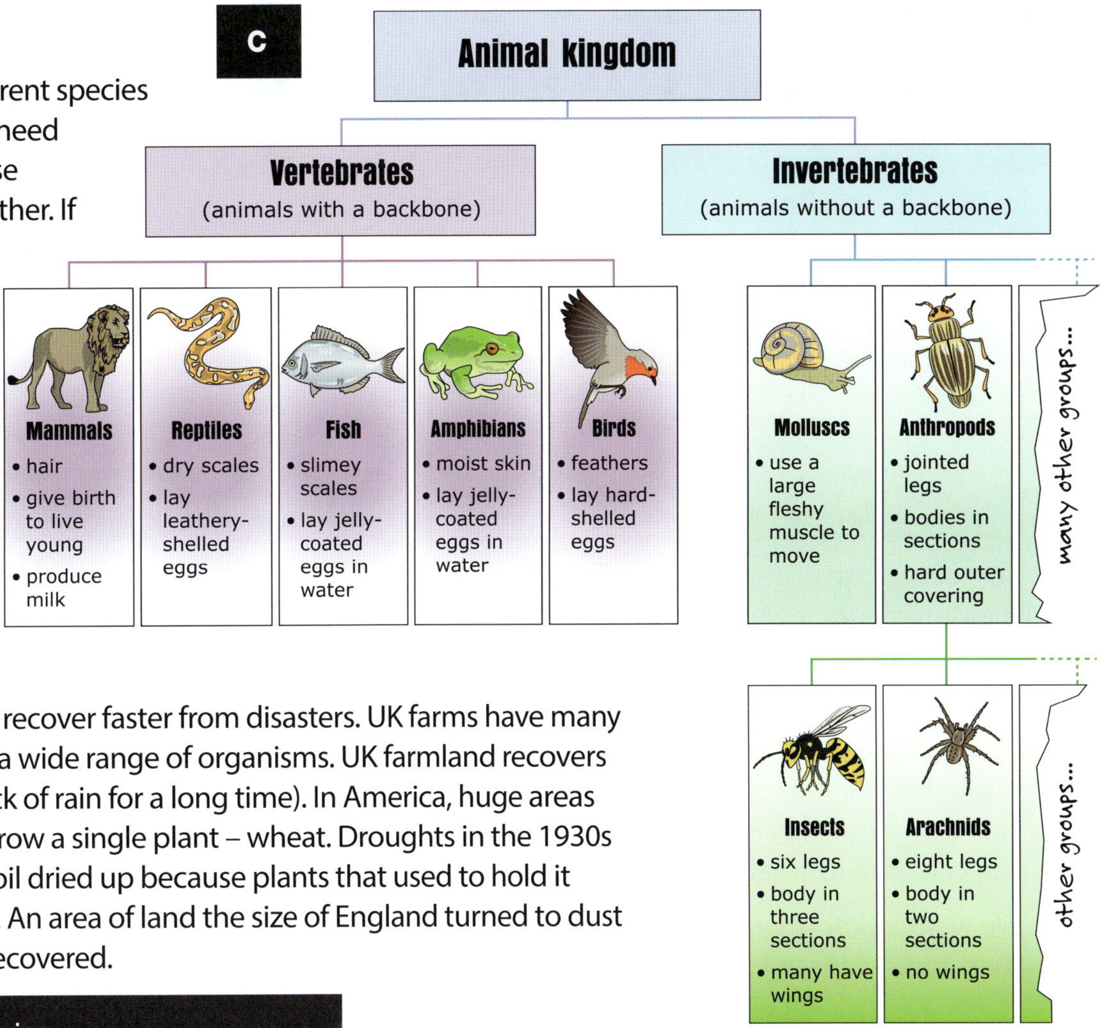

Diversity

Habitats containing many different species have greater **biodiversity**. We need to preserve biodiversity because organisms depend on one another. If an organism becomes **extinct** (dies out completely) it will affect other organisms in a habitat and may cause them to become extinct too.

There are many undiscovered substances in organisms that could be useful. If organisms become extinct, we may lose useful new products.

C Animal kingdom

Vertebrates (animals with a backbone)

- **Mammals**
  - hair
  - give birth to live young
  - produce milk
- **Reptiles**
  - dry scales
  - lay leathery-shelled eggs
- **Fish**
  - slimey scales
  - lay jelly-coated eggs in water
- **Amphibians**
  - moist skin
  - lay jelly-coated eggs in water
- **Birds**
  - feathers
  - lay hard-shelled eggs

Invertebrates (animals without a backbone)

- **Molluscs**
  - use a large fleshy muscle to move
- **Anthropods**
  - jointed legs
  - bodies in sections
  - hard outer covering

...many other groups...

- **Insects**
  - six legs
  - body in three sections
  - many have wings
- **Arachnids**
  - eight legs
  - body in two sections
  - no wings

...other groups...

Areas with greater biodiversity recover faster from disasters. UK farms have many hedges, providing habitats for a wide range of organisms. UK farmland recovers quite quickly from drought (lack of rain for a long time). In America, huge areas of land were ploughed up to grow a single plant – wheat. Droughts in the 1930s caused the wheat to die. The soil dried up because plants that used to hold it together were no longer there. An area of land the size of England turned to dust and some parts still have not recovered.

E | a dust storm in 1930s America

D | In Singapore, the plant on which this butterfly depended became extinct. So did the butterfly.

5 In diagram C, which characteristics of birds are the same as reptiles, and which are different?

6 What do you notice about how scientific names are written?

7 Which of these habitats do you think has the greatest biodiversity: tropical rainforest, Arctic, desert? Explain your reasoning.

8 Suggest why biodiversity should be preserved.

I can ...

- interpret scientific organism names
- describe how organisms are classified
- explain the importance of biodiversity.

87

8Ba ACCURACY AND ESTIMATES

UK NC, CEE

HOW DO YOU USE A SAMPLE TO ESTIMATE A SIZE?

Accuracy is a measure of how close a value is to its real value. The closer a measure is to the real value, the more accurate it is.

> **1**
> a) The real mass of a jar containing sunflower seeds is 1.853624 kg. Which balance in diagram A shows a value closest to this figure?
> b) Which is the least accurate balance? Explain your answer.

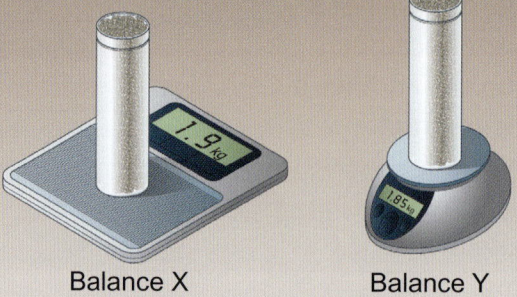

Balance X reads 1.9 kg
Balance Y reads 1.85 kg
Balance Z reads 1853.6 g

A | Different balances have different levels of accuracy.

Sometimes we do not need very accurate measurements. If we just wanted to know if the jar in A has a mass of more than 1 kg, the least accurate balance would be fine to use.

An **estimate** is an approximate value. We use estimates when we do not need accurate values to explain or describe something. You can calculate estimates using **samples**.

B | This art installation contains an estimated eight million ceramic sunflower seeds.

We want to know whether there are more than 1000 seeds in jar C. We could:

- count all the seeds
- count out 1000 seeds and then see if there are any remaining
- count the number of seeds in a sample and use that to calculate an estimate.

Worked example

Jar C is 30 cm tall. We take out the seeds from the top 1 cm (a sample). There are 46 of them. Now, we work out how much bigger the whole jar is compared with the sample.

× 30   1 cm contains   46 seeds   × 30
       30 cm contains   1380 seeds

This is an estimate because we have assumed that there are exactly 46 seeds in every 1 cm section of the jar.

> **2** A sweet jar is 50 cm tall. Sweets are taken from the top 5 cm. There are 24 sweets. Estimate the total number of sweets in the jar. Show all your working.
>
> **3** Why is the answer to question 2 an estimate?

C | A sample is a small amount taken from something much bigger.

WORKING SCIENTIFICALLY

D | When planning an estimate, think about the balance between the time it takes and the accuracy you need to draw a conclusion.

A larger sample gives more accurate results but takes longer to count. You need to balance time and accuracy when planning to estimate a quantity.

Sampling organisms

Scientists use samples to estimate **populations** (the numbers of organisms). Samples can be taken using a square frame called a **quadrat**, which is placed in different places around a habitat. In each place, the organisms inside it are observed, and those of interest are counted. If you know the area of the habitat and the area covered by the quadrats, you can estimate the total populations of the organisms.

A quadrat needs to be placed at **random**. This means that there is an equal chance of the quadrat being placed in any part of the habitat. There are different methods to randomly choose where quadrats are placed. Doing this means that the person placing the quadrat does not influence which parts of an area are sampled.

E | using a quadrat

Worked example

We want to estimate the number of dandelions in a lawn. The lawn is a rectangle 20 m long and 12.5 m wide:

area of lawn = 20 × 12.5 = 250 m^2

A quadrat is a square with sides 0.5 m:

area of quadrat = 0.5 × 0.5 = 0.25 m^2

The quadrat is placed 20 times. Four dandelions are counted in total:

total area sampled = 20 × 0.25 = 5 m^2

Now, we work out how much bigger the whole lawn area is compared with the sample:

×50 ⟳ 5 m^2 contains   4 dandelions ⟳ ×50
       250 m^2 contains 200 dandelions

The estimated number of dandelions is 200.

We have assumed there are 4 dandelions in every 5 m^2 of lawn.

4
a| A lawn has an area of 250 m^2. Using a quadrat, 15 daisy plants are found in a 10 m^2 sample. Estimate the daisy plant population in the whole lawn. Show all your working.

b| Explain why your answer is an estimate and not an accurate value.

c| What is the advantage of placing a quadrat more times?

d| What is the disadvantage of this?

I can ...
- use samples to calculate estimates
- use accuracy and time taken as criteria for evaluation.

89

8Bb TYPES OF REPRODUCTION

UK NC, CEE

WHAT ARE SEXUAL AND ASEXUAL REPRODUCTION?

Sexual reproduction occurs when two organisms breed and produce new organisms. Members of the same species can reproduce sexually to produce offspring that can also reproduce sexually.

Members of two different species cannot usually reproduce, but if they do, the offspring are called **hybrids**. Hybrids cannot reproduce sexually; they are not **fertile**.

1 What is needed for sexual reproduction to happen?

2 a| Which of the fruits in photo A is a hybrid?
b| Why can't the tree that produces this fruit reproduce?

A | A plumcot is the fruit from a hybrid of a plum tree and an apricot tree.

Sexual reproduction produces offspring that do not look identical to their parents; they have some characteristics from one parent and some from the other. These characteristics are **inherited** and so **variation** in these characteristics is called **inherited variation**.

3 Describe one characteristic the plumcot has inherited from:
a| apricots   b| plums.

In sexual reproduction, the parents produce sex cells or **gametes**. A male gamete and a female gamete join together to form a **fertilised egg cell** or **zygote**. The gametes carry the instructions for making a new organism, but each and every gamete made by a parent contains slightly different instructions for characteristics. This means that different offspring with the same parents will vary, and not look identical.

B | Some flowers show a lot of inherited variation.

FACT

The male gametes of mosses and ferns are swimming sperm cells. The male gametes of flowering plants and conifers cannot swim and are found inside pollen grains.

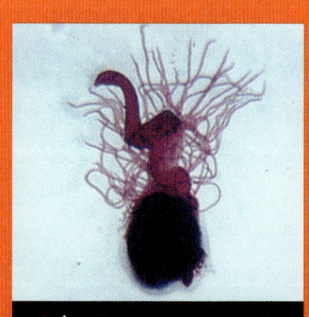

C | a fern sperm cell (magnification × 100)

4 What inherited variation is seen in photo B?

5 In humans what gametes are produced by:
a| males   b| females?

6 Explain why brothers do not usually look exactly alike.

Asexual reproduction

Plants can reproduce sexually, but many also use **asexual reproduction**. This type of reproduction does not need gametes. Instead, part of the parent plant forms a new plant. This means that the offspring will be identical to the parent.

Strawberry plants grow **runners**, which spread over the ground and sprout roots at intervals. Once the new plants have opened their leaves and can photosynthesise, the runner rots away.

Potato plants grow underground stems. The ends of these grow to form potato **tubers** (potatoes). They contain a store of food (starch). Each tuber can grow into a new potato plant.

D | Strawberry plants use runners for asexual reproduction.

> **7** What do strawberry plants use to reproduce:
> a| sexually   b| asexually?
>
> **8** Tony has seven tubers from one plant in his garden, called *Cyclamen persicum*. When he plants the tubers, why can he be sure that they will all grow into plants that look the same?

Gardeners use asexual reproduction to produce identical new plants quickly and cheaply. Often, they cut off a leaf or side stem from a plant and put it in moist soil. This is called taking a cutting. The cuttings grow roots and form new plants.

Asexual reproduction produces offspring that are all exactly the same as the parent. Asexual reproduction does not produce inherited variation but does allow plants to spread much faster than by using sexual reproduction.

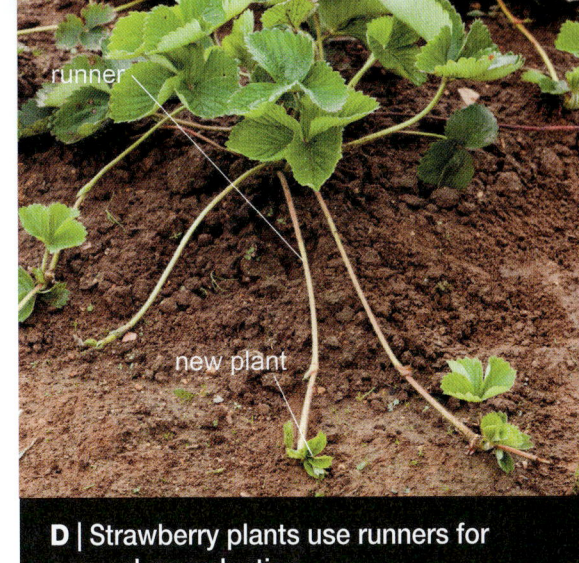

E | Potato plants use tubers for asexual reproduction.

F | taking a cutting

> **9** a| How is taking a cutting an example of asexual reproduction?
>
> b| Suggest one advantage of taking cuttings compared with collecting seeds from plants and growing them.

I can ...

- recall the differences between sexual and asexual reproduction
- recall examples of asexual reproduction in plants
- explain characteristics of offspring produced by sexual and asexual reproduction

UK NC, CEE

8Bc POLLINATION

WHAT ARE FLOWERS FOR?

Flowering plants use flowers for sexual reproduction. Most flowers contain both male and female reproductive organs.

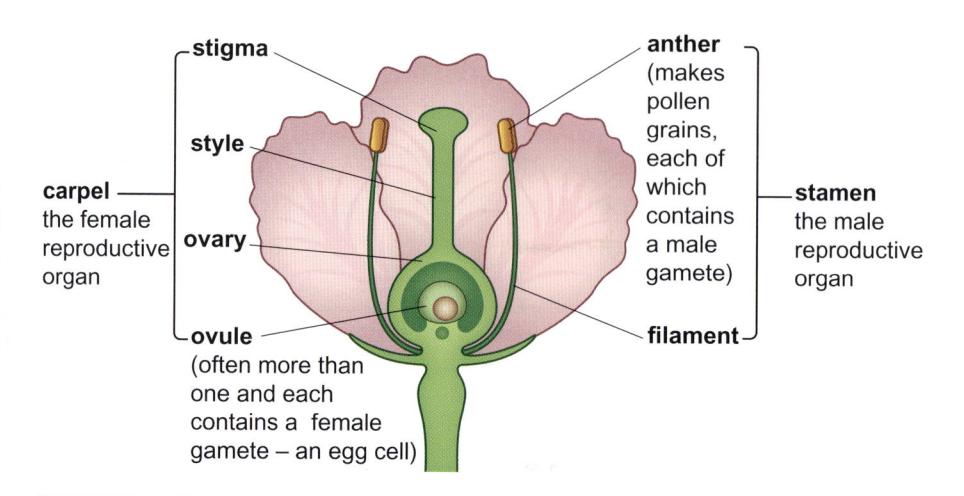

> **1**
> a| Name the male reproductive organ in plants.
> b| List its parts.

Each **pollen grain** contains a male gamete (sex cell). Pollen grains ripen inside anthers, which then split open. The grains are carried away and transferred to the stigmas of other flowers. This is called **pollination** and is carried out by animals, wind or water. Flowers have different structures depending on how they are pollinated.

Plants that use animal pollinators have flowers with petals. They attract the animals (mainly insects) with scent, colours and nectar to eat. Some plants also make extra pollen as a food for visiting insects. The structure of animal-pollinated flowers makes sure that visiting animals either collect or leave pollen grains.

Flower diagram labels:
- **stigma**
- **style**
- **carpel** — the female reproductive organ
- **ovary**
- **ovule** (often more than one and each contains a female gamete – an egg cell)
- **anther** (makes pollen grains, each of which contains a male gamete)
- **stamen** — the male reproductive organ
- **filament**

A | Most flowers have all these parts, although arranged differently.

B | A ripe lily anther: this has split open to reveal tiny pollen grains.

C | This plant is pollinated by bats.

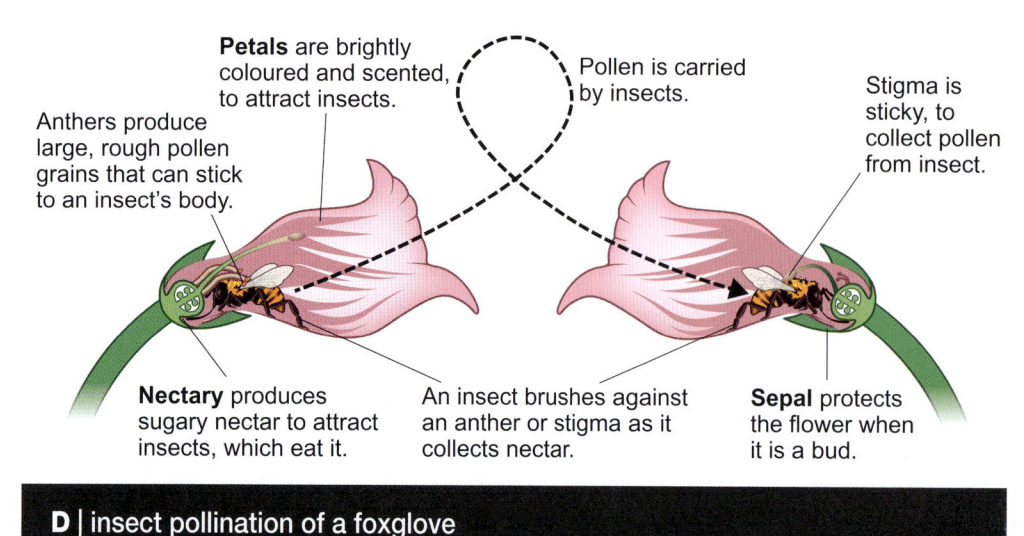

Foxglove pollination labels:
- **Petals** are brightly coloured and scented, to attract insects.
- **Anthers** produce large, rough pollen grains that can stick to an insect's body.
- Pollen is carried by insects.
- **Stigma** is sticky, to collect pollen from insect.
- **Nectary** produces sugary nectar to attract insects, which eat it.
- An insect brushes against an anther or stigma as it collects nectar.
- **Sepal** protects the flower when it is a bud.

D | insect pollination of a foxglove

> **2** What happens in pollination?
>
> **3** Suggest two parts that you would find in an egg cell.
>
> **4**
> a| What is the function of the stigma?
> b| How is it adapted to this function in insect-pollinated plants?

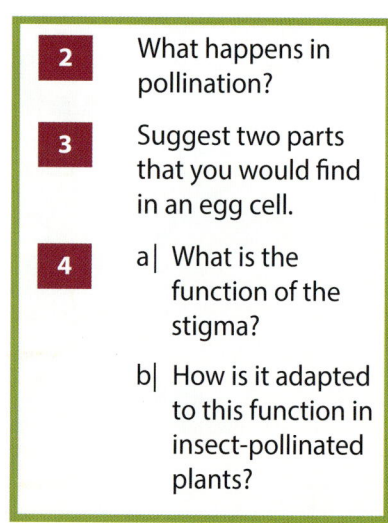

Hazel trees and grasses use the wind to spread their pollen. Wind-pollinated flowers look different from insect-pollinated flowers and do not have petals.

> **5** How can you tell that a flower is insect-pollinated and not wind-pollinated? Suggest three ways.

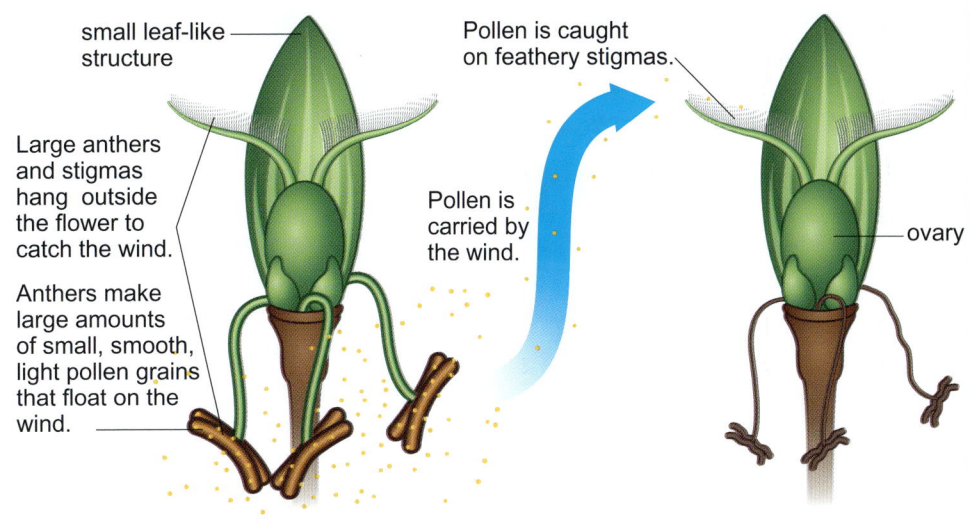

small leaf-like structure

Large anthers and stigmas hang outside the flower to catch the wind.

Anthers make large amounts of small, smooth, light pollen grains that float on the wind.

Pollen is caught on feathery stigmas.

Pollen is carried by the wind.

ovary

F | grass flowers shedding pollen

E | wind pollination of grass

Cross-pollination

Sexual reproduction should produce offspring with characteristics from two parents. If pollen grains from a plant land on the stigma of the *same* plant, this cannot happen. Plants try to stop this **self-pollination** and ensure **cross-pollination**. In some species (e.g. holly, nutmeg), half the plants have flowers with female reproductive organs and half the plants have male flowers. In other species, all the anthers on a plant mature and release their pollen before the stigmas become ready to receive pollen.

> **6** Look at photos G and H. Which shows pollen from an insect-pollinated plant? Explain your reasoning.

G × 1400

H × 1000

> **7** How are pollen grains from wind-pollinated flowers adapted to their function?

> **8** a| What is meant by cross-pollination?
> b| Explain why plants have ways of avoiding self-pollination.

FACT

Honey bees use nectar to make honey. It takes the nectar from about four million flowers to produce 1 kg of honey. The nectar is collected by worker bees, which only survive for 5–6 weeks; it is exhausting work! Back at the hive, the bees add enzymes to the nectar to break down complex sugars, turning them into simple sugars (such as glucose).

I can ...

- explain how the structures of flowers and pollen allow pollination, by animals or wind
- explain how plants ensure cross-pollination.

8Bc AIR QUALITY

HOW AND WHY DO WE CHECK AIR QUALITY?

Air quality is a measure of how clean the air is. Air contains many substances including pollen. The amount of pollen in air depends on the time of year. People who suffer from hayfever or asthma need to know how much pollen there is in the air because it can make these conditions worse.

Pollen can also cause problems in some factories, especially where tiny components such as microchips are made. A pollen grain can damage a chip as it is being made.

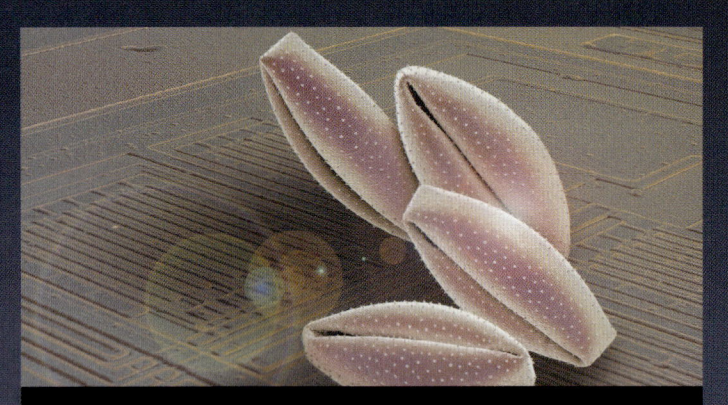

B | Pollen grains may be larger than lines of circuits on a microchip.

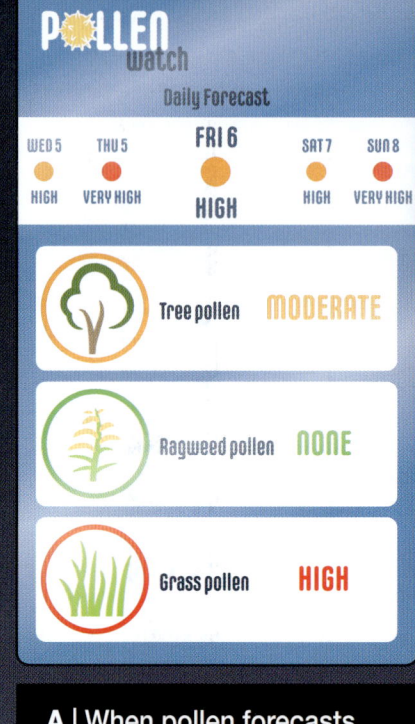

A | When pollen forecasts are high, people with breathing problems may choose to stay indoors or take more medication.

Air quality engineer

An air quality engineer monitors the levels of pollen, dust, gases and other substances in the air in a factory or office. The data from monitoring equipment is compared with acceptable levels to identify if the air quality is suitable for people or machines. The air quality engineer reports their findings and may need to find ways to improve the air quality.

An air quality engineer needs a degree in science with further training in environmental or chemical engineering.

C | Air is filtered to remove dust and pollen from areas where sensitive equipment is being used or made. Monitoring equipment takes regular samples from the air and alerts the air quality engineer if dust and pollen levels rise above a certain level.

STEM

1 Why do plants produce pollen?

2 Why do pollen concentrations vary in the air?

3 a | Suggest why pollen forecasting on a phone app usually only estimates if pollen levels are going to be 'low', 'medium' or 'high'.

b | Suggest why pollen level measurements in a microchip factory need to be more accurate.

Calculating concentrations

The levels of substances in the air are shown as **concentrations**. A concentration is the amount of something in a given volume. The concentration of pollen in the air can be measured as the number of grains in 1 m^3 of air (e.g. 10 000 grains/m^3). In liquid solutions, a concentration is the mass of solute dissolved in a certain volume of solvent (for example, 0.5 g/cm^3). Calculating concentrations using the same units allows you to compare them.

- If there are 400 grains of pollen in 100 cm^3 of air, then the concentration of pollen grains is $\frac{400}{100}$ = 4 grains/cm^3.
- If 10 g of salt is dissolved in 100 cm^3 of water, then the concentration of the salt solution is $\frac{10}{100}$ = 0.1 g/cm^3.

4 2000 cm^3 of air is filtered through a machine, which traps 268 pollen grains. Calculate the concentration of pollen grains in grains/cm^3.

5 a | 3 g of salt is dissolved in 25 cm^3 of water. Calculate the concentration of the solution in g/cm^3.

b | 15 g of salt is dissolved in 200 cm^3 of water. Compare the concentration of this solution with the one in part **a** to say which is the more concentrated.

ACTIVITY

Pollen in the air can be trapped using sticky tape. Stick squares of double-sided sticky tape to some microscope slides. Leave the slides in different positions. Later, add a drop of stain to the tape and cover with a coverslip. Using a microscope, compare the slides and order them by the amount of pollen they collected.

Different areas, weather, time of day or year can be compared to see what effect they have on the number of pollen grains in the air.

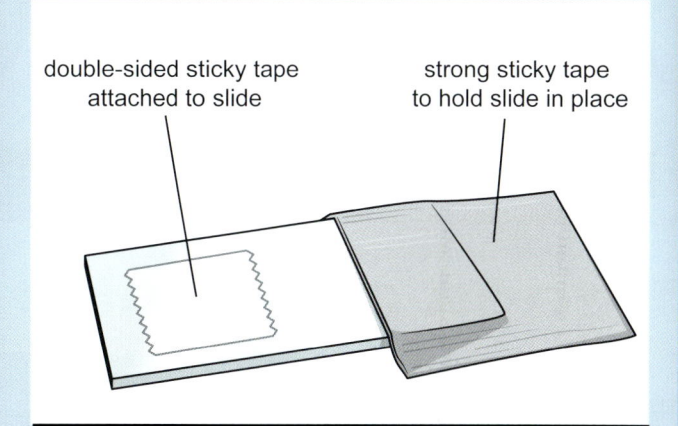

double-sided sticky tape attached to slide

strong sticky tape to hold slide in place

D | slide prepared for collecting pollen

6 Explain why the method in the activity will not give accurate enough measurements for inside a microchip factory.

95

8Bd FERTILISATION AND DISPERSAL

UK NC, CEE

HOW DOES FERTILISATION LEAD TO THE FORMATION OF A SEED?

If a pollen grain reaches a stigma of the same species, it can grow a **pollen tube**. The stigma makes a sugary solution, providing a source of energy for the pollen tube to grow down the style and into the ovary. Eventually the tube reaches an ovule.

The next stage is **fertilisation**, in which the egg cell and the male gamete from the pollen grain join together and their nuclei fuse into one. This forms a **zygote** (fertilised egg cell).

The zygote splits into two (using a process called **cell division**). These cells divide again and again to form an **embryo**. The embryo develops a tiny root and a tiny shoot.

A Pollen grains are carried to the stigmas of flowers. If the pollen grain is from the same species as the flower, it will grow a pollen tube.

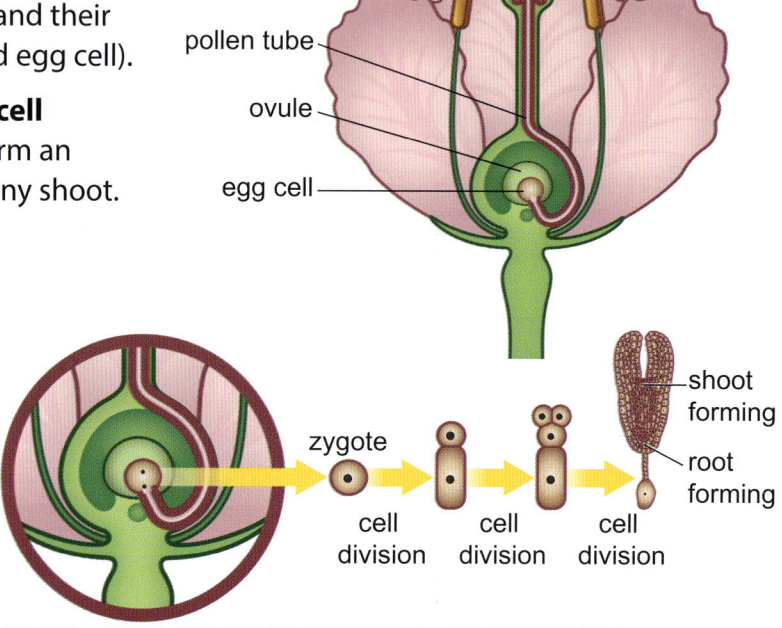

B | An embryo is formed by cell division.

1. a) Describe how the nuclei from an egg cell and the male gamete reach one another, after pollination.
   b) What is formed after the nuclei have fused?
   c) What is the name of this process?

2. How many cells will one cell become after cell division has happened three times?

3. What does the zygote go on to form?

Seeds and fruits

The ovule becomes the **seed**. Inside the seed is the embryo, together with a store of food (such as starch). A hard **seed coat** forms around the seed to protect it. When the seed starts to **germinate**, it uses the store of food to allow the embryo to grow. The ovary expands and becomes the **fruit** around the seed.

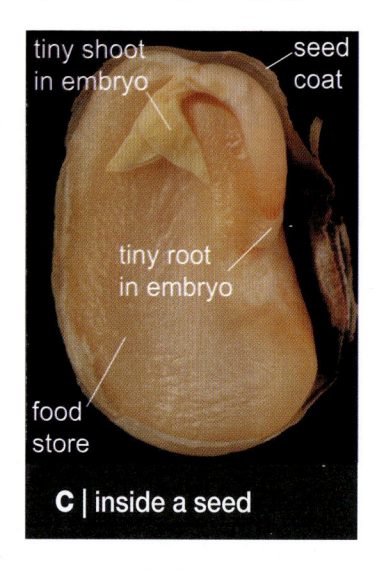

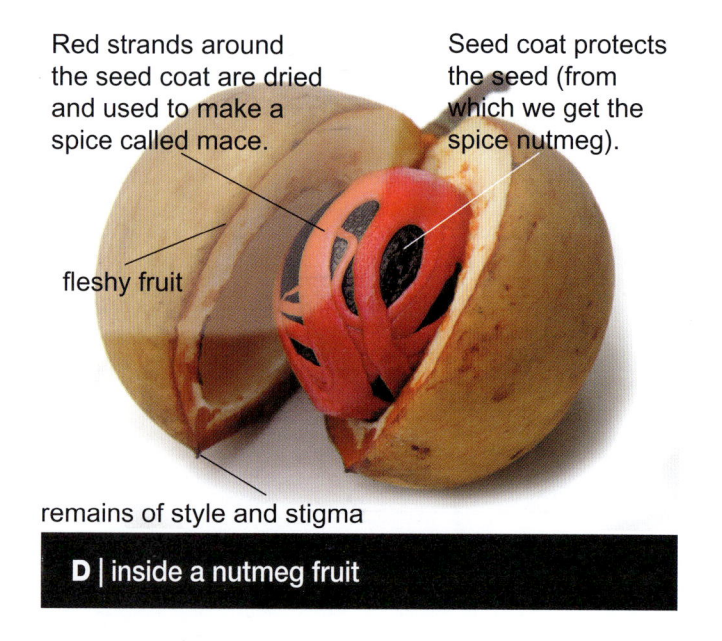

C | inside a seed

D | inside a nutmeg fruit

Red strands around the seed coat are dried and used to make a spice called mace.

Seed coat protects the seed (from which we get the spice nutmeg).

4	What part takes up most of a seed?
5	Look at photo D. From what part of the flower did the fleshy fruit develop?

FACT

Nutmeg spice is obtained from nutmeg tree seeds. In the 16th century, these trees only grew on a few tiny islands in Indonesia but their seeds were worth more than their weight in gold. The Portuguese, Dutch and the British had many battles for control of the islands. Eventually, in 1667, the British did a deal with the Dutch and swapped a nutmeg island for the island of Manhattan – the centre of what is now New York.

Seed dispersal

Fruits spread seeds away from the parent plants. This is called **seed dispersal**.

Some fruits are fleshy. They are soft, juicy and often good to eat. Many of them are brightly coloured to attract animals to eat them. The flesh of the fruit is easily digested but the seeds are protected from the digestive systems of the animals. The seeds are **egested** (passed out) by the animals in their **faeces**.

Other fruits are dry. They use animals, wind, water and even explosions to disperse their seeds.

Seed dispersal allows plant species to spread to new areas. It also means that the new plants are not in **competition** with their parents.

Plants compete with one another for resources (e.g. light, water). The more plants in an area, the greater the competition. If offspring grow away from their parents, there will be less competition between them.

E | fleshy fruits

F | These are all dry fruits. Himalayan balsam fruits explode, coconut fruits float in water, cocklebur fruits are carried by animals and dandelion fruits float in the air.

6	Identify the plants a–d in photo F and explain how the fruits disperse the seeds.
7	a| How do tomatoes spread tomato seeds? b| What protects the seeds? c| Why do the seeds need protection?
8	Why is it important for dandelion seeds to be spread away from the parent plants?

I can ...

- describe how pollination leads to fertilisation
- describe the formation of seeds and fruits
- explain the functions of seeds and fruits.

97

8Be GERMINATION AND GROWTH

UK NC, iLS, CEE

HOW DOES GERMINATION OCCUR?

A seed needs **resources** for germination to occur.

> 1. What is germination?
>
> 2. Describe the stages of germination. Include at least three stages.

Water allows the cells in the embryo to swell up and start cell division. It softens the seed coat too, allowing the embryo to grow through it. Water also lets substances called enzymes start breaking down the food store. The food is turned into smaller molecules, such as glucose, that the plant uses for growth.

The energy for growth comes from **respiration**, a process in which oxygen is used to release energy from glucose. It happens in the **mitochondria** of cells and can be summarised as a **word equation**:

glucose + oxygen → carbon dioxide + water (+ energy)

Germination needs warmth. Chemical reactions, such as those in respiration, are very slow if it is too cold.

Life processes, such as respiration, occur extremely slowly in a seed. It is still alive but it is **dormant**. Most seeds remain dormant until the resources for germination are available. Some seeds must be frozen before they will germinate. This makes sure that they only germinate after winter, when more resources are available in the spring.

A | germination

> 3. a) What are the raw materials needed for respiration?
>
>   b) What are the products of respiration?
>
> 4. List three resources that seeds need for germination.
>
> 5. Suggest why some plants make many fruits.
>
> 6. Explain how an embryo grows.
>
> 7. Why does the mass of a seed decrease during germination?

B | Some plants have seeds that lie dormant in the soil until after a fire. They then grow quickly when there is little competition from other plants.

FACT

Some seeds can remain dormant for a very long time. In 2005, a Judean date palm was grown from a seed found in a dry pot in Roman ruins that were being excavated. The seed was 2000 years old.

After germination, leaves make food for the plant by **photosynthesis**; carbon dioxide and water are used to make glucose (a type of sugar). The plant then converts the glucose into **starch**, to store it. The mass of material produced is **biomass**. Oxygen is a **byproduct** of this process, which we can summarise as follows:

$$\text{carbon dioxide} + \text{water} \xrightarrow[\text{chlorophyll}]{\text{light energy}} \text{oxygen} + \text{glucose}$$

Photosynthesis needs energy, which is transferred by light from the Sun. A green substance called **chlorophyll**, found inside **chloroplasts**, traps the energy and transfers it to glucose molecules, which store it.

Plants need small amounts of nutrients called **mineral salts** from the soil. The most important are compounds containing the elements nitrogen, phosphorus and potassium. They help the plant to grow. When a plant can reproduce, its **life cycle** starts again. An example is shown in diagram D.

> **8** a| What gases from the air does a plant need?
> b| Why does it need them?
>
> **9** a| What additional resources does a seedling need compared with a germinating seed?
> b| Why does it need these extra resources?

Interdependence

Many plants depend on insects for pollination and the insects depend on the plants for food, such as nectar. We say that they are **interdependent**. Humans also depend on the insects and the plants, because many plants do not form seeds and fruits for us to eat if they are not pollinated.

Plants and animals rely on one another in other ways. Many animals use plants for shelter. The seedlings from seeds dispersed through being eaten by animals also gain from a supply of mineral salts from the animals' droppings.

> **10** How are animals and plants interdependent for the gases they need?
>
> **11** Numbers of honeybees have been decreasing recently. Explain how this might affect humans.

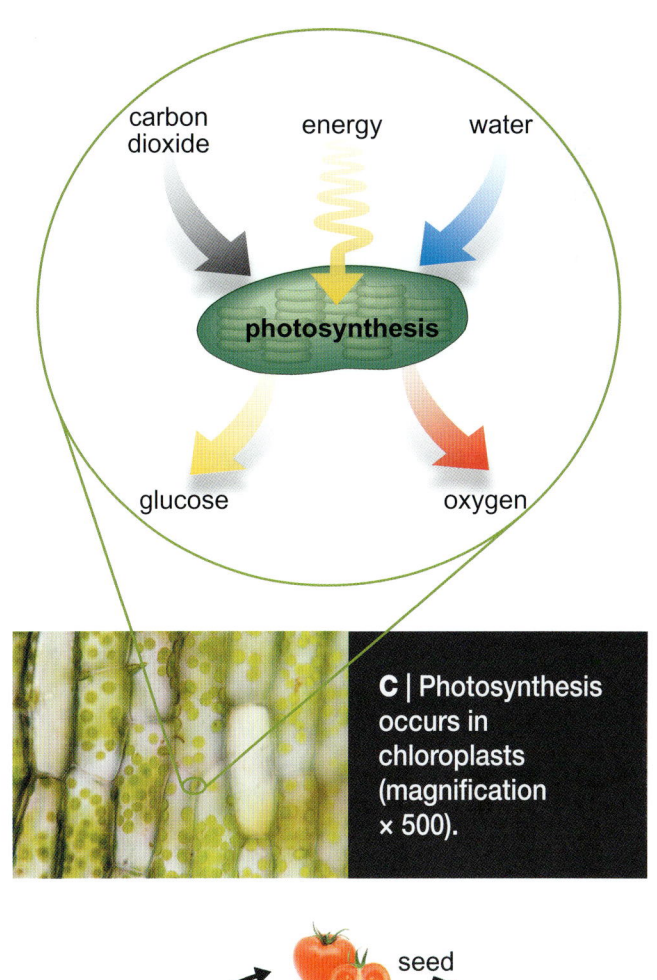

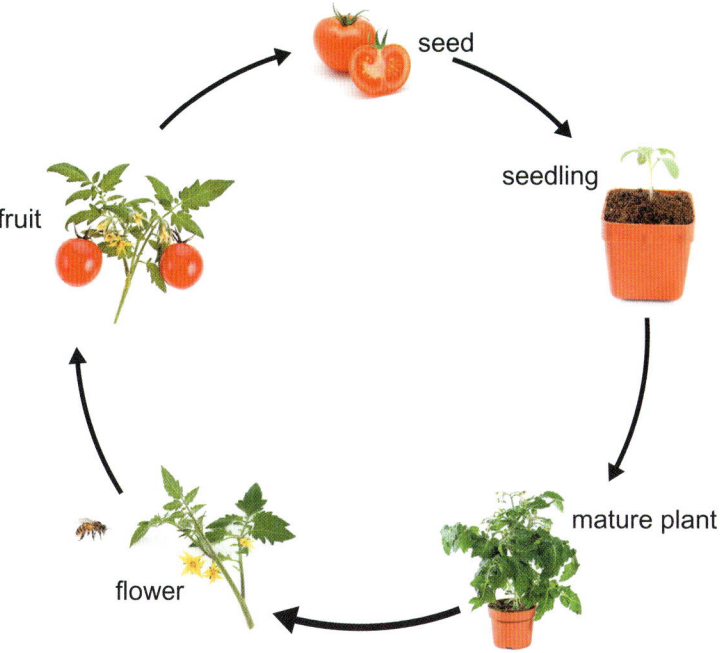

C | Photosynthesis occurs in chloroplasts (magnification × 500).

D | life cycle of a tomato plant

I can ...
- describe what happens in germination
- explain why seeds and plants need certain resources
- describe how organisms are interdependent.

8Be ANIMALS USING PLANTS

HOW DO ANIMALS USE PLANTS?

Like humans, animals have a whole range of uses for plants, other than for food.

Woodpecker finches, on the Galapagos Islands, use cactus spines to pick insects out of tree branches.

Male bowerbirds attract females by building large nests (or bowers) and decorating them with flowers, fruits, tubers and other useful or decorative objects.

In parts of Africa, crested rats chew up the bark of arrow poison trees and smear it on their fur, to kill predators. Local hunters also use the bark to make a deadly poison for their arrows. Traditional medicines are made using it too. The flower nectar is poisonous to birds but not bees, which collect it. The tree's fruit is highly poisonous to humans when unripe but once ripe, and purple in colour, it is safe to eat.

B | Crested rats (*Lophiomys imhausi*) grow up to 45 cm long.

Flower mantises are camouflaged to look like certain flowers. They hide and wait for other insects to visit the flowers.

C | an orchid mantis on a flower

A | the nest of a bowerbird (*Amblyornis inornatus*) from New Guinea

1. Which kingdom does each of the organisms on this page belong to?
2. What is the point of giving organisms scientific names?
3. Which genus does the crested rat belong to?
4. List the named items in the bowerbird's nest. Describe what *plants* use each of these items for.
5. Why are flowers good places for flower mantises to wait?
6. How does the arrow poison tree disperse its seeds? Explain your reasoning.
7. Write a paragraph to describe how the arrow poison tree and other organisms are interdependent.

HAVE YOUR SAY

It has been suggested that arrow poison trees are removed from an area outside a new town. What do you think of this idea?

8Ca WATER SPORTS AND BREATHING

The World Bog Snorkelling Championships are held every August in Llanwrtyd Wells, Wales. Competitors have to swim a total length of 110 metres as fast they can. The competitors obtain the air that they need via a snorkel.

Most swimmers do not use snorkels. They swim in such a way that they can take regular breaths. The breathing rate of a swimmer depends on the amount of air they need to complete a race as quickly as possible.

A | bog snorkelling

crest of the wave
breath taken in the trough of the wave

B | In front crawl, swimmers create a wave. The crest of the wave is just in front of the swimmer, so they can turn their heads to the side and breathe air from the trough of the wave.

C | a surfer holding his breath

Some water sports require people to hold their breath. Surfers practice holding their breath underwater to prepare for when they are submerged by giant waves.

1
a| What gas from the air do we need to breathe in?
b| What process is this gas needed for?
c| Where does this process occur?
d| How is this gas carried around your body?

2 Exhaled air contains more of one gas than inhaled air. What is this gas called?

3
a| List the organs through which air travels in your body.
b| Name one organ that causes air to be inhaled and exhaled.

4
a| What is a person's breathing rate?
b| When someone starts to do exercise, what happens to their breathing and heartbeat rates?
c| Explain why these rates change.

5 Surfers breathe quickly and deeply after being underwater for a long time. Suggest why.

8Ca AEROBIC RESPIRATION

UK NC, iLS, CEE

WHAT IS AEROBIC RESPIRATION?

Sporting events often have doctors and paramedics ready for immediate action. In an emergency they can quickly help a person. They attach monitors to measure things like heartbeat rate and temperature. The measurements are used to work out how to help the patient.

One monitor measures oxygen saturation (or 'sats'), which is shown as a percentage. A value of 100 per cent means that the blood is fully saturated and carrying as much oxygen as it can. Most people have an oxygen saturation of 95–100 per cent. If it drops below 80 per cent, organs can be damaged.

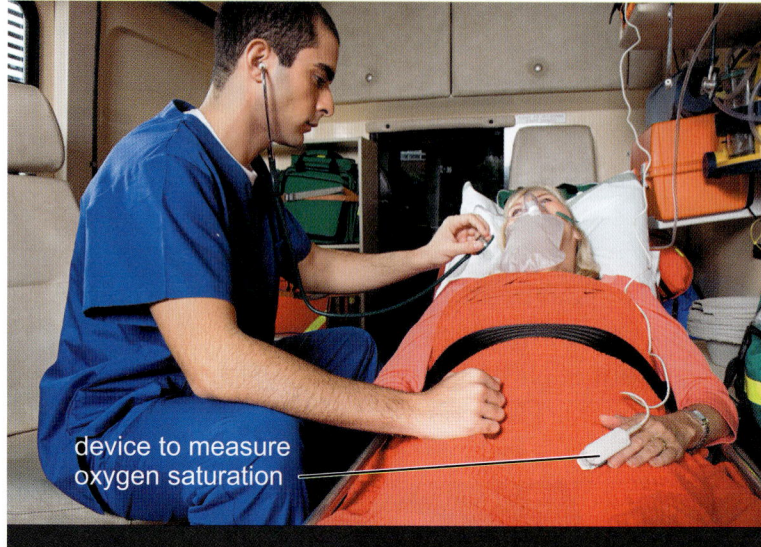

A | a paramedic measuring oxygen saturation in a patient

1 Steve has had an accident and the doctor says that his 'sats are low'.
 a| What does this mean?
 b| What substance will the doctor give Steve?
 c| What might happen if Steve is not given this?

Discovering oxygen

The Romans also had doctors at sports events. One, called Galen of Pergamon (129–c.200), was asked to look after a rich man's gladiator team. The gladiators fought one another in front of large crowds of people. They were often badly injured, and many died from their wounds. However, Galen was very successful at saving the gladiators' lives and so other doctors thought his ideas must be right. They continued to think he was right for the next 1500 years.

One of Galen's ideas was that the heart created warmth. He imagined that it contained a slow fire and thought that we breathed air to cool the heart. It was not until the 17th century that scientists started to test ideas about breathing.

In 1660, Robert Boyle (1627–1691) placed a burning candle in a jar and sucked out all the air. He repeated this with a mouse. Diagram B shows his results.

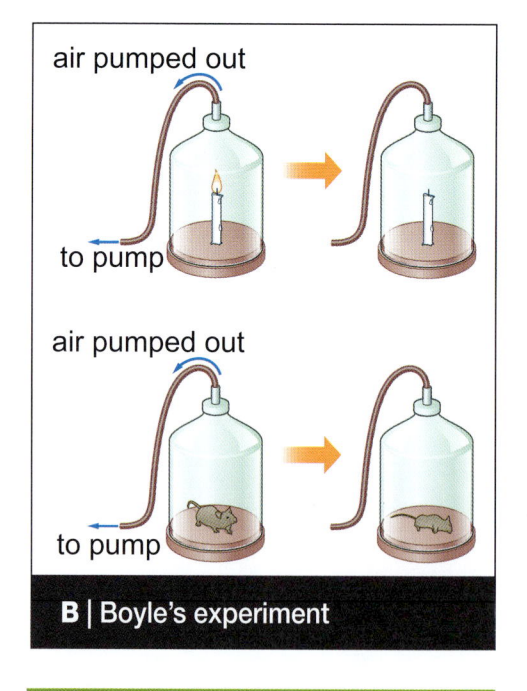

B | Boyle's experiment

2 What is meant by testing an idea scientifically?

3 Suggest the conclusion Boyle drew from his experiment.

Boyle's assistant, John Mayow (1641–1679), did further experiments. He discovered that only a certain part of the air was needed to keep a candle burning and a small animal alive (see diagram C).

Later, Joseph Priestley (1733–1804) and Antoine Lavoisier (1743–1794) showed that this part of the air was oxygen, which makes up about 21 per cent of the air.

4
a| What was Mayow's evidence that burning only needs a certain part of the air?
b| What made him think that the same part of the air was needed for both burning and keeping animals alive?

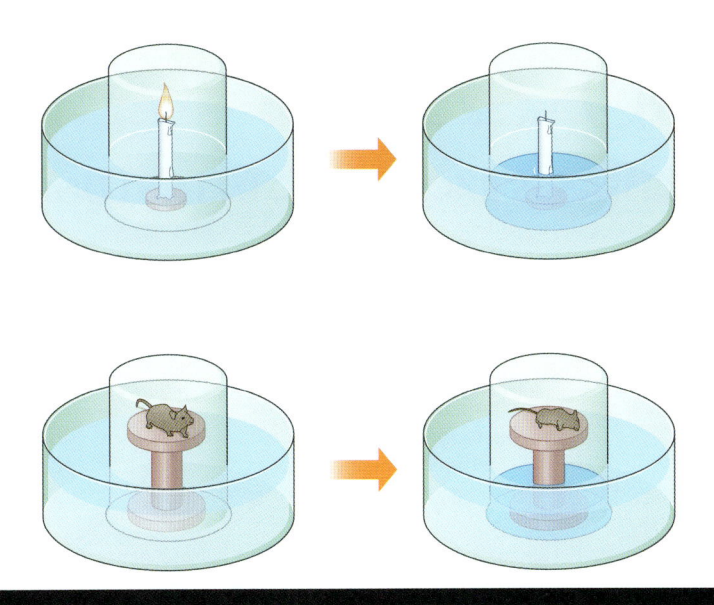

C | Mayow's experiment

FACT

Some cruise ships and spas now offer oxygen therapy, which allows people to breathe a mixture of 5 per cent normal air and 95 per cent oxygen. The gases may be bubbled through coloured liquids, which produce different smells. Some scientists, however, think that this type of oxygen therapy could be harmful.

D

Today we know that the mitochondria in cells use oxygen to release the energy stored in a type of sugar called **glucose**. The release of energy occurs in a series of chemical reactions called **aerobic respiration** (aerobic means requiring air). The energy is transferred to a compound called **ATP**, which then releases energy for the cell as it is needed.

Respiration happens in all parts of our bodies and some of the released energy keeps our bodies warm. We can sum up aerobic respiration as a **word equation**.

oxygen + glucose $\longrightarrow$ carbon dioxide + water (+ energy)

The word equation for the **combustion** (burning) of glucose is the same, but aerobic respiration occurs in a different way, using a series of slower reactions.

5 Beaker X contains peas that are starting to grow. Beaker Y contains boiled peas. In which beaker will:
a| the temperature rise? Explain your reasoning.
b| carbon dioxide be made? Explain your reasoning.

6
a| Suggest how aerobic respiration is like burning.
b| Suggest one way in which aerobic respiration and burning are different.

7
a| Write out the word equation for aerobic respiration.
b| Suggest one way in which this is a good model for respiration and one way in which it is a poor one.

I can ...
- recall what happens in aerobic respiration.

8Cb GAS EXCHANGE SYSTEM

UK NC, CEE

HOW ARE GASES EXCHANGED IN THE LUNGS?

John Mayow built a model to show that it is the moving of the ribs and **diaphragm** that causes the lungs to get bigger and smaller (it is not the lungs themselves).

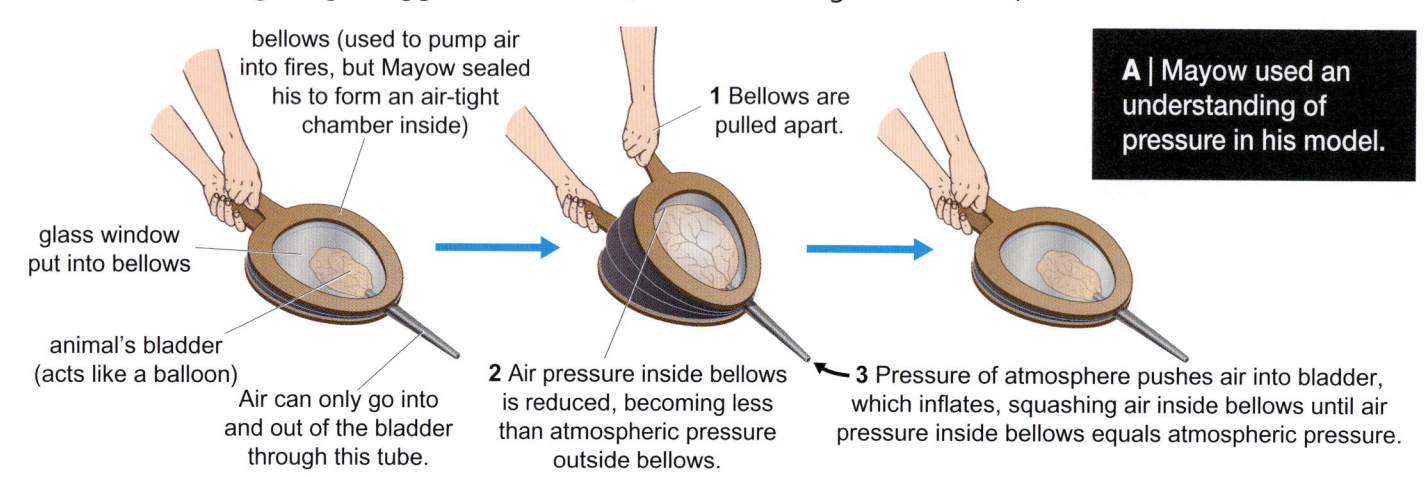

- bellows (used to pump air into fires, but Mayow sealed his to form an air-tight chamber inside)
- glass window put into bellows
- animal's bladder (acts like a balloon)
- Air can only go into and out of the bladder through this tube.

1 Bellows are pulled apart.

2 Air pressure inside bellows is reduced, becoming less than atmospheric pressure outside bellows.

3 Pressure of atmosphere pushes air into bladder, which inflates, squashing air inside bellows until air pressure inside bellows equals atmospheric pressure.

A | Mayow used an understanding of pressure in his model.

Breathing is when muscles between the ribs and in the diaphragm change the size of the lungs. The movement of air into and out of the lungs is called **ventilation**. Diagram B shows how inhalation (breathing in) happens. During exhalation (breathing out), the reverse happens.

B | inhalation (breathing in)

- Pressure in the lungs is reduced, so atmospheric pressure pushes air in.
- The muscles between and attached to the ribs contract, pulling the ribs up and out.
- The muscles in the diaphragm contract, moving it downwards.

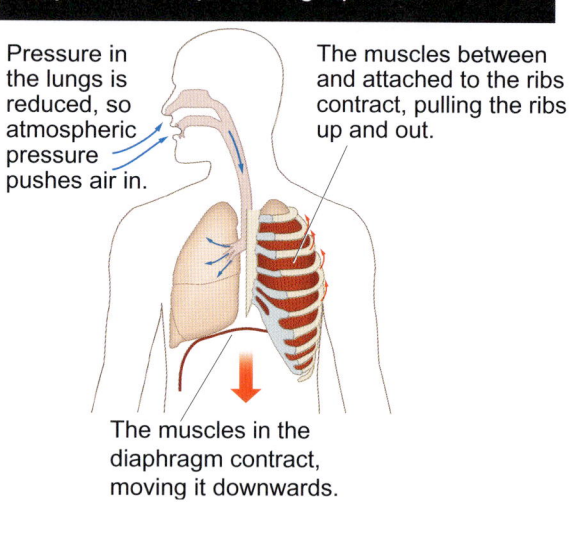

1. What do the bellows and bladder in Mayow's model represent?
2. What do muscles in the diaphragm do to cause inhalation?
3. Write three labels that could be added to the last drawing in diagram A, explaining why air leaves the bladder when the bellows are closed.

To work well, the lungs need to be kept clean. Some cells in the tubes in the lungs produce a sticky liquid called **mucus**. It traps dirt, dust and microorganisms. Tiny hairs on other cells, called **cilia**, sweep the mucus out of the lungs and into the oesophagus where it can be swallowed.

The chemicals and heat in cigarette smoke stop the cilia working. Mucus then collects in the lungs.

4. How are cells in the gas exchange system specialised to keep the lungs clean?

C | **Ciliated epithelial cells** help to keep the lungs clean.

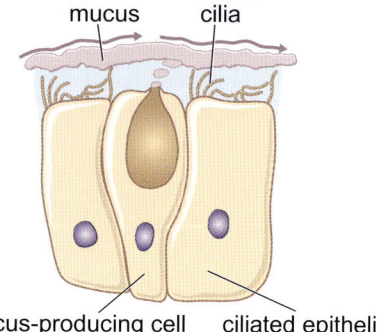

- mucus
- cilia
- mucus-producing cell
- ciliated epithelial cell

104

In the lungs, some of the oxygen from the air enters the blood. At the same time, some of the carbon dioxide in the blood plasma enters the air in the lungs. This swapping of gases is called **gas exchange**.

Gas exchange occurs by **diffusion**, when there is an overall movement of particles from a place where there are a lot of them to a place where there are fewer of them.

> **5** What happens during gas exchange in the lungs?
>
> **6** a| What is diffusion?
> b| What causes some oxygen molecules to move into the blood and other molecules to move out of it?

The lungs are adapted for gas exchange by having about 700 million little pockets called alveoli (pronounced 'al-**vee**-O-lee'). This gives the lungs a large **surface area**. The larger the surface area, the faster diffusion occurs.

The alveoli have walls that are only one cell thick. The blood **capillaries** surrounding them also have thin walls. These thin walls mean that diffusion happens more quickly.

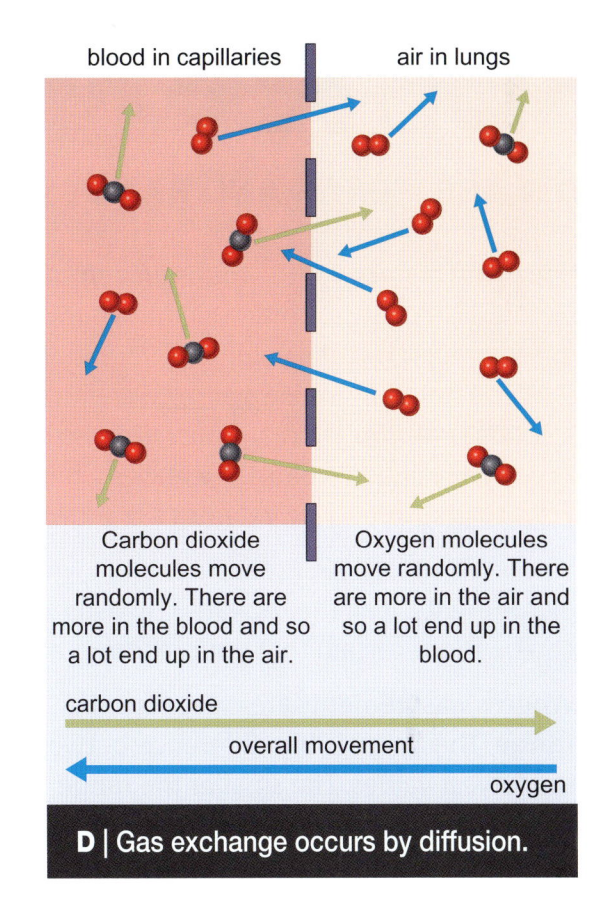

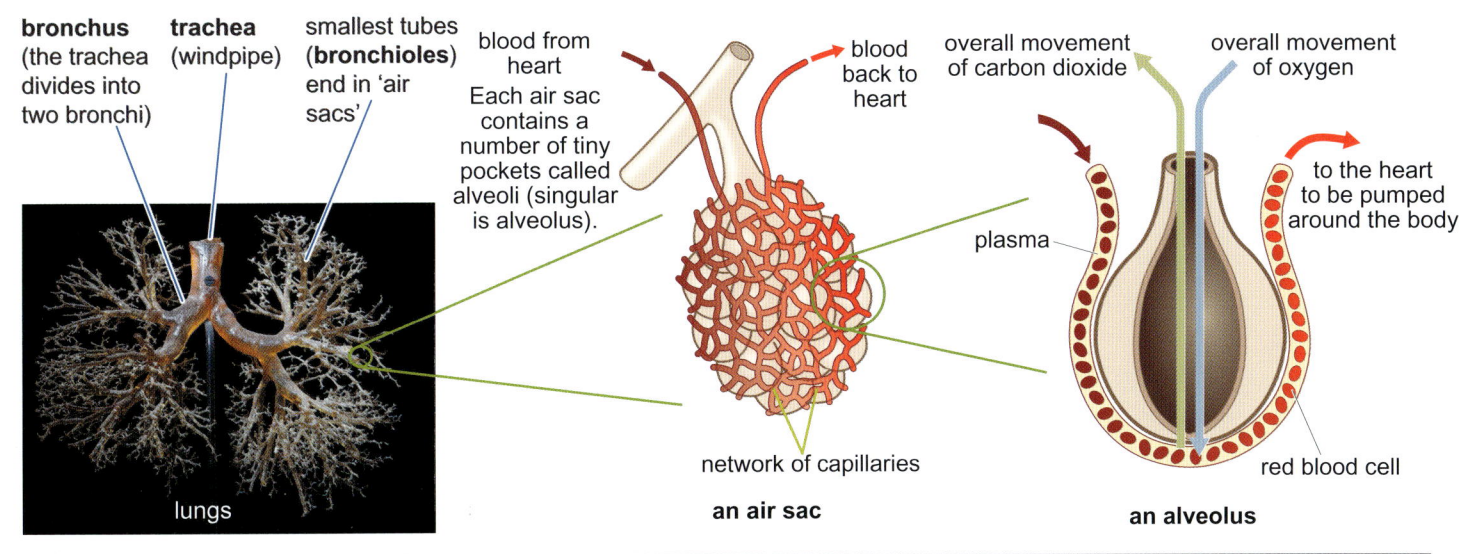

D | Gas exchange occurs by diffusion.

bronchus (the trachea divides into two bronchi)
trachea (windpipe)
smallest tubes (**bronchioles**) end in 'air sacs'

Each air sac contains a number of tiny pockets called alveoli (singular is alveolus).

lungs
an air sac
an alveolus
network of capillaries
blood from heart
blood back to heart
overall movement of carbon dioxide
overall movement of oxygen
plasma
to the heart to be pumped around the body
red blood cell

E | There are thousands of tiny, branched tubes inside the lungs, many of which are kept open with rings of a tough tissue called **cartilage**. These tubes end in air sacs, which contain the alveoli.

> **7** In order, list the organs through which air passes when we inhale.
>
> **8** Explain what effect a decrease in lung surface area would have on the speed of gas exchange.
>
> **9** Explain why gas exchange can be reduced in smokers.

I can ...

- recall the functions of the organs in the gas exchange system
- explain how the structure of the lungs allows efficient gas exchange.

8Cb MEANS AND RANGES

HOW ARE MEANS AND RANGES CALCULATED AND WHY DO WE USE THEM?

Your **vital capacity** is the maximum amount of air you can exhale after taking as much air into your lungs as you can. It is a measure of the total volume of your lungs. The volume of air that you normally inhale and exhale with each breath is called the **tidal volume**. Doing regular exercise can increase your vital capacity. Your tidal volume increases when you exercise. Two ways to measure these volumes are shown in photos A and B.

You often repeat your measurements when you do experiments. If all the repeated measurements are similar, you can be more certain that your readings are correct.

When measurements are close together, they have a small **range**. The range is the difference between the highest and the lowest values. The smaller the range in a repeated set of measurements, the more you can be sure that the results are correct.

A | This student is using a lung volume bag to measure tidal volume. All the air is removed from the bag and then you blow one normal breath into it. If you push the air from your breath along the bag, you can read off the volume on a scale.

B | This diver is having her tidal volume measured using a spirometer linked to a computer. It measures the volume of air she breathes in and out with every breath.

1
a| Why do you take repeated measurements in an experiment?
b| Look at photos A and B. Which method is easier for taking repeated measurements?
c| Suggest one disadvantage of this method.

2 Hitesh and Josie measured their tidal volumes just before and just after exercise. Their results are shown in table C.
a| Calculate the range of each set of results.
b| Which set of results can you be most sure of being correct? Explain your reasoning.

C

	Tidal volume (cm^3)			
	1st try	2nd try	3rd try	4th try
Hitesh before exercise	450	440	420	430
Josie before exercise	350	350	310	300
Hitesh after exercise	1010	1100	1050	990
Josie after exercise	750	950	840	900

WORKING SCIENTIFICALLY

Means

The true value of a repeated reading is usually somewhere between the highest and lowest readings. To **estimate** the true value from a group of repeated readings, we can calculate a **mean**.

To do this:

- we add up all repeated readings
- then we divide by the number of readings.

The more repeated measurements there are, the closer the mean is likely to be to the real value for the measurement.

Using more repeats also helps you to identify **anomalous results (outliers)**. These are results that are very different from all the other repeated measurements or that do not follow the same pattern as other measurements. If you can say what caused a result to be anomalous, you can leave it out when you calculate a mean.

Worked example

Mean tidal volume for Hitesh's results before exercise:

$$450 + 440 + 420 + 430 = 1740$$

$$\frac{1740}{4} = 435 \text{ cm}^3$$

How total vital capacity depends on height

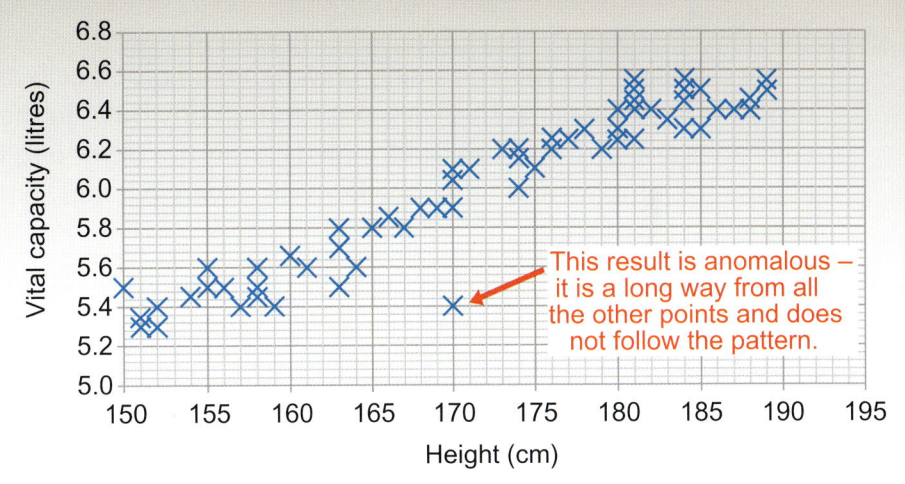

This result is anomalous – it is a long way from all the other points and does not follow the pattern.

D | This scatter graph is from a scientific paper, which was looking for a relationship between height and vital capacity in men.

3 Calculate the means for Hitesh's and Josie's other sets of results.

4 What is an anomalous result?

Method

A | Find your pulse and count how many beats you can feel in 15 seconds.

B | Use this value to calculate your pulse rate (in beats per minute).

C | Count how many times you inhale in 15 seconds.

D | Use this value to calculate your breathing rate (in breaths per minute).

E | Now do 2 minutes of exercise.

F | As soon as you stop, measure your pulse and breathing rates again.

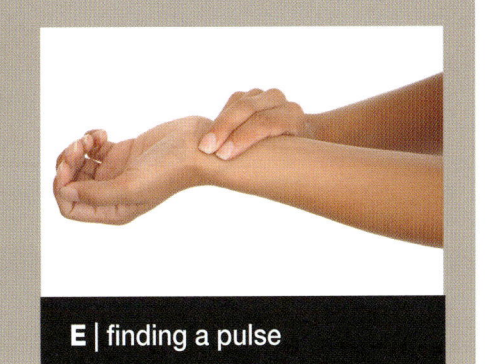

E | finding a pulse

5 Look at the Method above for finding your pulse and breathing rate.
  a| Suggest an exercise you could do in step E.
  b| You should repeat steps A–F. Why?
  c| How many times would you repeat them? Explain your reasoning.
  d| How will you work out means for your results?

6 Make a prediction about what the results will show.

I can ...

- recall why means and ranges are used
- calculate means and ranges.

107

8Cc GETTING OXYGEN

UK NC, iLS, CEE

HOW DOES OXYGEN GET FROM THE LUNGS TO THE REST OF OUR BODIES?

When oxygen gets into the blood, it enters **red blood cells** where it sticks to molecules of **haemoglobin** (pronounced 'hee-mow-**glow**-bin'). This makes the cells change colour, from dark browny-red to bright red.

From the lungs, blood enters the heart to be pumped out to the rest of the body through **blood vessels** called **arteries**. These divide into tiny capillaries.

In the capillaries, oxygen gradually leaves the red blood cells and dissolves in the plasma. This leaks out through tiny holes in the capillaries and forms **tissue fluid**, which carries the oxygen to the cells. Plasma has glucose and other nutrients dissolved in it and so these are also in the tissue fluid.

Waste products from cells dissolve in the tissue fluid and return to other capillaries, which connect to **veins**. Veins carry blood back towards the heart.

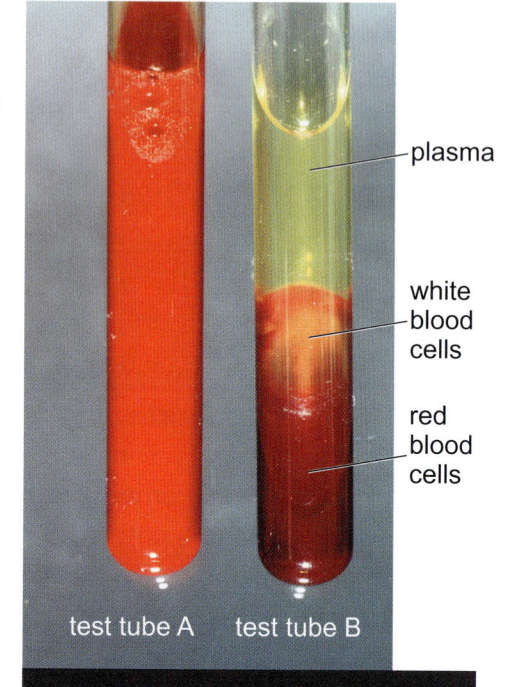

A | The different parts of blood can be separated, as has been done in test tube B. Blood contains liquid plasma, red blood cells and white blood cells (which fight infections).

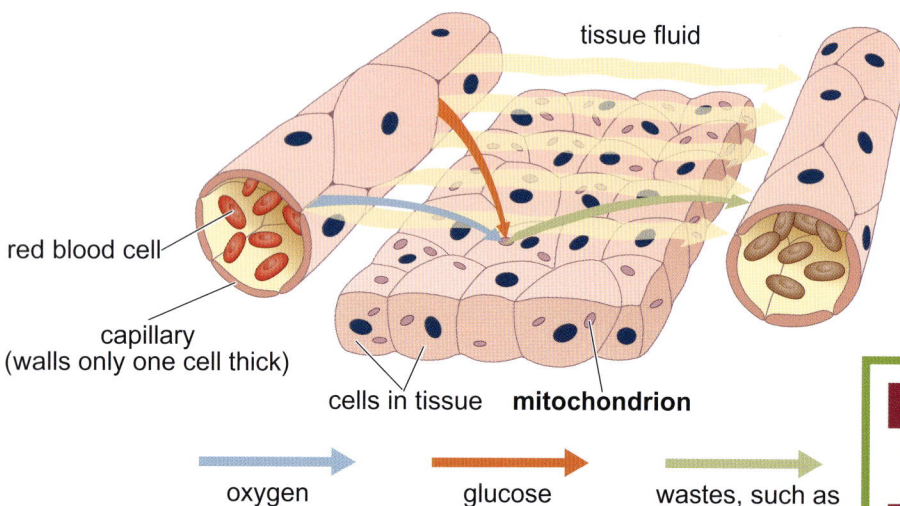

B | how oxygen, glucose and wastes are transported to and from cells in tissues

When you exercise, your muscle cells work harder and so must release more energy, using aerobic respiration. They need more oxygen and glucose. Your breathing rate increases to get extra oxygen into your blood, and your heartbeat rate increases to pump blood to the muscles more quickly.

1. Are the red blood cells in test tube B in photo A carrying oxygen? Explain your reasoning.

2. a| Name a waste gas produced by cells.
   b| What process produces this substance?
   c| Where in a cell is it produced?
   d| Describe how it is excreted from the body.

3. How is glucose carried to cells?

4. a| Explain why a boy's breathing rate doubles during a swimming race.
   b| Explain why his pulse rate also changes when he is racing.

108

C | Free divers swim slowly to avoid using too much oxygen.

Lack of oxygen

Without enough oxygen your cells can start to die. This can happen because of:

- narrowed blood vessels
- poisons
- poor gas exchange in the lungs.

To avoid heat loss when it is cold, the blood vessels in your skin become narrow and less blood reaches the cells. If this causes cells to die, it results in frostbite.

D | frostbite

In **cardiovascular disease**, blood vessels become narrower due to a fatty substance collecting inside them. If this reduces blood flow too much, then cells start dying. More of the fatty substance builds up in smokers. **Heart disease** is a type of cardiovascular disease in which the blood supply to the heart muscles is reduced. This can cause a **heart attack** (in which heart muscle cells die).

Faulty gas appliances can produce **carbon monoxide**, a poisonous gas also found in cigarette smoke. The gas sticks to haemoglobin and so stops red blood cells carrying so much oxygen.

Tar in tobacco smoke and dust both irritate the alveoli in the lungs. Over a long time this causes the alveoli to break apart (**emphysema**), reducing their surface area.

Cigarette smoke can also trigger **asthma**, in which the tiny tubes in the lungs become narrow and start filling with mucus. Less air can get into and out of the lungs, causing shortness of breath.

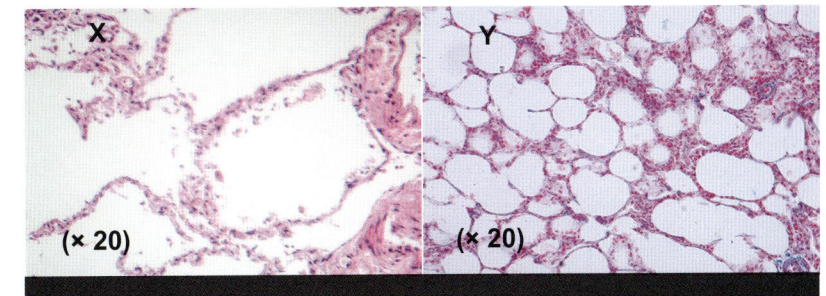

FACT

Carbon monoxide turns muscle and red blood cells bright red. It can be used to package meat (the bright red colour lasts a long time and makes the meat look fresh).

X (× 20)   Y (× 20)

E | Microscope specimens from two lungs; one is from someone with emphysema.

5 Why does blood from a smoker contain less oxygen than blood from a non-smoker? Give as many reasons as you can.

6 Look at the photos in E.
   a) Which specimen is from someone with emphysema? Explain your reasoning.
   b) Would this person have a higher or lower breathing rate than someone without emphysema? Explain your reasoning.

I can ...

- describe the effects of exercise on breathing and heartbeat rates
- describe how substances reach respiring cells from the blood and how waste products are returned to the blood
- describe the causes, and explain the effects of, reduced oxygen supply on the body.

8Cc EPIDEMIOLOGY

HOW CAN WE USE DATA TO IDENTIFY THE CAUSE OF DISEASE?

Epidemiologists are scientists who study links between how diseases are caused and how they spread. This involves gathering large amounts of data and analysing it to identify a relationship or **correlation**.

Correlation is when two variables change together. A correlation does not necessarily mean that one variable affects the other. The correlation may be due to chance, or another variable may cause the changes in two other variables. Graph A shows how ice cream sales and shark attacks change with time along a certain coast.

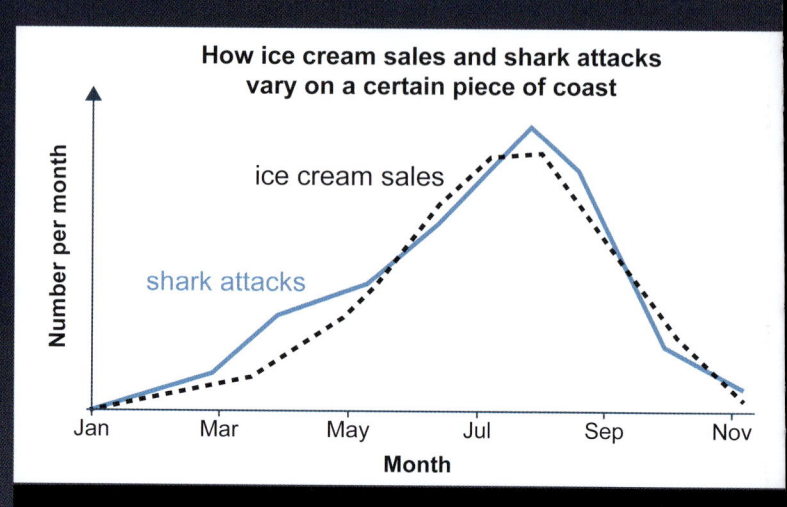

A | Is there a correlation between the number of ice creams sold and the number of shark attacks?

1
a | Does graph A show a correlation between sales of ice cream and shark attacks? Give a reason for your answer.
b | Does graph A show that sales of ice cream cause shark attacks? Give a reason for your answer.
c | The amount of sunshine per day on this piece of coast shows a similar pattern of change over the year. How can this extra information help explain the correlation shown in the graph?

Lung cancer and smoking

Lung cancer is a disease that destroys the lungs. In the 1950s an epidemiologist called Richard Doll (1912–2005) tried to work out what was causing a big rise in the number of lung cancer patients. Doll collected lots of data from lung cancer patients and found a correlation between lung cancer and smoking tobacco. Further studies showed the same correlation.

Scientists often use scatter graphs to look for a correlation between two variables. On a scatter graph, when most of the points form a pattern or a line, there is correlation. Scatter graph C shows a correlation from a study on smoking. The points will not show any pattern if there is no correlation (as shown in graph D).

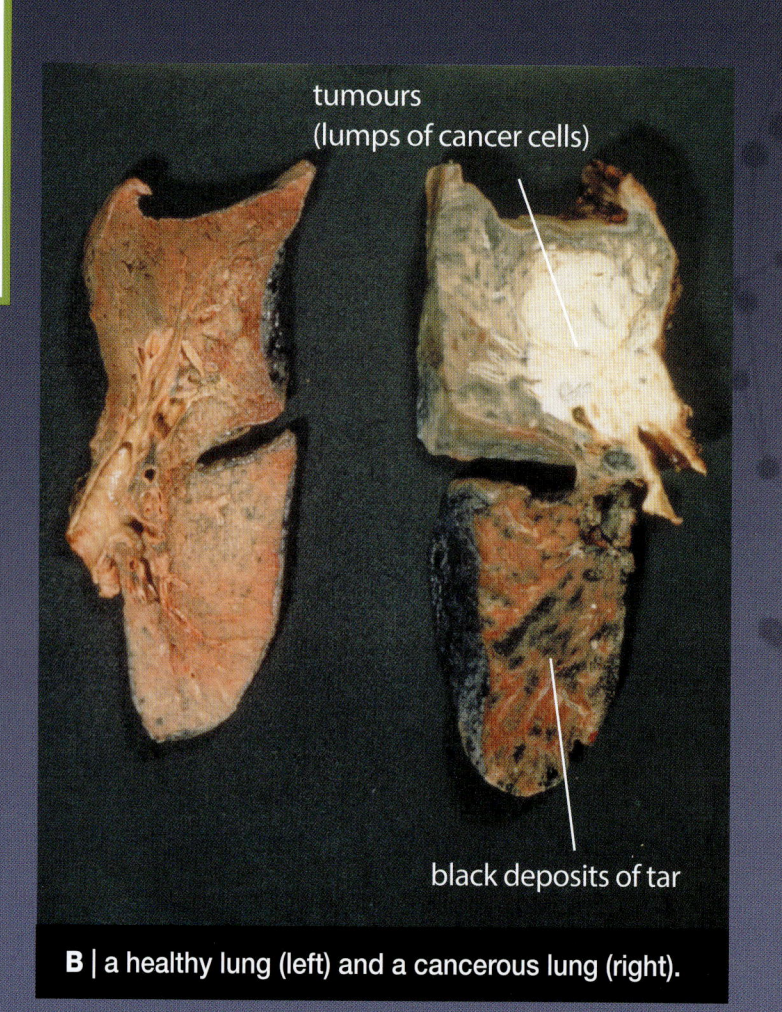

B | a healthy lung (left) and a cancerous lung (right).

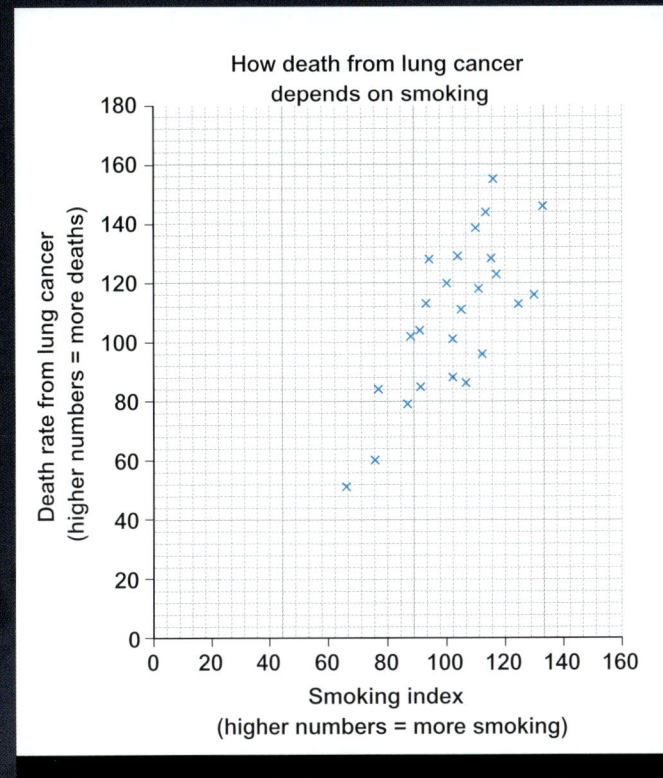

C | results from a study on smoking carried out in 1978

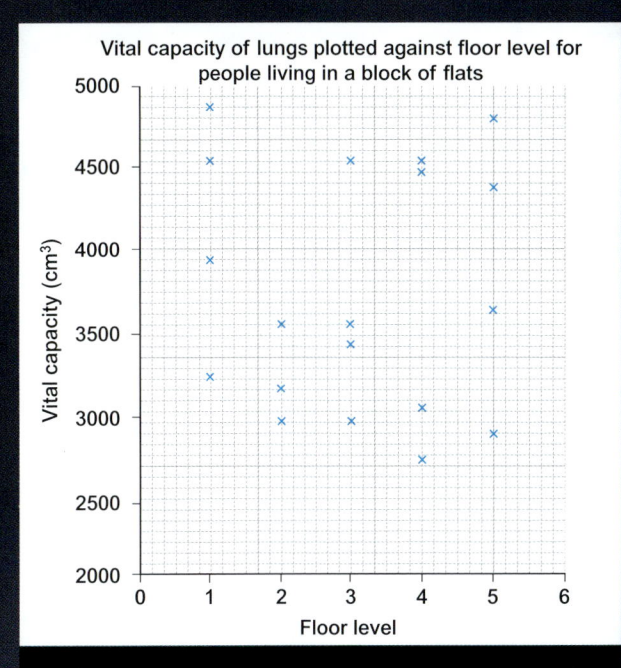

Graph: How death from lung cancer depends on smoking. X-axis: Smoking index (higher numbers = more smoking), 0 to 160. Y-axis: Death rate from lung cancer (higher numbers = more deaths), 0 to 180.

D | When the points on a scatter graph do not form a line or pattern, then there is no correlation between the two variables.

Graph: Vital capacity of lungs plotted against floor level for people living in a block of flats. X-axis: Floor level, 0 to 6. Y-axis: Vital capacity (cm^3), 2000 to 5000.

An epidemiologist needs a degree in a biological science, or in statistics. Many epidemiologists also have a doctorate (a further research degree) in epidemiology and they must all be very good at maths.

2 Describe the correlation shown in scatter graph C.

3 Experiments carried out by other scientists showed that many substances in tobacco smoke cause cells to become cancerous. Use this fact to explain the correlation shown in graph C.

PRACTICAL

Vital capacity is the largest volume of breath you can take after breathing out. It can be measured using a simple respirometer (see page 106).

- Collect measurements on vital capacity for as many people as you can.
- For those same people, collect data for another one or more continuous variables (e.g. age, height, pulse rate).
- Construct a spreadsheet to record all the measurements for each person.
- Use your spreadsheet to construct scatter graphs of lung volume against each of the other measurements you took.
- Use your scatter graphs to identify any correlations between vital capacity and the other measurements.

4 Compare any correlations in your scatter graphs. Which measurement correlates most strongly with vital capacity? Explain how you worked out your answer.

8Cd COMPARING GAS EXCHANGE

HOW DO WE DETECT GAS EXCHANGE IN DIFFERENT ORGANISMS?

To spend long periods underwater, humans take oxygen with them to breathe. Water-living mammals, however, have adaptations so they can go for a long time without breathing. For example, elephant seals have an organ in their bodies that stores blood that is full of oxygen.

A | HydroBOB underwater scooters

B | Elephant seals can stay underwater for 2 hours.

Not all the oxygen in a breath of air goes into the blood, so exhaled air still contains a lot of oxygen (table C). This means that most of the oxygen in a diver's air tank is lost in exhaled bubbles. Some divers, though, use rebreather apparatus. This contains calcium hydroxide, which removes carbon dioxide from their exhaled air and recirculates the remaining air for them to breathe.

A solution of calcium hydroxide is called **limewater**. It is a clear and colourless liquid that turns cloudy as it absorbs carbon dioxide, so is used to test for this gas.

Carbon dioxide dissolves in water to form an acidic solution. This means that respiration can also be detected using an **indicator**. For example, **hydrogen carbonate indicator** is pink in water but turns yellow as carbon dioxide is added and the **pH** drops.

Another way of detecting respiration is to look for a temperature rise, because some of the energy released by respiration warms up a cell's surroundings.

1. a| What adaptation do elephant seals have to help them go for a long time without breathing?
   b| Explain how this adaptation works.

2. Allan is diving and uses a tank of air in 30 minutes. Will the same tank of air last for more or less time if Allan uses a HydroBOB? Explain your reasoning.

3. Explain why the quantities of each of the five items in table C are or are not different between inhaled and exhaled air.

C	Inhaled air (%)	Exhaled air (%)
nitrogen	78	78
oxygen	21	16
carbon dioxide	0.04	4
water vapour	variable	greater
temperature	variable	warmer

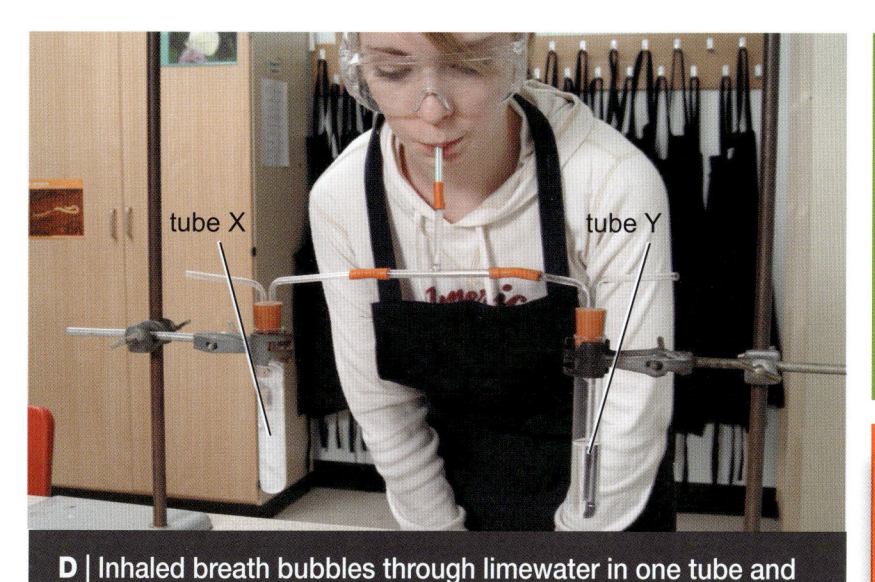

D | Inhaled breath bubbles through limewater in one tube and exhaled breath bubbles through limewater in the other.

> **4**
> Look at photo D.
> a| Through which tube is the girl's exhaled breath flowing?
> b| How can you tell?
> c| If the contents of tubes X and Y are replaced with water containing hydrogen carbonate indicator, explain what will happen as the girl breathes in and out.

FACT

It has long been a dream to develop an artificial gill for divers to use. This photo shows what one might look like, but it is not a reality … yet.

F

Gills

Mammals use lungs to get oxygen and so must breathe air. However, some animals never breathe air because they can extract oxygen from water, often using **gills**.

Water flows in through a fish's mouth.

In the gills, water flows over a fine network of feathery strands, where oxygen diffuses into the blood and carbon dioxide diffuses out.

E | gas exchange using gills

Stomata allow gases (such as oxygen, carbon dioxide and water vapour) to diffuse into and out of a leaf.

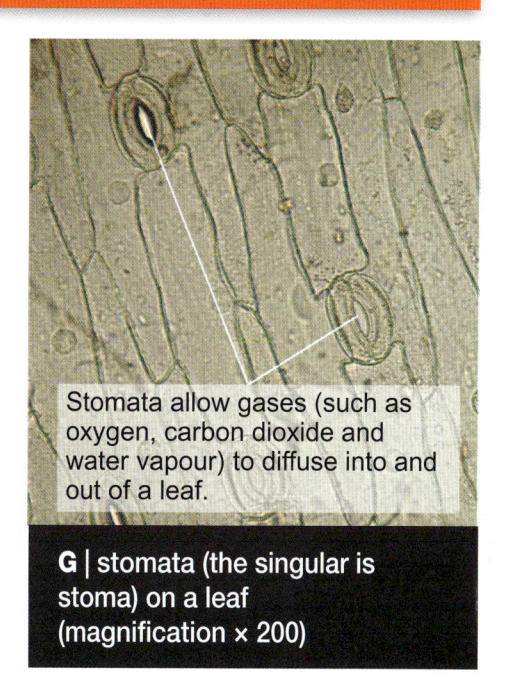

G | stomata (the singular is stoma) on a leaf (magnification × 200)

Plants

For **photosynthesis**, plants need carbon dioxide to make glucose. Plant cells then release energy from the glucose using aerobic respiration, which happens in all cells, all the time. To allow gases in and out, land plants have tiny holes in their leaves called **stomata**.

> **5**
> a| What substances do plants need for aerobic respiration?
> b| How do they get these substances?
>
> **6** Explain why fish tanks often become more acidic with time.
>
> **7** What are the similarities and differences between gas exchange in mammals and fish?

I can …
- recall how to detect aerobic respiration
- describe how gas exchange occurs in different organisms.

113

UK NC, iLS, CEE

8Ce ANAEROBIC RESPIRATION

HOW DOES ANAEROBIC RESPIRATION OCCUR?

If you hold your breath, the amount of carbon dioxide in your blood plasma increases. If it reaches a certain level, your brain causes you to breathe. This is why you cannot hold your breath for too long, although people can train themselves to hold their breath for longer times.

> **1** What substances does aerobic respiration produce?
>
> **2** Explain why the breath-holding competitor in photo A remains motionless.

Oxygen is stored by haemoglobin in red blood cells, so it can be carried around your body. Your muscle cells can also store some oxygen. After holding your breath for a long time, you breathe faster to get rid of the extra carbon dioxide in your blood and to replace the oxygen used up from your blood and muscles.

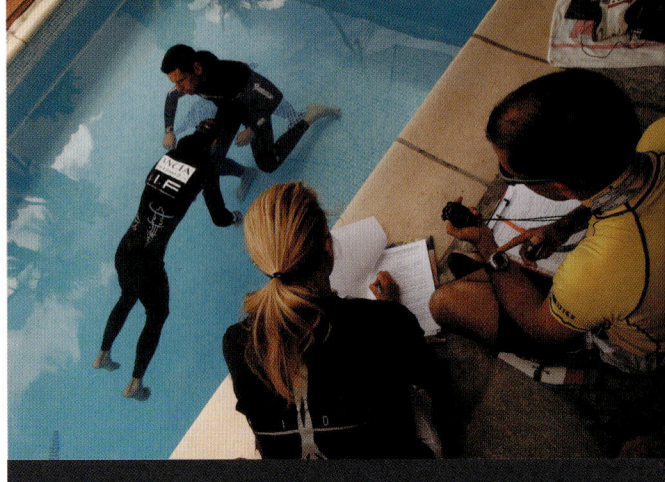

A | The world record for holding your breath floating face-down in a swimming pool is 11 minutes and 54 seconds. This was set by Branko Petrović in Dubai in 2014.

B | Underwater ice hockey players rely on anaerobic respiration to swim fast suddenly without breathing.

Exercise

During **aerobic exercise** your body continuously gets enough oxygen to replace the oxygen being used by **contracting** muscle cells. You can do aerobic exercise, such as slow swimming, for long periods of time.

During strenuous exercise, oxygen is used up faster than it is replaced. When this happens, **anaerobic respiration** occurs in the cytoplasm of your muscle cells. This does not need oxygen. We can summarise anaerobic respiration in humans as:

glucose ⟶ lactic acid (+ some energy)

C | Taking breaths slows swimmers down. So in short sprint events competitors only breathe once or twice and some do not breathe at all.

Anaerobic respiration does not release as much energy from glucose as aerobic respiration, and so does not form as much ATP. Anaerobic respiration also makes muscles tire quickly. However, anaerobic respiration allows animals to move suddenly and very quickly (for example, to sprint away from a predator).

> **3** What processes use up glucose in underwater ice hockey players as they sprint for the puck?
>
> **4** a| Suggest why sprint swimming is an anaerobic exercise.
> b| Why can't a swimmer sprint for a long time?
>
> **5** Write a paragraph to compare aerobic and anaerobic respiration. Use a table of similarities and differences to plan your paragraph.

FACT

Scientists are still not sure why muscles become sore a day or so after doing strenuous exercise. One hypothesis is that the body damages some cells in overworked muscles in the process of rebuilding these muscles.

The effect of exercise on demand for oxygen

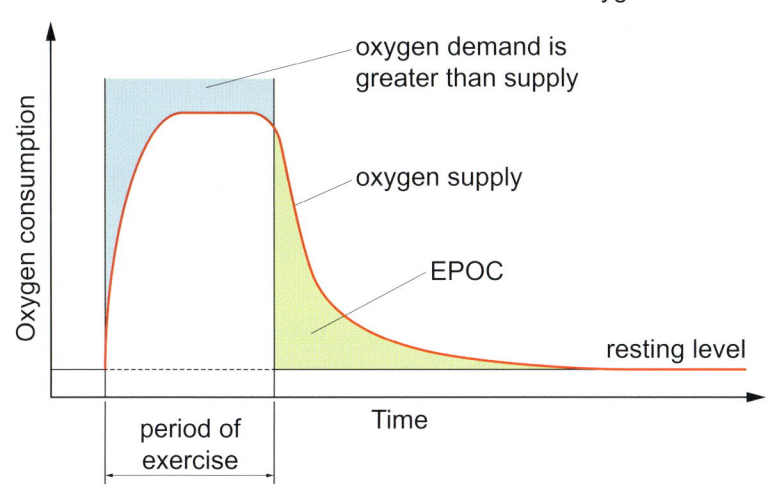

[Graph showing oxygen consumption vs time, with labels: "oxygen demand is greater than supply", "oxygen supply", "EPOC", "resting level", "period of exercise"]

D | EPOC occurs if your body does not get enough oxygen during exercise.

E | Sports scientists can find out how much anaerobic respiration happens in an athlete's body by measuring lactic acid levels in the blood.

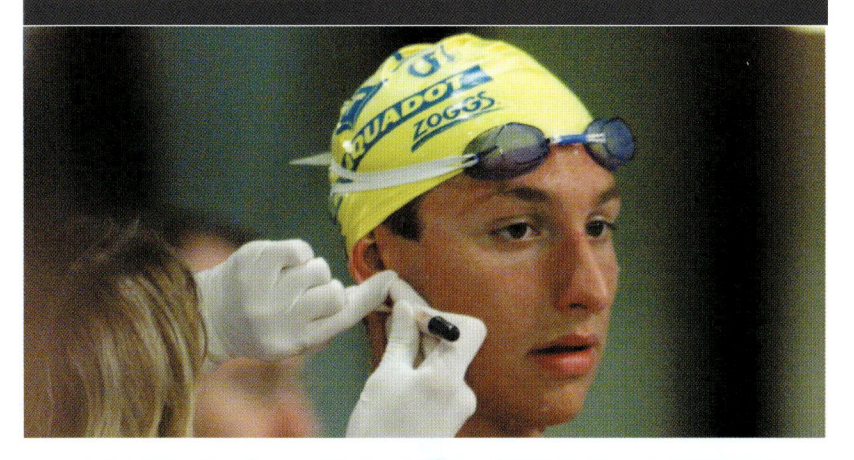

EPOC

Lactic acid from muscles enters the blood and is carried to the liver, where it is converted back into glucose. This process needs a lot of energy, which can come from aerobic respiration in liver cells.

After exercise you need extra oxygen for many processes, including helping to turn lactic acid back into glucose and replacing the oxygen lost from blood and muscle cells. This need for extra oxygen is called **excess post-exercise oxygen consumption** – or **EPOC** for short. It is also sometimes called the **oxygen debt**. Your breathing and heartbeat rates remain high after you stop exercising to get extra oxygen to your cells.

> **6** Describe one way in which the body gets rid of lactic acid.
>
> **7** After hard exercise, why does your:
> a| breathing rate remain high
> b| heartbeat rate remain high?
>
> **8** What causes EPOC? Give as many reasons as you can.

I can ...

- recall what happens in anaerobic respiration
- describe the effects of anaerobic respiration during and after hard exercise.

8Ce FITNESS TRAINING

HOW DOES TRAINING CHANGE THE BODY'S SYSTEMS?

Sports training increases the size of muscles, which become stronger. But it is not just arm and leg muscles that get stronger – the muscles in the gas exchange and circulatory systems also become stronger.

In the gas exchange system, the stronger the breathing muscles are, the bigger the lungs can become. The more air that you can take into your lungs, the more oxygen gets into your blood. Training also increases the number of capillaries in the lungs.

The heart is mainly made of muscle tissue. Training helps to make heart muscle beat more strongly and so the volume of blood that the heart pumps in each beat increases.

The more exercise someone does, the fitter they are. Fitter people have slower resting pulse and breathing rates, and these rates return to their resting rates after exercise more quickly than in less fit people.

A | Different sports increase the size and strength of different skeletal muscles, but all sports training strengthens muscles in the gas exchange and circulatory systems.

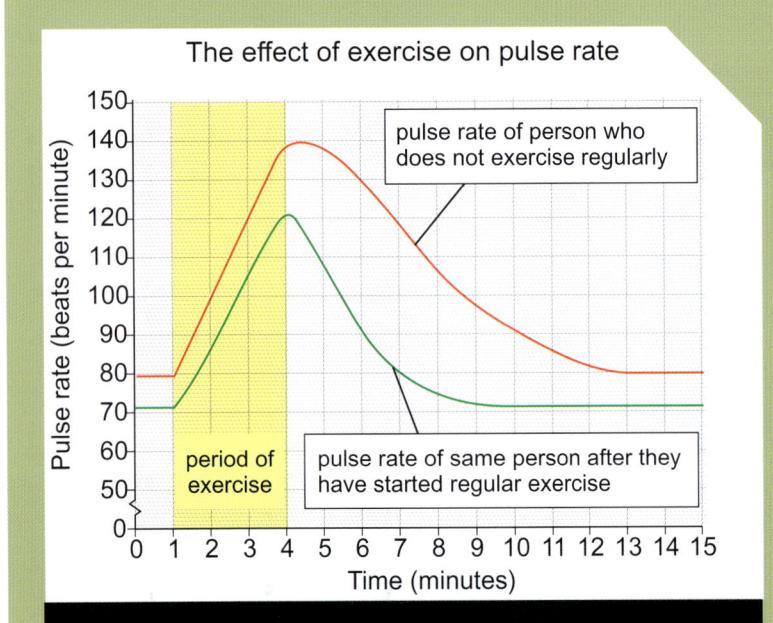

B | The fitter you are, the more quickly your pulse rate returns to its resting rate.

1. Look at graph B.
   a| What sort of respiration is occurring before exercise?
   b| What substances are needed for this type of respiration?
   c| How could you detect the gas produced?
   d| What type of respiration starts to increase when exercising hard?

2. Where are the breathing muscles found?

3. How does oxygen get from your lungs to a muscle cell in your leg?

4. Explain why competitive athletes do not smoke. Give as many reasons as you can.

5. a| Write a paragraph to explain the shape of the red line on graph B.
   b| What happens when the person starts to do regular exercise?
   c| Why does this happen?

HAVE YOUR SAY

Should people do sport throughout their lives?

8Da THE BLACK DEATH

During the 14th century, a disease called the Black Death (or plague) spread across Asia, the Middle East and Europe. The disease caused the deaths of between 75 and 200 million people, reducing the population of Europe by 45–50%. So many people were dying that their bodies were often hastily buried in mass graves.

A | an engraving showing a plague pit in London, UK

There were many later outbreaks of the disease but no one knew its cause. A 14th-century suggestion blamed planets lining up in the sky. In the 17th century, bad air produced by rotting things was blamed. In the late 19th century, a microorganism called *Yersinia pestis* was shown to be the cause.

The disease causes blood vessels to split open and leak blood, which then clots (sets hard). The clots stop blood from reaching tissues and so cells die and turn black.

The 'beak' was filled with herbs to keep 'bad air' away.

The long cloak, boots, gloves and mask were to stop 'bad air' reaching the doctor's body.

B | Doctors in the 17th century wore special costumes, which they thought would stop them getting the plague.

1. a| What life processes do all organisms carry out?
   b| Suggest what the word 'microorganism' means.
2. *Yersinia pestis* belongs to a kingdom called the prokaryotes. Give the names of three other kingdoms of organisms.
3. What would have happened to the bodies of people buried in plague pits?
4. Describe one way in which microorganisms are useful.
5. Explain why human cells need a good supply of blood in order to survive.
6. Some microorganisms feed on the dead cells inside plague victims. What sort of respiration will these microorganisms use? Explain your reasoning.

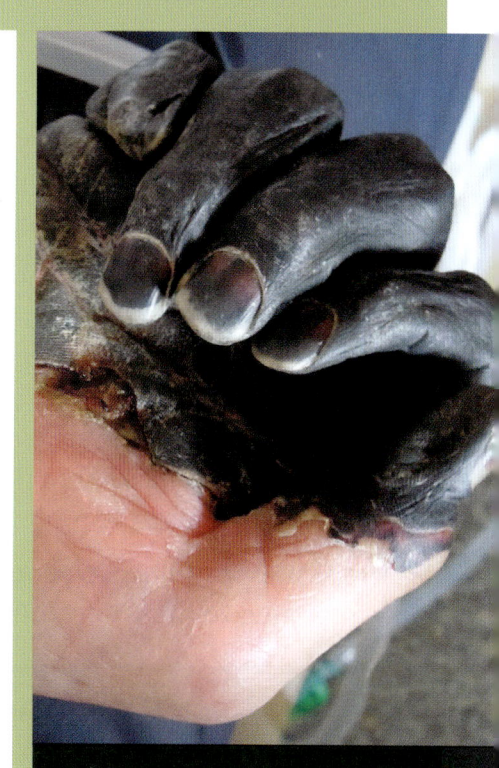

C | There are still up to 3000 cases of plague around the world each year but it can now be treated.

8Da UNICELLULAR OR MULTICELLULAR

UK NC, iLS, CEE

HOW DO DIFFERENT SPECIES OF UNICELLULAR ORGANISM VARY?

An organism is a living thing. All organisms carry out seven life processes: movement, reproduction, sensitivity, growth, respiration, excretion, nutrition.

Organisms are all based on **cells**. Organisms made of many cells are said to be **multicellular**. An adult human is made up of about 37 million million cells!

Cells of the same type are grouped together as tissues. Different tissues form organs and organs work together in organ systems. Large multicellular organisms use organ systems to help them carry out the life processes.

> 1. Name one organ system that helps humans carry out each life process.
> 2. Are plants multicellular? Explain your reasoning.

Some organisms are made of just one cell but this cell still carries out all seven life processes. One-celled organisms are described as being **unicellular**. They are also called **microorganisms** because they are very small. You usually need a microscope to see them.

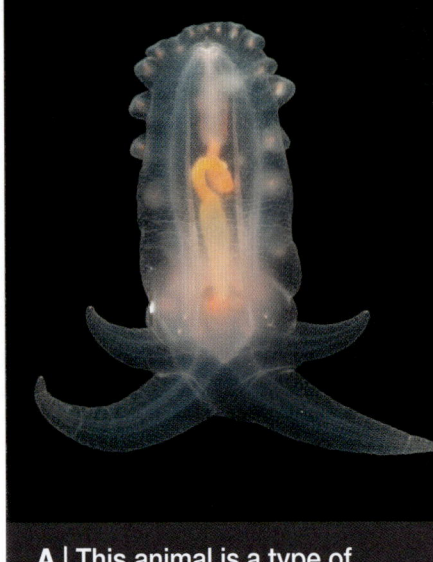

A | This animal is a type of sea cucumber. The tissue that covers it is transparent, so you can see the different organs in its digestive system.

Diffusion

All matter is made of particles that are constantly moving. So particles can move without anything moving them. This causes an overall movement of particles from where there are many of them to where there are fewer, and this is **diffusion**.

Materials that a unicellular organism needs (e.g. oxygen) can diffuse into the cell and diffuse around inside the cell. There is a size limit, though; if a cell were too big, it might not be able to fill up with all the materials it needs quickly enough. Cells need large **surface area : volume ratios** (see page 81) to be able to take enough of the substances they need from their surroundings. The bigger the surface area : volume ratio, the more surface area a cell has per unit volume.

The tissues in multicellular organisms need to have raw materials transported to them because diffusion would be too slow.

Diffusion fills this cell with enough of the materials.

This cell cannot get filled with enough of the materials.

B | Diffusion may not be fast enough to allow a larger cell to get enough of the materials it needs. This is because larger cells have smaller surface area : volume ratios.

> 3. Why might a unicellular organism need oxygen?
> 4. How does oxygen get into a unicellular organism?
> 5. a| Which organ system carries materials to human tissues?
>   b| Why do multicellular organisms need efficient transport systems?

Kingdoms

Organisms are classified into five **kingdoms** based on what their cells look like.

Yersinia pestis, which causes plague, is a **bacterium**. All bacteria are in the **prokaryote** kingdom. Unicellular **protoctists** are larger than bacteria. Unicellular **fungi** (e.g. yeasts) are usually smaller than protoctists but bigger than bacteria.

Viruses

Viruses are much smaller than bacteria and cause diseases like chicken pox, influenza (flu) and measles. They have no cell wall, no mitochondria, no nucleus and cannot live without being inside a living cell. Since they do not carry out the life processes for themselves, they are not living organisms and there is no virus kingdom.

Virus particles have a very simple structure, mainly consisting of a protein coat that contains a strand of **genes**. The genes contain the instructions for making new viruses. When a virus gets into a cell, these genes cause the cell to make new copies of the virus, which then burst out of the cell. This is known as **replication**.

Viruses are **parasites**, which means that they live on or in an organism (the **host**) and harm it. The term **obligate parasite** can be used to describe viruses (obligate means that they cannot reproduce without being in their hosts).

C

Cell part	Prokaryotes (all unicellular)	Protoctists (mainly unicellular)	Fungi (mainly multicellular)	Plants (all multicellular)	Animals (all multicellular)
cytoplasm	✔	✔	✔	✔	✔
cell membrane	✔	✔	✔	✔	✔
nucleus	✘	✔	✔	✔	✔
mitochondria	✘	✔	✔	✔	✔
cell wall	✔	✘/✔ (some only)	✔	✔	✘
chloroplasts	✘	✘/✔ (some only)	✘	✔	✘

D | Structure of a virus

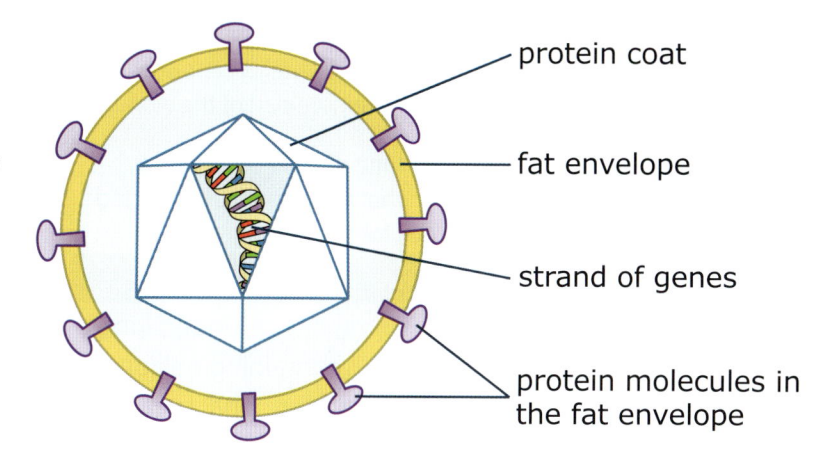

- protein coat
- fat envelope
- strand of genes
- protein molecules in the fat envelope

FACT

Most unicellular organisms are microscopic but a bubble alga consists of one cell that can grow up to 5 cm in diameter.

E — bubble alga

6 a | Name a host of the influenza virus.
  b | Explain why this virus damages tissues in its host.

7 One cell from an organism has a cell wall but no mitochondria. Will this organism be unicellular or multicellular? Explain your reasoning.

8 Which kingdoms contain organisms that can make their own food?

9 Why is there no virus kingdom?

I can ...

- use cell features to identify members of different kingdoms
- explain differences between unicellular and multicellular organisms.

TACKLING DISEASES

8Da

HOW DO MICROBIOLOGISTS HELP IN THE TREATMENT AND PREVENTION OF DISEASES?

A **pathogen** is something that can spread between organisms and cause disease. Most pathogens are microorganisms.

Microbiologists study microorganisms. Some work in hospitals to identify pathogens, using microscopes to examine fluids taken from patients. However, scientists are developing devices with advanced scanning technology to do this work automatically and speed up the process. Identifying pathogens helps doctors to plan effective treatments.

1 Name a pathogen and the disease it causes.

2 Suggest why a hand-held device to detect pathogens would be useful in a relief centre set up after an emergency in a remote part of the world.

3 Tuberculosis (TB) is a lung disease caused by a bacterium. Suggest what fluid would be collected and examined to look for this pathogen.

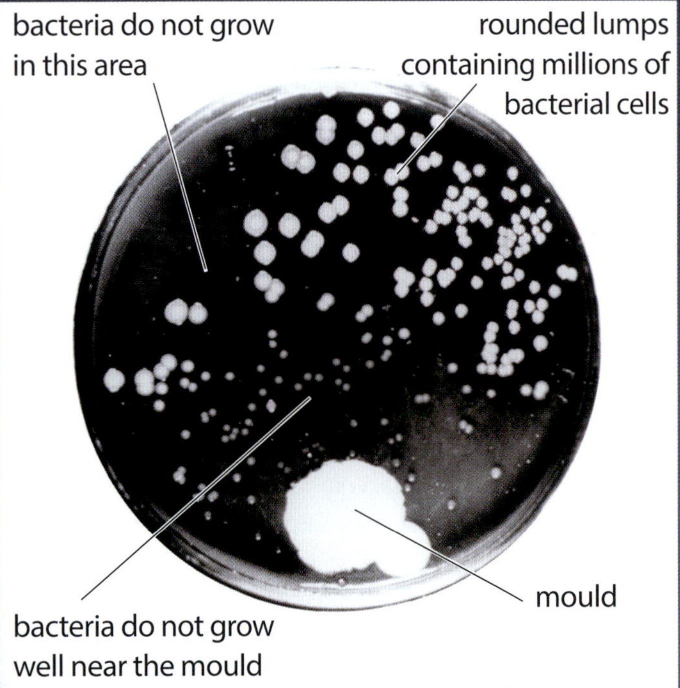

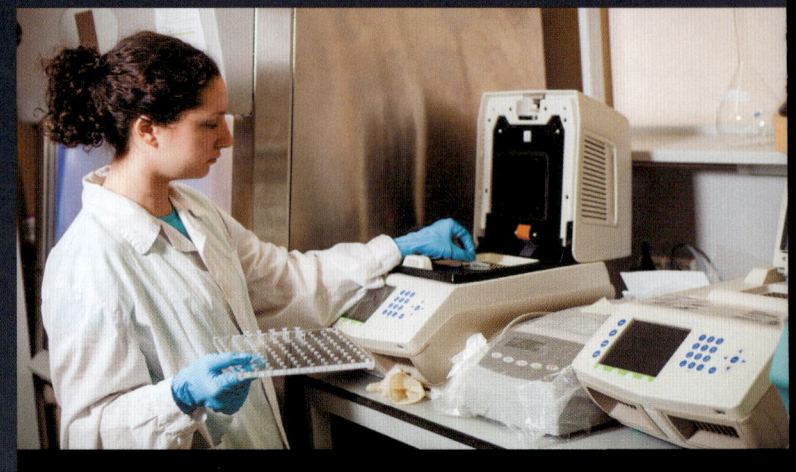

A | Machines such as this can identify pathogens from blood samples in 2–3 hours.

Antibiotics

Alexander Fleming (1881–1955) was a Scottish microbiologist. In 1928 he was growing bacteria on some jelly to study. Some mould (a type of fungus) got onto the jelly and also started to grow. He noticed that the bacteria did not grow near the mould. He came up with the idea that the mould was releasing a substance that doctors could use to kill bacteria. He had **invented** the first **antibiotic** (penicillin).

Many microbiologists have developed this idea and made new antibiotics. They have **innovated** using Fleming's original invention. There are now many antibiotics, and each type is used against different species of bacteria.

Over time bacteria become less affected by antibiotics. They become **resistant**. The more that antibiotics are used, the more types of bacteria become resistant to them. This makes some diseases harder to treat and increases the cost to treat them.

Many scientists think that doctors should stop giving people so many antibiotics and look for other ways to cure diseases. Some farmers give animals antibiotics to *stop* them getting diseases and scientists think that this is also causing resistance.

- bacteria do not grow in this area
- rounded lumps containing millions of bacterial cells
- mould
- bacteria do not grow well near the mould

B | Fleming's dish of jelly

STEM

4 Penicillin was used to treat many bacterial diseases. Explain why it is not used so much now.

5 a | Explain why farmers use antibiotics.
b | What problem does this cause?

6 An invention is a new discovery. What is an innovation?

7 Suggest why more innovation is needed for antibiotics.

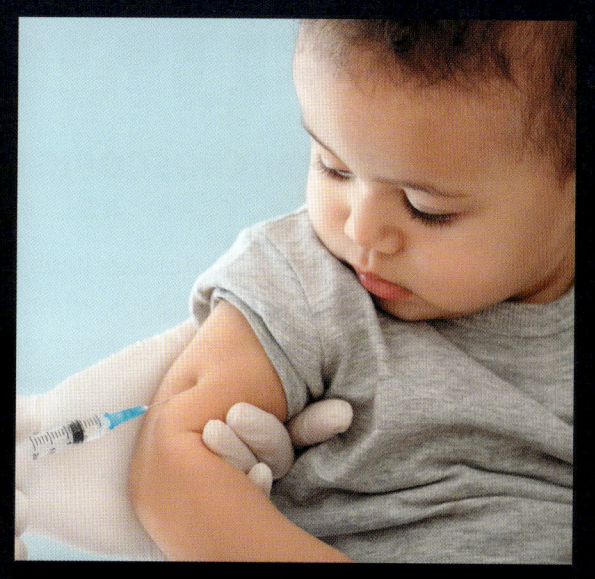

Vaccines

Antibiotics do not affect viruses and so viral diseases can be more difficult to treat. It is better to stop them spreading. This can be done using **vaccines**.

A vaccine is a substance put into the body that causes some of your white blood cells to become able to destroy a certain virus or bacterium. A vaccine makes you **immune** to a certain disease (meaning that you will not get the disease).

C | This child is getting a vaccine to protect her from three viral diseases: measles, mumps and rubella (MMR). If most people in a community are vaccinated the viruses cannot spread and cause diseases.

8 Why will an antibiotic not cure measles?

9 In a community, a disease is less likely to spread from an infected person if many people are vaccinated against that disease. Explain this observation.

Hygiene

Another important way to stop pathogens spreading is to keep yourself and your surroundings clean. Disinfectants are good at killing microorganisms and soaps are good at getting them off your skin.

D

PRACTICAL

Cinnamon powder can be used as a model to represent microorganisms. Work in a group to plan and carry out an experiment to find out which is the best method to get a mixture of oil and cinnamon powder off your hands: washing with cold water, with cold water and soap, with warm water or with warm water and soap.

1 Write a report about your experiment (including how you made it a fair test).

2 Use your results to produce a poster about hand washing in school.

8Db MICROSCOPIC FUNGI

UK NC, iLS, CEE

HOW DO WE USE MICROSCOPIC FUNGI?

Ringworm is a common skin disease. It was thought to be caused by worms until the 1840s, when David Gruby (1810–1898) used a microscope to discover a fungus in the 'rings'. This was **evidence** that a microorganism caused the disease. A fungus also causes athlete's foot.

Advances in microscopes in the 19th century allowed more discoveries of microscopic fungi. Unicellular yeasts were discovered and were seen to use **budding** to reproduce. Budding is a type of **asexual reproduction** in which a daughter cell grows out of a parent cell.

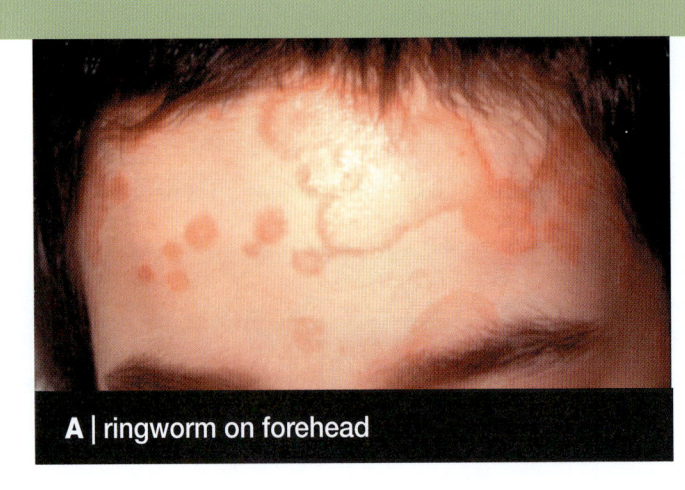

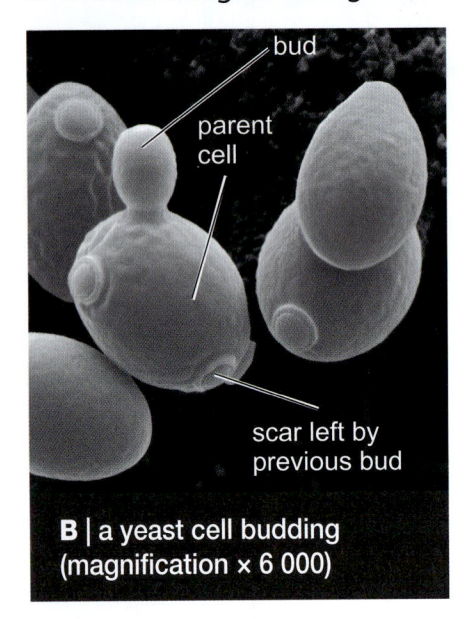

A | ringworm on forehead

B | a yeast cell budding (magnification × 6 000)

Like all cells, the nucleus of a yeast parent cell contains long strands of a molecule called **DNA**. Sections of the DNA (**genes**) contain the instructions for making proteins and for an organism's inherited characteristics. In budding, the nucleus copies itself (including all the DNA). The new nucleus then moves into the bud. The bud has identical inherited characteristics to the parent cell and eventually splits from it.

Louis Pasteur (1882–1895) discovered that yeasts produce carbon dioxide and ethanol. He also found that giving air to yeast cells made them stop making ethanol. He concluded that yeasts could use two forms of **respiration** – **aerobic** (with oxygen) and **anaerobic** (without oxygen).

> 1 Why was the cause of ringworm not known until the 1840s?
>
> 2 a| What form of asexual reproduction do yeast use?
>   b| Explain why the new cell formed in asexual reproduction has identical characteristics to the parent cell?

Baking

We now know that, compared with anaerobic respiration, aerobic respiration releases more energy from glucose and also produces much more carbon dioxide:

glucose + oxygen → carbon dioxide + water (+ energy)
(a sugar)

Bread dough is stretched and folded to get air into it. The yeast cells respire aerobically and bubbles of gas make the dough rise.

C | Bread dough is left to rise in a warm place before baking.

> 3 What is inside the bubbles that cause bread dough to rise?
>
> 4 Why do bakers try to get a lot of air into bread dough?
>
> 5 Where in a yeast cell does aerobic respiration occur?

Anaerobic respiration

The anaerobic respiration of microorganisms is called **fermentation**. In yeast, this process produces ethanol. Plants can also use this type of anaerobic respiration (for example, when their roots are waterlogged).

glucose → carbon dioxide + ethanol (+ some energy)

> **6** What liquid is produced when yeast cells ferment?
>
> **7** If bread dough is made so that it contains very little air, the dough still rises a bit. What process allows this to happen?
>
> **8** Energy in a cell is stored in molecules of ATP. Which type of respiration produces more ATP? Explain your reasoning.

D sugar solution being fermented by yeast — carbon dioxide gas escaping

Growth curves

For yeast cells to grow and reproduce they need resources such as moisture, sugar and warmth. This is why bread dough is left in a warm place for it to rise. A few yeast cells soon become millions but the **population** of cells will not keep growing forever. Eventually the sugar runs out and the population stops growing. Something that slows down or stops a process is called a **limiting factor**.

How a yeast population changes with time

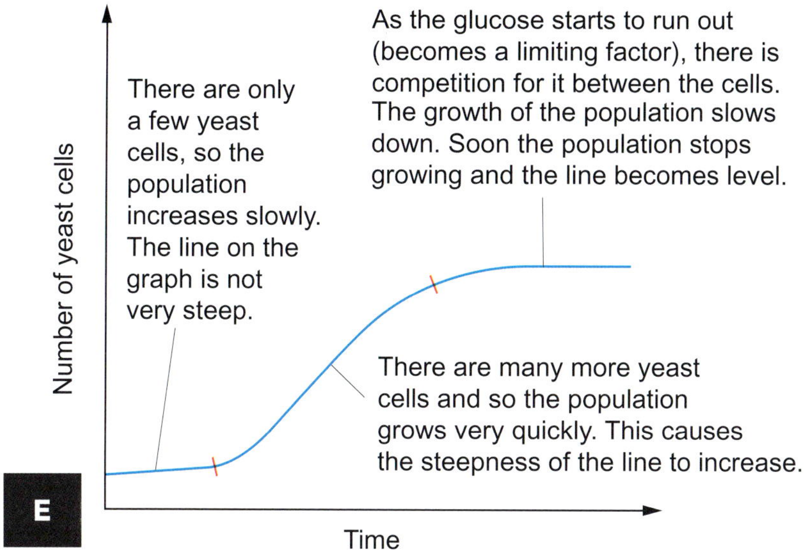

Number of yeast cells vs Time

- There are only a few yeast cells, so the population increases slowly. The line on the graph is not very steep.
- There are many more yeast cells and so the population grows very quickly. This causes the steepness of the line to increase.
- As the glucose starts to run out (becomes a limiting factor), there is competition for it between the cells. The growth of the population slows down. Soon the population stops growing and the line becomes level.

E

FACT

Cacao beans are fermented using yeast, during chocolate production. Bacteria then convert the ethanol into ethanoic acid. The ethanol, ethanoic acid and the heat that is produced, develop flavours in the bean and kill off the seedling as it tries to germinate.

F

> **9** a| List three resources that yeast cells need to grow and reproduce.
>
> b| Which resource is most likely to be the limiting factor that causes a population of yeast cells to stop increasing? Explain your reasoning.

I can ...

- describe the ways in which yeast respire
- explain the use of yeasts in baking
- describe how yeasts reproduce and the factors that limit this.

123

UK NC, iLS, CEE

8Dc BACTERIA

WHAT ARE THE FEATURES OF BACTERIA?

In the 19th century, scientists thought that rotting things could produce living organisms (the theory of spontaneous generation). They also thought that 'bad air' given off by rotting materials caused diseases (miasma theory).

In the 1860s, French scientist Louis Pasteur showed that rotting only occurred when microorganisms got into things, and that diseases could be caused by bacteria. These ideas led to the discovery of the bacteria that cause many diseases, such as **tuberculosis (TB)**. Pasteur also went on to develop some of the first **vaccines**.

> 1 Give the name of a disease caused by a bacterium.
>
> 2 Which are the yeast cells in photo A? Explain your reasoning.

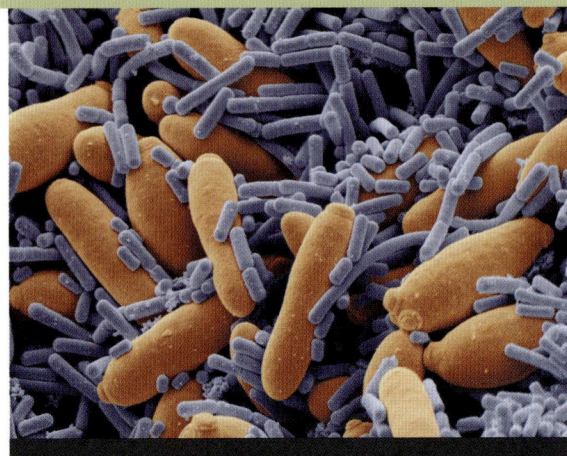

A | Kefir is a fermented milk drink, made using yeast and lactic acid bacteria. Its sour taste is due to the acid produced by anaerobic respiration of the bacteria. (× 4000)

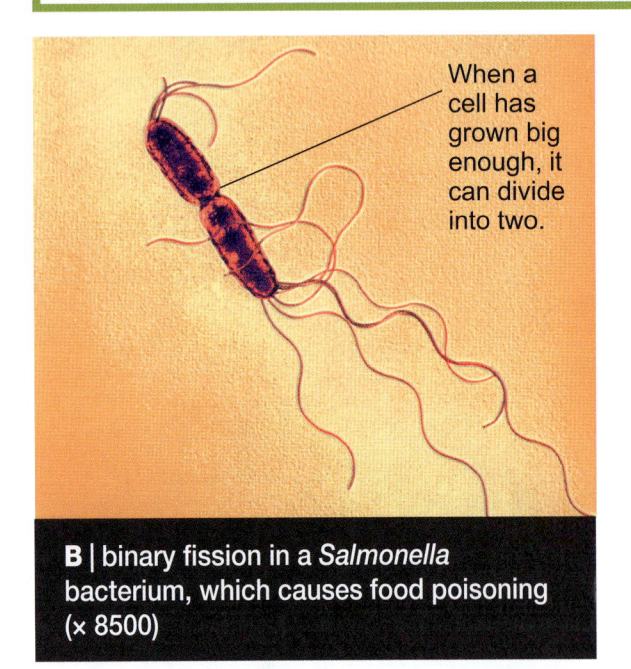

Pasteur examined drinks (such as milk) that turn sour. He found that in sour drinks, there was always lactic acid and certain bacteria. He also concluded that the bacteria use a type of anaerobic respiration that produces lactic acid:

glucose → lactic acid (+ some energy)

Like yeast, bacteria grow well if they have nutrients (such as sugar), warmth and moisture. They use the nutrients for respiration and making substances for growth and reproduction. When it is warmer, the **enzymes** making new substances work faster, so the bacteria grow faster. Moisture stops the cells drying out.

Bacteria use a method of asexual reproduction called **binary fission**. In this process, one cell grows and then splits evenly into two identical parts.

When a cell has grown big enough, it can divide into two.

B | binary fission in a *Salmonella* bacterium, which causes food poisoning (× 8500)

Yoghurt and cheese

Lactic acid bacteria are used to turn milk into yoghurt. The lactic acid they produce turns the milk sour and thickens it, which is why unsweetened yoghurt tastes sour. These bacteria are often used to make the sour milk needed to make cheese.

> 3 Draw a table to compare budding and binary fission.
>
> 4 Explain why milk lasts longer when stored in a fridge (rather than left at room temperature).
>
> 5 Sketch a graph to show how the numbers of bacterial cells in a jug of fresh milk might change with time. (*Hint*: Look back at page 123.)

6
a| What sort of respiration occurs in the bacteria used to make yoghurt?
b| What substance does this produce?
c| What are the effects of this substance on milk?

Bacterial cells

Bacteria are prokaryotes. Members of this kingdom do not have nuclei, and the information to control a cell is found in a circular **chromosome** (made of DNA).

- flagellum (for movement)
- circular chromosome made of DNA (found in an area of the cell called the nucleoid)
- slime capsule (stops the cell drying out)
- cell wall (gives the cell its shape and provides protection)
- cell surface membrane (controls what enters and leaves the cell)
- cytoplasm (which does not contain mitochondria but does contain plasmids (tiny loops of DNA), which control some of the cell's characteristics)

D | This bacterium causes cholera, a disease that causes terrible diarrhoea and vomiting. It often kills people.

Some bacteria swim using **flagella** (pronounced '*fla-**jel**-la*'). Each flagellum spins to move a cell forward, similar to a boat's propeller.

Different species of bacteria have different shapes and sizes. They can be identified using a **statement key**, such as the one shown in F.

7 Use the statement key F to identify the bacteria shown on these pages.

8 Describe the functions of the parts of a bacterial cell.

9 Compare the different types of respiration in humans, yeast and bacteria.

FACT

Many species of bacteria can be used to make cheese, as long as they produce lactic acid. Some cheeses have mould added to them, which makes 'blue cheese'.

C

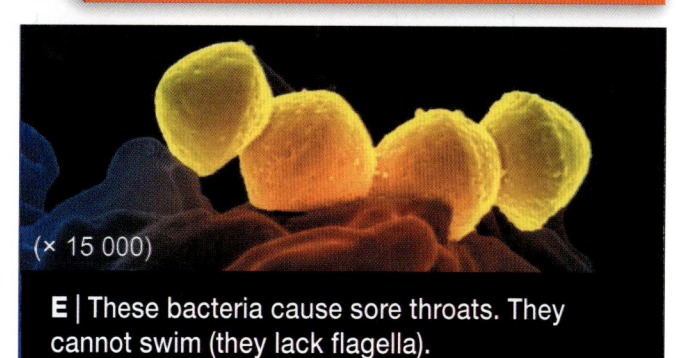

(× 15 000)

E | These bacteria cause sore throats. They cannot swim (they lack flagella).

1	shaped like a straight rod	GO TO 2
	not shaped like a straight rod	GO TO 5
2	has one or more flagella	GO TO 3
	does not have flagella	GO TO 4
3	one flagellum	*Pseudomonas aeruginosa*
	many flagella	*Salmonella typhimurium*
4	long, thin, with smooth outer layer	*Lactobacillus delbrueckii*
	short, with rough outer layer	*Yersinia pestis*
5	round shape	GO TO 6
	comma-shaped	*Vibrio cholerae*
6	in groups, like bunches of grapes	*Staphylococcus aureus*
	in a chain	*Streptococcus pyogenes*

F | At the top, choose the description that matches your bacterium. Follow the 'GO TO' instruction to find the next pair of sentences. Keep choosing sentences until you get to a name.

I can ...

- explain why anaerobic bacteria are used to make yoghurt and cheese
- describe the functions of the parts of a bacterial cell
- describe how bacteria reproduce
- use a statement key.

UK NC, iLS, CEE

8Dc PIE CHARTS

HOW ARE PIE CHARTS DRAWN AND WHY DO WE USE THEM?

At the start of the Crimean War (1853–1856), thousands of soldiers were dying of cholera (although no one knew what caused this disease).

In November 1854, a British nurse called Florence Nightingale arrived in the Crimea. She started cleaning up the dirty rooms in the main hospital. About six months later, the drains were cleared. After these changes, the number of soldiers dying from diseases dropped dramatically.

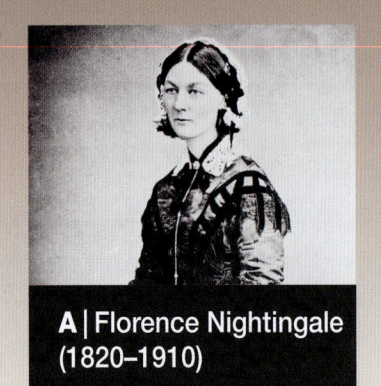

A | Florence Nightingale (1820–1910)

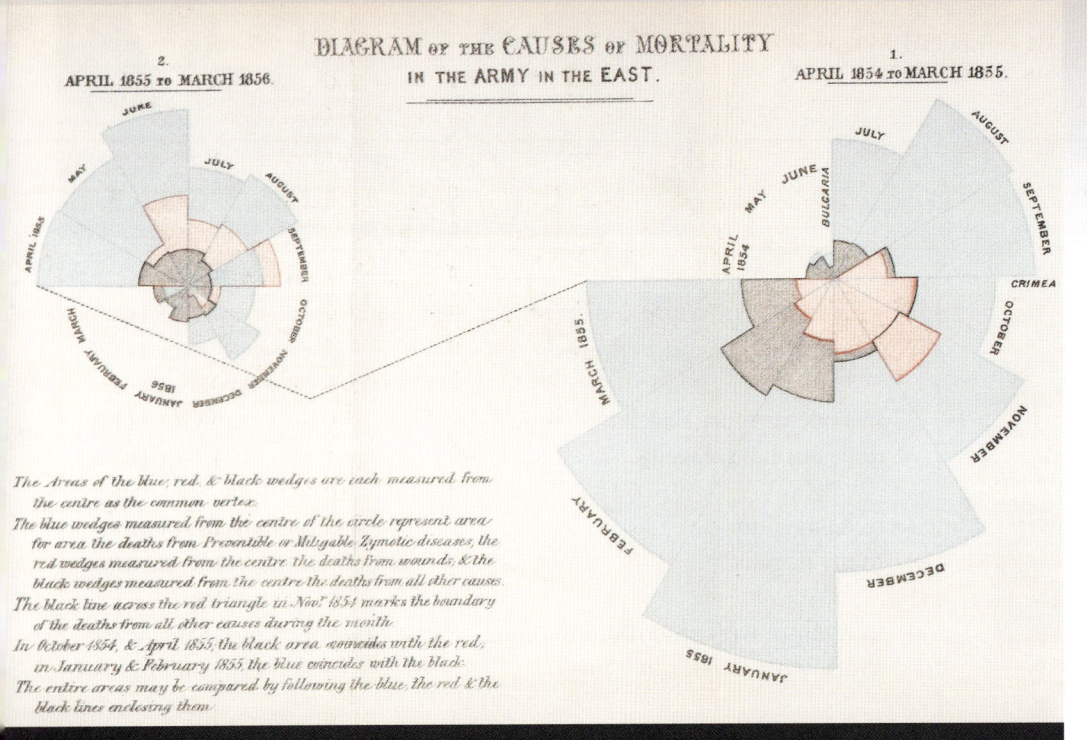

Florence Nightingale became certain that cleaning the hospital and clearing the drains had saved many lives. Back in the UK, she started raising money for a nursing school. She thought that showing the data as diagrams would make it easier for people to understand how cleaning had helped. So she published leaflets with different sorts of diagrams.

The money was raised and Florence Nightingale's school opened in 1860. Her teaching emphasised the importance of cleanliness. It soon became clear why cleanliness was so important, because scientists started to understand how microorganisms caused diseases and how they were spread by poor hygiene and dirty water.

B | This is Florence Nightingale's most famous diagram. Like a pie chart, it uses area to show the contributions made by different factors. It shows that deaths from diseases were much lower in the second year of the war (left-hand chart) than in the first, after changes at the hospital.

Drawing pie charts

The popularity of pie charts is partly thanks to Florence Nightingale's use of similar diagrams. Pie charts are used to show the contribution of something to a whole. A larger sector (slice) shows a bigger contribution. Diagram C shows how some of Florence Nightingale's data might be shown today. The data used is in table D.

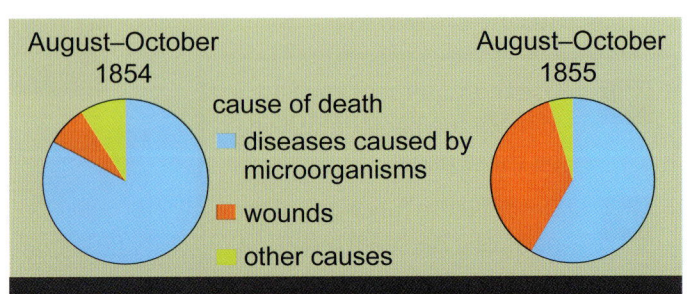

C | deaths in the three months before Florence Nightingale arrived and in the same period the following year

August–October 1854 | August–October 1855

cause of death
- diseases caused by microorganisms
- wounds
- other causes

126

WORKING SCIENTIFICALLY

The different sectors on a pie chart are drawn using angles. A bigger angle gives a bigger sector. To draw pie charts we need to work out the angles required to represent each sector.

Step 1: Find the total number of items (deaths in this case). For 1854, this is 83 + 8 + 9 = 100.

Step 2: Work out the angle for one item (1% of deaths in this case). To do this, take the number of degrees in a circle (360) and divide it by the total number of deaths (100):

$$\frac{360}{100} = 3.6°$$

Step 3: Work out the angle for each cause of death. Round each answer to the nearest whole degree:

microorganism diseases:
1% is 3.6°
× 83
83% is 299°

wounds:
1% is 3.6°
× 8
8% is 29°

other causes:
1% is 3.6°
× 9
9% is 32°

Step 4: Next, draw a circle using a pair of compasses. Then draw a vertical line (radius) from the centre to the edge.

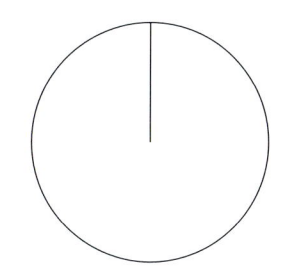

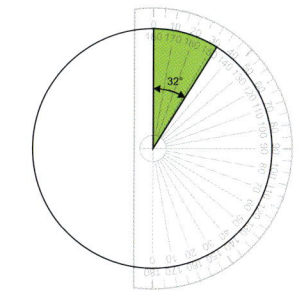

Step 5: Use a protractor on this line to measure the angle of a sector and draw it.

Step 6: Use the line you have just drawn to measure and draw the next sector. Keep doing this until you have drawn all the sectors.

Step 7: Add labels or a key to say what each sector represents.

D	Percentage of deaths caused by …		
Date	micro-organism diseases	wounds	other causes
August–October 1854	83	8	9
August–October 1855	59	36	5

1
a| What data do the pie charts in diagram C show?
b| How did the percentage of deaths caused by diseases change?
c| Are deaths from diseases in August to October 1855 more or less than half the total number of deaths? Explain your reasoning.
d| Are deaths from diseases in August to October 1854 more or less than three-quarters of the total number of deaths? Explain your reasoning.

2 Use table D to draw the pie chart on the right of diagram C. Show your working.

3 For which of these would it be best to use a pie chart:
a| how the number of bacterial cells changes during a day
b| the numbers of different species of bacteria found in human intestines
c| how the speed of yeast cell growth depends on temperature?

I can …
- interpret and draw pie charts.

UK NC, iLS, CEE

8Dd PROTOCTISTS

WHAT ARE THE FEATURES OF PROTOCTISTS?

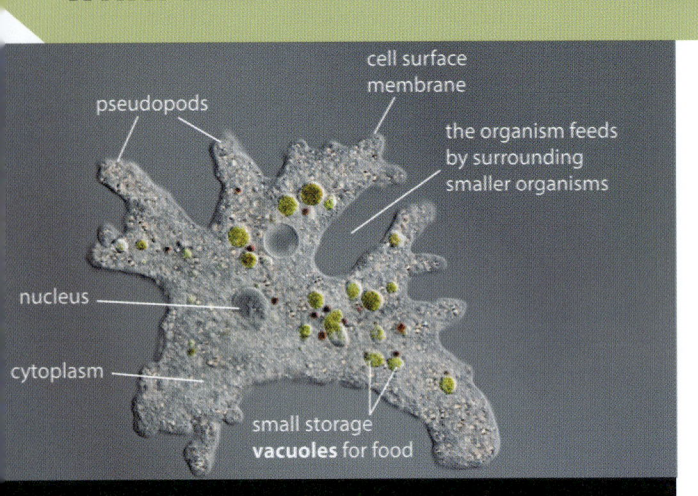

Protoctists are mostly unicellular but exist in many different shapes and sizes. Some cause diseases, such as malaria.

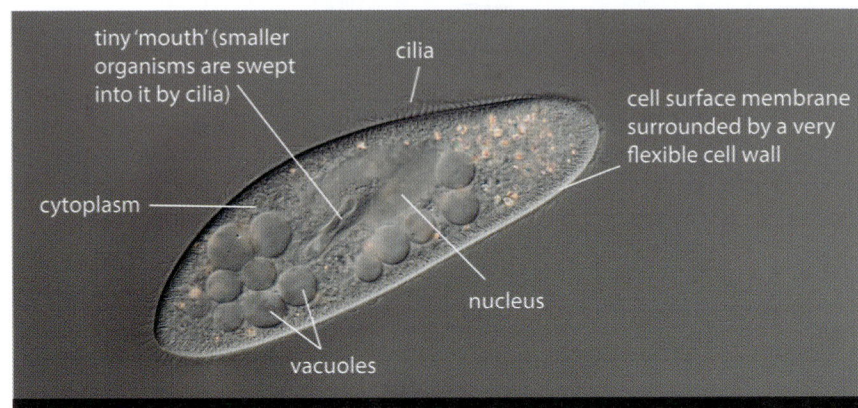

A | An *Amoeba* cell moves by stretching out **pseudopods** and then pulling the rest of the cell towards them. Amoeba live in water and can cause amoebic dysentery, which gives you severe diarrhoea with blood. (× 1000)

B | A *Paramecium* cell moves using tiny waving hairs, called **cilia**. (× 500)

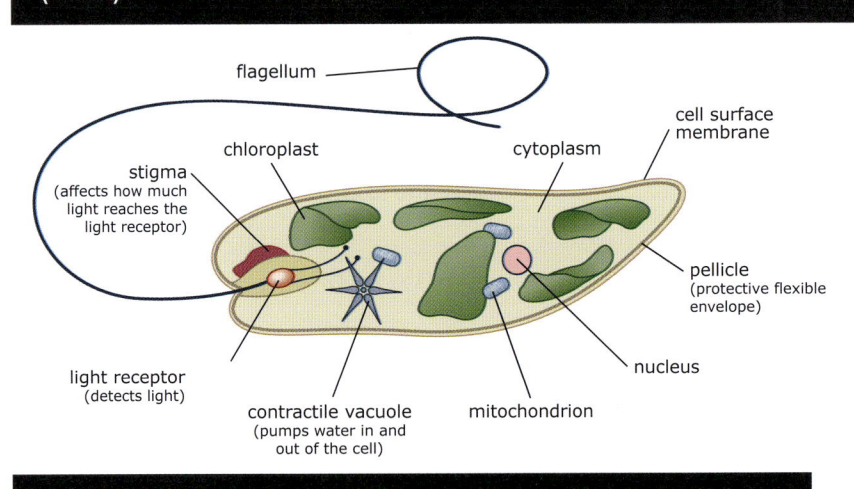

C | Algae are protoctists that can photosynthesise. Some, such as *Euglena*, have flagella but others cannot move. (× 1500)

1. a| Which internal part needed for respiration is only shown in diagram C but is also found in *Amoeba* and *Paramecium*?
   b| Draw a table to compare the features of the three protoctists A, B and C.
   c| Compare the ways the three organisms get their nutrition.
2. *Amoeba* reproduce using binary fission. Draw a diagram of this.

FACT

Some algae emit light when disturbed. This bioluminescence can produce amazing scenes along beaches at night, as waves stir up the algae.

Like plants, algae use **photosynthesis** to produce **organic molecules** (molecules that contain carbon atoms joined together):

$$\text{carbon dioxide} + \text{water} \xrightarrow[\text{chlorophyll}]{\text{light energy}} \text{glucose} + \text{oxygen}$$

3. Explain how animals depend on photosynthesis.
4. a| State the reactants in photosynthesis.
   b| State the product that is organic.

Most life on Earth depends on photosynthesising **producers**, such as plants and algae. Inside chloroplasts, a green substance called **chlorophyll** traps energy transferred from the Sun by light. This energy is used to join carbon dioxide and water, to make glucose. Some of this energy is stored in the glucose and substances made from glucose. This energy can be transferred to other organisms, which we show using **food chains, food webs** and **pyramids of numbers**.

The bars in a pyramid of numbers represent the numbers of organisms. At each **trophic level**, organisms transfer some of the energy in their food out of their bodies (e.g. by moving or as waste). There is less energy available for the next level, so there are fewer animals in the next level.

Pyramids of numbers do not take into account the size of the organisms, and so are sometimes not pyramid-shaped. A better way to show how energy is lost from the trophic levels is to use a **pyramid of biomass**. This shows the mass of living material at each trophic level (diagram F).

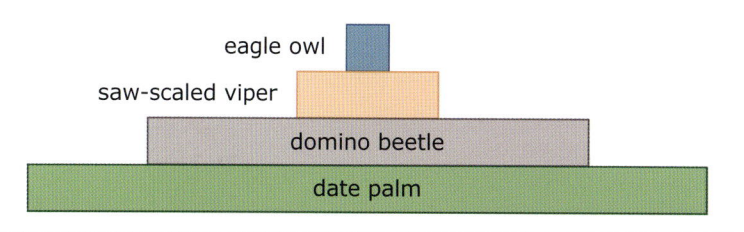

5 a| State two resources *Amoeba* and *Paramecium* need from their environments.
b| What additional resource do algae need?

E | pyramid of numbers for organisms in an Arabian desert

- eagle owl — tertiary consumer
- saw-scaled viper — secondary consumer
- domino beetle — primary consumer
- date palm — producer

6 a| Draw a food chain from pyramid of numbers E.
b| Which organism in food chain E is a herbivore?
c| Describe how energy from the Sun has been transferred to this organism.
d| Suggest two ways in which energy is 'lost' (and not stored inside the organism).

F | a pyramid of biomass for organisms in an Arabian desert

- eagle owl
- saw-scaled viper
- domino beetle
- date palm

7 Explain the shape of pyramid of biomass F.

8 Using examples from this page, explain why a pyramid of biomass is better at showing energy flow through a food chain.

Some photosynthetic protoctists found in the sea produce poisons that are not broken down inside the bodies of fish. The poison becomes concentrated in the bodies of a few large fish. Eating these fish causes a very serious illness called ciguatera (pronounced 'sig-wa-**tair**-a').

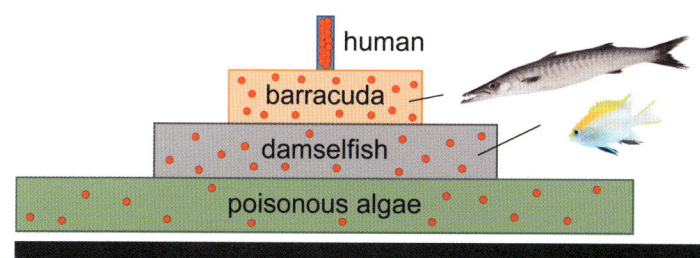

G | Some poisons can become more and more concentrated along a food chain.

- human
- barracuda
- damselfish
- poisonous algae

9 In 2014, Australian fishermen caught a large Spanish mackerel. They ate the fish but were soon seriously ill. Suggest what had happened.

I can ...

- describe the functions of the common parts of protoctist cells
- describe how algae make their own food, and explain the importance of this.

8De DECOMPOSERS AND CARBON

UK NC, iLS, CEE

HOW ARE MICROORGANISMS IMPORTANT IN THE CARBON CYCLE?

Microorganisms are an important part of an **ecosystem** because they are **decomposers**; they break down dead organisms and animal wastes in a process called **decay**. This allows substances inside the dead organisms and wastes to be used again by other organisms.

1. What is a decomposer?
2. What do you think the decomposer in photo B is feeding on?
3. Why are decomposers important in an ecosystem?

Bacteria, fungi and protoctists can all be decomposers. The process of decay is helped by the way in which many of them feed (as shown in diagram C).

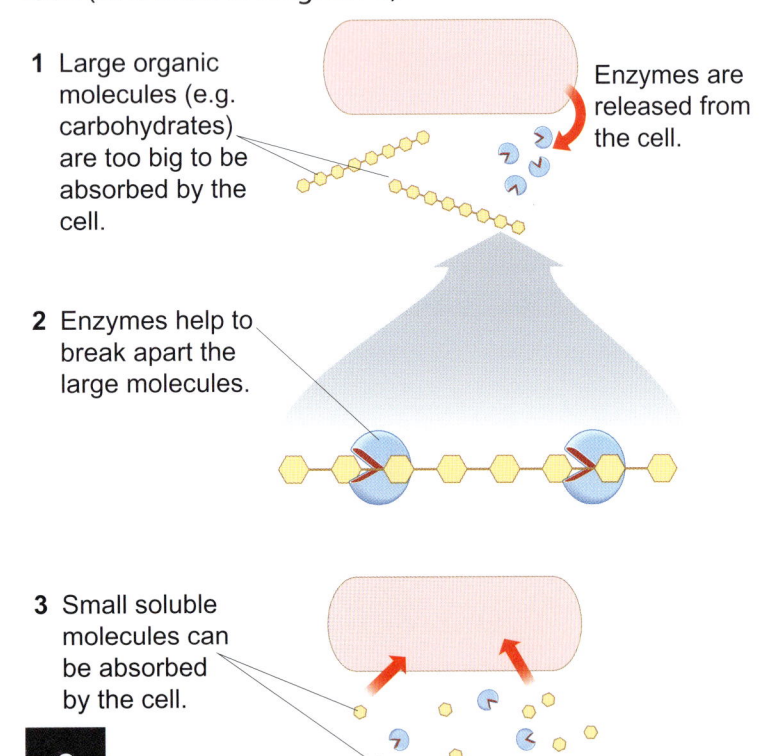

1. Large organic molecules (e.g. carbohydrates) are too big to be absorbed by the cell.
   Enzymes are released from the cell.
2. Enzymes help to break apart the large molecules.
3. Small soluble molecules can be absorbed by the cell.

C

Microorganisms use digested molecules for respiration and to produce new substances for growth.

A | Microorganisms cause decay.

B | This decomposer is a protoctist called dog's vomit slime mould. You can see microorganisms when there are millions of cells growing in the same place.

D | Gases from respiring decomposers inside this dead Bryde's whale made it swell up until it was about to explode.

4
a| What do bacteria use to digest their food?
b| Why do they need to use these substances?
c| What process is shown by the arrows in part 3 of diagram C?

5 Name a gas you would expect to find inside the whale in photo D. Explain your reasoning.

Kitchen and garden waste can be put on a compost heap. Decomposers decay this material to form compost. This is added to the soil because it contains nutrients called mineral salts. These are needed for plant growth, and include nitrates (which contain a source of nitrogen).

6 Suggest why the compost in photo E is:
a| steaming   b| acidic.

Recycling carbon

Most substances in cells are organic compounds. These include **carbohydrates**, **proteins** and **fats**. Decomposers recycle the carbon in these compounds. We use a model called the **carbon cycle** to show this.

FACT

Some bacteria in your gut use a type of anaerobic respiration that produces methane. Others produce hydrogen. These gases form flatulence, which only smells when it contains sulfur compounds. Cabbages are rich in sulfur compounds!

E | compost

7 What decomposer helps to make bread?

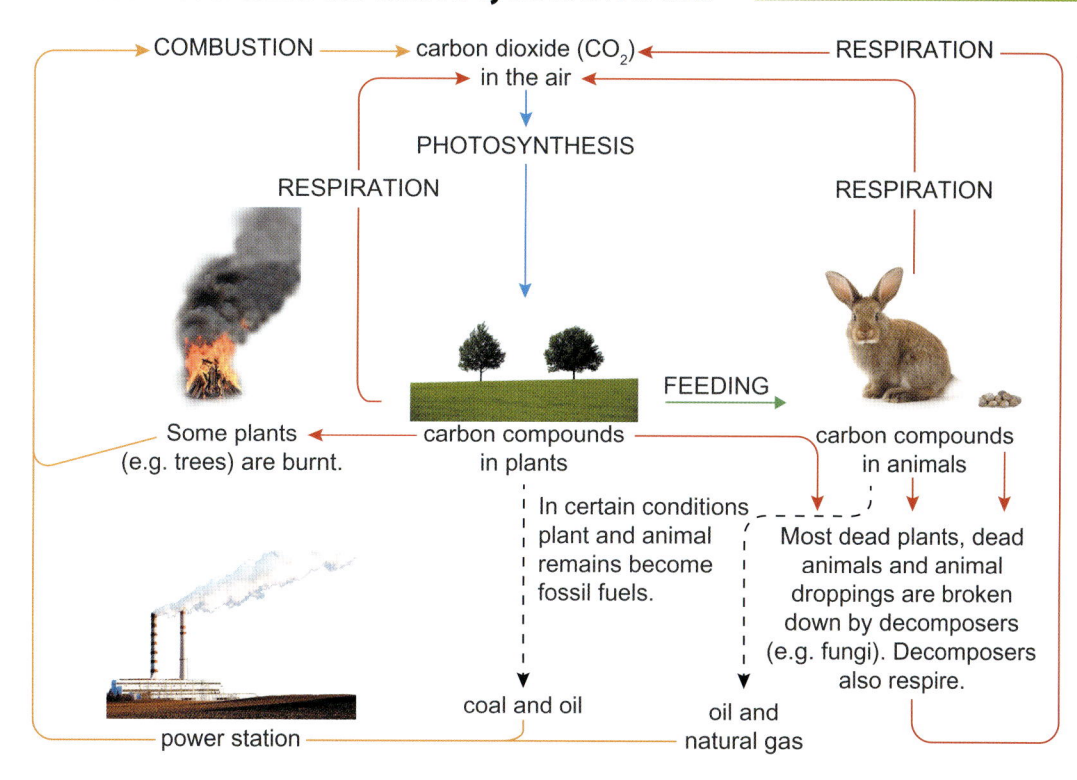

8 State the names of some compounds that contain carbon in an ecosystem. Give as many as you can.

9 Draw a diagram to show how plants and animals are interdependent (depend upon one another).

10 In the last 300 years, the amount of carbon dioxide in the atmosphere has increased. Suggest why.

Carbon cycle diagram: COMBUSTION → carbon dioxide (CO_2) in the air ← RESPIRATION; PHOTOSYNTHESIS; RESPIRATION; Some plants (e.g. trees) are burnt; carbon compounds in plants; FEEDING → carbon compounds in animals; In certain conditions plant and animal remains become fossil fuels; Most dead plants, dead animals and animal droppings are broken down by decomposers (e.g. fungi). Decomposers also respire; coal and oil; oil and natural gas; power station.

F | The carbon cycle shows how carbon is recycled, and how photosynthesis and respiration help to maintain the balance of gases in the atmosphere.

I can ...
- explain the importance of decomposers
- model the recycling of carbon in an ecosystem using the carbon cycle.

8De BLACK DEATH HYPOTHESES

HOW DO WE KNOW WHAT CAUSED BLACK DEATH?

In 1894, one of Louis Pasteur's students, Alexandre Yersin (1863–1943), went to investigate a plague outbreak in Hong Kong. He discovered a bacterium in the victims' bodies. He also found the bacterium in black rats and so scientists thought that blood-sucking fleas carried the bacteria between rats and humans, as the fleas fed.

Not all scientists accepted this hypothesis. Many thought that Black Death in the 14th century had spread too quickly for rats and fleas to be responsible. In 2001, another hypothesis was presented: Black Death and plague are different diseases and Black Death was caused by a virus.

In 2014, engineers on a large underground rail project in London discovered a 14th-century plague pit. Scientists used new technology to find and identify bacterial chromosomes in the bodies. The chromosomes were from *Yersinia pestis*. The chromosomes also matched those of bacteria from recent plague victims in Madagascar in 2013. Scientists now think that the bacterium can be spread through the air by coughs and sneezes, as well as by rats and fleas.

(× 8 000)

A | *Yersinia pestis* causes plague.

B | the plague pit uncovered in Clerkenwell, London by workers on the underground rail project

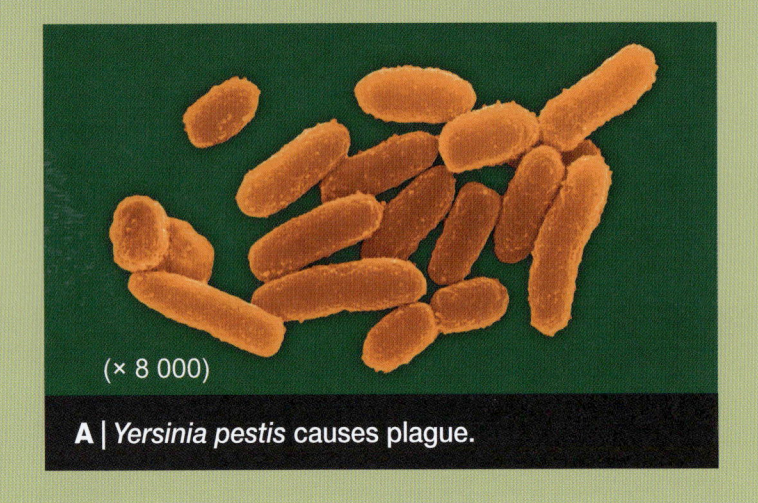

1. a| Which kingdoms do bacteria and humans belong to?
   b| What are the differences between these two kingdoms?
2. a| Why are the bodies of plague victims reduced to skeletons?
   b| Why is this useful for the environment?
   c| Why is this process slower if bodies are buried?
3. Scientists find many different types of microorganisms underground. However, they do not find living algae. Explain why.
4. Explain why *Yersinia pestis* cannot move on its own.
5. Draw a diagram to show how *Yersinia pestis* reproduces.
6. a| What is the function of the chromosome in a bacterium?
   b| State the location of chromosomes in protoctists.
7. Sketch a graph to show how the number of microorganisms on a plague victim changes over time. Label your graph to explain its shape.

HAVE YOUR SAY

Should we vaccinate everyone against plague?

9Aa MONSTERS AND MYTH

A story says that the bones in photo A are from a terrible fire-breathing dragon that roamed Poland long ago. The creature was slain by Krak, a shoemaker's apprentice who later became king. The city of Krakow was built in his honour.

The bones are obviously not from a dragon. They are probably from a whale and a mammoth. Myths often originate from people finding the bones of extinct creatures, which they cannot explain. The idea of one-eyed giants (Cyclops) from Ancient Greek mythology probably came from the discovery of mammoth or elephant skulls, which have a large central hole for the animal's trunk.

In 1676, Robert Plot (a university professor) was given part of an enormous thighbone. He concluded that it was from a giant human. It was actually a dinosaur bone but no one knew about dinosaurs at the time.

Later, William Buckland (1784–1856) carefully studied a set of huge bones. In a **scientific paper** published in 1824, he hypothesised that the bones came from a large extinct reptile. Its **species** name is now *Megalosaurus bucklandii*, in his honour, and it was the first dinosaur described in a science **journal**. However, many scientists at the time were not convinced by Buckland's hypothesis because he was quite eccentric. He sometimes gave lectures to his students on horseback.

A | 'dragon bones' hanging in the city of Krakow, Poland

B | an elephant skull

C | a model of *Megalosaurus bucklandii* and a human

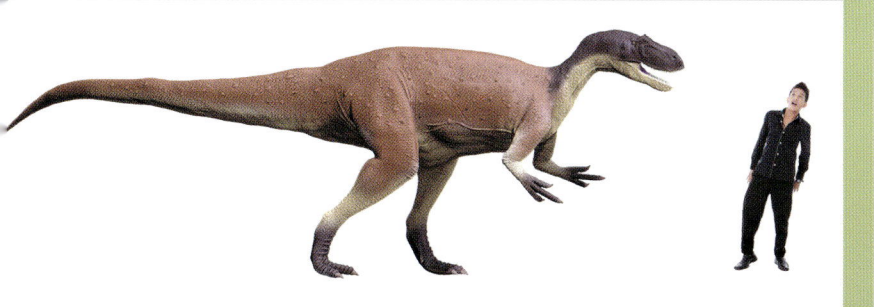

1. a| What does 'extinct' mean?
   b| Suggest a way in which extinction happens.

2. a| What **variation** is there between the two species in photo C?
   b| How can variation be caused? Give two ways.

3. What is a species?

4. What **genus** is Buckland's dinosaur in?

5. DNA is a substance found in cells. Where in the cell is it found?

9Aa ENVIRONMENTAL VARIATION

UK NC, iLS, CEE

WHAT CAUSES ENVIRONMENTAL VARIATION?

The monster pumpkins in photo A did not get that big by chance. The plants were carefully looked after and given all the **resources** they needed, including additional light, water, warmth and mineral salts.

An organism's surroundings are its **environment**. In all environments there are **environmental factors** that can change the organism. There are **abiotic factors** or **physical environmental** factors (e.g. temperature, the amount of light). There are also **biotic factors**, which are the activities of other organisms (e.g. competition, predation, infectious disease).

A | The pumpkins in this growing competition did not break any records – the world's heaviest pumpkin had a mass of 1190 kg.

1 Suggest what abiotic factors allowed the pumpkins in photo A to grow so big.

2 a| Describe two physical environmental factors in your environment at the moment.

b| Apart from physical factors, what other environmental factors are in your environment?

FACT

In 2008, some Japanese cherry tree seeds spent 6 months in space. When planted back on Earth the trees flowered 6 years early. Scientists are still trying to work out why.

The features of an organism are its **characteristics**. The differences between the characteristics of organisms are known as variation. **Environmental variation** is variation caused by an organism's environment.

In humans, examples of environmental variation include scars and hairstyles. Scars are made by physical environmental factors, such as fire or sharp objects. Hairstyles follow fashion, which is an environmental factor caused by other people in your environment.

3 a| Describe the environmental variation shown in photos B, C and D.

b| Suggest what environmental factor has caused the variation in each case.

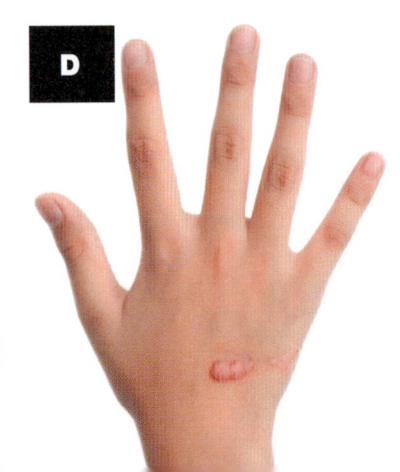

Continuous and discontinuous

Pumpkins, such as the ones shown in photo A, can have a large spread of different sizes, from very small to enormous, and everything in between. Variation that can have any value between two points is **continuous variation**. Variation that can only have a value from a limited set of possible values is **discontinuous variation**.

4 a| Identify a type of environmental variation in photo E.

b| State whether this is continuous or discontinuous. Explain your reasoning.

5 Explain whether each example of variation in photos B, C and D is continuous or discontinuous.

E | In humans, hair length is an example of continuous variation. Wearing glasses or contact lenses is discontinuous.

Classification

Classification is sorting organisms into groups. The smallest group an organism is classified into is its **species**. Members of the same species can reproduce with one another and their offspring will also be able to reproduce.

Sometimes environmental variation makes classification difficult. In 2003 some ancient human bones were discovered on Flores Island in Indonesia. The bones were from adults who were just over 1 m tall – much shorter than human adults today. Some scientists think that the bones were from our own species of human but that a shortage of a mineral called iodine in the diet meant that the people did not grow very tall. Other scientists think that these people were from a different species, which is now extinct.

6 A plant growing on a seashore has pink flowers at the top of a stem, which has pairs of oval leaves along its 10 cm length. On a nearby island there are similar plants but they are over 50 cm tall and have dark purple flowers. Scientists took seeds from plants in both areas and grew them in the laboratory. They all grew to look the same.

a| What does this tell you about the plants from the two areas?

b| Use this example to explain how environmental variation can make it difficult to identify plant species.

F | A team led by Professor Mike Morwood (on the right) say that their evidence supports the hypothesis that the Flores Island people were a different species to humans.

I can ...
- identify different types of environmental variation and explain their causes
- explain how environmental variation can cause problems with classification.

9Ab INHERITED VARIATION

HOW IS INHERITED VARIATION CAUSED?

Offspring get a mixture of characteristics from their **parents**. We say they **inherit** these characteristics. The variation in these characteristics is **inherited variation**. Examples include human eye colour, dimpled chins and blood groups.

A | inherited variation in dragon fruit

1. Give three examples of inherited variation in dragon fruit (photo A).

2. a| Look at photo B. From which parent has the child wearing glasses inherited her myopia?
   b| Give another characteristic that the children have inherited from one parent.

3. What is the difference between environmental and inherited variation?

B | Children inherit characteristics from their parents.

The instructions for inherited characteristics are stored in **genetic information** (which is found in the **genes** inside the **nuclei** of cells). In **sexual reproduction**, two **gametes** (one male and one female) **fuse** during **fertilisation** to produce a **zygote**. Since the zygote contains genetic information from two parents, the offspring will have some characteristics of each parent.

Every gamete contains slightly different genetic information; no two gametes are identical. For example, in people with dimpled chins, some of their gametes carry the instructions for a dimpled chin and some of their gametes may not. Since all gametes are different, brothers and sisters do not look exactly the same.

FACT
Humans share a lot of genetic information with 'great apes' (e.g. 99% with chimpanzees, 98% with gorillas). These species share many characteristics but look very different.

C | Brothers (and sisters) share similar characteristics (but only identical twins look identical).

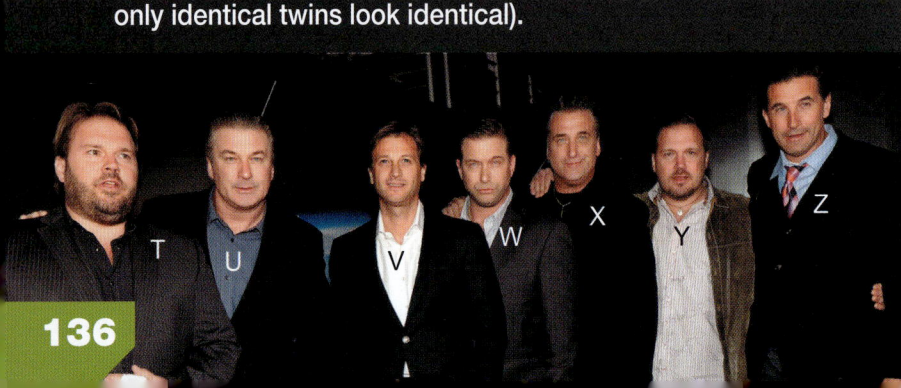

4. List the brothers in photo C.

5. Where in a gamete is genetic information stored?

6. List three of your characteristics caused by genetic information.

Inherited variation can also be continuous or discontinuous. One example of discontinuous inherited variation is blood group. Every person has one of four different blood groups, referred to as A, B, AB or O. Other examples of discontinuous inherited variation include having a dimpled chin and shoe size.

Examples of continuous inherited variation include human height and skin colour. However, like many characteristics, these can also be affected by environmental factors. For example, tall parents are likely to produce tall children but children can only grow tall if they eat a healthy diet.

7 Explain why foot length is an example of continuous variation but shoe size is discontinuous.

8 What factors affect how tall people grow?

9 Suggest a variation in tomatoes caused by both genetic information and environmental factors. Explain your reasoning.

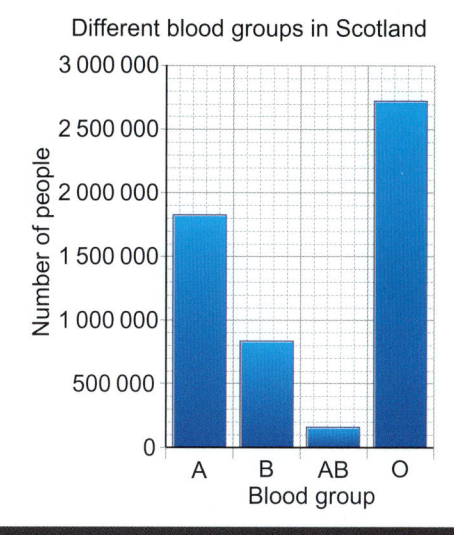

D | Data about discontinuous variation can be plotted on a bar chart, with gaps between the bars.

E | Height and skin colour are both affected by genetic information and environmental factors. Diet can affect height, and sunlight makes skin darker.

The measurements for a characteristic that shows continuous variation can be put into groups (as shown on the *x*-axis in graph F). Plotting a bar chart of this grouped data usually gives a 'bell shape'. We can make this more obvious if we join the tops of the bars with a smooth curve. This shape is known as a **normal distribution** (and is the shape we often see in characteristics that show continuous variation).

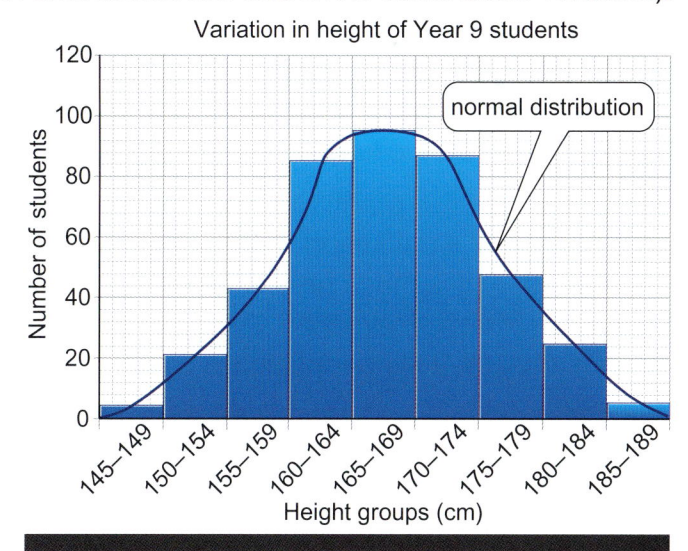

F | Data about continuous variation can be put into groups and then plotted on a bar chart without gaps between the bars.

10 a| State whether variation in each of the characteristics below is inherited, environmental or both, and whether each is continuous or discontinuous. Present your answer as a table.

natural eye colour	skin colour	having a scar	hair length	naturally curly hair
blood group	speaking Arabic	dimpled chin	wearing a watch	height

b| Suggest one characteristic you would expect to show a normal distribution.

I can ...
- identify different types of inherited variation
- explain how sexual reproduction causes inherited variation
- identify a normal distribution.

UK NC, CEE

9Ab PROBABILITY

HOW DO WE USE STATISTICS AND PROBABILITY?

Statistics is collecting, analysing and presenting data. We use statistics when we:

- collect data (e.g. using **samples** to **estimate** values)
- draw conclusions (e.g. finding **correlations** using scatter graphs or calculating averages)
- present findings (e.g. drawing graphs)
- make predictions.

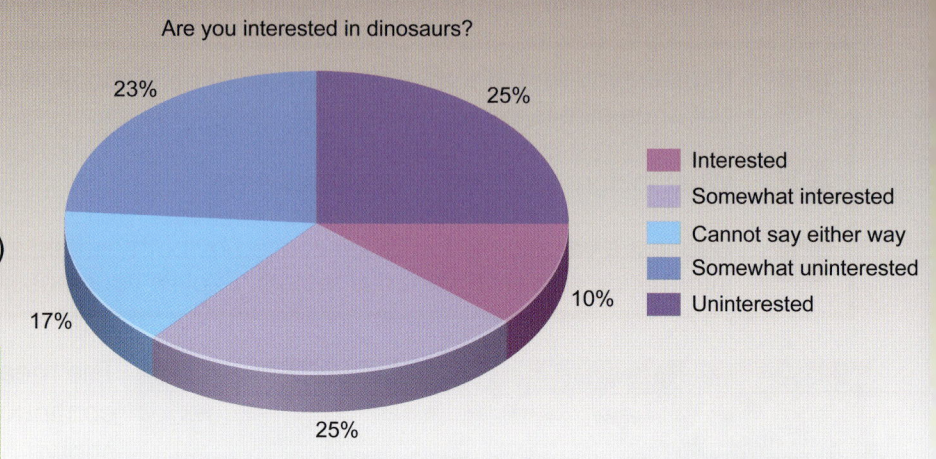

Are you interested in dinosaurs?

- 25% Interested
- 10% Somewhat interested
- 25% Cannot say either way
- 17% Somewhat uninterested
- 23% Uninterested

A | 13 867 people in Japan were asked how interested they were in dinosaurs. The findings could be used to decide whether to use dinosaurs in an advert.

1 What sort of chart is chart A?

2 The results from the survey in chart A have been converted into percentages. What is a percentage?

Using statistics

Clothing manufacturers collect measurements from people. They then draw conclusions by calculating averages and drawing graphs. For example, a company could use graph B to predict how many shirts with a certain sleeve length they are going to sell.

You could also use graph B to work out how likely it is that a shopper would need 95 cm long sleeves. You can see that there is a much greater chance of a shopper needing a 90 cm sleeve than a 95 cm sleeve. The chance of something happening is called its **probability**.

3 What is probability?

4 Look at graph B. Is a shopper picked at random more likely to need 84 cm sleeves or 94 cm sleeves?

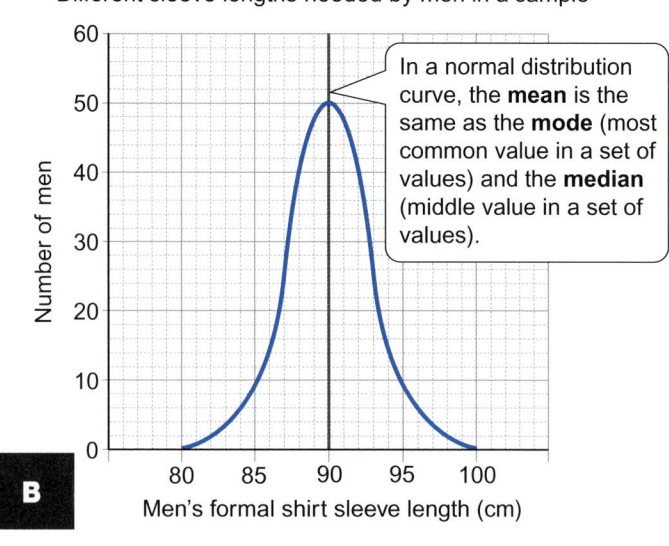

Different sleeve lengths needed by men in a sample

In a normal distribution curve, the **mean** is the same as the **mode** (most common value in a set of values) and the **median** (middle value in a set of values).

B Men's formal shirt sleeve length (cm)

Probabilities are often shown as percentages. This is how often a particular outcome occurs in every 100 times something happens. If you flipped a coin 100 times, and it landed on one side 52 times, the probability of it landing on this side was 52/100 or 52%. This is the experimental probability. We can show probability on a scale, such as diagram C. The probability of an impossible event is 0%. The probability of an event that is certain to happen is 100%.

WORKING SCIENTIFICALLY

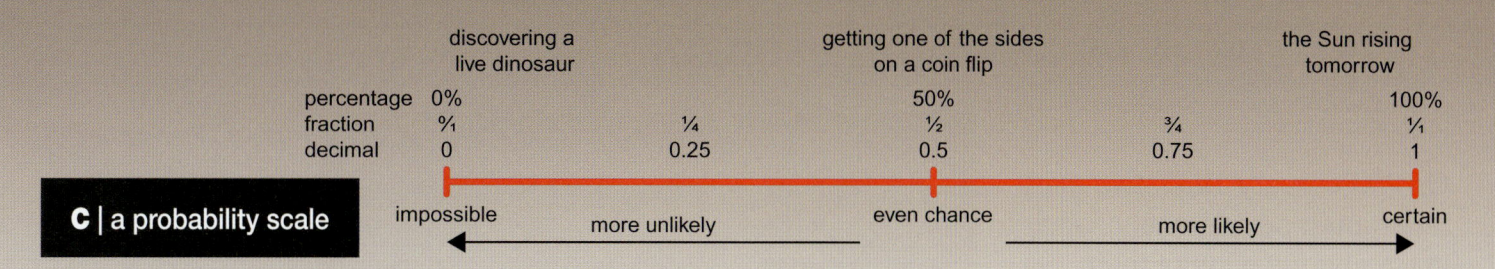

	discovering a live dinosaur		getting one of the sides on a coin flip		the Sun rising tomorrow
percentage	0%		50%		100%
fraction	0/1	¼	½	¾	1/1
decimal	0	0.25	0.5	0.75	1

C | a probability scale

impossible ← more unlikely — even chance — more likely → certain

Method

A | Throw two dice 100 times and each time add the two numbers to get a score.

B | Record the number of times you get each score in a tally chart.

C | Calculate the experimental probability of getting each of the 11 different possible numbers.

Probabilities can be given as decimals. To change a percentage to a decimal, write it as a fraction over 100 and then divide. For example, 52% = 52/100 = 0.52.

Probabilities can also be shown as fractions. For example, with the six-sided dice there is a 1/6 probability of rolling a '1' and a 5/6 probability of rolling 'not 1'.

If there is a 76% chance of rain, it means that if you had that period of time 100 times over, on 76 occasions it would rain in your area.

D | Weather apps show theoretical probabilities, worked out using computer models. A theoretical probability is what you would expect to happen.

Probability and inheritance

Some diseases and conditions are caused by the genetic information in our cells. People with one of these conditions may want to know the theoretical probability of passing it on to their children. An example is achondroplasia (*'ack-on-drO-**play**-zee-a'*). People with achondroplasia do not grow very tall (up to about 130 cm).

- If neither parent has achondroplasia, the theoretical probability of their child having it is 0.003%.
- If one parent has achondroplasia, the theoretical probability of a child having it is 50%.
- If both parents have achondroplasia, the theoretical probability of a child having it is 75%.

5 Carry out the instructions in the Method. Give your answers as percentages and decimals.

6 What is the theoretical probability, as a decimal, that a child will have achondroplasia if one parent has it?

7 What is the theoretical probability of throwing a number less than three with one dice? Give your answer as a fraction, a decimal and a percentage.

I can ...
- explain what probability is
- calculate probabilities and display them in different forms.

139

UK NC, CEE

9Ac DNA

HOW IS GENETIC INFORMATION STORED?

On 28 February 1953, two men interrupted people eating lunch in Cambridge. One of them announced: 'We have discovered the secret of life.' Their names were James Watson and Francis Crick. They had just made a cardboard model of a substance called **DNA**.

Watson and Crick used their own and other scientists' data to build their model. They showed their first attempt to Rosalind Franklin, who told them it was wrong.

Along with Maurice Wilkins, Rosalind Franklin had been taking photos of DNA using X-rays.

Rosalind Franklin (1920–1958)

Maurice Wilkins (1916–2004)

James Watson (born 1928)

Francis Crick (1916–2004)

A | Watson and Crick made a model of DNA, showing that it consists of two joined spiral strands – a 'double helix'. They used data from other scientists, including Maurice Wilkins and Rosalind Franklin.

Photo B is one of her photos, which Wilkins showed to Watson at the start of 1953. Although it looks like a blurry X, Watson knew that only spiral molecules could form this pattern. With this information, Watson and Crick finished their model. They published a paper about it in a journal called *Nature* on 25 April 1953. Wilkins and Franklin published their work in the same edition. Afterwards, Franklin worked on other things but Wilkins spent some years testing Watson and Crick's hypothesis, and making small corrections to their model.

> 1 Suggest how Watson and Crick were able to find other scientists' data.
>
> 2 Draw a table to show what each scientist in photo A did to help discover the structure of DNA.

Chromosomes

DNA is found in structures called **chromosomes** inside the nuclei of cells. Each chromosome contains one enormously long DNA molecule. Genetic information is stored in sections of a DNA molecule, called **genes**.

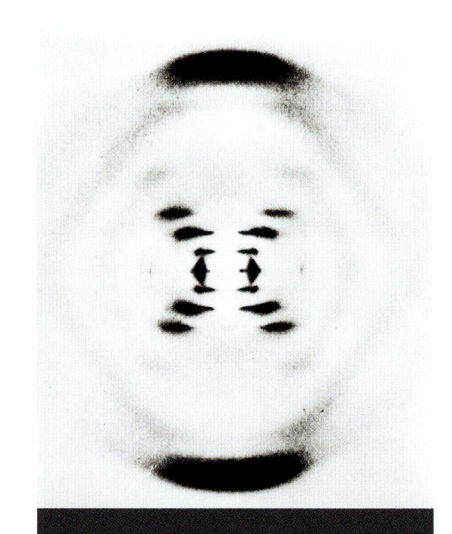

B | Rosalind Franklin's X-ray photo. Cross shapes are made by spiral molecules.

FACT

Your biggest chromosome contains 4316 genes. If stretched out, its DNA molecule would be 8.5 cm long.

Genes control inherited characteristics. A few characteristics (such as the ABO blood group) are controlled by one gene. Most characteristics are controlled by many genes.

A human cell nucleus contains 46 **chromosomes**, which contain **genes**.

Each chromosome contains a single molecule of DNA.

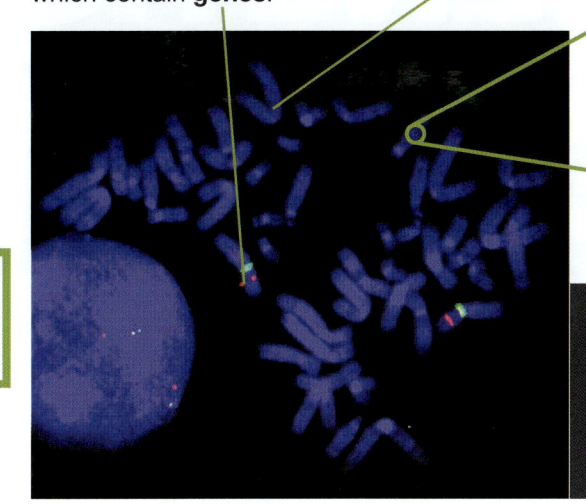

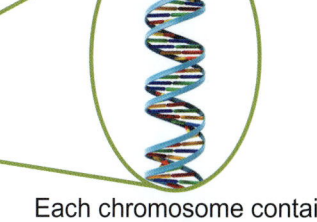

C | Two different genes on these chromosomes have been stained so that they glow (one green and one red).

3 Give two examples of characteristics controlled by genes.

Most of your cells contain 23 *pairs* of chromosomes (46 in all). Both chromosomes in a pair contain the same genes and are the same size, apart from the **sex chromosomes**. Girls have two X sex chromosomes, which are the same size. Boys have one X and one much smaller Y sex chromosome.

Unlike body cells, gametes only contain 23 chromosomes. When two gametes fuse, the resulting zygote has 46 chromosomes, as shown in diagram E. After a zygote has formed, **cell division** occurs over and over again, forming a ball of cells. Each of these cells contains identical copies of the same 46 chromosomes.

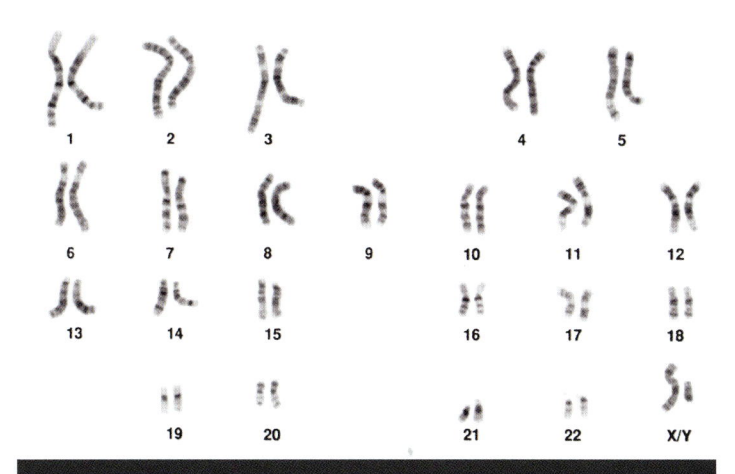

D | chromosome pairs (× 3000)

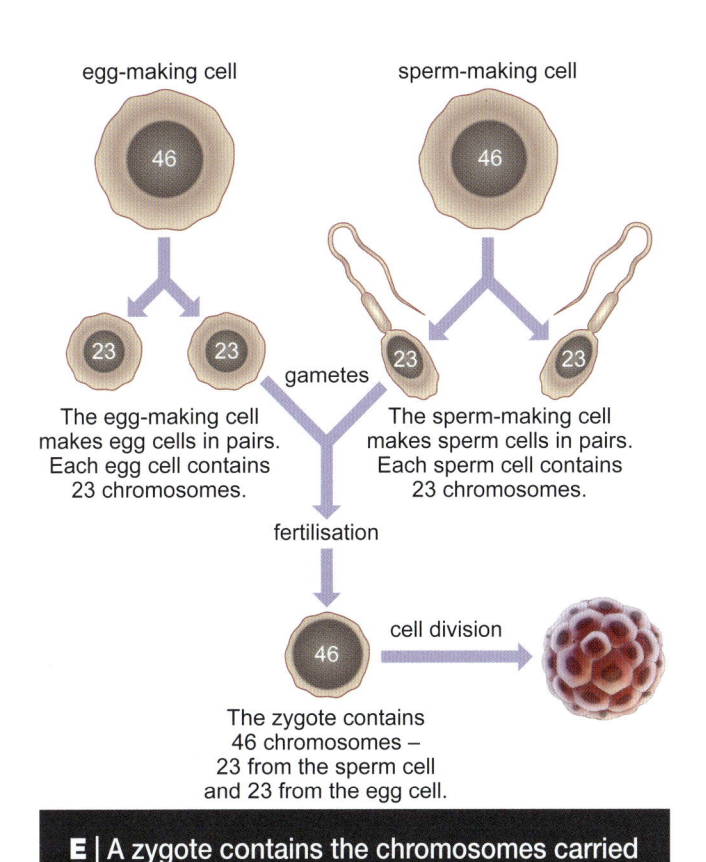

egg-making cell   sperm-making cell

46   46

23 23   23 23
gametes

The egg-making cell makes egg cells in pairs. Each egg cell contains 23 chromosomes.

The sperm-making cell makes sperm cells in pairs. Each sperm cell contains 23 chromosomes.

fertilisation

46   cell division

The zygote contains 46 chromosomes – 23 from the sperm cell and 23 from the egg cell.

E | A zygote contains the chromosomes carried in both the egg cell and the sperm cell.

4 What sex is the person whose chromosomes are shown in photo D? Explain your reasoning.

5 How many chromosomes does the nucleus of each of these cells contain:

a | sperm cell   b | heart muscle cell
c | egg-making cell   d | zygote?

6 a | Look at photo C. Two different genes have been stained so that they glow. How many copies of each gene are there?

b | Explain why there are this number of copies.

7 Draw a diagram to show how DNA, chromosomes, genetic information and genes are linked.

I can ...

- outline how the structure of DNA was discovered
- explain the importance of DNA
- describe the relationship between chromosomes, DNA, genes, genetic information and nuclei.

141

9Ac GENETIC COUNSELLING

HOW CAN SCIENCE AND TECHNOLOGY HELP PEOPLE WITH GENETIC DISEASES?

Each body cell contains two copies of each chromosome and so carries two copies of every gene. There are usually small differences between the two copies of a gene and sometimes these differences cause problems.

Most genes carry the instructions to make a protein. These instructions are given by a precise sequence of four substances in the DNA of a gene. The substances are represented by letters: A, T, G, C. Any slight change in the sequence can alter the protein, which can change a person's characteristics. Diagram A shows an example.

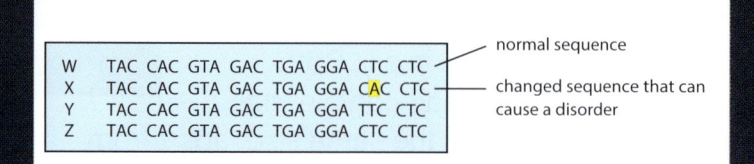

```
W   TAC CAC GTA GAC TGA GGA CTC CTC    — normal sequence
X   TAC CAC GTA GAC TGA GGA CAC CTC    — changed sequence that can
Y   TAC CAC GTA GAC TGA GGA TTC CTC      cause a disorder
Z   TAC CAC GTA GAC TGA GGA CTC CTC
```

A | These four DNA sequences are from genetic tests to find the A, T, G, C sequence in a haemoglobin gene in four people. Person W has the normal gene. Person X produces faulty haemoglobin (people with this sequence may have a painful disorder called sickle cell anaemia, in which red blood cells can stick together).

1 Give the total number of chromosomes found in a normal body cell.

2 Look at diagram A. Explain which sequences produce faulty haemoglobin.

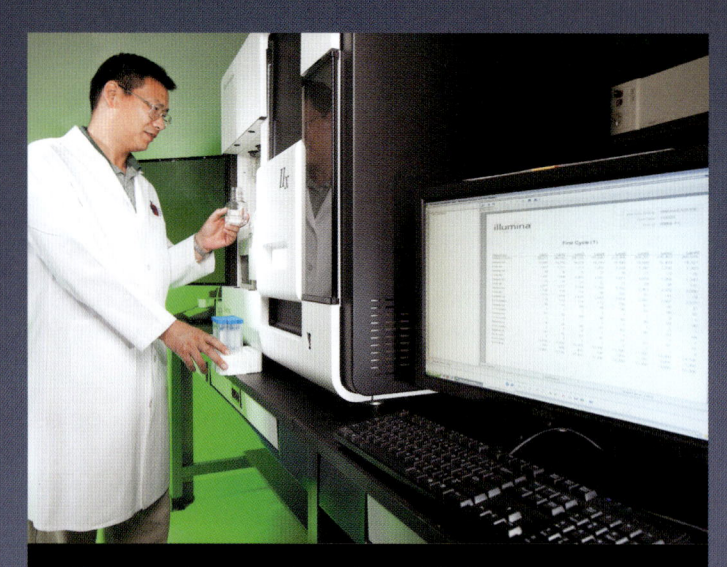

B | Technology, such as these 'DNA sequencers', find the DNA sequence of people's genes very quickly.

Each gene can exist in slightly different versions, caused by slight changes in the sequence of A, T, G and C in its DNA. Some versions of a gene cause genetic disorders – problems that may need medical treatment.

Some disorders affect people all their lives, others only affect people as they get older. Some people 'carry' changes in their chromosomes or genes that do not affect them but may affect their children.

Help and advice

A genetic counsellor organises tests for people to see if their cells contain versions of genes that may cause problems. They interpret the test results and advise people on how a genetic disorder may affect their lives and how to cope.

STEM

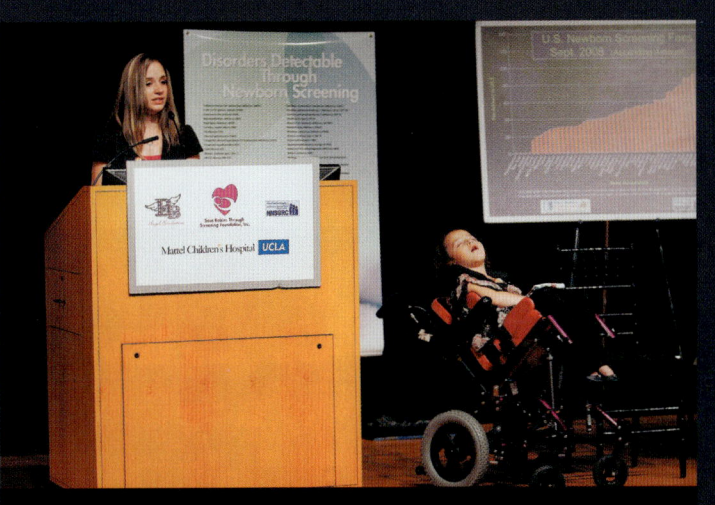

Genetic counsellors are not medical doctors. They usually do a university degree in biology and then a masters degree in genetic counselling, together with training on how to talk to people and ask appropriate questions. Genetic counsellors need to be clear communicators and explain complex ideas in simple ways.

They also need to be able to apply their knowledge of what chromosomes and genes look like, so that they can spot things that do not fit a normal pattern.

C | This woman is explaining the benefits of genetic tests for newborn babies. Her daughter has GA1, a disorder in which certain substances collect in her body and damage her tissues. Early treatment means that less damage is caused.

3 Suggest why genetic tests on babies are becoming more common.

4 Suggest why couples who want to start a family may see a genetic counsellor.

5 A test report reads: "The patient has one copy of the ε4 variant of the APOE gene. The probability of developing Alzheimer's disease before the age of 85 is 20% (compared with 13% for the general population)." How would you explain this simply to the patient?

ACTIVITY

Photo D shows the results of a genetic test to look at a person's chromosomes.

1 Use your knowledge of chromosomes to identify what is unusual about the person.

2 This person does not suffer any problems. However, a woman with chromosomes like this has a 10% chance of having a baby with Down's syndrome. There is no increased risk of a baby with Down's syndrome if the man has these chromosomes.

   a Find out the effects of Down's syndrome.

   b You are the genetic counsellor for the person with the chromosomes shown in photo D. The person tells you they want to start a family. Write down what you would say.

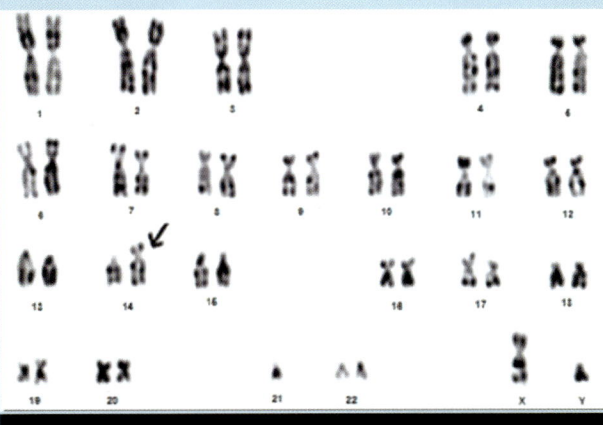

D | Chromosomes can appear as X-shapes as well as I-shapes.

9Ad GENES AND EXTINCTION

HOW CAN GENETIC INFORMATION CAUSE EXTINCTION?

Around 65 million years ago, 75% of the Earth's species became extinct, including the dinosaurs. Many scientists think that a giant meteorite hit the Earth, throwing so much dust into the atmosphere that it blocked out the sunlight. Evidence for this includes the remains of a 180 km wide crater near Mexico, which was formed at this time.

> **1**
> a| State one physical environmental factor that the meteorite changed in habitats on Earth.
>
> b| Explain the effect this may have had on animal populations.

A | The meteorite impact 65 million years ago released more energy than a million nuclear bombs.

The **adaptations** of an organism are due to its genes. Changes in an **ecosystem** can affect species in an area because they may no longer be so well adapted to the new conditions. The organisms can become **endangered** or even **extinct**.

This includes changes in abiotic factors, such as rainfall. It also includes changes in biotic factors, such as competition from other organisms, disease and human activities (e.g. hunting, clearing habitats, using poisons).

B | Thylacines were killed in Tasmania to protect sheep. The last one died in 1936.

Competition

Grey squirrels were brought to the UK from the USA in the 1870s and now the red squirrels that are **native** to the UK are rare. One inherited variation between the species is that greys store more fat in their bodies. So, if there is little food during a long winter, greys are more likely to survive. Greys are better adapted than reds.

In woodland, greys and reds are in **competition** for food. Greys can digest unripe acorns but reds cannot. So, greys eat the acorns before the reds, meaning the reds get less food. When food is limited, more of the better-fed greys survive and reproduce. Grey squirrel populations then increase faster, leaving even less food for reds.

C | The Hawaiian silversword plant became endangered because goats, which were introduced by humans, ate it. Strict protection, introduced in 1992, saved it from extinction.

Grey squirrels also carry squirrel pox. This disease does not affect greys but it kills reds.

grey squirrel
- eyes on side of head for good all-round vision, to spot predators
- long, bushy tail for balance
- long, strong hind legs for leaping
- sharp claws for gripping tree trunks

red squirrel

D | Red and grey squirrels share many adaptations but greys are bigger than reds.

2 How are squirrels adapted for:
a | climbing trees
b | balancing on branches?

3 a | Why might a squirrel population decrease during a long winter?
b | How are grey squirrels better adapted to long winters than reds?
c | Explain how genes are responsible for this.

4 Why have red squirrels disappeared from most of the UK?

5 Conifer trees have smaller seeds and thinner, more flexible branches than trees with broad leaves. Suggest why red squirrels may be better adapted to conifer forests than greys.

Preserving biodiversity

We lose the opportunity to make use of species that become extinct. Extinctions also upset ecosystems and change **food webs**. So, we need to preserve the **biodiversity** (number of different species) on Earth.

Ways of doing this include banning the hunting of certain animals, setting up nature reserves and starting breeding programmes. We can also store parts of organisms (e.g. seeds, gametes) that can be used to produce the organisms again if they become extinct. These materials are stored at low temperatures in **gene banks**.

FACT

This 'frozen zoo' contains gametes from 9000 species of animals.

E

6 Red squirrels died out in some parts of the UK in the 1980s. There are plans to reintroduce them. What could be done to help the reintroduced red squirrels to survive?

7 Suggest one reason for saving the silversword plant.

8 Predict an effect of global warming on the population of polar bears. Explain your reasoning.

9 Explain how a gene bank can allow a plant species to survive if it becomes extinct in the wild.

I can ...
- explain how organisms become endangered or extinct
- explain how adaptations affect the survival of organisms
- explain some ways of preserving biodiversity

9Ae NATURAL SELECTION

WHAT IS DARWIN'S THEORY OF EVOLUTION?

Photo A shows inherited variation in peppered moths. The speckle pattern varies and some moths have genes that make them black.

> **1** What causes inherited variation?

In the 1850s most peppered moths around Manchester in the UK were pale. By 1895, 98% of them were black. During this time many factories were built. These produced huge amounts of soot, turning buildings and trees black. Birds could easily spot the pale moths on the blackened buildings and trees, and so more pale ones were eaten. The black moths were harder to spot and so more of them survived and reproduced, and their numbers increased.

This is an example of **natural selection** caused by a change in the environment. The environment is 'selecting' certain genetic variations in characteristics, which are passed on to the next generation.

A | The pale peppered moth is hard to spot on the trunk of a tree but is easy to spot on a black background. The opposite is true for the black peppered moth.

> **2** a| Explain why black peppered moths survived better around Manchester than pale ones at the end of the 19th century.
>
> b| Use the term 'genes' to explain why the number of black moths gradually increased.
>
> **3** a| Manchester now has many fewer factories. Predict how the number of black moths has changed.
>
> b| Use the idea of natural selection to explain your prediction.

Salty seas

The shoreline in photo B is not made of sand … but the bones of millions of fish. The Salton Sea in California was originally full of fresh water, but got more and more salty. This caused most of the fish species to die out.

B | The Salton Sea formed between 1905 and 1907 when a river flooded a low-lying area. The sea is 25% more salty than the Pacific Ocean, which has killed most of the fish.

The only fish still living in the Salton Sea are of a species called tilapia. They are usually found in fresh or slightly salty water. If tilapia from a freshwater lake are put into water from the Salton Sea, they die. The tilapia in the Salton Sea have become better adapted to more salty water.

This gradual change in an adaptation is due to natural selection. When the Salton Sea started getting salty, by chance some tilapia had genetic variations that allowed them to cope better with the salt. More of these fish survived than those that could not cope so well with the salt. So, more of the 'salt-tolerant' fish reproduced, and the next generation of tilapia therefore contained more of the 'salt-tolerant' fish. As the sea got saltier, this process happened over and over again. Today all the Salton Sea tilapia fish can cope with very salty water.

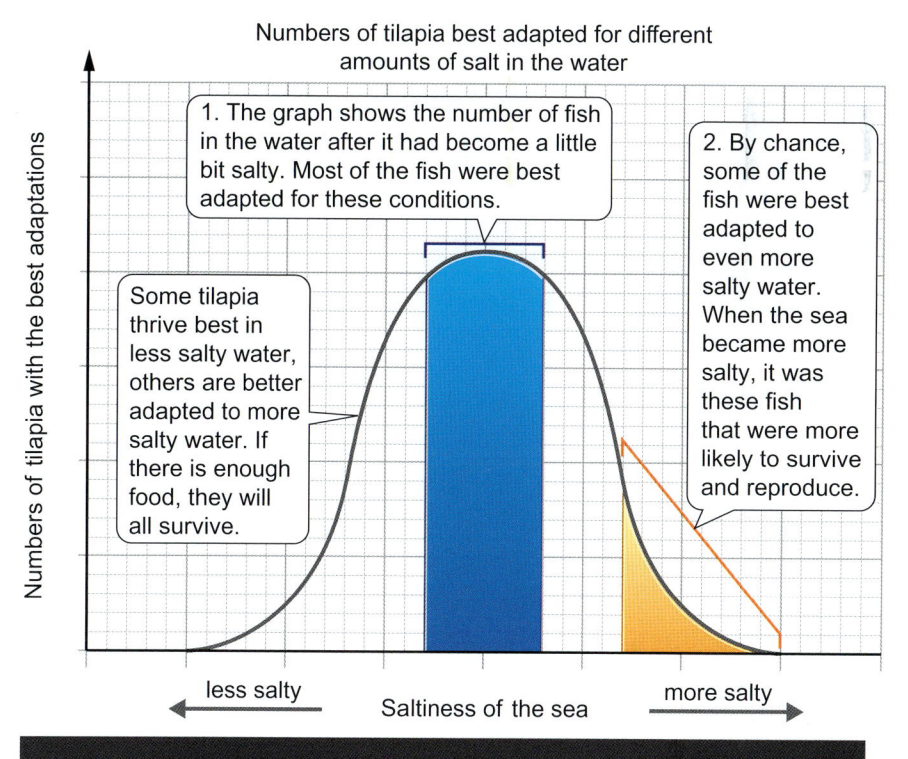

Numbers of tilapia best adapted for different amounts of salt in the water

1. The graph shows the number of fish in the water after it had become a little bit salty. Most of the fish were best adapted for these conditions.

2. By chance, some of the fish were best adapted to even more salty water. When the sea became more salty, it was these fish that were more likely to survive and reproduce.

Some tilapia thrive best in less salty water, others are better adapted to more salty water. If there is enough food, they will all survive.

C | Environmental change often causes natural selection.

4
a| What characteristic has been 'naturally selected' in fish in the Salton Sea?
b| How has this selection occurred?

Evolution

A change over time in the characteristics of organisms is known as **evolution**. Charles Darwin (1809–1882) and Alfred Russel Wallace (1823–1913) both developed a hypothesis that natural selection causes evolution. This is now usually called 'Darwin's theory of evolution'.

Darwin's theory says that as natural selection occurs, a population can evolve into a new species. Many scientists now think that some dinosaurs evolved into birds over millions and millions of years.

5
a| What is a hypothesis?
b| How does a hypothesis become a theory?

6 What is evolution?

7 Explain how natural selection can produce a new species if two populations of the same organism become separated. (*Hint:* Think about the definition of a species.)

D | Microraptor was a dinosaur with feathers and four wings. Microraptor fossils are 125–120 million years old.

I can ...
- recall that individuals in a population vary genetically
- explain how natural selection works on these variations

147

9Ae RECREATING ANIMALS

CAN WE BRING EXTINCT ANIMALS BACK TO LIFE?

Woolly mammoths became extinct about 4000 years ago, probably due to hunting by humans and the Earth getting warmer. We know that they were hunted because spear marks have been found in mammoth remains. We also know that the Earth started getting warmer about 10 000 years ago. Scientists think that as this happened the plants that mammoths ate could only be found further and further north, and so the mammoths' habitat got smaller and smaller.

A | The largest mammoths were about 4 m tall with a mass of about 8 tonnes.

- large size (larger objects transfer energy to their surroundings less quickly, keeping them warmer)
- thick, oily hair to keep it warm
- tusks help to push snow out of the way to find food
- large feet to stop it sinking into the snow

B | remains of a baby woolly mammoth discovered in ice in northern Russia

Many scientists think that woolly mammoths and elephants evolved from one species, about 6 million years ago. Elephants evolved to cope with hot conditions (such as having large ears to cool their blood) and mammoths evolved to cope with the cold.

DNA can be found in frozen mammoth remains. Some scientists think we could use this to recreate a mammoth, using a process called cloning. This could help us to better understand how current global warming might affect endangered species. However, a 'cloned mammoth' may not behave in a natural way, so the experiment may not be valid. It is unlikely we could clone dinosaurs because their DNA will have decomposed after 65 million years.

1. What environmental variation has been found in mammoth remains?
2. Give two examples of inherited variation between elephants and mammoths.
3. Woolly mammoths had 58 chromosomes.
   a | What long molecule do chromosomes contain?
   b | How many chromosomes would a mammoth sperm cell have?
   c | What sections of chromosomes contain instructions for a cell?
4. a | Explain how mammoths were adapted to their habitat.
   b | How might their adaptations have limited them to only living in certain areas of the world?
5. Suggest how mammoths may have evolved their hair, when the species they evolved from had very little hair.

HAVE YOUR SAY

Should we recreate mammoths using cloning? Write an argument for or against.

9Ba ON A FARM

Farmers use **criteria** to decide whether it is worthwhile to farm in a certain way. Criteria are a set of standards used to judge things. Some criteria that a farmer may use are:

- the amount of profit
- the harm done to the environment
- the effect on family life.

The costs of growing crops include seeds, machinery, fertiliser, pesticides, diesel and wages for workers. A farmer then needs to know how much the crop can be sold for. The values of crops go up and down, so the farmer may not be sure how much the crop will be worth when it is ready to be sold.

Some farmers try to avoid harming the environment by using very few chemicals. This is known as **organic farming**. Organic foods are often expensive to produce and so cost more in the shops.

A | Wheat covers the greatest area of farmed land. It is used for foods, animal feed and to make biofuels.

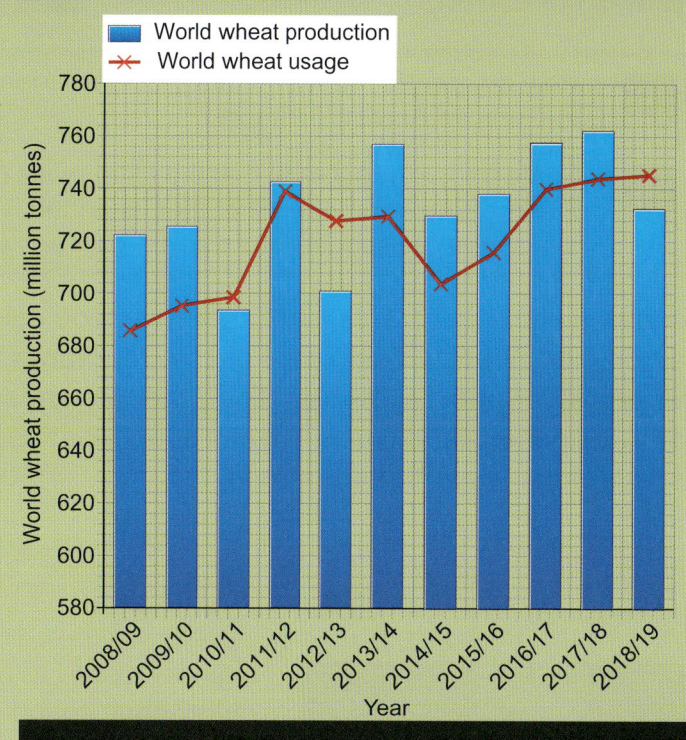

B | world wheat production and usage

C | Organic farming can be labour intensive. This farmer is removing weeds from his potato crop. The yellow flowers belong to mustard plants. They attract an insect pest called wireworm away from the potato plants.

1. a | What process do wheat plants use to make their own food?
   b | Suggest the name of a carbohydrate that wheat plants store in their seeds.
   c | Explain the effect of a lot of cloudy weather during a year on the amount of wheat that is harvested.

2. Look at graph B. Suggest one year in which the price of wheat was high. Explain your reasoning.

3. Why do farmers use fertilisers on their crops?

4. Explain why the farmer in photo C needs to plant mustard to protect his potatoes.

9Ba REACTIONS IN PLANTS

UK NC, iLS, CEE

WHAT CHEMICAL REACTIONS HAPPEN IN PLANTS?

The Greek scientist Aristotle (384–322 BCE) thought that roots sucked up soil for plants to eat. Belgian scientist Jan Baptista van Helmont (1580–1644) did the experiment in diagram A and showed that this was not correct.

A | Van Helmont planted a small tree and gave it only water, as he watched it grow for 5 years. He measured the masses of the pot, soil and the tree before and after the 5-year period.

willow tree (mass = 76.74 kg)

small willow tree (mass = 2.27 kg)

5 years watered regularly

mass of pot + dry soil = 90.72 kg

mass of pot + dry soil = 90.66 kg

> **1** How do van Helmont's results provide evidence to disprove Aristotle's theory?
>
> **2** Some people suggested that the extra mass of the tree came from the water that he added. Was this a sensible suggestion? Explain your answer.

Today we know that plants make their own food using carbon dioxide and water. These are the **reactants (raw materials)** for **photosynthesis**. The **products** are a sugar, called **glucose**, and oxygen. We can show what happens using word and **symbol equations**.

carbon dioxide + water → glucose + oxygen

$6CO_2 + 6H_2O \rightarrow C_6H_{12}O_6 + 6O_2$

Light is needed to make photosynthesis happen. A substance called **chlorophyll**, found inside **chloroplasts** in many plant cells, captures the energy transferred by light. This energy then becomes stored in the glucose.

Photosynthesis can occur at different **rates** (speeds). With less light, or a shortage of a raw material, photosynthesis is slower. A variable that slows down the rate is a **limiting factor**.

B | bubbles of oxygen being produced by an aquatic plant

> **3** List the reactants in photosynthesis.
>
> **4** Where in a plant cell does photosynthesis occur?
>
> **5** Why do plants in a field only photosynthesise during the day?
>
> **6** Draw a flow chart to show how energy from the Sun becomes stored in a plant.
>
> **7** The faster Canadian pondweed photosynthesises, the more oxygen bubbles it produces. Explain how three different limiting factors can prevent the number of bubbles increasing.

Aerobic respiration

Every living cell in a plant needs a supply of glucose for energy. Energy is needed to help the plant grow and to make new substances. The chemical energy stored in the glucose is released by **aerobic respiration** (which is the opposite of photosynthesis):

glucose + oxygen → carbon dioxide + water (+ energy)

$C_6H_{12}O_6 + 6O_2 \rightarrow 6CO_2 + 6H_2O$ (+ energy)

The energy released from glucose is transferred to molecules of ATP, which store energy for a cell until it is needed.

Photosynthesis only happens when there is light but respiration happens *all* the time. During the day, a plant produces more oxygen from photosynthesis than it needs for respiration and so oxygen is given off.

Glucose is carried to all parts of a plant in the form of sugars dissolved in water. **Phloem vessels**, which are made from chains of living phloem cells, carry the sugar solution. This is how roots get glucose for respiration. They also need oxygen, which they get from the soil. If soil becomes flooded or waterlogged, roots cannot get enough oxygen and so the plant can die.

D | cross-section through a leaf (showing green chloroplasts in cells that photosynthesise, xylem and phloem vessels)

8 What is the test for carbon dioxide?

9 Graph C shows the levels of oxygen and carbon dioxide in the water around a pondweed plant.

C How the concentrations of two gases dissolved in water vary over 18 hours in a beaker containing pondweed

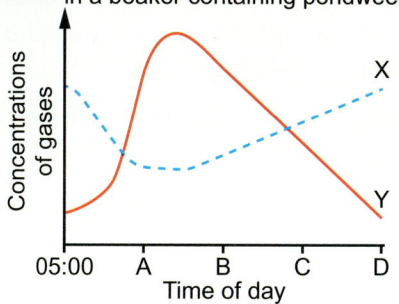

a | Which letter (A–D) do you think represents a time of 23:00?

b | Which line shows the oxygen concentration, X or Y?

c | Explain why line X goes up between letters B and D.

FACT

E

Mangrove plants are adapted to living in waterlogged areas by having special roots (pneumatophores) that poke up above the surface of the water to get air.

10 Why do root cells need oxygen?

11 Why is flooding of fields a problem for growing crops?

I can ...

- explain what happens when plants photosynthesise and respire
- explain how the rate of photosynthesis can be affected.

9Bb PLANT ADAPTATIONS

HOW ARE PLANTS ADAPTED FOR GETTING WHAT THEY NEED?

Roots hold plants in place and absorb water (containing dissolved **mineral salts**). Plants need chemical elements from mineral salts to stay healthy. For example:

- nitrogen from nitrate salts is needed to make proteins
- magnesium is needed to make chlorophyll
- plant root cells need potassium to be able to absorb water properly.

The other elements that plants need are carbon, oxygen and hydrogen. These are all supplied by water from the ground and carbon dioxide and oxygen from the air.

Water

Roots are **adapted** to their function by being branched and spread out, helping them to get water from a large volume of soil. They also have **root hair cells** to give them a large **surface area** so they can quickly absorb water.

FACT
One rye grass plant can grow roots with a total length of over 600 km in about 4 months.

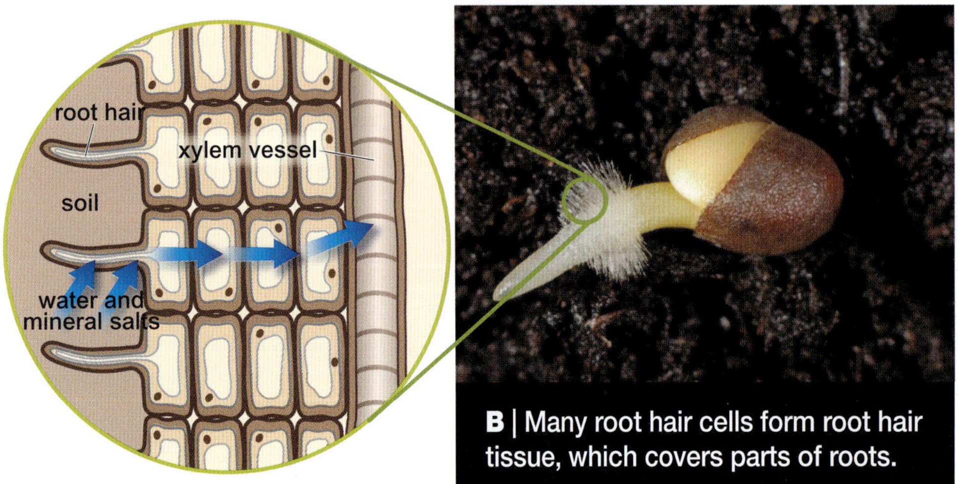

A | Venus flytraps live in soils that are low in mineral salts. They have leaves with specialised cells that form 'trigger hairs'. If an insect touches a hair more than once, a signal is sent to cells in the 'hinge'. These cells change shape and the trap shuts. Enzymes then digest the insect, releasing mineral salts.

1
a| Suggest why a Venus flytrap hair needs to be touched more than once.
b| State the source of potassium for a Venus flytrap.
c| Why might it die without this source?

Once absorbed, water passes to **xylem vessels** in the centre of the root. These long tubes are formed when chains of xylem cells become hollow, as they die. The tubes carry water and dissolved mineral salts to the leaves.

Water is needed for many reasons, such as photosynthesis, keeping leaves cool, and filling up cells to keep them expanded and firm. If there is too little water, the cells sag and the plant droops – it **wilts**.

B | Many root hair cells form root hair tissue, which covers parts of roots.

2. Describe the route that water takes from the soil to a leaf.
3. How are the following cells adapted for their functions:
   a) xylem cells   b) root hair cells?

C | In this radial arrangement of leaves the upper ones do not shade the lower ones much.

Carbon dioxide

Stomata are small holes in a leaf that are opened and closed by **guard cells**. Stomata are shut at night and open when it is light. Gases, such as carbon dioxide, enter and leave the leaf by **diffusion** through open stomata. Leaves are thin, so the carbon dioxide does not have to diffuse very far into a leaf before getting to cells. Plants also lose water and oxygen through stomata. This swapping of different gases is **gas exchange**.

Diffusion is faster at higher temperatures and so gas exchange is faster (including loss of water). Diffusion is also faster when there is a greater difference between the concentration of a gas inside and outside of a leaf.

E | a stoma (× 2500)

Light

The leaves of many plants are broad (wide) and have a large surface area for trapping light. They are often arranged on a plant so that the upper leaves do not shade the lower ones too much.

Inside a leaf, there are different layers of tissue. **Epidermis cells** produce a waxy layer (**cuticle**) to stop the leaves losing too much water. **Palisade cells** are adapted to their function by containing lots of chloroplasts (where photosynthesis occurs). The chloroplasts move nearer to the surface of the leaf in dim light. They move in the opposite direction in bright light to stop them being damaged.

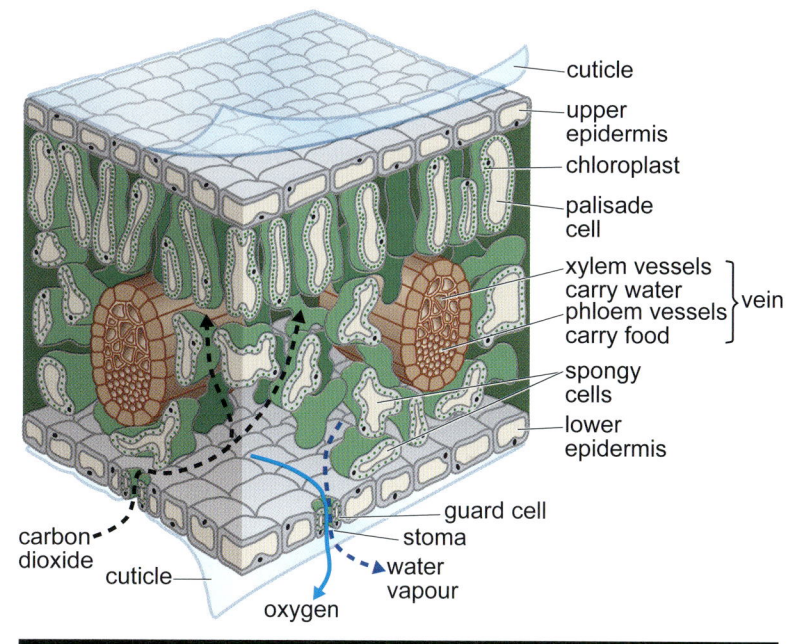

D | inside a leaf

4. In which cells, in diagram D, will no photosynthesis occur?
5. Why do you think stomata shut at night?
6. What cells control gas exchange?
7. Describe how a leaf is adapted to allow palisade cells to get all the resources they need.

I can ...
- describe how leaves, roots and stems are adapted for their functions
- explain how substances enter and leave plants.

153

9Bc PLANT PRODUCTS

UK NC, CEE

WHY DO PLANTS MAKE LIPIDS, CARBOHYDRATES AND PROTEINS?

Most life on Earth depends on photosynthetic organisms. They help maintain the balance of carbon dioxide and oxygen in the atmosphere, and they produce substances that other organisms use for energy and growth. All the substances found in a plant depend on the glucose from photosynthesis for their production.

Carbohydrates

The glucose molecules made in photosynthesis can be linked together to form a **polymer** called **starch**. This molecule stays in the chloroplasts until photosynthesis stops. The starch is then broken down into small sugar molecules and transported to **phloem vessels** (see page 151), in which they are carried to other parts of the plant.

> 1 When is starch broken down in chloroplasts, during the day or night? Explain your reasoning.

In some plants, these sugars are converted back into starch in storage organs, such as potatoes, or seeds. The sugars are also used to make another polymer called **cellulose**, which is used to make plant cell walls.

You can test for starch by using iodine solution. This turns the starch a blue-black colour, as shown in photo B.

Lipids

Plants make many different **lipids**. These are a group of insoluble substances that include **fats** and **oils**.

The cuticle of a plant leaf contains lipids to make it waterproof. Plants also use lipids to make parts of cells, for example cell membranes. Fats and oils are often found in plant seeds, where they are used as energy stores. They can also be found in the flesh of some fruits, such as avocado, to encourage animals to eat the fruits and so disperse the seeds.

> 5 What substance must plants produce in order to make lipids?
>
> 6 Give one use that humans have for plant lipids.

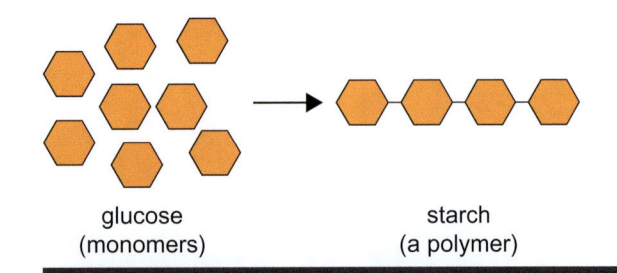

glucose (monomers) → starch (a polymer)

A | The monomer used to make starch is glucose.

The leaf is treated to remove all the chlorophyll and then iodine solution is added.

B | A variegated leaf (it has areas of white) being tested with iodine solution.

> 2 What would happen if you added iodine solution to potato chips? Explain your reasoning.
>
> 3 Explain the results of the test shown in photo B.
>
> 4 Why do seeds need starch?

C | Rapeseed (or canola) has yellow flowers and is grown to produce oil (e.g. for cooking). Mobile beehives may be brought in to help pollination and so increase the number of seeds formed.

Proteins

Proteins are another a type of polymer. They are long chains of molecules called **amino acids** (of which there are many different kinds). However, to make amino acids a plant needs a good supply of nitrogen from mineral salts called **nitrates**.

Proteins have many functions. All enzymes are proteins, such as those needed for photosynthesis and respiration. Seeds also contain a store of protein to supply amino acids to make new proteins as a seedling starts to grow.

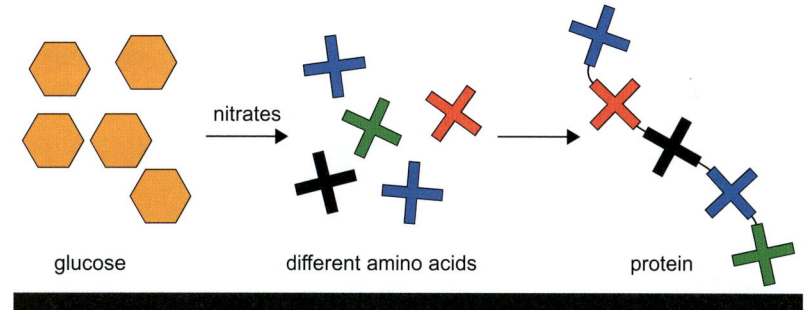

D | proteins are chains of amino acids

glucose   different amino acids   protein

7 Give two uses for each of lipids, carbohydrates and proteins in plants.

8 Why do plants not grow well if there is a lack of nitrates in the soil?

Seeds

Seeds contain a store of all the resources that a new seedling will need to grow, until its leaves can open and start to photosynthesise. Diagram E shows what happens during **germination**.

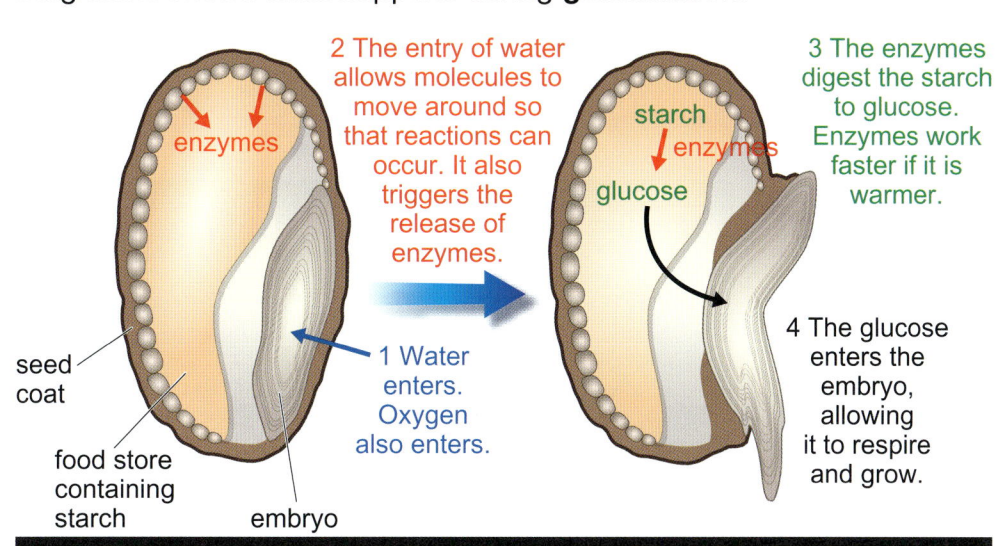

E | processes that occur during germination

1. Water enters. Oxygen also enters.
2. The entry of water allows molecules to move around so that reactions can occur. It also triggers the release of enzymes.
3. The enzymes digest the starch to glucose. Enzymes work faster if it is warmer.
4. The glucose enters the embryo, allowing it to respire and grow.

FACT

Just five seeds from the castor oil plant can be enough to kill an adult human. The seeds contain a protein called ricin, one of the most poisonous natural substances.

9 What are the enzymes in diagram E made out of?

10 List three substances you would expect to find in a seed and explain the function of each.

You can test for the glucose produced in a seed using Benedict's reagent. This is a blue solution, which turns orange and red when heated with glucose.

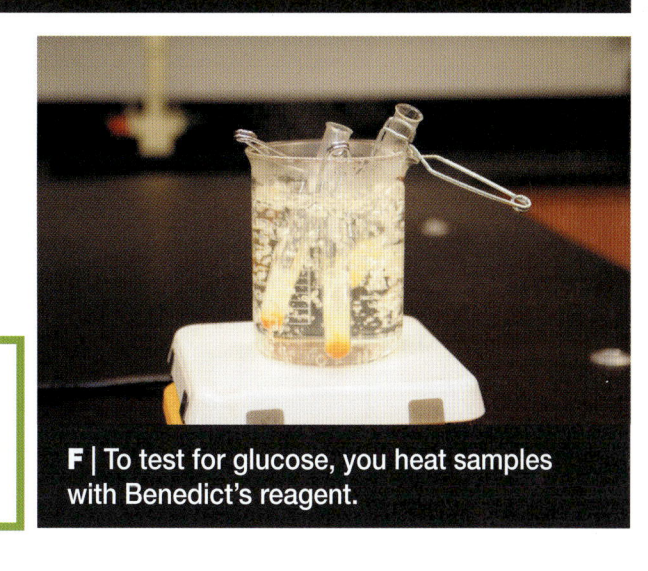

F | To test for glucose, you heat samples with Benedict's reagent.

11 Explain whether the samples in photo F contain glucose.

I can ...
- explain how and why plants make different substances
- explain the importance of nitrates.

9Bd GROWING CROPS

HOW DO FARMERS MAKE SURE THEIR CROPS GROW WELL?

UK NC, iLS, CEE

Farmers want to get as much useful product (**yield**) from their crops and land as possible.

Forests are cut down to make farmland. Hedgerows are removed to create more space for big machines. Machines can plant and harvest crops faster than humans. Greenhouses can also be used to make sure that plants have the best conditions for growth and protect crops from changes in abiotic factors (e.g. temperature, wind, rain).

Fertilisers

Fertilisers contain mineral salts that help plant growth, such as potassium, phosphates and nitrates. Farmers use cheap artificial fertilisers and natural ones such as manure (animal waste). Microorganisms, called **decomposers**, break down manure and release the mineral salts, but this can take a long time.

A | The maize at the top was grown in soil that lacks phosphates. The maize at the bottom was grown in the same conditions and for the same amount of time but with phosphate fertiliser added.

> **1** Describe the effect of too little phosphate.
>
> **2** a| Write down two other mineral salts that plants need.
> b| Why do plants need these?

Pesticides

Pesticides kill **pests** (organisms that damage crops). **Insecticides** kill insect pests. **Fungicides** kill fungi that cause plant diseases.

Herbicides (**weedkillers**) kill weeds, which **compete** with the crop plants for water, light and mineral salts. The size of a crop and its yield are reduced by competition from weed growth. Modern herbicides are **selective**; they kill weed plants with broad leaves but not crop plants with narrow leaves (such as wheat).

B | A blocked sprayer nozzle has meant that a selective herbicide has not been applied to all of this field.

> **3** In low-income countries, families grow their own crops. Explain the effect an increase in the following will have on their food supply.
> a| number of people in a family
> b| number of pests
>
> **4** a| Suggest why a farmer might want to use a selective herbicide.
> b| Suggest why farmers in low-income countries may not use selective herbicides.

Varieties

A **variety** is a group of plants that have been bred to have certain characteristics. Some differences between varieties are not easy to see. For example, the modern wheat variety in photo C is much less likely to get a disease called 'rust' than the old variety.

Different varieties are sometimes bred with each other to produce offspring that hopefully have the characteristics of both breeds. This is **cross-breeding** and is one way of creating a new variety.

Wheat variety grown widely today

Wheat variety from the 1950s

C | wheat varieties

D | Cross-breeding could be used to remove the bitter taste from this apple variety but keep its red flesh.

5. a) Why would the apples in photo D not be sold in shops?

   b) What could be done to make a red-fleshed apple that could be sold?

6. Look at photo C. Suggest two reasons why the 1950s variety of wheat is not grown today.

New varieties are also created using **selective breeding**. This is when only plants with certain characteristics are used to breed. For example, a breeder may want to produce a variety of wheat that is short, so the wind is less likely to blow it over. Two short parent plants are bred. Then only the shortest offspring are selected and used to breed the next generation. In the next generation only the shortest plants are selected and bred. This process is repeated and repeated, and over many generations a new variety of short wheat is produced.

E | wild carrots (on the left) and a modern variety

FACT

Orange carrots were selectively bred in the Netherlands in the 1500s. Some people think that this was to show support for William of Orange (who was fighting for Dutch independence) but it is more likely that it was to make carrots less bitter.

7. Describe how wild carrots would have been selectively bred to produce the variety we grow today.

8. Farms in the UK today produce 35% more food per m^2 than they did in 1973. Explain how.

I can ...

- describe how pests and human populations alter the food supply
- explain ways in which farmers boost food production
- explain some ways in which plant varieties are created.

9Bd PROTECTING WILD PLANTS

HOW CAN HUMANS' NEED FOR FOOD BE BALANCED WITH THE NEEDS OF WILD PLANTS?

Many plants and animals are found in particular areas of the world and nowhere else. They are well adapted to their environment. We say these species are **endemic** to the area.

Human activities, such as farming, tourism and building are using more land. This changes the environment and reduces the space for other plants and animals that live there.

A | The dragon's blood tree is endemic to the islands of Socotra, near Yemen.

Ecological audits

Plant ecologists have a university degree in plant science or environmental sciences. They are often asked to carry out ecological audits, during which they carefully study the plants in the area. They identify the different species, assess how rare they are, and how likely they are to be damaged by human activities.

Different types of communication are important for plant ecologists. They must write detailed records in a very clear and logical way, to communicate their findings about the plants in an area. Their records may be used to prepare field guides to help others identify the plants.

Their records may also be used by the IUCN (International Union for Conservation of Nature) in their database of organisms called the Red List, which shows how rare or at risk a species is. Information in field guides and websites must be well organised so that it is easy to find.

1. How can farming harm wild plants?
2. What is an endemic species?
3. Why are endemic plants most at risk from human activities?

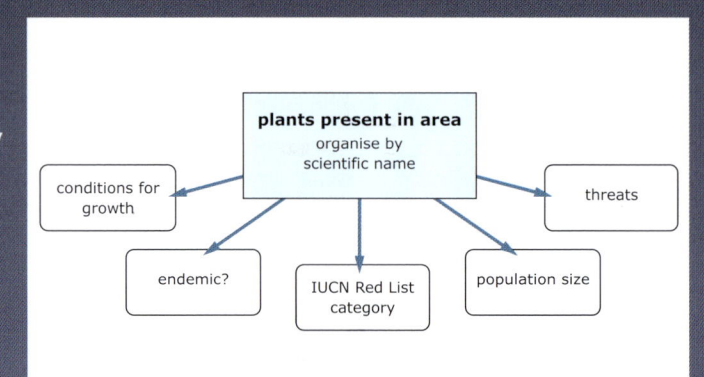

B | Preparing the structure of a plant database as part of an ecological audit.

STEM

Plant ecologists write reports on their findings from ecological audits. These will include clear recommendations about how to reduce the impact of human activity on plants, using evidence from an audit. The reports are used by conservation organisations, such as the IUCN, and by governments when they are deciding whether to protect an area, and how best to protect it.

Plant ecologists may also communicate with local farmers about how they farm their land, so endemic plants are not affected. Then they need to use language and terms that farmers understand.

IUCN Red List categories

Extinct

Extinct in the wild

Threatened:
- Critically endangered
- Endangered
- Vulnerable

Near threatened

Least concern

Species are classified according to population size, rate of decline in population, area of distribution and fragmentation of population.

C | The IUCN Red List database identifies the risk of extinction for thousands of species.

D | A large area of the Kurdistan mountains has been given Key Biodiversity Area status because many endemic plants grow there. This status tells governments and conservation organisations that an area is worth protecting. It is hoped that the area will now become a national park.

4 Suggest how a plant ecologist might identify a plant in a particular area.

5 Explain why a report for a government organisation may be written differently than one for local farmers.

E | Laws and regulations can encourage farmers to farm in ways that protect wild plants, such as by smaller-scale farming.

ACTIVITY

As a group, consider an area where human activities are expanding into natural areas.

1. Describe how a plant ecologist would carry out an ecological audit to find out if the area should be given Key Biodiversity Area (KBA) status.

2. Design a layout for a clear, structured report to be written about the audit. Include how you would present the evidence and the criteria for deciding whether to recommend KBA status or not.

9Be FARMING PROBLEMS

UK NC, iLS, CEE

WHAT PROBLEMS CAN FARMING CAUSE?

Clearing land (to make space for crops or machinery) destroys habitats, reducing the populations of organisms.

FACT
Worldwide, about 12 hectares (the area of 17 soccer pitches) of trees are cut down every minute.

A | This rainforest was cleared to graze cattle. The steep slopes are now prone to erosion.

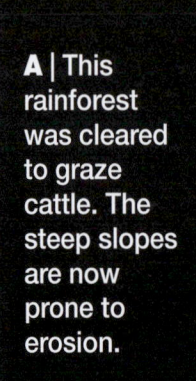

Fertilisers

Fertilisers can wash into rivers and lakes. The very rich supply of nutrients (**eutrophication**) causes fast growth of **algae** and plants, which block out light causing a lot of them to die. As decomposer bacteria break down the dead material, they use up the oxygen in the water, causing fish to die (as shown in photo B). Animal waste fertilisers (e.g. manure) may also contain harmful microorganisms.

B | fish killed due to a lack of oxygen

Pesticides

Insecticides can kill helpful insects that eat pests or pollinate plants. Some insecticides are **persistent** (do not break down in the environment). Predators in a food chain may eat many animals containing small amounts of insecticide meaning that the top predator gets a large amount of the substance, which may harm it.

In 2014, the EU banned the use of some 'neonicotinoid' insecticides on flowering crops. These insecticides made the plants poisonous for most of the growing season. The ban was based on evidence that the insecticide made nectar and pollen poisonous to bees.

Selective herbicides only kill plants that have broad leaves and so a crop, like wheat, is not affected. However, many plants in hedges have broad leaves and are killed.

C | Animal waste fertilisers (e.g. manure) can also cause eutrophication, and may contain harmful microorgansims. They also smell!

---

1. Explain why an increase in bacteria in a lake can reduce the populations of fish.
2. Why do extra nitrates in lakes cause algae and plants to grow quickly?
3. Draw a flow chart to explain why the fish in photo B have died.

4
a| Draw out a food web of the following: Sparrowhawks eat sparrows and dormice. Wheat is eaten by caterpillars and aphids. Caterpillars feed on hazel trees, as do dormice. Sparrows feed on aphids and caterpillars.

b| This food web is from a hedge next to a wheat field. What would happen to the populations of the organisms if a farmer sprayed the wheat with:

  i | a general insecticide

  ii | a selective herbicide?

5 Suggest why neonicotinoids were banned for use on rapeseed crops but not on wheat.

Varieties

Farmers often plant the same variety of crop. Since all the plants are identical, if one gets a disease then all the others will. A new disease can wipe out the whole crop.

Planting a single crop variety over a large area reduces biodiversity. The food webs become smaller, and if a disaster hits the area it takes much longer to recover than if the area was very biodiverse.

6 In 19th century Ireland, most people survived by growing and eating one variety of potato (called lumper). Between 1845 and 1852 more than a million people starved. Suggest why.

7 A huge area of land is planted with wheat for many years. The farmer wants to grow rapeseed instead. Explain why the rapeseed may not give a good yield.

D | This area is all planted with one variety of oil palm. The whole area was originally rainforest.

Plants remove carbon dioxide from the atmosphere when they photosynthesise. Carbon is 'stored' in trees but the carbon in crops is soon released back into the atmosphere, when the crops are used for food or fuel. Due to the destruction of forests and burning of fossil fuels, the amount of carbon dioxide in the atmosphere has been increasing for the last 200 years, which is thought to be causing **global warming**.

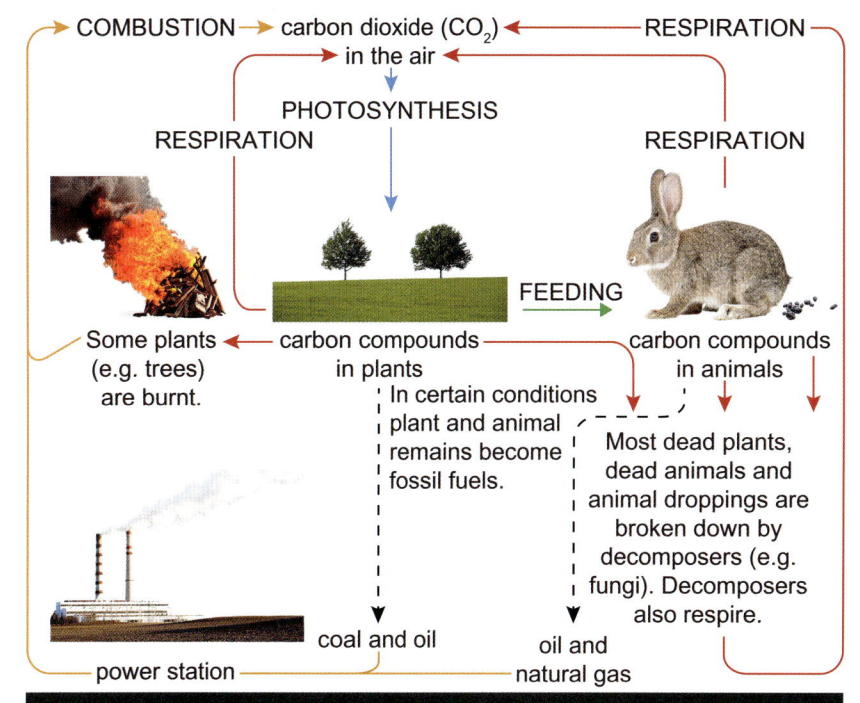

E | The **carbon cycle** shows the processes by which carbon dioxide is removed from and released into the atmosphere.

We need to conserve habitats so that species do not die out and so that future generations can enjoy them. To do this, we may need to change the way we farm, build towns and produce energy. Developing the things we need, without destroying habitats is called **sustainable development**.

8 Explain two ways in which a farmer could grow crops more sustainably.

9 Draw a table to show the advantages and disadvantages of clearing land, insecticides, herbicides and fertilisers.

I can ...

- use models, for example food webs and the carbon cycle, to explain changes in an ecosystem
- recognise the advantages and disadvantages of different farming methods

UK NC, iLS, CEE

9Be BIAS AND VALIDITY

WHAT ARE BIAS AND VALIDITY?

Bias is a shift away from a true meaning or value. Sometimes it is done on purpose and sometimes by mistake.

Intentional bias

Herbicide-tolerant (or HT) soybean is a variety that is not killed by a selective herbicide called glyphosate, which kills common weeds (such as milkweed). Milkweed plants are important for monarch butterflies, as they lay their eggs on them. The bars on graph B show the numbers of monarch butterflies that migrated from the USA to Mexico each winter. Some scientists think that increased planting of HT soybean means that farmers are getting rid of more milkweed, reducing butterfly numbers. Others blame the reduction of butterflies on deforestation in Mexico and new weather patterns.

A | HT soybean growing

B HT soybean growing and monarch butterflies in Mexico 1996 – 2013

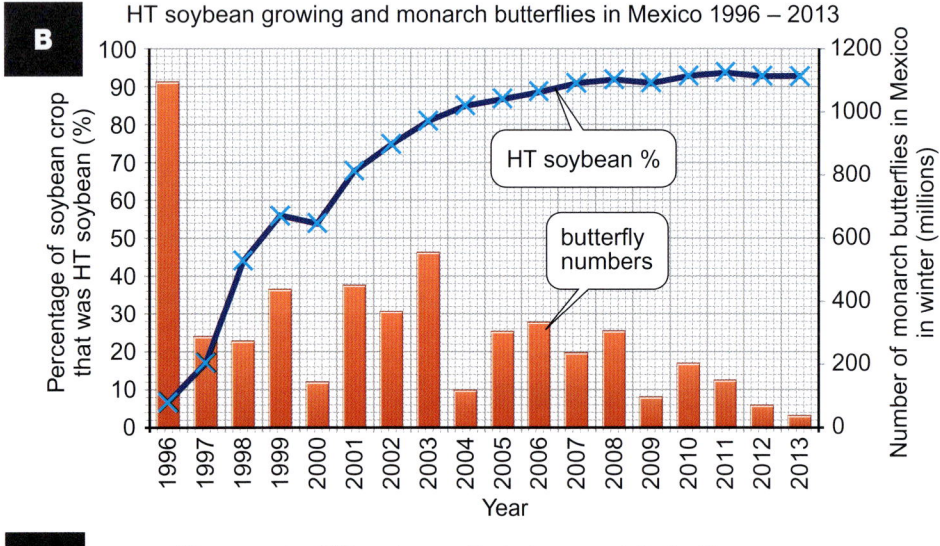

C How growing HT soybean affected monarch butterflies in Mexico 1997 – 2003

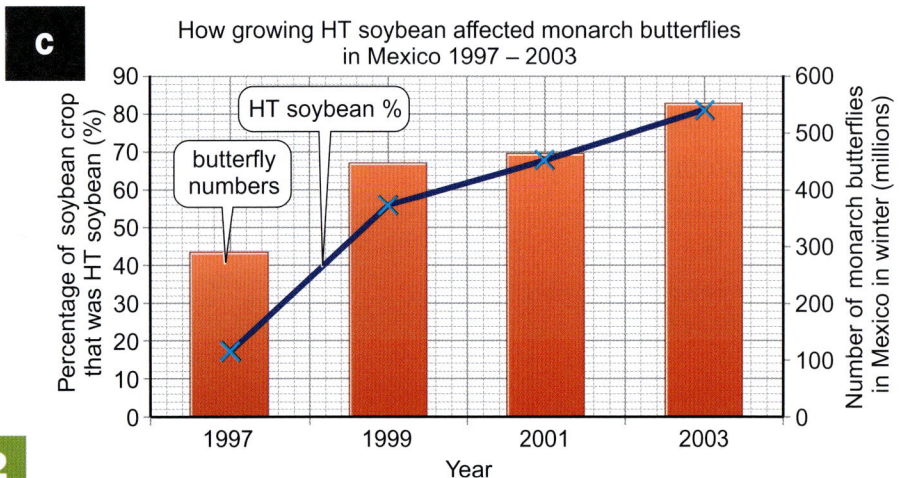

Sometimes people do not present all the data from investigations and only choose data that support their ideas. Graph C shows how data could be selected from graph B to show bias.

1
a| What is graph C trying to get you to believe?
b| Explain how this graph is biased.
c| Suggest who might create a graph like this. Explain your reasoning.

2 Which figures would you use from graph B to show a continual decrease in monarch butterflies?

WORKING SCIENTIFICALLY

What someone says or writes is 'balanced' if the points in favour *and* the points against something are considered equally. Bias occurs when the points selected do not give the full picture. Cartoon E shows how information from table D could be used in a biased way.

D | advantages and disadvantages of growing HT soybean

Advantages	Disadvantages
easier management of weeds	expensive
fewer glyphosate sprayings needed than with other herbicides	with time, weeds unaffected by glyphosate become more common meaning that other herbicides may be needed
glyphosate is not persistent	HT soybean may grow as a weed in other crops and could be difficult to control

Speech bubble: "We all know that HT soybean is bad news. It's incredibly expensive and creates weeds that are impossible to control."

Sign: DOWN WITH GLYPHOSATE

E | bias against HT soybean

3 Why is what the person is saying in cartoon E biased?

4 Write a biased paragraph to encourage farmers to plant HT soybean.

Accidental bias

Bias can be caused by **systematic error**, when readings are all shifted away from the true values by the same amount. For example, a thermometer with an incorrectly printed scale may always read 1 °C higher than the correct temperature.

Sampling can also cause accidental bias. Samples must be taken at **random** and should not be chosen. Otherwise, scientists might only take samples from interesting areas or areas that are likely to give the data that they expect. The estimated numbers of monarch butterflies in graph B were calculated from samples. The scientists used a computer program to randomly choose the sample areas in which to count the butterflies.

5 Scientists used a computer to randomly choose trees to sample in a Mexican forest. They then counted monarch butterflies on the trunks of the trees, in the parts they could reach. Why could this sampling cause bias?

6 "Graph B clearly shows that as more HT soybean has been planted, the number of monarch butterflies in Mexico in winter has decreased." Explain why this is not a valid conclusion. (*Hint:* think about what a percentage tells you.)

Validity

Something is **valid** if it does what it is supposed to do. A fair test is valid because only the effects of the independent variable are measured. Results are valid if they correctly measure what was supposed to be measured. A valid conclusion for an investigation is drawn using only the results of the investigation.

I can ...
- identify bias
- explain different sources of bias
- explain whether something is valid.

163

9Be ORGANIC FARMING

IS ORGANIC FARMING BETTER THAN INTENSIVE FARMING?

In organic farming, only natural fertilisers, such as manure, are used. And only small amounts of naturally occurring substances can be used as pesticides, for example sulfur or copper sulfate.

Organic farmers do not plant the same crops in the same place every year, but rotate (change) their crops. They make sure that one crop in the rotation is a plant that adds nitrates to the soil, such as clover. They also use organisms to reduce the numbers of pest organisms – this is known as biological control.

A | Powdery mildew fungus grows over plant leaves but can be treated organically using copper sulfate mixed with calcium hydroxide. However, this mixture harms some soil microorganisms and helpful insects.

B | Hoverfly larvae are used to control aphids.

Some people prefer to eat organic foods. This may be because they think they are healthier than conventionally farmed foods. There is little evidence for this though. Some people do not like the idea of artificial substances being on or in plants they eat. Others think that artificial pesticides and fertilisers cause too much environmental damage.

Studies have shown that organic farms do have a greater biodiversity than conventional farms. However, organic farms take up much more space to provide the same amount of food. Organic foods can also be very expensive.

1. Powdery mildew affects photosynthesis in plants.
   a) Describe what happens in photosynthesis.
   b) Explain what effect powdery mildew would have on photosynthesis.
   c) Explain how this would affect a farmer's yield.

2. Small amounts of magnesium mineral salts are needed to make chlorophyll.
   a) What is chlorophyll?
   b) Describe how magnesium salts travel from the soil into the leaves.
   c) Explain how roots and stems are adapted to this function.

3. Name a helpful insect and explain why it is helpful to farmers.

HAVE YOUR SAY

Do you think we should make all farming organic?

9Ca THREAT FROM DISEASE

HOW HAS LIFE EXPECTANCY CHANGED?

In England and Wales in the 1840s, the median (average) age of death was 46 but today it is 83 years old. Many factors have made this change possible.

One major factor has been understanding how **hygiene** prevents diseases. Hygiene means keeping things clean, such as keeping drinking water separate from sewage that contains human faeces. Sewage contains **pathogens**, which are microorganisms that cause diseases such as cholera and typhoid.

Diet has generally improved since the 1840s, which means people are healthier and stronger and can fight off diseases better. **Immunisation**, particularly in childhood, helps protect people throughout their lives against particular diseases.

It is estimated that in 1940s and 1950s, a disease called polio paralysed or killed about half a million people worldwide every year. The virus that causes polio attacks the nervous system, which stops signals being sent along certain nerves to muscles. Thanks to an international immunisation programme there are only a few hundred cases each year in the world today.

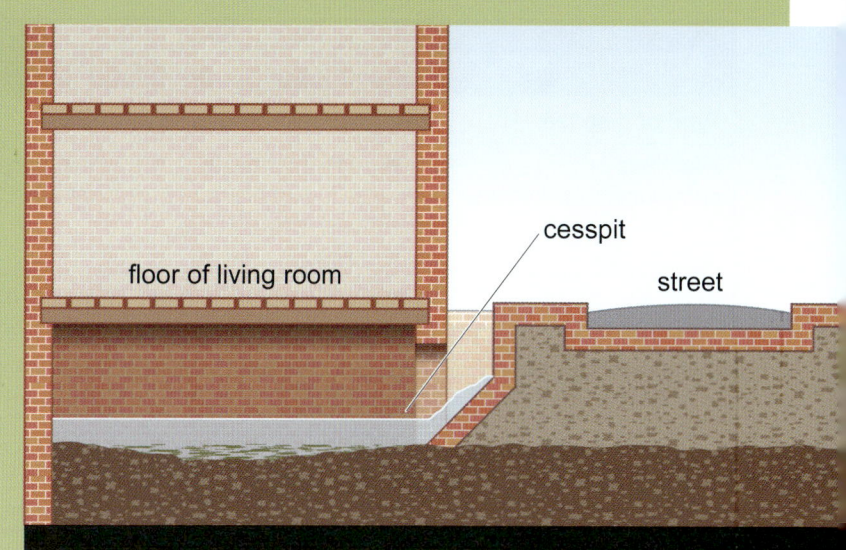

A | People used to dump their waste in open cesspits under their homes, but now sewage is removed from buildings in pipes.

Medicines also developed greatly in the 20th century, including the introduction of **antibiotics** that help people recover from bacterial diseases.

The main causes of death in richer countries are now from diseases caused by changes inside the body rather than from infections.

B | These children cannot walk unaided because damage to their nervous system caused by polio stopped their leg muscles working properly.

1. A poor diet can cause deficiency diseases. Define the term deficiency disease, giving an example.

2. Name two groups of microorganisms.

3. Explain why damage to nerves can affect muscles.

4. Explain what is meant in the text where it says that polio affected an *estimated* half a million people.

5. Medicines taken by mouth are absorbed into the blood and enter cells by diffusion. Explain how diffusion happens.

iLS, CEE

9Ca DISEASES

HOW ARE VIRUSES LINKED TO DISEASE?

A **disease** is something that makes you ill. Diseases have many causes, as shown in table A.

A | types of diseases, some examples and their causes

Type of disease	Example	Cause
infectious or communicable disease	athlete's foot, cholera, influenza (flu), malaria, pneumonia, polio, Ebola, chickenpox	microorganism (e.g. bacterium, fungus, protoctist, virus) that gets into the body and changes how it works
deficiency disease	anaemia, kwashiorkor, night blindness, rickets, scurvy	lack of a nutrient that the body needs for healthy growth and development (the lack of different nutrients causes different diseases)
genetic or inherited disease/disorder	sickle cell disease, haemophilia	a fault in the DNA (genetic material) in a cell that changes how the cell works
lifestyle disease	lung cancer, cardiovascular disease	factors in the way we live increase the risk of getting these diseases, e.g. smoking tobacco, eating unhealthily, too little exercise
autoimmune disease	type 1 diabetes	when the body's immune system attacks and damages cells in the body

B | A sneeze or cough can send out droplets containing infectious pathogens at over 60 kilometres an hour to a distance of over 5 metres.

Diseases caused by **pathogens** are called **communicable** or **infectious diseases**, because the pathogen that causes the disease can be passed from person to person. Other types of disease cannot be passed from person to person, and so are **non-communicable diseases**.

> **1**
> a | Give one example of a non-communicable disease.
> b | Explain why your example is non-communicable.
>
> **2** Explain how you could become infected with cholera. (*Hint:* look at page 165 to help you.)

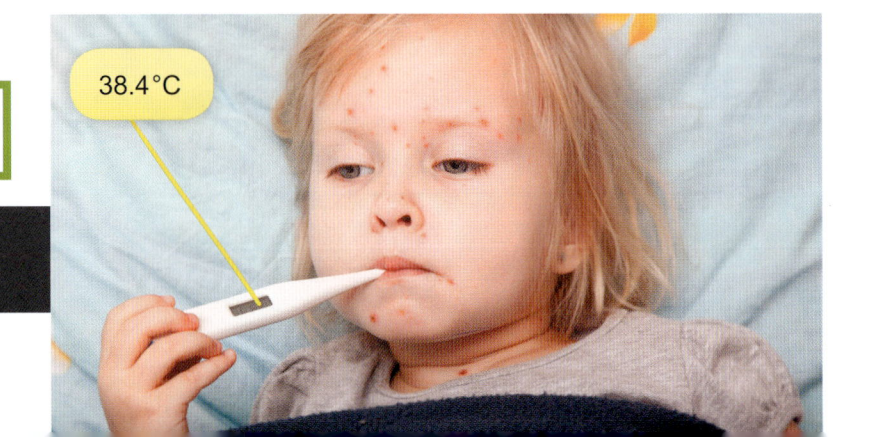

The obvious effects of a disease are its **symptoms**. For example, the symptoms of some infectious diseases are a raised temperature and/or a rash.

> **3** Look at photo C. What are the symptoms of chickenpox?

C | This child has chickenpox, which is a disease caused by a virus.

38.4 °C

166

Immunity

Your body uses different types of **white blood cell** to kill pathogens that get inside you.

Phagocytes can **ingest** microorganisms (they surround and digest them), as shown in photo D.

Lymphocytes make **antibodies**, which are proteins that stick to microorganisms. The antibodies make it easier for microorganisms to be ingested. Antibodies can also make microorganisms stick together or burst open.

Lymphocytes make new, specific antibodies to attach to each different sort of pathogen that infects you. This takes time, which is why you get ill before you get better again.

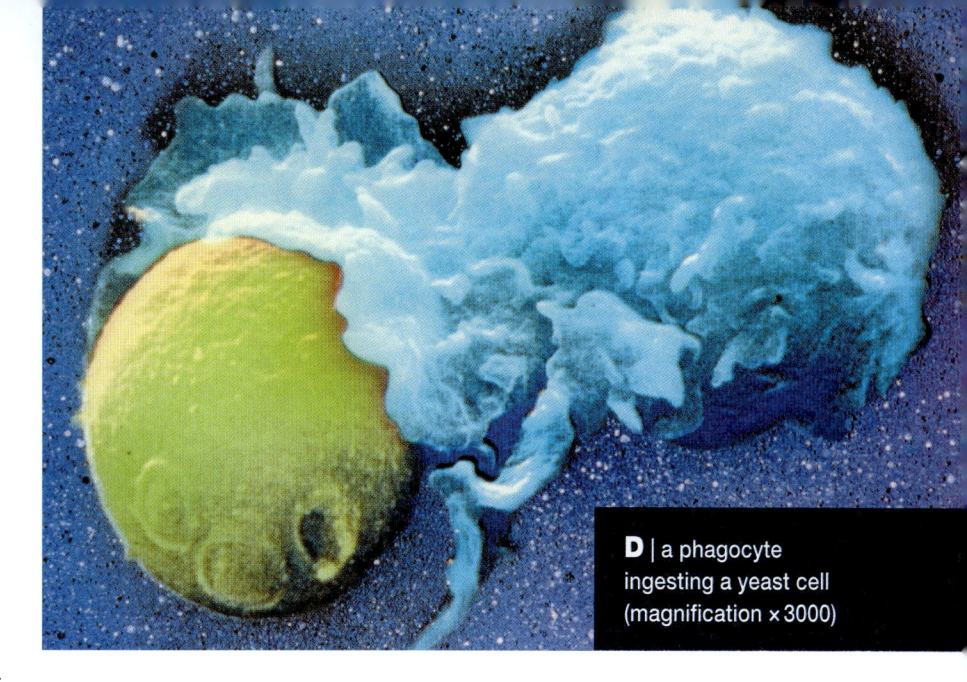

D | a phagocyte ingesting a yeast cell (magnification ×3000)

E | Lymphocytes are white blood cells that make specific antibodies to attach to each different type of microorgansm that they find.

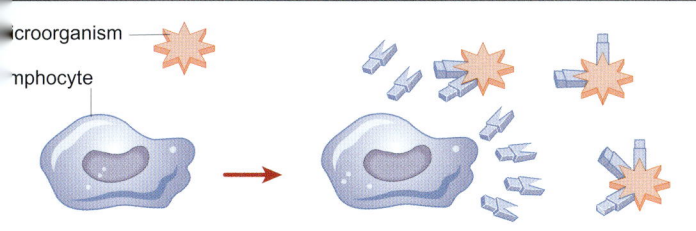

microorganism
lymphocyte

When a lymphocyte encounters a microorganism, it starts to make antibodies

The antibodies are made specifically to fit into the outside of that particular microorganism. Each type of microorganism has a different surface an so needs a different type of antibody.

After an infection some lymphocytes (**memory cells**) remain ready to produce the antibodies that attach to that pathogen. So, the next time that microorganism gets inside you, the correct antibodies are produced very quickly and in much greater numbers. That is why you only get many infectious diseases once (e.g. measles). You become **immune** to the disease.

Vaccines contain parts of the surface coating of a microorganism. Lymphocytes then create antibodies against these parts, and memory cells are formed. So, you become immune to the disease without having the disease.

4   a| List three things antibodies can do to microorganisms.
b| Explain why people are often ill before getting better when infected by a new pathogen.

5   Antibodies are said to be 'specific' for a certain microorganism. State what this means.

6   What does it mean if you are immune to a disease?

7   Explain why viruses are not classed as living organisms.

8   Explain how vaccinations stops the spread of a disease in a community.

FACT

Pithovirus sibericum is the largest known virus, about the size of many bacteria. *Pithovirus* was found in 30 000-year-old ice from Russia and could still infect protoctists called *Amoeba*.

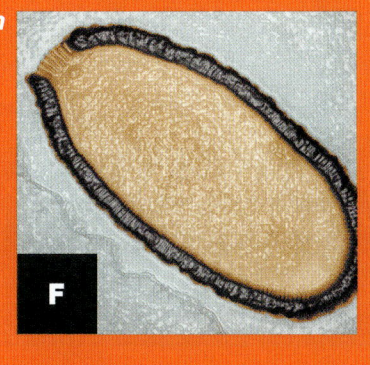

F

I can ...

- give examples of different kinds of diseases and describe how they are caused
- describe the ways in which white blood cells destroy microorganisms in the body, and explain how this can lead to immunity.

9Ca VETERINARY SCIENCE

HOW DO VETS HELP TREAT DISEASES IN ANIMALS?

In 1999 in New York, some elderly people developed swollen brains. At the same time, crows started to die from swollen brains, as did birds in the Bronx Zoo. Dr Tracey McNamara, a zoo vet, knew these symptoms suggested a viral disease. She wondered if the same virus was infecting the people and birds.

Blood samples were taken from the people and the birds and analysed by scientists. All the samples contained West Nile virus (originally from Africa). It is spread by mosquitoes, which collect and pass on the virus as they feed on the blood of people and animals. The virus had not been seen in the USA before.

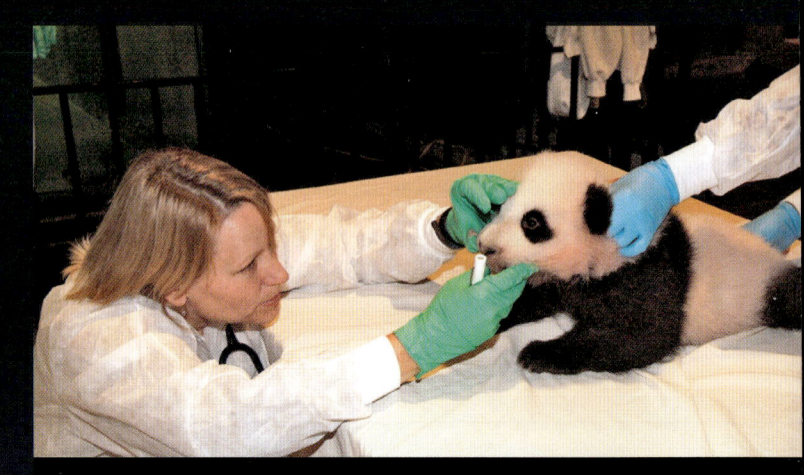

A | Zoos have vets to look after the animals.

1. State two pieces of evidence that supported the idea that the people and birds had the same disease.

2. Suggest one way in which the virus spread to the USA from Africa.

B | Many vets work with farm animals. This vet is vaccinating cattle.

Vets are expert problem-solvers and use a systematic approach to work out what problems animals have. This involves examining them for signs of disease and talking to people who have been near the animals to find out as much as possible. Vets examine this information and apply their knowledge of diseases. They may want to do tests to collect more evidence, before giving a **diagnosis**.

Being a vet

There are many types of veterinary surgeon (or 'vet'). Some treat farm animals and others work in zoos. Some specialise in certain animals and others treat many different species.

Vets train at a university or a specialist veterinary college for four or five years. To be accepted onto a degree course you need to be good at biology, chemistry and maths and have worked with animals (e.g. volunteering at a zoo, working on a farm).

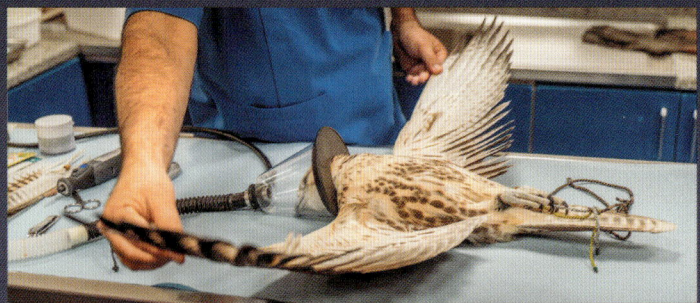

C | Some vets specialise in birds. This falcon has been anaesthetised so it can be examined.

3. Explain why farm animals are vaccinated.

STEM

Treating animals

Like humans, animals may need drugs to treat certain diseases. A vet must prescribe the correct medicine and calculate the amount to give (the dose). The dose depends on the species of animal and its mass.

Antibiotics last for different lengths of time inside different animals. The speed at which this happens is measured in a **half-life** – the time it takes for half the antibiotic molecules to be broken down. Species in which an antibiotic has a longer half-life need fewer doses.

Species	Dose (mg of antibiotic/kg of animal)	Half-life (hours)
cat	8	166.0
rhesus macaque	8	8.0
squirrel monkey	8	2.6

D | Doses of an antibiotic called cefovecin for different animals.

4
a | Explain why Dr McNamara did not prescribe antibiotics to treat animals affected by West Nile virus.
b | Suggest one way to stop the spread of the West Nile virus in a zoo.

5 Look at table D.
a | Calculate the dose for a 20 kg squirrel monkey.
b | Explain why a squirrel monkey will need more doses over time than a cat.

E | It is important to know the masses of animals in zoos so that they can be given the correct doses of medicines.

ACTIVITY

Table E gives some information about an antibiotic called ceftiofur.

1. To be effective, the concentration of ceftiofur in a ball python must be above 2.5 mg/kg. After the first dose, calculate the number of days until another dose is needed.

Species	Dose (mg/kg)	Half-life (hours)
alpaca	6.6	45
American black duck	6.6	32
ball python	10	64
goat	15	37

E

2. Design a model to teach vet students about half-lives. Write a list of apparatus and instructions for a teacher, using information from table E for examples.

9Cb CONTROL SYSTEMS

HOW ARE THE BODY'S RESPONSES CONTROLLED?

A virus causes the childhood infection chickenpox. After the infection has cleared up, some of the viruses remain inside nerve cells. Many years later the viruses may leave the nerve cells and cause a disease called shingles.

Nervous system

The **nervous system** is the organ system that helps us to sense changes in our surroundings and inside our bodies. It also allows our bodies to respond rapidly to those changes. The organs of the **central nervous system** (CNS) are the **brain** and **spinal cord**. The CNS is linked to the rest of the body by organs called nerves. All these organs contain nerve tissue formed from nerve cells.

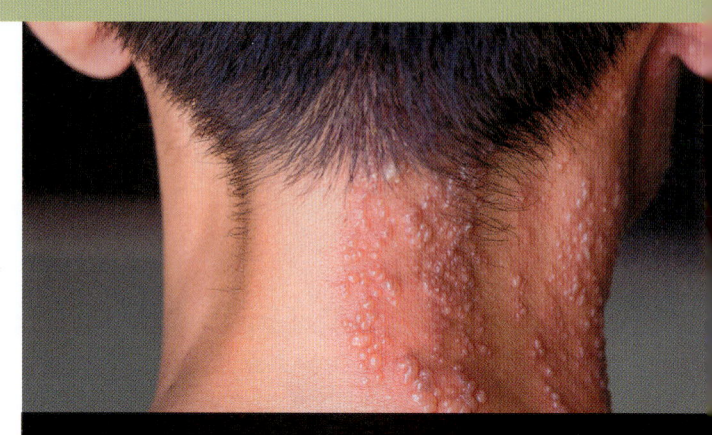

A | Symptoms of shingles include headache, fever and a painful rash on an area of skin linked to a single large nerve.

B | some organs of the human nervous system — brain, spinal cord, nerves

Changes that we sense are called **stimuli**. Stimuli are detected by **receptor cells** in **sense organs**, such as the eyes, ears and skin.

When a stimulus is detected, a receptor cell produces electrical signals. These signals are called **impulses** and travel along nerves, usually to the brain via the spinal cord. The brain processes the information from receptor cells and sends electrical impulses back out along other nerves to **effectors**, such as muscles and glands. Muscle cells respond to these impulses by contracting. Cells in some glands respond by releasing hormones into the blood.

C | This cap measures electrical responses to see which parts of the brain are active during a task.

1. Name as many organs, tissues and cells in the human nervous system as you can.

2. Describe the functions of the organs, tissues and cells that you named in question 1.

3. Draw a flow chart to show the path that the impulses take from touch receptors in the skin of the fingers to the muscles that lift your hand as you pick up a pen.

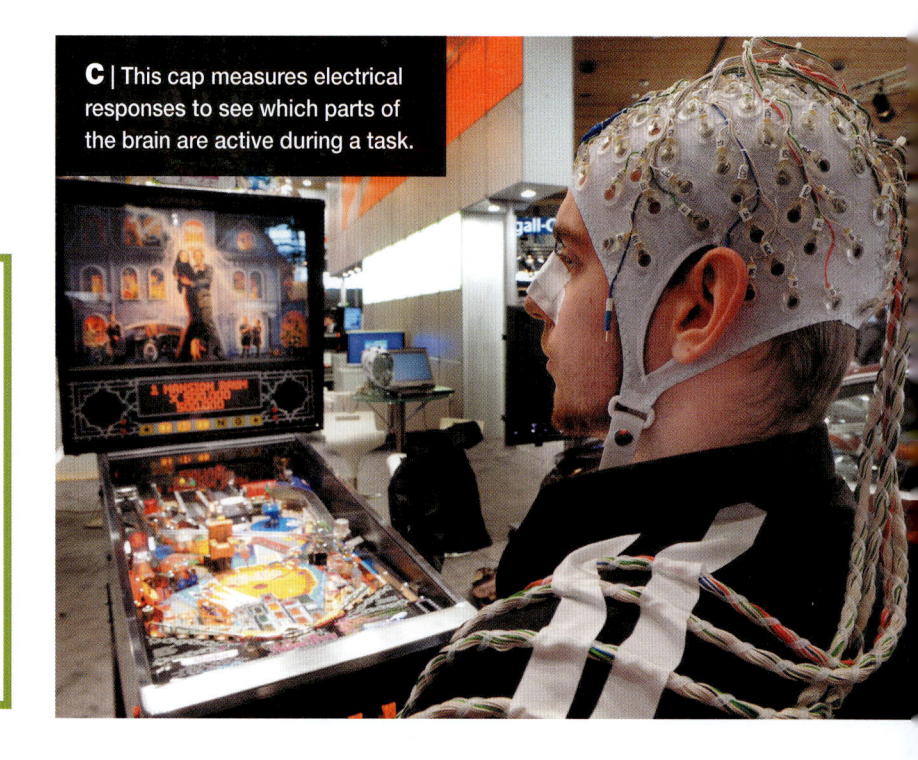

Hormonal system

Hormones are substances that act as chemical messengers in the body. They are made in organs called **glands**, which release them into the blood plasma. **Target cells** or **target organs** respond to hormones in the blood by changing what they are doing. For example, the hormone adrenaline increases the pulse rate.

Sometimes a hormone from one gland causes the release of a different hormone from another gland. For example, a hormone from the ovaries (oestrogen) causes the pituitary gland to release a hormone that triggers ovulation.

gland: thyroid
hormone: thyroxine
target organs: many
response: controls normal rate of many functions of body e.g. respiration

gland: adrenal
hormone: adrenaline
target organs: many including heart and lungs
response: increases heart rate and breathing rate

gland: ovary
hormone: oestrogen
target organs: many
response: controls changes in a girl's body during puberty, and some changes in the menstrual cycle

gland: pituitary
hormone: growth hormone
target organs: many
response: controls normal growth of children

gland: pancreas
hormone: insulin
target cells: muscle and liver cells
response: cells take up glucose from blood

gland: testis
hormone: testosterone
target organs: many
response: controls changes in a boy's body during puberty

D | the positions of important glands, and some of the effects of the hormones they produce

FACT

In 2014 the world's tallest and smallest men met. Sultan Kosen is 2.51 m tall, and Chandra Dangi is 0.55 m tall. Both heights have been caused by problems with the amount of hormones their bodies make.

E

Comparing systems

Having two different response systems means we can respond in different ways to different stimuli.

F | Comparison of nervous and hormonal systems

Nervous system	Hormonal system
electrical impulses along nerves	chemical messengers in blood
short, rapid response to stimulus	longer, slower response to stimulus
impulses act only on the effector connected to the nerve	messengers can act on many target organs at the same time

4 State what is meant by a hormone.

5 Name one target organ for adrenaline.

6 Suggest two target cells for the hormone testosterone. Explain your answer.

7 Identify two glands that might not be working properly in Sultan Kosen and Chandra Dangi, and suggest why the men are such extreme heights.

8 You tread on something sharp. Suggest which control system is best for responding to this stimulus. Explain your answer.

9 When we see something dangerous, we start to release adrenaline.
  a | Sketch a flow chart to show the pathways and organs involved in this response.
  b | Explain how this response prepares the body for dealing with a dangerous situation.

I can ...

- describe how the nervous system works
- describe how hormones affect the body

9Cc TREATING DISEASES

HOW DO WE TREAT DIFFERENT TYPES OF DISEASE?

A **drug** is a substance that affects how the body works. **Medicines** are drugs that are used to help treat or prevent disease. To treat communicable diseases, we may use **antibiotics** (to kill bacteria) or antivirals (to stop viruses **replicating**). We also use **vaccines** to help stop us being ill when particular pathogens infect us.

Other types of drugs treat some lifestyle diseases, such as heart disease. Nutritional deficiency diseases may be treated by adding nutrients to the diet.

> 1. Explain why medicines are drugs.
> 2. Explain why a doctor gives a patient an antibiotic for an ear infection.
> 3. Describe how scurvy can be treated.

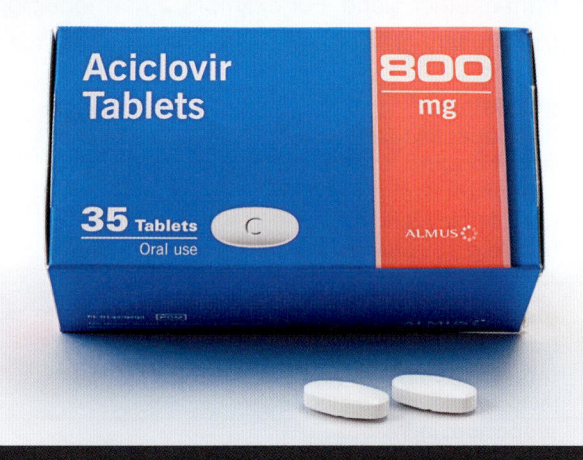

A | a common antiviral medicine

B | Lavinia Warren (1841–1919) at the age of about 20. As an adult she was 81 cm tall. Today people with this condition can be treated.

Genetic disorders are caused by genes. People are born with these disorders and may need treatment throughout their lives. Examples include sickle cell anaemia and some types of growth hormone deficiency (which causes lack of growth).

Autoimmune diseases are due to white blood cells attacking parts of the body. Scientists are not sure why this happens. In type 1 diabetes, for example, the tissue that produces insulin is destroyed. This results in high levels of glucose in the blood, which can damage organs.

> 4. a | State the organs in which insulin and growth hormone are produced. (*Hint:* Look at page 171.)
>   b | Explain why organ damage can be caused by type 1 diabetes.

Transgenic organisms

People whose bodies do not make hormones need injections of those hormones. In the past, human growth hormone was extracted from dead bodies, and insulin was extracted from other animals (such as cattle). This is expensive and slow.

These protein hormones are now made by **genetically modified** or **genetically engineered** bacteria (their DNA has been altered by scientists). The genes for the hormones are taken from human chromosomes and put into the DNA of bacteria. The **transgenic** bacteria then make the hormones. (Transgenic means they contain DNA from more than one species.)

> **5** Name the molecule on which genes are found.
>
> **6** Scientists can remove genes from organisms. Explain how this can create a genetically modified organism that is *not* transgenic.

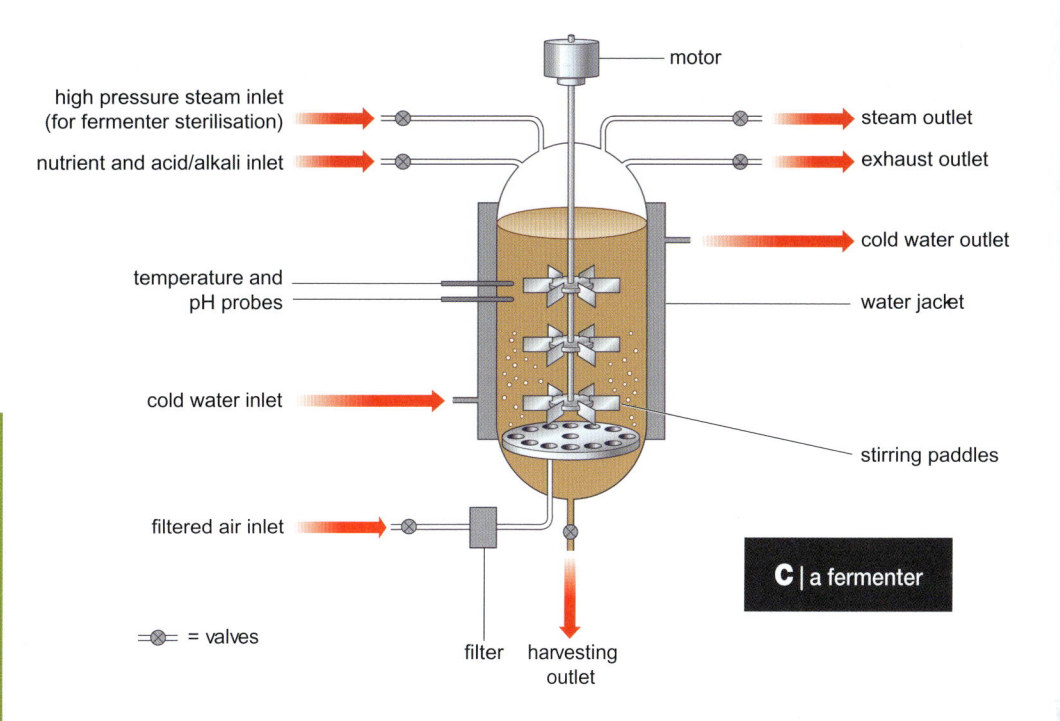

C | a fermenter

To produce a lot of hormone, the transgenic bacteria are grown in large **fermenters** (diagram C). Fermenters provide the best conditions for the bacteria to grow and reproduce quickly, and produce a lot of the hormone. At regular intervals, the fermenter is drained and the hormone is extracted.

Aseptic precautions are needed – the fermenter and anything that goes into it are **sterilised** (all microorganisms are killed). This stops other microorganisms growing, which might be harmful or reduce hormone production.

Oxygen and nutrients are added, including carbohydrates for the bacteria to feed on. Stirrers agitate the mixture so that the bacteria do not sink to the bottom. This also mixes the nutrients and oxygen and helps to keep the temperature even.

All **enzymes** (including those that make hormones) work best at a certain temperature and pH, so these factors are monitored. A water jacket cools the fermenter to maintain the best temperature, and acids or alkalis are added to keep the pH constant.

> **7** Describe how the fermenter is sterilised.
>
> **8** a | Give the reason why air is bubbled into the fermenter.
> b | Explain why this air needs to be filtered.

FACT

Scientists are now making transgenic animals. These types of cows, in Argentina, produce insulin in their milk.

D

I can ...

- explain how large amounts of human hormones can be produced quickly using genetically modified bacteria.

173

9Cc MEDIAN AND QUARTILES

WHAT DO THE MEDIAN AND QUARTILES OF A SET OF DATA TELL US?

Different people vary in their response to medicines. So, medicines are tested in clinical trials. In these trials, scientists often analyse the data by dividing the people into groups. For example, a test group might be divided into smaller groups based on resting pulse rate. A group might be split into half – those with pulse rates of 65 or more beats per minute (bpm), and those with rates of less than 65 bpm. Scientists can then see if a drug has different effects depending on someone's pulse rate.

To divide a group into half, you need to find the middle value when the values are written in order. This is the **median**. We can also divide a dataset into quarters to identify the **quartiles**. Quartiles are the values that are one-quarter and three-quarters into the set of values. Diagram B shows an example.

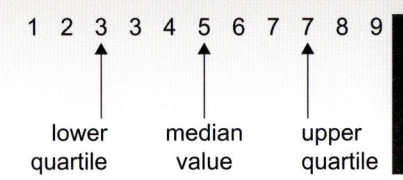

1 2 **3** 3 4 **5** 6 7 **7** 8 9

↑ lower quartile   ↑ median value   ↑ upper quartile

B | The median and quartiles in a set of values. (Remember, the values must be put in order first.)

The **interquartile range** is the difference between the upper quartile (UQ) and lower quartile (LQ) values in a dataset. For the example shown in diagram B, it is:

7 − 3 = 4

> **1** Using numbered steps:
> a | write out how to find the median of a dataset
> b | write out how to find the lower quartile and upper quartile of a dataset.
>
> **2** a | Find the median value, and the lower and upper quartile values, in this dataset:
> 28 13 4 25 21 14 6 19 35 17 22 34 11 16 8
> b | Calculate the interquartile range for the dataset in part a.

Some variables, such as height, can take any value and so show **continuous variation**. For a population, a continuous variable plotted against numbers of organisms often forms a bell-shaped curve. For example, the heights of most of the population are close to the middle value, and few people are much taller or shorter. This is called the **normal distribution**.

We can show the median and quartile values on a normal distribution, as shown in graph D.

Statins are a new wonder drug
Statins in new health scare
Health experts warn against statins
Statins help you live longer

A | Many people with heart disease take statins to help prevent heart attacks. Clinical trials have shown that some people may be harmed by taking statins.

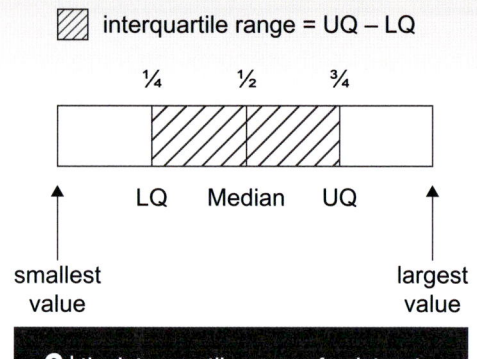

▨ interquartile range = UQ − LQ

¼   ½   ¾

↑ smallest value   LQ   Median   UQ   ↑ largest value

C | the interquartile range of a dataset

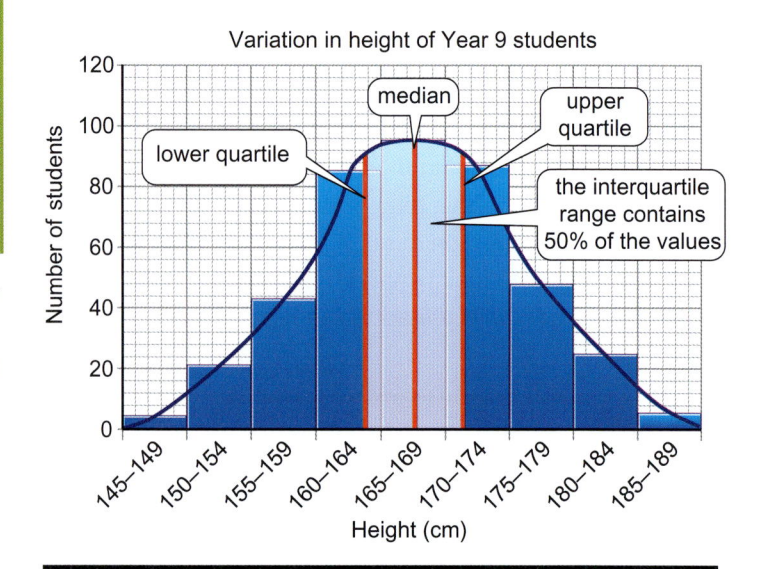

Variation in height of Year 9 students

(histogram showing number of students vs height (cm) in bins: 145–149, 150–154, 155–159, 160–164, 165–169, 170–174, 175–179, 180–184, 185–189, with labels for lower quartile, median, upper quartile, and "the interquartile range contains 50% of the values")

D | variation in height of students shows a normal distribution

WORKING SCIENTIFICALLY

The interquartile range ignores extreme values in a data set, and shows the range of the middle 50 per cent of the data. This is a more useful measure for comparing the variation in two different groups, because extreme values can bias a comparison if the ranges of all the data are compared. A small interquartile range shows that the individuals in a population show little variation, while a large interquartile range means there is a lot of variation.

3 If you looked at the two trees in E, on which tree would you see leaves that are much shorter or longer than others? Explain your answer.

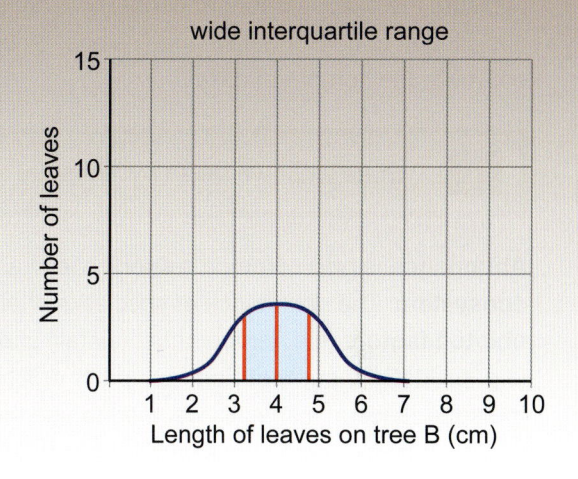

E | The leaf lengths on two trees of the same species show different normal distributions.

In medicine testing, data about features that might affect how well the drug works are collected. The graph and chart in F show the results of a test to see how a statin affected the risk of heart disease. Splitting the results into quartiles makes it easier to see how the drug worked well for many people but not for everyone.

F | The people in the study were measured for their normal ability to absorb cholesterol from their diets. The data for cholesterol absorption were split into quartiles of cholesterol absorption (graph on left). Then, the quartiles were compared for a change in the risk of heart attack after using statins (chart on right).

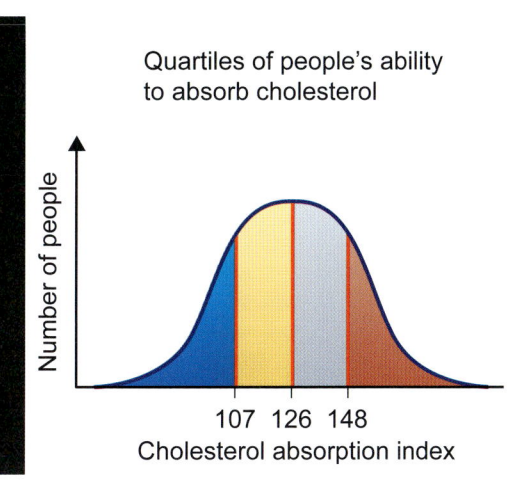

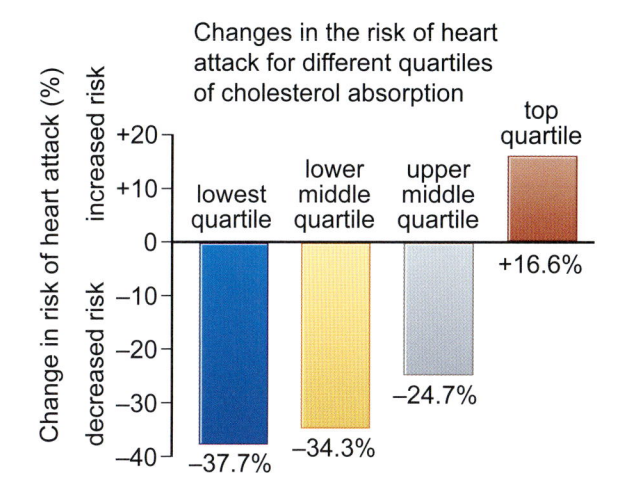

4 Look at F.

a | Explain why the data for cholesterol absorption were split into quartiles.

b | Calculate the interquartile range for the data on cholesterol absorption.

c | Explain what the charts show about the effect of cholesterol absorption on the success of reducing heart attack risk after using statins.

I can ...

- calculate the median, quartiles and interquartile range of a simple dataset
- interpret the use of quartiles in comparing variation in a large continuous dataset.

175

iLS, CEE

9Cd ECOLOGY

HOW CAN WE ESTIMATE ABUNDANCE?

When there is an outbreak of a disease, it is often difficult to measure the exact number of people who are infected because it is difficult to collect data in many areas. Scientists need to **estimate** the number of cases.

> **1** State what we mean by 'estimate'.

Abundance is how common a **species** is in a **habitat** or **ecosystem**. The abundance of species is often affected by **abiotoc factors** (e.g. temperature, rainfall) and **biotic factors** (e.g. **predation**, **competition** from other organisms). To measure the abundance of a species we need to use the right method for finding that species. Some examples are shown in B.

A | Victims of a viral disease called Ebola are very infectious and need to be moved away from towns and villages by people in full protective gear. An estimate of the number of victims allows aid agencies to calculate how many people and how much equipment they need.

B | Different methods are used to find different species. A quadrat is used to sample static or slow-moving organisms in an area. Beating a tree causes organisms to fall onto a cloth. Small organisms in tall plants are trapped in sweep nets, and small animals that run across the ground can fall into pitfall traps.

One measure of abundance is **population** size. It is rare that you can find all the organisms in a population, or have time to count them all. Therefore, we take **samples** to estimate the population size.

For the estimate, you must know the number of organisms in a sample, the size of the sample area and the size of the whole area:

> **2** Some lions move into an area where gazelles (their prey) live.
> a| Give the name of the factor that will now affect the gazelles.
> b| Suggest the effect of this factor.
>
> **3** Explain which method you would use to find:
> a| ground beetles
> b| insects in long grass.

$$\text{population size} = \text{number of organisms in sample} \times \frac{\text{total size of area where the organism lives}}{\text{area of sample}}$$

The **accuracy** of the estimate is how close it is to the true value if every organism were counted. Estimates are more accurate if:

- the sample size is larger (but this takes longer to do)
- it is easy to find organisms in the sample area
- the organisms are spread across an area (rather than being clumped).

Distribution

Distribution is how organisms are spread out in the area. Diagram C shows the three main types.

Random | Regular | Clumped

C | Distribution of organisms may be randomly scattered, regularly spaced or clumped together.

Sometimes it is easy to see how organisms are distributed and sometimes it is not. When it is not easy to see, scientists sample along a line or belt. This is known as a transect survey (shown in photo E). If there is an even distribution, the organism will be found in every sample. If the distribution is clumped, the organism will only be found in some samples.

When you do any survey of organisms in a habitat, you can also count the number of different species. This gives information about the **biodiversity** of an area (how many different species are in the **community**).

FACT

Estimating the number of tigers in the wild is difficult because small numbers are spread over large areas. Sampling by taking photographs and analysing faeces suggests there are only 3000–4000 tigers left.

4
a| On a rocky shore there were three crabs in a 0.5 m × 0.5 m quadrat. Estimate the total crab population on the rocks, which covered an area of 60 m long by 10 m wide.

b| There are an estimated 7000 limpets living in the same area. Which organism is more abundant?

D | Gannets nest in large colonies.

E | Carrying out a belt transect survey.

5
a| Look at photo D. Describe the distribution of the birds. Explain your answer.

b| Suggest how you could estimate the number of gannets on the small island.

6 The crabs in question 4 are only found in a few small pools between the rocks.

a| State how the crabs are distributed.

b| Suggest the effect of this on the accuracy of your population estimate. Explain your answer.

7 There are many different types of grass, which all have slightly different leaf shapes. How would you find out which of four different species was the most abundant in a large field?

I can ...

- identify suitable apparatus for measuring distribution and abundance
- use data from abundance investigations to estimate population size.

177

9Ce IN AND OUT

WHY IS SURFACE AREA: VOLUME RATIO IMPORTANT?

During the Second World War, one-sixth of the deaths of Allied soldiers in tropical areas were caused by a disease called tropical sprue.

This disease reduces the surface area of the small intestine and so reduces the **diffusion** of nutrients from the small intestine into the blood. This can lead to deficiency diseases.

A | Diseases such as tropical sprue and coeliac disease reduce the surface area for absorbing digested food substances.

Normal healthy villi increase the surface area of the small intestine for absorption of digested food substances.

A person with tropical sprue has damaged, flattened villi.

> **1** A lack of vitamin B12 getting into the body causes a problem called anaemia.
>
> a | Explain how vitamin B12 can diffuse into the body.
>
> b | Explain how tropical sprue could cause anaemia.

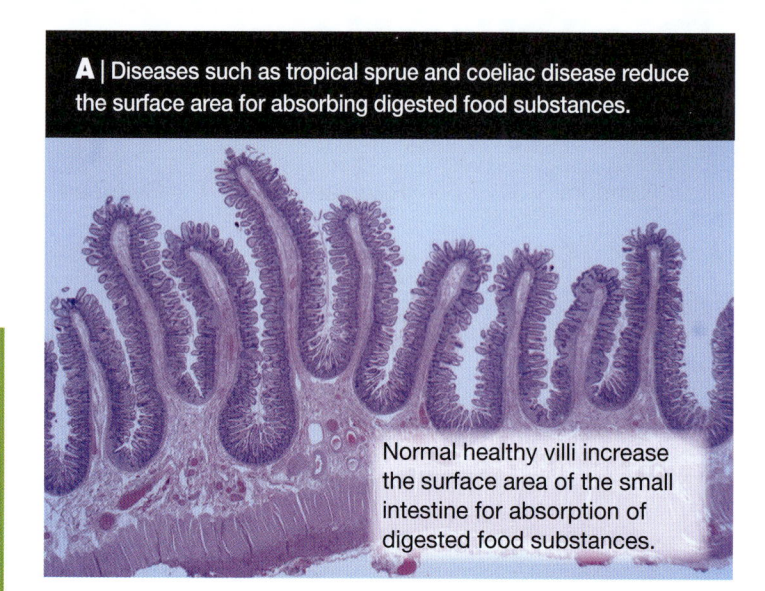

SA:V ratio

Unicellular organisms have a large enough surface area that diffusion can supply their inside volume with enough of what they need. Larger organisms have too little outside surface area compared with their volume to do this. So they have organs with large surface areas compared to their volumes, in order to quickly absorb substances. Transport systems then carry those substances to all their cells.

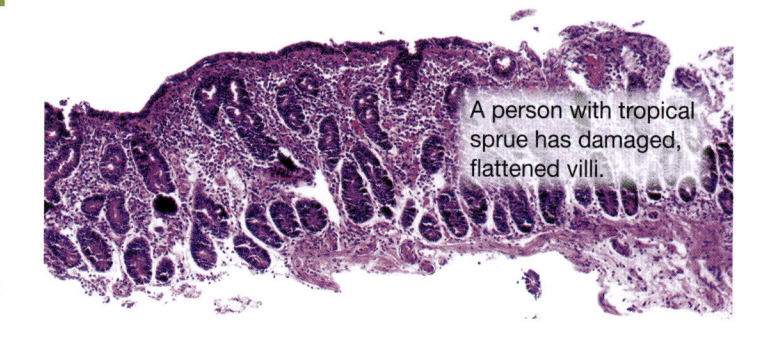

> **2** a | Explain how oxygen molecules enter an aerobically respiring unicellular organism.
>
> b | Many unicellular organisms split into two after reaching a certain size. Using ideas about surface area, explain why this is useful.
>
> **3** a | Name a human organ that exchanges gases with air.
>
> b | Describe how the surface of this organ is adapted to increase its surface area.

Comparing surface area to volume is important in biology. We calculate it as a figure called the **surface area : volume (SA:V) ratio**. Diagram B shows this calculation for a cuboid. The bigger the surface area : volume ratio, the more surface area something has per unit volume. Cells need large surface area : volume ratios to be able to take enough of the substances they need from their surroundings.

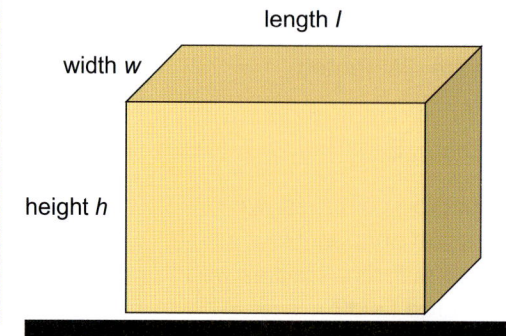

length l
width w
height h

surface area:
- two sides have an area of $l \times h$
- two sides have an area of $l \times w$
- two sides have an area of $w \times h$

so total surface area =
    $2(l \times h) + 2(l \times w) + 2(w \times h)$
volume = $l \times w \times h$
SA:V ratio = surface area/volume

B | calculating the SA:V ratio of a cuboid

The SA:V ratio is also important when organisms lose substances and energy. For example, mammals and birds use energy to keep their bodies warm. This energy is transferred to the environment across their surfaces. The rate (speed) of transfer is faster for small animals than bigger ones because small animals have a larger SA:V ratio. Smaller animals cool faster than larger ones.

4
a| Calculate the SA:V ratio of a cuboid where *l* is 3 cm, *w* is 2 cm and *h* is 1 cm. Show all your working.

b| Compare the SA:V ratio for the cuboid in part a with the SA:V ratio of a cuboid that has *l* = 6 cm, *w* = 4 cm and *h* = 2 cm.

5
a| For each anteater in photo C, work out the number of ants eaten per gram of body mass.

b| Suggest a reason for the difference in these values.

C | A typical silky anteater has a mass of less than 400 g and eats up to 5000 ants a day. A typical giant anteater has a mass of 40 kg and eats up to 30 000 ants each day.

Osmosis

Small molecules can pass through tiny holes in some membranes by **diffusion**. Membranes that only allow some molecules to pass through them are **partially permeable membranes**.

Osmosis is a type of diffusion. It is the overall movement of molecules of a **solvent** through a partially permeable membrane (from where there are more of the molecules to where there are fewer). Like diffusion, osmosis is faster at higher temperatures (because particles move faster). And like diffusion, it is also faster when there is greater concentration difference between one place and another (the **concentration gradient**).

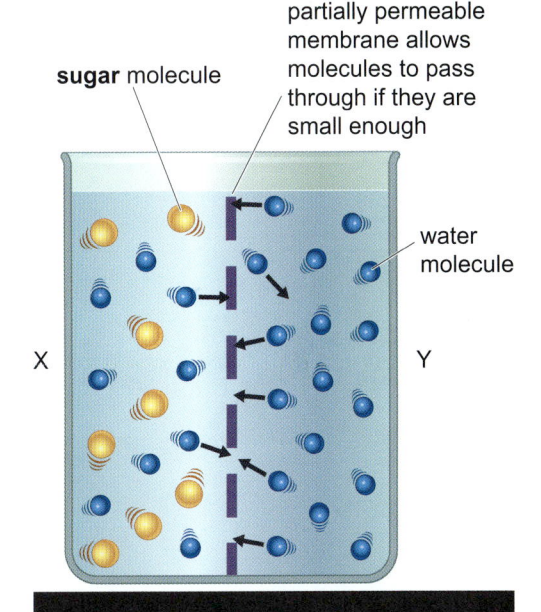

D | Osmosis occurs if solutions on each side of a partially permeable membrane contain different concentrations of water molecules.

6 Look at diagram D.

a| Which liquid (X or Y) contains more water molecules?

b| In which direction is the overall movement of water molecules?

c| Name this process and explain how it ocurs.

FACT

Normal red blood cells are smooth. People with kidney disease may have lumpy or spiky red blood cells because the liquid plasma around them contains more urea than normal and draws water out of the cells by osmosis.

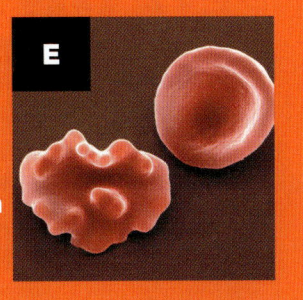

7 Use ideas about osmosis to explain the shape of the cells in photo E.

8 Explain how tropical sprue can cause diarrhoea by osmosis.

I can ...

- give examples of how surface area : volume ratio affects organisms
- describe how osmosis happens.

179

9Ce COMBATTING PANDEMICS

HOW CAN INFECTIOUS DISEASES CAUSE DEATHS ACROSS THE WORLD?

An infectious disease that infects many people over a short time across several countries is called a **pandemic**. Many people thought that with vaccination, antibiotics and better hygiene, new dangerous infectious diseases were unlikely to become pandemics. However, recently there have been outbreaks of diseases (e.g. Ebola) that have spread from one country to neighbouring countries, and sometimes to other parts of the world.

Scientists are also concerned about the risk of a pandemic of many viral diseases including Ebola, SARS, bird flu and swine flu. These diseases cannot be treated with antibiotics because they are caused by viruses. An infected person can pass on the virus to others before they show symptoms of the disease. An outbreak of SARS started in China in 2002 and rapidly spread to 37 countries. It was controlled by isolating infected people and anyone they had been in contact with.

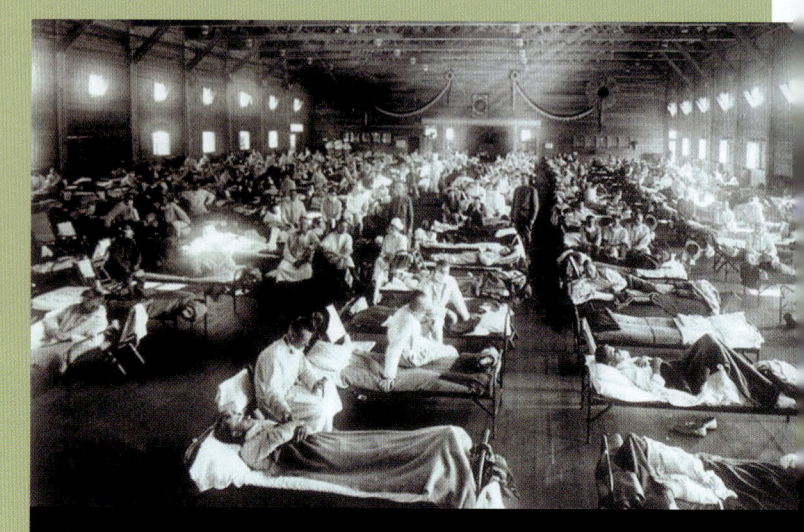

A | 'Spanish flu' killed between 50 and 100 million people across the world in 1918–19. Emergency treatment centres were needed to care for millions of patients.

B | To try to prevent infectious diseases spreading from one country to another, checks are often put in place. For instance, people who arrive in a country with a high temperature may be put in isolation.

C | Various organisations work together to plan and practise how to deal with the spread of a serious infectious disease.

1. Was 'Spanish flu' a pandemic? Explain your answer.
2. Explain why rapid international travel makes a pandemic more likely.
3. Explain why isolation can be used to prevent a pandemic.
4. Suggest why some countries are more able to control a highly infectious disease than others.

HAVE YOUR SAY

Should all countries contribute money to pay for developing vaccines or medicines to treat new infectious diseases as soon as they are identified?

9D CLEAR WRITING

We need people to understand our instructions and points of view quickly and easily. So, we must communicate ideas in a clear and logical way, without too many words.

For longer pieces of writing, we often use a plan to put information into a logical order. Table B shows some common ways to plan writing for different purposes.

A | Using symbols is clear whatever language you speak, and avoids problems with spelling.

Plan method	Purpose of writing	Examples
tables	making comparisons	
	problems and solutions	traditional / organic / artificial fertiliser / manure
	lists of items	
flow charts	causes and effects	fertiliser → eutrophication
	sequences	
concept maps	summaries	farming → traditional, organic; traditional → artificial; organic → natural
bullet points	lists of items	• herbicide
	summaries	• fungicide • insecticide

B

1. Draw out a plan for a paragraph to compare the advantages and disadvantages of using selective weedkillers (*Hint*: Look at page 156).

We then use the plan to write a paragraph. This needs a clear structure.

Paragraphs often start with a short 'topic sentence'. It sums up one main idea, which the rest of the paragraph explores in more detail. For example: 'Weedkillers can damage an ecosystem'.

There are then some supporting sentences. They describe or explain the main idea in more detail, providing examples and evidence to back up the main point.

Longer paragraphs usually end with a summary sentence. This links together all the ideas in the paragraph.

2. Write a topic sentence for a paragraph to explain how cacti can grow in deserts.

3. Some people compare a clearly structured paragraph to a burger. Draw a burger between two buns and label it to show how it can act as a model for a paragraph.

9D1 ANIMAL SMUGGLING

PROJECT 1

It's not every day that you sit next to an iguana on an aeroplane, but passengers on a recent flight to the Bahamas had some rare reptilian company.

Thirteen Bahamian rock iguanas had arrived in the United Kingdom from the Bahamas in February, in less comfortable circumstances. Wrapped in socks and shoved into suitcases, they had then been loaded into an aircraft hold for a nine-hour flight. Staff carrying out customs checks at London discovered the animals. One had already died.

A | one of the Bahamian iguanas

Bahamian rock iguanas (*Cyclura rileyi*) are critically endangered and trading them is banned under the CITES agreement. Grant Miller, head of the UK Border Force CITES team, said: "Not only has Border Force made sure that the criminals responsible for smuggling these animals are behind bars, we're also proud to have been able to play a part in safeguarding the future of this species."

According to the World Wide Fund for Nature, the illegal trafficking of live animals is worth about $16 billion US dollars per year, so continued hard work is needed to bring the problem under control.

It is not only endangered animals that are smuggled. Many countries keep animals at a special centre for a few weeks, after they arrive. The animals can then be checked to make sure that they are healthy and free from disease. Some people try to smuggle their pets into countries to avoid this 'quarantine period'.

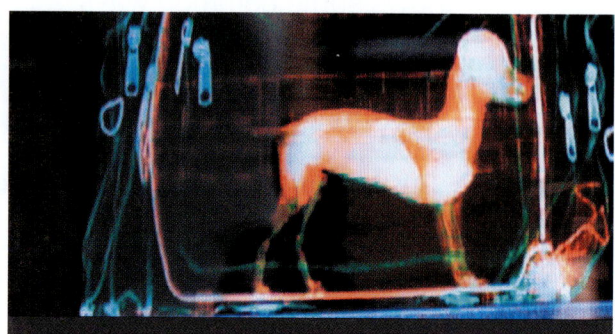

B | This dog was found, using an X-ray machine, in hand luggage at Dublin airport.

In airports, animals are found in luggage using X-rays and dogs that have been trained to sniff out other animals. But animals are also smuggled through sea ports in shipping containers and these are more difficult to detect due to the large sizes of the containers. Various detection methods are used, including sensors that detect temperature and carbon dioxide concentrations inside the containers.

---

1. This story is from an online news site. The editor wants readers' questions to be answered, explaining the science. Choose one of the questions below and write a detailed answer for the site.
   a| Why is it important that the Bahamian rock iguanas are returned to where they came from?
   b| Why are temperature and carbon dioxide detectors useful in detecting concealed animals?
   c| How do animals become critically endangered?
   d| Why can illegal smuggling be a danger to the natural environment of a country?

2. Find out about CITES. Write a paragraph describing its purpose and how it works.

3. When writing a story, science journalists use 'press releases', information from online resources (such as encyclopaedias) and their own scientific knowledge. Search for a 'press release' about 'animal smuggling' or 'animal trafficking' and write an article for an online newspaper. Use a variety of sources and show where you have got all your information from. Use no more than 350 words.

9D2 ENZYME INVESTIGATION

PROJECT 2

Some tougher meats are often cooked or served with certain fruits. This is not just to make them taste nice but because the fruits contain substances that help to make the meat more tender; they tenderise it.

These fruits contain enzymes. Enzymes are molecules that speed up chemical reactions without being changed. Many enzymes help to break down large molecules into smaller ones. There are lots of enzymes of this type in your digestive system.

The enzymes in some fruits can break down the proteins in the meat. This means that long strands of protein are broken down into shorter ones, and the meat is easier to chew.

Gelatine is a 'gelling agent'. It is used in some countries in cooking to make jellies, and is made from an animal protein called collagen. There is a lot of collagen in tendons, ligaments and skin. When gelatine is cooked, its long strands of protein form a tangled mesh. As it cools, the long protein strands trap water and the gelatine forms a jelly. If enzymes are added to break down the protein in gelatine, the protein strands become too short to become tangled up. This means that the mesh does not form and the jelly will not 'set'.

A | Pineapple can be used to tenderise chicken.

FACT

Workers in pineapple-canning factories wear protective clothing to stop the fruits causing skin damage.

the mesh of fibres traps water and flavourings

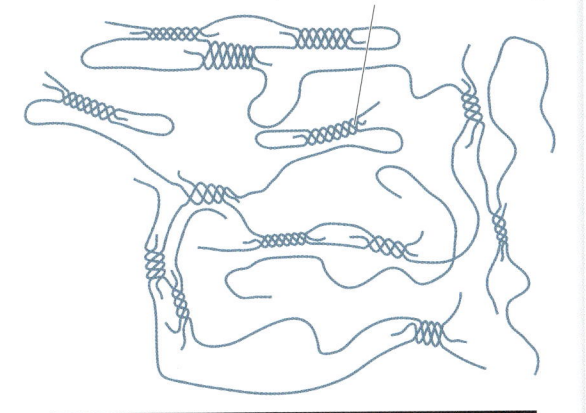

B | The long strands of collagen in gelatine form a tangled mesh when cooked. This mesh traps water as it cools, and so a 'jelly' is formed.

Planning

Working in a group, plan an investigation of your choice to find out how fruits affect gelling agents. There are some ideas below.

- Which fruits contain enzymes that break down proteins?
- Do fruits that stop gelatine forming a jelly also work on vegetarian gelling agents such as agar?
- Does cooking the fruits make a difference to how well their enzymes break down proteins?
- Do canned fruits work as well as fresh ones?
- Do fruit juices contain enzymes that break down proteins?

If you are able to carry out your investigation, write a report about it. Include a conclusion based on your evidence, and an evaluation.

! Check that others in your class are not allergic to any fruits you decide to try. Remember do not *eat* or drink in a lab.

9D3 TEETH

COMMUNICATING WITH THE PUBLIC

Animals use their teeth to chop and grind up their food, making it easier to swallow and starting the process of digestion. Predators may also use their teeth to kill their prey. Animals that lose their teeth often die of starvation.

The enamel on your teeth is the hardest material in your body. It cannot be replaced naturally and is gradually worn away by chewing. Enamel is destroyed more quickly by acids in your food and by acids produced by bacteria. The bacteria form a layer of plaque, which needs to be removed by regular brushing. Bacteria can also infect your gums and cause gum disease. Sometimes they can infect the tissue under a tooth or in your jaw, causing a pus-filled abscess.

Fluoride helps to strengthen the enamel, making it more resistant to wearing away. Fluoride is found in toothpastes and in tap water in some areas. However, dentists recommend that your teeth are checked every six months. Problems can then be spotted and dealt with early, and hardened plaque can be removed.

Destruction of the enamel results in holes (cavities) and, if a dentist does not fill them, they can cause toothache. In severe cases, the tooth can become infected with bacteria and can die, and fall out.

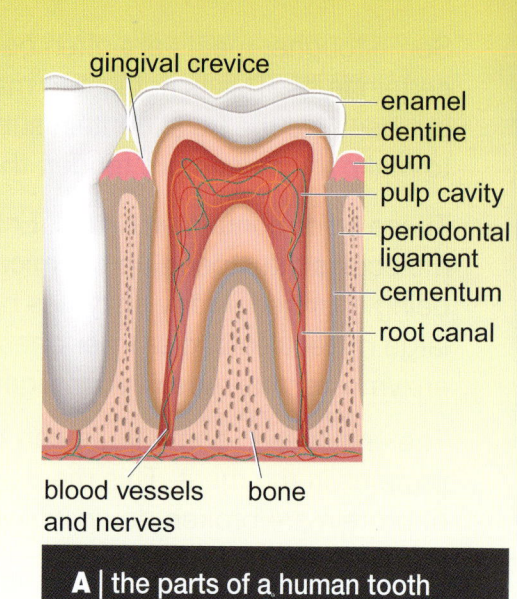

A | the parts of a human tooth

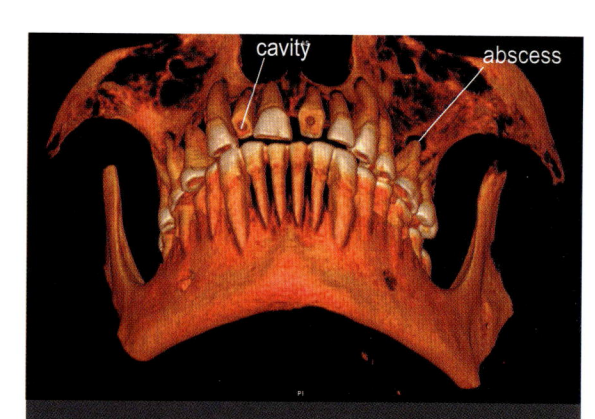

B | This scan of an Ancient Egyptian mummy shows that the man inside may have died of an infection caused by an abscess. His teeth were full of cavities and he must have been in extreme pain.

PROJECT 3

1. A dentist wants a waiting room leaflet entitled 'Looking after your teeth means looking after your diet'. Design and write a leaflet using information from this page, what you know about diet and bacteria, and some research. You should provide explanations for the recommendations that you make, and include:
   - the problems with too many of the wrong sorts of foods in your diet
   - what plaque is and how it is formed
   - how bacteria feed.

2. A dentist may treat an abscess using antibiotics. Do some research to find out how your body fights infections like this and why antibiotics may be needed. You should include what antibiotics are, how they work and why it is important to finish a course of antibiotics. Present your report as a leaflet to be inserted into a packet of antibiotic tablets.

HAVE YOUR SAY

Research and prepare an argument in favour of or against adding fluoride to a water supply.

GLOSSARY

Pronunciation note: A capital 'O' is said as in 'so'

abiotic factor	Something that is abiotic has nothing to do with living organisms (e.g. temperature, the wind).	antibody	A protein made by white blood cells (lymphocytes) that helps to fight microorganisms that might cause diseases.
abundance	The number of organisms in an area. Also called 'population size'.	anus (**ay**-nus)	The opening at the end of the gut.
accuracy (**ack**-U-rass-ee)	A measure of how close a value is to its real value.	apparatus	Pieces of equipment.
accurate (**ack**-yer-it)	A measurement that is close to the true value.	apex predator	Another term for top predator.
acne (**ack**-nee)	Spots on the skin.	artery	A blood vessel that carries blood away from the heart.
adaptation (add-app-**tay**-shun)	The features that something has to enable it to do a certain job or survive in a particular place.	aseptic precautions	Any method to ensure that living microorganisms do not come into contact with something.
adapted	If something has adaptations for a certain job or for survival in a particular place, it is said to be adapted for that job or place.	asexual reproduction	Producing new organisms from one parent only.
addictive	If something makes you feel that you need to have more of it, it is said to be addictive.	asthma	A condition in which the tiny tubes leading to the alveoli become narrow and start to fill with mucus.
adolescence (add-ol-**less**-sense)	A time when physical and emotional changes occur in teenagers.	ATP	compound that is used to store energy in cells until it is needed. ATP stands for adenosine triphosphate.
aerobic exercise (air-**O**-bick)	An exercise in which all the energy needed can be supplied by aerobic respiration.	backbone	A series of small bones (vertebrae) that form a chain to support the main part of some animals' bodies.
aerobic respiration (air-**O**-bick)	A type of respiration in which oxygen is used to release energy from substances, such as glucose.	bacterium	A type of prokaryote microorganism. Plural is bacteria.
afterbirth	When the placenta is pushed out through the vagina after the baby has been born.	balanced diet	Eating a variety of foods to provide all the things the body needs.
aim	What you are trying to find out or do.	ball and socket joint	A joint where one bone can swivel and move in any direction.
algae	Types of protoctists that can photosynthesise.	bar chart	A chart where the lengths or heights of bars (rectangles) represent the values of the variables.
alveolus (al-vee-**O**-lus)	A small pocket in the lungs, in which gases are exchanged between the air and the blood. Plural is alveoli.	bias (**bye**-as)	A shift away from a correct meaning or value.
amino acid	Substance used to make proteins.	biceps	A muscle in the upper arm, used to help pull up the lower arm.
amnion (**am**-nee-on)	A bag containing amniotic fluid.	binary fission	When a cell splits into two.
amniotic fluid (am-nee-**ot**-ick **floo**-id)	The liquid surrounding the growing embryo and protecting it.	biodegradable	Capable of being decomposed (broken down) by organisms in the soil.
anaemia (an-**ee**-me-a)	A deficiency disease caused by a lack of iron. Causes tiredness and shortness of breath.	biodiversity (bI-O-die-**ver**-sit-ee)	The range of different species of organisms in an area.
anaerobic respiration (an-air-**O**-bick)	A type of respiration that does not need oxygen.	biofuel	A fuel made from plants or animal wastes.
		biomass	The mass of organisms living in an area.
		biomechanics	The study of how muscles and bones work together.
analogy (an-al-**O**-jee)	A model that compares something complicated to something that is easier to understand.	biotic factor	An activity of an organism that affects another organism (such as competition or predation).
animal	A member of the animal kingdom. Animals are multicellular and have cells without cell walls.	bladder	The organ that stores urine.
		blood vessel	A tube that carries blood around the body.
anomalous (uh-**nom**-uh-luh s)	Something that does not fit a pattern. When talking about water, this means that water does not behave in the same way as other liquids when it freezes.	bone marrow	The tissue inside bones in which blood cells are made.
		brain	The organ of the nervous system that controls the body and coordinates responses to changes inside and outside the body.
anomalous result (uh-**nom**-uh-luh s)	A measurement that does not fit the same pattern as other measurements from the same experiment.	breathing	The movement of muscles that make the lungs expand and contract.
antagonistic pair (an-**tag**-on-is-tic)	Two muscles that work a hinged joint by pulling a bone in opposite directions.	breathing rate	The number of times you inhale and exhale in one minute.
anther	A male reproductive organ in plants that produces pollen grains.	breathing system (bree-thing)	The organ system that allows an exchange of gases between the blood and the lungs. Also known as the gas exchange system.
antibiotic	Medicine that helps people recover from a bacterial infection by killing the pathogen.	bronchiole	Smallest of the airway tubes in the lungs, leading to the alveoli.

185

bronchus (*bron*-kus)	The trachea splits into two tubes; one bronchus goes into the left lung and the other goes into the right lung. Plural is bronchi.
budding	A type of asexual reproduction in which a new small cell, a bud, grows out from a parent cell.
bulb	An underground plant organ. Some plants only have leaves at certain times of the year and remain as bulbs at other times.
byproduct	A substance produced by a chemical reaction that is not the desired product. For example, the desired product of photosynthesis is glucose, and oxygen is a byproduct.
caffeine (*caff*-een)	A stimulant that increases the speed at which nerves carry impulses. Found in coffee, tea and cola drinks.
cannabis	A drug that can cause memory loss with long-term misuse.
capillary	A thin-walled blood vessel that carries blood from arteries to veins.
carbohydrate	A nutrient that is used as the main source of energy.
carbon cycle	A model used to show how carbon compounds are recycled in an ecosystem.
carbon dioxide	A waste gas produced by respiration.
carbon monoxide	A poisonous gas produced by carbon burning without enough oxygen. Found in cigarette smoke.
cardiovascular disease	A disease in which blood vessels are narrowed by a build-up of a fatty substance. This reduces blood flow.
carnivore	An animal that eats other animals.
carpel	The set of female reproductive organs in plants (ovary, style and stigma).
cartilage	Tough, flexible body tissue found in the ears, nose, many joints and in the larger airway tubes in the lungs (in which it forms strong rings to keep the airways open).
catalyst (*cat*-a-list)	A substance that speeds up a chemical reaction, without itself being used up.
cell	The basic unit of all life. All organisms are made of cells.
cell division (*sell*)	The splitting of a cell to form two identical cells.
cell surface membrane	The membrane that controls what goes into and out of a cell.
cellulose (*sell*-you-lOhs)	A strong plant material used to make cell walls.
cell wall	The tough wall around plant cells. It helps to support and protect the cell.
central nervous system	The brain and spinal cord.
cervix (*sir*-vicks)	The ring of muscle at the bottom of the uterus in females.
chamber	A space inside the heart that blood moves through as the heart pumps.
characteristic	A feature of an organism.
chlorophyll (*klor*-O-fill)	The green substance found inside chloroplasts. It traps energy transferred by light.
chloroplast (*klo*r-O-plast)	A green disc containing chlorophyll. Found in plant cells. Where the plant makes food, using photosynthesis.
chromosome (*krow*-mO-sOwm)	A structure found in the nuclei of cells that contains instructions for organisms and their cells. Each chromosome contains one very long DNA molecule.
ciliated epithelial cell (*sill*-ee-ate-ted) (ep-ith-*ee*-lee-al)	A cell in the tubes leading to and from the lungs that has cilia growing on its surface.
cilium (*sil*-lee-ah)	A small hair-like structure on the surface of some cells. Plural is cilia.
circulatory system (sir-cu-*late*-or-ee)	An organ system that carries oxygen and food around the body.
circumcision (sir-cum-*siz*-shun)	Removal of the foreskin.
claim	A statement that is supposed to be true.
classification	Sorting things into groups.
classify	To sort things into groups.
coarse focusing wheel	The wheel on a microscope that moves parts of the microscope a large amount to get the image into focus.
cocaine	A very powerful and harmful stimulant that can cause blocked arteries and mental problems with long-term misuse.
combustion	Burning, usually in air. The reaction gives out energy, which is transferred to the surroundings by heating or light.
communicable disease	A disease that can be passed from an infected person to an uninfected person. Also called 'infectious disease'.
communication	The transfer of information.
community	All the different species of organism that live in a habitat.
competition (com-pet-*ish*-un)	There is competition between organisms that need the same things as each other. We say that they compete for those things.
concentration gradient	The difference between two concentrations. There will be an overall movement of particles down a concentration gradient, from higher concentration to lower concentration.
conclusion (con-*cloo*-shun)	An explanation of how or why something happens, which is backed up by evidence. You use evidence to 'draw' a conclusion.
constipation	When the intestines get blocked.
consumer	An animal that consumes (eats) other organisms.
continuous	Data values that can change gradually and can have any value (between two limits) are continuous (e.g. human height).
continuous variation	When the value of a variable changes in a continuous way, it shows 'continuous variation'.
contract	To get smaller. When a muscle contracts it uses energy to get shorter and fatter.
contraction (con-*track*-shun)	The uterus muscles squeezing.
convention	A standard way of doing something or representing something, so that everyone understands what is meant.
correlation (cor-al-*lay*-shun)	When two things happen together, such as one variable increasing (or decreasing) as another increases, or two variables changing with the time in a similar way.
coverslip	A thin piece of glass used to hold a specimen in place on a slide. It also keeps the specimen flat and stops it drying out.
Crick, Francis	Scientist who, along with James Watson, worked out the structure of DNA.
criteria (cry-*teer*-ee-a)	A set of standards by which to judge things.
cross-breeding	When sexual reproduction occurs between different varieties or breeds.
cross-pollination (poll-in-*ay*-shun)	When pollen is transferred from one plant to a different plant of the same species.
cubic centimetre (cm^3)	A unit used for measuring volume.
cuticle (*cyou*-tick-ul)	The waxy covering on the outside of many leaves.
cytoplasm (site-O-*plaz*-m)	The watery jelly inside a cell where the cell's activities take place.
daily changes	Changes in the physical environmental factors that happen during a day (e.g. it gets dark at night).
data	Observations or measurements collected in investigations.
decay	The breakdown of dead organisms or animal wastes, which allows the substances they contain to be recycled.
deciduous (des-*sid*-yoo-us)	Plants that lose their leaves in winter.
decomposer	An organism that feeds on dead organisms or animal wastes, causing them to decay.
defecation	Getting rid of undigested food from your gut.

deficiency disease	A disease caused by a lack of a nutrient.
dependent variable (dee-**pend**-ent **var**-ee-able)	The variable that is measured in an investigation. The values of the dependent variable depend on those of the independent variable.
depressant	A drug that decreases the speed at which nerves carry impulses.
diagnosis	A conclusion about what is wrong with an organism. It is based on evidence from symptoms and tests.
diaphragm (**dye**-a-fram)	An organ containing a lot of muscle tissue, which contracts and moves downwards to increase the volume of the lungs when inhaling.
diet	The food that you eat.
diffusion (diff-**you**-zshun)	When particles spread and mix with each other without anything moving them. Diffusion into and out of cells occurs for particles that are small enough to pass through the cell surface membrane.
digested	When food has been broken down it has been 'digested'.
digestion (dye-**jes**-jun)	A process that breaks food into soluble substances in our bodies.
digestive juice	A liquid containing enzymes that break down food.
digestive system (die-**jest**-iv)	An organ system that breaks down food.
discontinuous	Data values that can only have one of a set number of options are discontinuous (e.g. shoe sizes, days of the week and blood group).
discontinuous variation	When the value of a variable changes in a discontinuous way it shows 'discontinuous variation'.
discrete (dis-**kreet**)	Data that involves a limited number of values (numbers).
disease	Something that makes you ill, such as infection by a pathogen or not having a healthy diet.
distribution	How the organisms are spread throughout an area, such as evenly, randomly or clumped.
DNA	A large molecule that contains genes. Short for deoxyribonucleic acid.
dormant	If something is dormant its life processes are very slow.
double circulatory system	A circulatory system with two main loops, in which blood goes through the heart twice on its way around an animal's body.
double helix	Two helices joined so that they are in parallel.
drug	A substance that affects the way your body works.
ductile	A ductile material can be pulled into a wire, without breaking.
ecosystem	All the physical environmental factors and all the organisms that are found in a habitat.
ecstasy	A stimulant that can cause depression, mental illness and even death with long-term misuse.
effectors	Organs that bring about responses to changes inside the body and in the surroundings, such as muscles that cause movement and glands that produce hormones.
egestion (ee-**jes**-jun)	When faeces are pushed out of the anus.
egg cell	The female sex cell (gamete).
ejaculation	When semen is pumped out of a man's penis.
embryo (**em**-bree-O)	The tiny new life that grows by cell division from a fertilised egg cell.
emphysema (em-fee-**see**-ma)	A disease in which the lungs cannot take much oxygen out of the air because the walls of the alveoli have broken down.
endangered (en-**dayn**-jerd)	When a type of organism is in danger of ceasing to exist.
endemic	Belonging to a certain area, and only naturally found in that area.
energy	Something that is needed to make things happen or change.
environment	The conditions in a habitat caused by physical environmental factors and living organisms.
environmental variation	Differences between organisms caused by environmental factors.
enzyme	A substance that can speed up some processes in living things (e.g. breaking down food molecules).
epidermis cell	Cell that forms tissue covering the surface of an organ.
erection	When the penis becomes stiff.
estimate	An approximate answer, often calculated from a sample or using rounded values.
ethical questions	Questions about what people think is fair or right and wrong.
eutrophication	When a body of water contains excessive levels of nutrients (e.g. nitrates from fertilisers).
evaluate	Looking at the good and bad points about something, in order to reach an overall decision.
evaluation	Weighing up plus points and minus points to reach a judgement about something (e.g. how good something is, how well something does its job, how safe something is).
evaporation	When a liquid changes into a gas.
evergreen	Plants that do not lose their leaves in winter.
evidence	Data used to support an idea or show that it is wrong.
evolution	A change in one or more characteristics of a population over a long period of time.
excess post-exercise oxygen consumption (EPOC)	The need for extra oxygen after exercise, to break down lactic acid and replace the oxygen lost from blood and muscle cells.
excrete (ex-**creet**)	To get rid of waste. All organisms excrete.
exhalation	Breathing out. Also called expiration.
expiration	Breathing out. Also called exhalation.
external fertilisation	When fertilisation happens outside the bodies of the parents.
extinct	Something that no longer exists is extinct.
eyepiece lens	The part of the microscope you look down.
faeces (**fee**-sees)	Waste food material produced by the intestines.
fallopian tube	Another term for an oviduct.
fat	A nutrient that is stored to be used for energy in the future. It also acts as a thermal insulator.
fat tissue (**tiss**-you)	Tissue that stores fat. It is made of fat cells.
fermentation (fer-ment-**ay**-shun)	Anaerobic respiration occurring in microorganisms.
fermenter	A container in which microorganisms are cultured to produce a useful substance on a large scale - the product is collected from the solution in which the microorganisms have grown.
fertile	Able to produce offspring.
fertilisation (fert-ill-I-**zay**-shun)	Fusing of a male gamete with a female gamete.
fertilised egg cell (**fert**-ill-I-zed)	What is produced when two gametes fuse.
fibre (**fY**-ber)	A substance found in food that is not used up by the body. It helps to keep our intestines clean.
filament	A male reproductive organ in plants that supports the anther.
fine focusing wheel	The wheel on a microscope that moves parts of the microscope a small amount to bring the image into focus.
fixed joint	A place where two or more bones meet but cannot move.
flagellum (fla-**jel**-lum)	A tail-like structure that rotates, allowing a unicellular organism to move. Plural is flagella.
flexible joint	A place where two or more bones meet and can be moved (by muscles).
focus	To make an image clear and sharp. If an image is 'in focus' it is clear and sharp.

187

foetus (*fee*-tus)	An embryo is known as a foetus once it has developed a full set of organs.
food chain	A way of showing what eats what in a habitat.
foodpipe	An organ in the shape of a tube that takes food from your mouth to your stomach. Also called the 'gullet' or 'oesophagus'.
food web	Many food chains linked together, showing the flow of energy through organisms in a habitat.
force	A push, pull or twist.
foreskin	A covering of skin protecting the head of the penis.
fracture	Break.
Franklin, Rosalind	Scientist whose experiments produced evidence that helped Watson and Crick work out the structure of DNA.
frequency diagram (*free*-kwen-see)	Any chart or graph that shows a frequency (the number of things) on the y-axis.
fruit (*froot*)	Something used to carry the seeds of flowering plants. Can be fleshy or dry.
fuel	A substance that contains a store of chemical energy that can easily be transferred.
function (*funk*-shun)	The job or role something has.
fungicide (*fung*-giss-ide)	Pesticide that kills fungi.
fungus	A member of the fungus kingdom. A fungus can be multicellular or unicellular but does not make its own food. Plural is fungi.
fuse (*fewz*)	When two things join together to become one.
gamete (*gam*-meet)	A cell used for sexual reproduction.
gas exchange	When one gas is swapped for another. In the lungs, oxygen leaves the air and goes into the blood. At the same time, carbon dioxide leaves the blood and goes into the air in the lungs.
gas exchange system	The organ system that allows the exchange of gases in the lungs. Also known as the breathing system.
gene (*jeen*)	A length of DNA that contains the instructions for making a protein, and helps to produce an inherited characteristic of an organism.
gene bank	Any facility that stores genetic material from different organisms (e.g. seeds, gametes, tissue samples).
genetic engineering	When scientists make changes to the genetic material (the DNA) of an organism.
genetic information (*jen-et*-tick)	The inherited instructions that control your characteristics.
genetic modification	Altering the DNA of an organism.
genetic variation	Another term for 'inherited variation'.
genus (*jeen*-ous)	A group of similar organisms. The genus name is the first word in the scientific name for a species.
germinate	When a seed starts to grow.
germination (*jer-min-ay*-shun)	When a seed starts to grow.
gestation period (*jess-tay*-shun)	The length of time from fertilisation to birth.
gills	A series of flaps of tissue with a good blood supply just behind the head of an organism and used to take oxygen out of the water. Fish have gills.
gland	Tissue that makes and releases substances. The glands in the male reproductive system add liquids to sperm cells to make semen. Glands in the hormonal system produce hormones that are released into the blood.
global warming	Increased warming of the Earth's surface as a result of increased amounts of carbon dioxide and other greenhouse gases in the air.
glucose	An important sugar, which is used as a reactant in respiration. It is also a product of photosynthesis
grow	To increase in size. All organisms grow.
guard cell	One of a pair of cells that help to open and close a stoma.
gullet (*gull*-ett)	A more scientific name for the 'foodpipe'. Also called the 'oesophagus'.
gut	The organs that form the tube running from the mouth to the anus.
habitat	The place where an organism lives (e.g. woodland).
haemoglobin (hee-mow-*glow*-bin)	The substance that carries oxygen in red blood cells.
half-life	The time taken for half of a substance to disappear or be used up.
heart (*hart*)	The organ that pumps blood.
heart attack	When heart muscle cells start to die.
heart disease	A disease caused by narrowing of the arteries carrying blood to the muscles of the heart, so the heart muscles do not receive enough oxygen.
herbicide (*herb*-iss-ide)	Pesticide that kills plants. Also called a 'weedkiller'.
herbivore	An animal that eats plants.
heroin	A powerful depressant drug, which can have dangerous side-effects.
hibernation (hy-ber-*nay*-shun)	When animals hide away during the winter and become very inactive.
hinge joint	A joint that allows back and forth movement in one direction.
hormone	A chemical messenger that is released from a gland into the blood and carried around the body.
host	Organism that provides food and shelter for a parasite.
hybrid	An organism produced when members of two different species reproduce with each other.
hydrogen carbonate indicator	An indicator that is pink in water but turns yellow as carbon dioxide is added and the pH drops.
hygiene (*hi*-jean)	Keeping things clean, and killing microorganisms to reduce risk of infection.
hypothesis (hy-*poth*-uh-sis)	An idea about how something works that can be tested using experiments. Plural = hypotheses.
image	A picture that forms in a mirror or on a screen, or is made by a lens. You see an image when looking down a microscope.
immune	When a person does not fall ill after infection with a pathogen because their white blood cells destroy the pathogen quickly.
immunisation (imm-you-ny-*say*-shun)	Protecting a person from a particular disease by getting their body to recognise and attack the pathogen that causes the disease.
implantation (im-plant-*ay*-shun)	When an embryo sinks into the lining of the uterus.
impulse	An electrical signal that travels in the nervous system.
independent variable	The variable that you chose the values of in an investigation.
indicator	A substance that changes colour in solutions of different acidity and alkalinity.
infectious disease	Another term for 'communicable disease'.
ingest	To take in something in order to digest it.
ingestion	Taking substances into the body. For example, we ingest food using our mouths.
inhalation	Breathing in. Also called inspiration.
inherited	A feature that an organism gets from a parent is inherited.
inherited variation	Differences between organisms passed on to offspring by their parents in reproduction.
innovation	When you innovate, you take something and make improvements to it.

insecticide (in-**sect**-iss-ide)	Pesticide that kills insects.
insoluble	Describes a substance that cannot dissolve in a certain liquid.
inspiration	Breathing in. Also called inhalation.
intercostal muscles	Muscles attached to the ribs. The muscles move the ribs during breathing.
interdependent	Organisms that depend on one another are said to be interdependent.
internal fertilisation	When fertilisation happens inside the body of a parent.
interquartile range	The difference between the lower quartile and the upper quartile in a data set: interquartile range = upper quartile – lower quartile.
inter-specific	Meaning between two species. For example, inter-specific competition is when organisms from different species compete with one another.
intra-specific	Meaning within the same species. For example, intra-specific competition is when organisms from the same species compete with one another.
invention	When you invent, you create something that has not been created before.
journal (scientific)	A scientific magazine in which scientists publish their findings by writing articles called scientific papers.
kidney	An organ used to clean the blood and make urine.
kilojoule (kJ) (**kill**-O-jool)	A unit for measuring energy. There are 1000 joules (J) in 1 kilojoule (kJ).
kingdom	There are five kingdoms into which organisms are divided: plants, animals, fungi, protoctists and prokaryotes.
kwashiorkor	A deficiency disease caused by a lack of protein.
labour	Labour starts when contractions begin in the uterus and ends when the afterbirth has come out.
large intestine	An organ in which water is removed from undigested food.
leaf	A plant organ used to make food by photosynthesis.
life cycle	The series of changes in an organism as it grows, matures and reproduces.
life process	A process that something does in order for it to be alive. The life processes that happen in all living things are movement, reproduction, sensitivity, growth, respiration, excretion and a need for nutrition.
ligament	A band of tissue that connects bones together.
limewater	A solution of calcium hydroxide. It is clear and colourless but turns 'milky' in contact with carbon dioxide.
limiting factor	Something that stops a population growing.
line of best fit	A line drawn on a scatter graph that goes through the middle of the points, so that about half the points are above the line and about half of them are below the line.
lipid	Fats (and oils) are part of a large group of similar substances called lipids.
liver	An organ used to make and destroy substances in your body. It also stores some substances.
locomotor system (**low**-cO-mow-ter)	An organ system that contains all your muscles and bones and allows you to move.
lung	An organ used to take oxygen out of the air and into the blood. Lungs also put waste carbon dioxide into the air.
lymphocyte	A type of white blood cell that makes antibodies.
magnification (mag-nif-ick-**ay**-shun)	How much bigger something appears compared with its actual size.
malnutrition (mal-new-**trish**-un)	A problem caused by having too much or too little of a nutrient in the diet. Obesity, starvation and deficiency diseases are all examples.
mammal	Animal that has hair and produces milk to feed its offspring.
mammary gland	A gland that produces milk. Mammary glands are contained in the breasts and in women produce milk after giving birth.
mass	The amount of matter that something is made from. Mass is measured in grams (g) and kilograms (kg).
mean	An average calculated by adding up the values of a set of measurements and dividing by the number of measurements.
median	The middle value in a set of numbers that has been written in order.
medicine (med-iss-in)	A drug that helps the body to ease the symptoms of a disease or cure the disease.
memory cell	A type of lymphocyte that is able to produce specific antibodies that will help to destroy a certain pathogen.
menopause (men-O-pors)	When the ovaries in women stop releasing egg cells.
menstrual cycle (**men**-strew-al)	A series of events lasting about a month, happening in the female reproductive system. The cycle causes ovulation and the lining of the uterus is replaced.
menstruation (men-strew-**ay**-shun)	When the lining of the uterus and a little blood pass out of the vagina as part of the menstrual cycle.
microorganism	An organism too small to be seen with the naked eye.
microvillus	A fold on the surface of a villus cell. Microvilli increase the surface area so that digested food is absorbed more quickly.
migration (my-**gray**-shun)	When animals move to different areas depending on the season.
mineral	An element that is a nutrient needed in small quantities for health (e.g. calcium). Minerals are found in foods and soils as compounds called mineral salts.
mineral salt	A compound containing an important element that is needed in small quantities for health (e.g. calcium). Plants get their mineral salts from the soil, animals get them from food.
mitochondria (my-tow-**kon**-dree-a)	Small structures (organelles) in the cytoplasm of all cells, where aerobic respiration occurs. Singular is mitochondrion.
mnemonic (nem-**on**-ick)	A pattern of letters or words that helps you to remember something.
model	A way of showing or representing something that helps you to think about it or find out about it.
move	To go from place to place. All organisms can move themselves or parts of themselves.
mucus	A sticky liquid produced by certain cells in the body, including some cells found in the tubes leading to and from the lungs.
multicellular	An organism made of many cells.
muscle cell (**muss**-ell)	Cell that can change its length and so move things.
muscle tissue (**muss**-ell **tiss**-you)	Tissue that can change shape and move things. There is muscle tissue in the heart.
native	Naturally found in a certain area.
natural selection	A process in which an organism is more likely to survive and reproduce than other members of the species because it possesses a certain inherited variation.
navel (**nave**-ell)	The scar left by the umbilical cord. Often called the 'belly button'.
nectary	A part of a flower that produces a sweet nectar, on which some animals like to feed.
nerve	An organ that is made of nerve cells (neurons) that carry impulses between the spinal cord and all other parts of the body (not the brain).
nervous system (**nerve**-us)	An organ system that contains your brain, spinal cord and all your nerves and carries impulses (signals) around the body. This system helps us to sense and respond quickly to changes inside and outside the body.
newton (N)	The unit for measuring force.
nicotine	An addictive drug found in tobacco smoke.
night blindness	A deficiency disease caused by a lack of vitamin A. A person with the disease cannot see very well in dim light.

nitrate (*ny*-trait)	Mineral salt needed by plants to make proteins.
nocturnal (*nock-ter*-nal)	Organisms that are active at night are nocturnal.
non-communicable disease	A disease that cannot be passed by the person who has it to other people around them, such as diseases caused by poor diet or unhealthy lifestyle, or diseases that are inherited.
normal distribution	When many things have a middle value with fewer things having greater or lesser values. This sort of data forms a bell shape on charts and graphs.
nucleus (*new-clee*-us)	The 'control centre' of a cell. Plural = nuclei.
nutrient (*new-tree*-ent)	A substance needed in the diet to provide raw materials for making new substances and for energy release.
nutrition (*new-trish*-un)	Substances that help organisms respire and grow. All organisms need nutrition.
obesity (*ob-ee-sit*-ee)	Being very overweight.
objective lens	The part of the microscope that is closest to the specimen.
obligate parasite	A parasite that cannot reproduce without being in its host.
observation	Something that you see happening.
oesophagus	The muscular tube that leads from the mouth to the stomach. Also called the 'gullet'.
offspring	The new organisms produced by reproduction.
oil	A liquid fat.
organ	A large part of a plant or animal that does an important job. Organs are made of different tissues working together.
organic farming	Producing foods without the use of lots of artificial chemical substances.
organic molecule	A molecule that is built using a chain of carbon atoms.
organism	A living thing.
organ system	A collection of organs working together to do an important job.
organ transplant	Taking an organ from one person to put it into another.
osmosis (*os-mo*-sis)	The type of diffusion that describes the overall movement of solvent molecules in a solution across a partially permeable membrane.
outlier	Another term for 'anomalous result'.
ovary (*O*-very)	A female reproductive organ. Produces egg cells.
oviduct	A tube that carries egg cells from the ovaries to the uterus in females. Fertilisation happens here.
ovulation	Release of an egg cell from an ovary.
ovule	Contains an egg cell in plants. An ovary contains ovules.
ovum/ova	Another term for egg cell.
oxygen	A gas that makes up about 21 per cent of the air. It is needed for aerobic respiration.
oxygen debt	An older term for EPOC.
palisade cell	Tall cell found in leaves that contains many chloroplasts.
pancreas	An organ that produces some digestive enzymes, as well as some hormones.
pandemic	An infectious disease that spreads to many people in more than one country in a short time.
parasite	Organism or virus that lives on or in a living host organism and takes food from it, causing harm to the host.
parent	An organism that has produced offspring.
partially permeable membrane	A membrane, such as the cell surface membrane, that lets some particles cross through it but not others.
pathogen (*path*-o-jen)	A microbe that causes disease, such as polio virus, cholera bacterium, malaria protoctist, mould fungus.
peer review	An evaluation of the quality of a scientific paper carried out by other scientists who work in the same area of science.
penis	Part of the male reproductive system in mammals.
persistent	A chemical substance that does not get broken down in nature very quickly is persistent. It stays around for a long time.
pest	An organism that damages things that humans want to use (e.g. a crop).
pesticide (*pess*-ti-side)	A chemical substance that kills pests.
pH	A numerical scale from 1 to 14 showing how acidic or alkaline a substance is. Acids have a pH below 7, neutral substances have a pH of 7 and alkalis have a pH greater than 7.
phagocyte	A type of white blood cell that can ingest pathogens.
phloem tissue/vessel (*flow*-em)	Tube made of living phloem cells that transports dissolved substances (e.g. sugars) around the plant.
photosynthesis (*fO-tow-sinth*-e-sis)	A process that plants use to make their own food. It needs light to work.
physical environmental factors	Physical (non-living) features of an environment (e.g. amount of rain; amount of light).
placenta (*plas-en*-ta)	This is attached to the uterus wall. It transfers oxygen and food out of the mother's blood into the foetus and transfers waste materials from the foetus into the mother's blood.
plant	A member of the plant kingdom. Plants have chloroplasts and so can photosynthesise.
plant kingdom	A group of organisms that have cells with cell walls made of cellulose and that are able to photosynthesise.
plasma	The liquid part of the blood.
pollen grain	The container for the male gamete in plants.
pollen tube	A tube that grows from a pollen grain down through the stigma and style and into the ovary.
pollination (*poll-in-ay*-shun)	The transfer of pollen from an anther to a stigma.
polymer	A substance made up of very long molecules containing repeating groups of atoms.
population (*pop-U-lay*-shun)	The number of a certain organism found in a certain area.
precise	Measurements that are close to one another.
predation (*pred-ay*-shun)	A biotic factor in which an animal (the prey) is killed and eaten by another (the predator).
predator (*pred-att*-er)	An animal that catches and eats other animals.
prediction	What you think will happen in an experiment.
prefix (*pree*-fix)	Something added to the beginning of a word to change its meaning. In 'kilometre', 'kilo' is the prefix.
pregnant	When a female animal has an embryo growing inside her uterus.
premature	When a baby is born much earlier than expected, it is premature.
pressure	The amount of force pushing on a certain area.
prey (*pray*)	An animal that is caught and eaten by another animal.
probability	The likelihood of something happening.
producer	An organism that makes its own food, such as a plant using photosynthesis. Producers form the first trophic level in a food web or food chain.
product (*prod*-uct)	A new substance made in a chemical reaction. In a word equation, products are written on the right side, after the arrow.
prokaryote (*prO-ka-ree*-oat)	A member of the prokaryote kingdom. Prokaryotes are all unicellular and have cells that lack nuclei.
proportional (*prO-por-shun*-al)	A relationship between two variables where one doubles if the other doubles. A graph of the two variables would be a straight line through the origin.
protein (*prO*-teen)	A nutrient used for growth and repair.
protoctist (*prO-tock*-tist)	A member of the protoctist kingdom. Many protoctists are unicellular.

pseudopod (*syoo*-dO-pod)	An extension from a cell that can extend and contract and so pull a cell in a certain direction.
puberty (*pew*-bert-ty)	A time during which big physical changes happen in the body.
pulse	A feeling of the heart beating that can be felt in arteries.
pulse rate	The number of times a pulse is felt in a minute.
pyramid of biomass	Diagram showing the biomass in each trophic level of a food chain.
pyramid of numbers	Diagram showing the numbers of different organisms at each trophic level in a food chain.
quadrat	A square frame, thrown randomly on the ground, which is used to sample plants in an area.
quartile	The values of one-quarter (lower quartile) and three-quarters (upper quartile) through a set of values that have been written in order.
random	When there is an equal chance for one event occurring as there is for any other events in the same set.
random error	An error that can be different for every reading.
range	The difference between the highest and lowest values in a set of data (usually ignoring any anomalous results).
rate	The rate at which something happens is its speed.
ratio	A way of comparing two different quantities. The two numbers are separated by a colon (:).
raw material	A substance used to make other substances.
reaction time	The time it takes you to respond to things happening around you.
recreational drug (*reck-ree-ay-shun-al*)	A drug used for its mind-altering effect and not as a medicine.
rectum	An organ that stores faeces before they are egested.
red blood cell	A blood cell that carries oxygen.
Reference Intake (RI)	The amount of a nutrient that people are advised to eat in a day.
relationship	A link between two variables, so that when one thing changes so does the other. Best seen by using a scatter graph. Also called a correlation.
relax	When a muscle relaxes it stops exerting a force and becomes thinner and longer.
replicate	To make copies. Viruses replicate (make copies of themselves) when they enter a living host cell.
replication	When a virus (or DNA) makes copies of itself.
reproduce	When organisms reproduce, they make more organisms like themselves.
reproductive organ	An organ used in sexual reproduction.
reproductive system	All the reproductive organs.
resistant	Unaffected or less affected by something.
resource (*rez-ors*)	Something needed by an organism. For example, plants need light as a resource and animals need food as a resource.
respiration (*res-per-ay-shun*)	A process in which energy is released from substances so it can be used by an organism. All organisms respire.
respiratory system	Another term for the breathing system.
response	A reaction to something (e.g. the release of hormone by a gland is a response to another hormone in the blood).
result	A measurement or observation from an experiment.
rickets	A deficiency disease caused by a lack of calcium (or a lack of vitamin D). It causes weak and poorly shaped bones.
root	A plant organ used to take water out of the soil.
root hair cell	Cell found in plant roots that has a large surface area to get water out of the ground quickly.
root hair tissue (*tiss-yoo*)	Tissue that helps roots get water out of the ground quickly. This tissue is made out of root hair cells.
runner	A stem that grows from certain plants (e.g. strawberry), from which new plants grow using asexual reproduction.
saliva (*sall-eye-va*)	A digestive juice. It contains an enzyme that breaks down starch into sugar.
salivary gland	Found in the mouth. It makes saliva.
sample	To take a small part of something to investigate. You use a sample to draw conclusions about what the larger whole is like.
scatter graph	A graph in which data for two variables is plotted as points. This allows you to see whether there is a relationship between the two variables. Lines (or curves) of best fit are often drawn through the points.
scientific method	Any way of testing that involves collecting information in order to show whether an idea is right or wrong. This is often done by developing a hypothesis that is tested by using it to make a prediction. The prediction is then tested using experiments.
scientific paper	An article written by scientists and published in a science magazine called a journal. It is like an investigation report but usually shows the results and conclusions drawn from many experiments.
scrotum (*scrow-tum*)	The bag of skin containing the testes in males.
scurvy	A deficiency disease caused by a lack of vitamin C. Joints hurt, the gums bleed and cuts take a long time to heal.
seasonal change	Change in the physical environmental factors of an environment that happens during the course of a year (e.g. it gets colder in winter).
seed	A small part of a plant formed by sexual reproduction that can grow into a new plant.
seed dispersal	The spreading of seeds away from a parent plant.
seed coat	The tough outer covering of a seed.
seedling	A newly germinated plant.
selective breeding	When humans choose an organism that has a certain characteristic and breed more of these organisms, often making that chosen characteristic more and more obvious.
selective (herbicide)	A herbicide that only kills certain types of plants.
self-pollination (*poll-in-ay-shun*)	When pollen is transferred from a flower on a plant to a stigma in the same flower or to another flower on the same plant.
semen (*see-men*)	The mixture of sperm and special fluids released by males during ejaculation.
sense	To detect things in the surroundings. All organisms can sense certain changes in their surroundings.
sense organs	Organs that contain receptor cells, such as the eye, ear, nose and skin.
sepal	A leaf-like structure that protects a flower bud.
sex cell	Another word for a gamete.
sex chromosome (*krow-mO-sOwm*)	Chromosome that determines the sex of an organism. In humans, males have one X sex chromosome and one Y sex chromosome, while females have two Xs.
sex hormones (*hor-moans*)	Natural chemicals released in the body that control the menstrual cycle and puberty.
sexual intercourse	During which semen is ejaculated into the end of the vagina.
sexual reproduction (*ree-prod-uck-shun*)	Reproduction that needs two individuals to produce a new organism of the same type.
side-effect	A harmful or unpleasant effect caused by a drug.
single circulatory system	A circulatory system with only one loop, in which blood goes through the heart once on its way around an animal's body.
skeleton	The structure that supports an organism and gives it its shape. It is made of 206 bones in an adult human.
skin	The organ that covers the body. It is used for protection and to detect changes in the environment (e.g. temperature).
skull	A collection of bones that protects the brain.
slide	A glass sheet that a specimen is put on.

small intestine	An organ in which most digestion happens. The soluble substances produced by digestion are absorbed into the blood here.
soluble	Describes a substance that can dissolve in a liquid.
solvent	A liquid in which a substance dissolves to make a solution. Some solvents (found in glues) can be dangerous.
specialised	If something has features that allow it to do a particular job it is said to be specialised.
species (*spee*-shees or *spee*-sees)	A group of organisms that can reproduce with each other to produce offspring that will also be able to reproduce.
specimen (*spess*-im-men)	The object you look at using a microscope.
sperm cell	The male sex cell (gamete).
sperm duct	The tube that carries sperm cells from the testes to the urethra.
spinal cord (*spy*-nal kord)	The large bundle of nerves that runs through the vertebrae (backbone). Nerve cells in the spinal cord carry electrical impulses to and from the brain to many other parts of the body.
stage	Part of a microscope. You put a slide on it.
stain	A dye used to colour parts of a cell to make them easier to see.
stamen	The set of male reproductive organs in plants (anther and filament).
starch	A type of insoluble carbohydrate found in plants. The glucose made in photosynthesis is used to make starch.
starvation	A form of malnutrition in which people lack many nutrients.
statement key	A series of descriptive statements used to work out what something is.
stem	A plant organ used to take water to and support the leaves.
sterilisation	Making something free from living microorganisms (usually by killing them).
stigma	Part of the female reproductive organs in a plant. It is where pollen lands.
stimulant (*stim*-you-lant)	A drug that increases the speed at which nerves carry messages (e.g. caffeine).
stimuli (*stim*-you-lie)	Changes inside and outside the body that the body detects and responds to.
stoma (*stO*-ma)	A tiny hole in a leaf through which gases can diffuse into and out of the leaf. Plural is stomata.
stomach (*stum*-ack)	An organ containing strong acid that mixes food up and digests proteins.
storage organ	An organ used by plants to store materials.
style	Part of the carpel in the female reproductive organs of a plant. It connects the stigma to the ovary.
substance abuse	Taking any substance in a way that causes harm to the body.
substance misuse	Another term for substance abuse.
sucrose	The sugar that is transported around plants. It is also known as table sugar.
sugar	A type of soluble carbohydrate. Glucose and sucrose are examples of sugars.
surface area	The total area of all the surfaces of a three-dimensional object.
surface area : volume ratio (SA:V)	The total amount of surface area of an object divided by its volume.
sustainable development	Developing the things humans need, without destroying habitats and ecosystems.
symbol equation (eck-*way*-shun)	A way of writing out what happens in a chemical reaction using symbols to represent the substances involved.
symptom (*simp*-tom)	Changes in the way the body works when it is affected by a disease, which help a doctor to work out what is wrong with you.
systematic error (sis-tem-*at*-ick)	An error that is the same for all readings, such as when forgetting to zero a balance before using it to measure a series of masses.
tar	A sticky substance found in cigarette smoke, which contains harmful compounds including some that can cause cancer.
target cell/organ	Cells or organs that respond to hormones by changing what they are doing.
tendon	A cord of tissue that connects a muscle to a bone.
testis	A male reproductive organ. Produces sperm cells. Plural = testes.
theory (*thear*-ree)	A hypothesis (or set of hypotheses) that explains how and why something happens. The predictions made using a theory should have been tested on several occasions and always found to work.
tidal volume	The volume of air that you inhale and exhale in each normal breath.
tissue (*tish*-you)	A part of an organ that does an important job. Each tissue is made up of a group of the same type of cells all doing the same job.
tissue fluid	The liquid formed when plasma leaks out of capillaries, carrying oxygen and food to cells.
top predator	A predator that is not prey to other animals.
trachea (track-*ee*-a)	An organ in the shape of a tube that takes air to and from your lungs. Also called the 'windpipe'.
transfer	When energy moves from one place to another.
transgenic	An organism is transgenic if genetic modification has added DNA from another species into it.
triceps	A muscle in the upper arm, used to help push down the lower arm.
trophic level (*trO*-fic *lev*-ell)	Feeding level in a food chain, such as producer, primary consumer, secondary consumer.
tuber (*tyew*-ber)	The swollen part of an underground stem used as a storage organ and as a method of asexual reproduction in some plants.
tuberculosis (TB)	A communicable bacterial disease that infects the lungs.
ultrasound scan	A picture of what is inside someone's body, created by an ultrasound scanner, using sound.
umbilical cord (um-*bill*-ick-al)	The tissue that carries food, oxygen and waste between the placenta and the growing embryo or foetus.
unicellular	An organism made of one cell.
urethra (you-*ree*-thra)	The tube that carries sperm cells from the testes and urine from the bladder.
urinary system (*your*-in-air-ee)	An organ system that cleans the blood and removes wastes in urine.
uterus (*you*-ter-ous)	The organ in females in which a baby develops.
vaccine	A substance introduced into the body to make a person immune to a certain pathogen.
vacuole (*vack*-you-oll)	Storage space in cells.
vagina (*vaj*-eye-na)	The tube in females leading from the cervix to the outside. The penis is placed here during sexual intercourse.
valid	Something is valid if it is doing what it is supposed to do. A measurement is valid if it measures what it is supposed to measure. A valid conclusion is drawn only from the data that the conclusion is supposed to be drawn from.
variable (*vair*-ee-ab-el)	Anything that can change and be measured.
variation (vair-ee-*ay*-shun)	The differences between things.
variety	A group of plants that has different characteristics from other plants of the same species.
vein	A blood vessel that carries blood towards the heart.

ventilation (vent-ill-**ay**-shun)	The movement of air in and out of your lungs.
vertebra (vert-teb-**bra**)	A small bone that forms part of the 'backbone'. Plural = vertebrae.
villus	A small finger-like part of the small intestine. Villi increase the surface area so that digested food is absorbed more quickly.
virus (**vy**-rus)	A non-living particle that is formed from an outer protein coat surrounding genetic material. It can change how a living cell functions when it enters a cell and causes the cell to make copies of the virus.
vital capacity	A measure of the total volume of your lungs. It is the total volume of air that you are able to exhale after taking as much air as you can into your lungs.
vitamin	A nutrient needed in small quantities for health (e.g. vitamin C).
Watson, James	Scientist, who along with Francis Crick, worked out the structure of DNA.
weedkiller	Another name for a 'herbicide'.
white blood cell	A blood cell that fights microorganisms.
Wilkins, Maurice	Scientist whose experiments produced evidence to support our current understanding of the structure of DNA.
wilting	When a plant droops because it has too little water.
windpipe	An organ in the shape of a tube that takes air to and from your lungs. Also called the 'trachea'.
word equation (eck-**way**-shun)	An equation in which the names of the reactant(s) are written on the left side, there is an arrow pointing from left to right and the names of the product(s) are written on the right side. A word equation is a type of model.
xylem tissue/vessel (**zy**-lem **tiss**-you)	Tube that carries water (and dissolved mineral salts) in plants. It is found in stems and roots and is made of xylem cells.
zygote (**zy**-goat)	Another term for fertilised egg cell.

STEM skills

The STEM pages in each unit focus on key STEM skills. These skills are listed and described below.

STEM skill	STEM skill description	STEM pages developing skill
Numeracy and use of maths	Using maths	8B, 8C 9A, 9C
Generation and analysis of data	Design ways of collecting and analysing data to reach answers.	8C
Critical analysis and evaluation	Give reasons why data (or proposed solutions) are or are not good enough (e.g. to answer questions, solve problems).	7C 8C
Application of knowledge	Apply knowledge to unfamiliar contexts to reach answers. Understanding of the principles of science and mathematics	7B, 7D 9A
Communication	Use language and maths to communicate ideas effectively.	9B
Innovation and invention	Combine ideas to reach answers.	8A, 8D
Problem-solving	Use reasoning and systematic approaches to reach answers.	7A

INDEX

abiotic factors 58, 134, 176
absorption of food 8, 78, 82–3
abundance 176
accidental bias 163
accuracy 88–9, 177
adaptation 58–9, 61, 64, 144, 152–3
addictive substances 50–1
adolescence 34
aerobic exercise 114
aerobic respiration 102–3, 122, 151
air quality 94–5
alcohol 30, 50, 51, 83
algae 160
allergies 183
alveoli 105, 109
amnion 29
anaemia 74
anaerobic respiration 114–5, 122–3, 124, 131
animal smuggling 182
animals, treating 169
anomalous results (outliers) 107
anthers 92
antibiotics 120, 165, 172
antibodies 31, 167
anus 78
Aristotle 150
arteries 40, 41, 42, 51
artificial limbs 48–9
aseptic precautions 173
asexual reproduction 91, 122
asthma 109
autoimmune diseases 172
backbone 44, 45
bacteria 79, 119, 124–5, 131
baking bread 122
balanced diets 74–5
Baptista van Helmont, Jan 150
bar charts 56, 57
bias 162–3
binary fission 124
biodiversity 86–7, 145, 177
biofuels 86
biomechanics 46
biotic factors 63, 134
Black Death 117, 132
bladder 8, 26, 37
blood 5, 29, 41
    cells 41, 44, 52, 108
    gas exchange 104–5
    and nutrients 12, 18, 29
    and oxygen 8, 12, 29, 31, 38, 41, 42, 108–9
    oxygen saturation ('sats') 102
blood vessels 18, 38, 40, 108
bone marrow 41, 44
bones 10, 11, 18, 41, 44–5, 46–7, 133, 135
brain 8, 19, 45, 47, 50–1
breathing 104
breathing system 18, 37, 38–9
bronchus 105
Buckland, William 133
budding 122
byproducts 99
cancer 110–11
capillaries 40, 41, 42
carbohydrates 70, 131, 154
carbon cycle 131, 161

carbon dioxide 9, 99
    diffusion in the lungs 105
    photosynthesis 128, 153
    in respiration 8, 37, 38, 40
    test for 112
carbon monoxide 109
carbon recycling 131, 161
carpel 92
cartilage 44, 45
catalysts 79
cell division 96, 141
cells 16–17, 18, 19, 20, 118–9, 133, 153
    bacteria 125
    blood 108
    egg 92
    protoctists 119, 128–9
    respiration 38, 40
    sex 90, 92
    surface area 80–81
    villus 83
    yeast 122–3
cellulose 154
central nervous system 170
characteristics of organisms 86, 134
chlorophyll 17, 99, 128–9, 150
chloroplasts 17, 99, 119, 129, 150
chromosomes 125, 140–1
    sex chromosomes 141
cilia 27, 35, 104, 128
circulatory system 18, 38, 41
classification 86–7, 135
clear writing 181
collagen 183
combustion 103
communicable diseases 166
communities 59, 177
comparison of systems 171
competition 62, 68, 97, 144–5, 156, 176
concentration gradient 179
constipation 70
continuous variation 135, 174
control systems 170–1
correlation 110, 138
Crick, Francis 140
criteria 37, 49
criteria for farming 149
crops 149, 158, 161
cross-breeding of crops 157
cross-pollination 93
cuticle 153
daily changes 61
Darwin, Charles 147
decay 130–1
decomposers 130–1, 156
deficiency diseases 74, 178
depressants 51
diagnosis 168
diaphragm 8, 37, 38, 39
diet 30, 70, 74–5, 165
diffusion 82, 105, 118, 153, 179
digestion 78–9
digestive system 8, 18, 37
dinosaurs 133
discontinuous variation 135
diseases 165, 166–7
    distribution 177
    treating 120–1, 172–3
DNA 122, 133, 140–1

dormancy 98
drugs 30, 50–2
ears 45, 46
ecological audits 158–9
ecology 176–7
ecosystems 59, 63, 130, 144
effectors 170
egestion 78, 97
egg cells 24–5, 27, 28, 34, 35, 59
embryos 28, 29, 30, 35, 96
emphysema 109
endangered species 24, 26, 32–3, 36, 144
energy 66
    respiration and 7, 38, 47
    transfer 72–3
environment 58–65, 134
environmental factors 134
environmental planners 65
environmental variation 134–5
enzymes 124, 130, 173, 183
epidemiology 110–11
epidermis cells 153
estimates 88–9, 107, 138, 176
eutrophication 160
evaporation 19
evidence 5, 21
evolution 147
excess post-exercise oxygen consumption (EPOC) 115
excretion 7, 8, 37, 38
exercise, aerobic 114
extinction 22, 24, 26, 32, 36, 62, 87, 144–5, 148
eyepiece lens 14
faeces 78, 97
farming 149
farming problems 160–1
fats 70, 131, 154
fermentation 123, 124
fermenters 173
fertilisation 24–5, 28–9, 90, 96–7, 136
fertilisers 156, 160
fibre, dietary 70
filaments 92
fitness 37
flagella 125
foetus 32–3
food 7, 8, 18, 33, 37
    plants 7, 9, 17
food chains and webs 62–3, 66–7, 129, 145
food labelling 69, 70–1, 84
foodpipe 8, 37
food technology 76–7
food testing 71
food webs 145
forces 46, 47
Franklin, Rosalind 140
fruits 96
fuels 72
fungi 119, 122–3
fungicides 156
fuse 24, 136
gametes 24–5, 26, 59, 90, 92, 136
gas exchange 104–5, 112–3, 153
gas exchange system 38
gene banks 145
genes 122, 136, 140–1, 142, 144–5
genetic counselling 142–3

genetic disorders 172
genetic information 136, 144
genetically engineered bacteria 173
genetically modified bacteria 173
genus 86, 133
germination 96, 98–9, 155
gestation period 30–1
gills 113
gland cells 170
glands 171
global warming 161
glucose 103, 114–5, 124, 150
    in photosynthesis 128
greener cities 62–3
growth 7, 73, 98–9, 123
    curves 123
guard cells 153
gullet 8, 37, 78
gut 78–9
habitat 176
haemoglobin 108, 114
half-life measurement 169
health 73
heart 5, 12–13, 17, 18, 29, 40
    and circulation 8, 12, 18, 37, 40, 41, 42–3
heart attack 75, 109
heart disease 75, 109
herbicides (weedkillers) 156
hibernation 61
hormonal system 171
hormones 171
hormones, sex 34, 36, 52
human organs 8–9
human reproduction 26–9
hybrids 55, 90
hydrogen carbonate indicator 112
hygiene 121, 165
hypotheses 22–3, 42
immunisation 165
immunity 167
implantation 28
impulses 47, 51, 170
indicators 112
infectious diseases 166
ingestion 78, 167
inheritance 90, 139
inherited variation 136–7
insecticides 156
insect pests 156
insoluble substances 78
intentional bias 162–3
interdependence 63, 99, 131
International Union for Conservation of Nature (IUCN) 158
interquartile range 174–5
intestines 78, 82–3
    large 78
    small 78, 82–3
joints 45
journals, scientific 133
keys (biological) 125
kidneys 8, 37
kilojoule (kJ) 72
kingdoms of organisms 86, 119
kwashiorkor 74
labelling of foods 69, 70–1, 84
labour 31

lactic acid 114–5, 124
large intestine 8, 37, 78
leaves 7, 9, 19, 60, 61
life cycles 35, 36, 99
life expectancy 165
life processes 6–7
ligaments 45
light 60, 153
limewater 112–3
limiting factor 123, 150
line of best fit 57
lipids 70, 154
liver 8, 37, 42, 50, 78
locomotor system 18, 46–7
lung cancer 110–11
lungs 8, 18, 37, 38, 39, 41, 44, 50, 104–5, 110–11
lymphocytes 167
magnification 14–15, 17
malnutrition 74
mammary glands 31
McNamara, Dr Tracy 168
mean values 107, 139
median values 138, 174
medicines 172
memory cells (lymphocytes) 167
menopause 27, 35
menstrual cycle 35
microorganisms 79, 118
microscopes 14–15, 16, 17, 20
microvilli 83
migration 61
mineral salts 73, 99, 152
minerals (in the diet) 70, 73
mitochondria 17, 47, 98, 108
mode 138
models 79
movement 6, 45
multicellular organisms 118
muscle cells 17, 39, 47, 170
muscles 18, 38, 39, 45, 46–7, 51, 114
native species 144
natural selection 146–7
nectary 92
nerves 19, 47
nervous system 18, 19, 45, 47, 51, 170
night blindness 74
nitrates 155
nocturnal animals 61
non-communicable diseases 166
normal distribution 56, 137, 174
nucleus (cell) 17, 20, 26, 27, 28, 39, 41, 136, 141
nutrients 12, 18, 35, 40, 70–1, 72–3, 160
nutrition 7, 8, 37
obesity 75
observations 22, 42
oesophagus 78
offspring 24, 25, 35, 36, 55, 136
oils 53, 70, 154
organic farming 149, 164
organic molecules 128
organisms 6–7, 24, 53
    and environment 58–61, 64–5
    variation 54–61
organs 5, 8–9, 12–13, 18–20, 37, 44
organ systems 18–19, 37
osmosis 179
ovaries 27, 28, 29, 34, 35, 52, 92
ovulation 35
ovules 92
oxygen 35, 40, 99, 114
    in blood 12, 18, 41, 105, 108–9

debt 115
lack of 109
    in respiration 7, 8, 37, 38, 40, 102–3, 122
    saturation ('sats') 102
palisade cells 153
pandemics 180
parents 136
partially permeable membranes 179
Pasteur, Louis 122, 124, 132
pathogens 120, 165, 166
penis 26, 28, 34
pesticides 67, 156, 160–1
pests of crops 156
petals 92
phagocytes 167
phloem vessels 151, 154
photosynthesis 9, 17, 61, 99, 113, 128, 150–1
physical environmental factors 58, 134
pie charts 126–7
placenta 28, 29, 30, 31, 35
plague 117, 132
plants 85, 100, 119
    adaptations 152–3
    classification 86–7
    gas exchange 113
    products 154–5
    protection 158–9
    reactions 150–1
plant organs 9
plant tissue 13
plasma 41, 82, 108
Plot, Robert 133
poisons 67
pollen grains 92–3
pollen tubes 96
pollination 92–3
polymers 154
populations 89
population size 176
predation 63, 176
predators 63
predictions 22–3
pregnancy 27, 28–9, 30–1
premature 31
pressure 29, 104
prey 63
probability 138–9
    inheritance 139
producers 129
products of a reaction 150
prokaryotes 119, 125
prosthetics 48–9
proteins 70, 131, 155
protoctists 119, 128–9
pseudopods 128
puberty 26, 27, 34–5
pulse rate 40, 43, 107, 116
pyramid of numbers 66, 129
quadrats 89
quartiles 174–5
random sampling 89, 163
range of measurements 106
rates of reaction 150
raw materials 70, 150
reaction times 51
receptor cells 170
recreational drugs 51
rectum 8, 37
recycling carbon 131
red blood cells 73, 108
Redi, Francesco 23
Reference Intakes (RIs) 75

relationships between variables 57
replicating viruses 172
reproduction 6, 22, 30–1, 35, 36, 55, 90–1, 122
    asexual 91, 122
    sexual 24–30, 59, 90, 136
reproductive system 26–7, 34–5
resources 98, 134
respiration 7, 8, 17, 37, 38, 40, 47, 72, 98
    aerobic 102–3, 122, 151
    anaerobic 114–5, 122–3, 124, 131
rickets 74
root hair cells 17, 19, 152
roots 9, 13, 19
runners 91
saliva 78
salivary glands 78
salty seas 146–7
samples 138, 176
sampling organisms 89
scatter graphs 57
scientific journals 133
scientific method 22–3, 42–3
scientific papers 133
scrotum 26
scurvy 74
seasonal changes 61
seed coat 96
seed dispersal 97
seeds 96–7, 155
selective breeding of crops 157
selective herbicides 156
self-pollination 93
sense organs 170
sensitivity 7
sepals 92
sex cells 24, 59
sex chromosomes 141
sex hormones 34, 36, 52
sexual reproduction 24, 30, 59, 90, 136
side-effects 50
skeleton 44–5, 46
small intestine 8, 37, 78, 82–3
smoking 30, 31, 50, 51, 110
soil 7, 9, 13
soluble substances 78
solvent 179
solvents 51
specialised cells 17
species 54, 55, 86, 133, 176
specimens 14–15
sperm cells 24–5, 26, 28, 34, 59
spinal cord 19, 47, 170
stamens 92
starch 70, 99, 154
starvation 75
statement keys 125
statistics 138–9
STEM 10–11
stems 9
sterilisation 173
stigmas 92
stimulants 51
stimuli 170
stomach 8, 37, 78
stomata 113, 153
storage organs 9
styles 92
substance misuse 50
sugars 70, 122–3
surface area 41, 152
    calculation 80–1
    of the lungs 105

surface area : volume (SA:V) 81, 118, 178–9
sustainable development 161
symbol equations 150
symptoms of disease 166
systematic error 163
systems
    comparing 171
    hormonal 171
    nervous 170
tar (in tobacco smoke) 109
target cells 171
target organs 171
teeth 184
tendons 45
testes 26, 34, 52
tissue fluid 108
tissues 12–13, 16–17, 18, 19, 20
    fat 12, 18
    muscle 12, 18, 39
    nerve 18
    root hair 13, 19
    xylem 13, 19
trachea 8, 37, 38, 105
training 116
transgenic bacteria 173
transgenic organisms 172–3
tubers 91
transplants 20
ultrasound 30
umbilical cord 29, 31
unicellular organisms 118
urinary system 18, 19
urine 5, 7, 8, 10, 26, 37, 58
uterus 27, 28, 29, 31, 35
vaccines 121, 124, 167, 172
vacuole 17, 128
vagina 27, 28, 31, 35
validity 163
variables 56–7
    dependent 56
    independent 56
variation 54–61, 90, 133
    continuous 54, 55, 56, 135
    discontinuous 57, 54, 55, 56, 135
    environmental 60–1, 134–5
    inherited 59, 136–7
variety of crops 161
variety of plants 157
veins 40, 108
ventilation 39, 104
vertebrae 44, 45
veterinary science 168–9
vets 168
villi 83
viruses 32, 33, 67, 119, 168
vitamins 70, 73, 74
Wallace, Alfred Russel 147
waste (from organisms) 7, 8, 37, 40
water 152
Watson, James 140
weedkiller (herbicides) 156
white blood cells 108, 167
Wilkins, Maurice 140
wilts 152
windpipe 8, 37, 38
word equations 98, 103
writing clearly 181
xylem vessels 152
yeasts 122–3
yield 156
yoghurt 124–5
zygotes 24, 27, 90, 96, 136, 141

Photographs
(Key: T-top; B-bottom; C-Centre; L-left; R-right)
123RF: Rune Kristoffersen 004cl1, Tul Chalothonrangsee 004cl2, Nico Smit 006br, Pat138241 007tr, Atic12 012t, Sebastian Kaulitzki 018bl/B, 018br, 019tc/D, 019tr/E, PaylessImages 38tc, Mykhailo Orlov 46tc, Konstantin Pelikh 49, Stockbroker 54b, Ondrej Prosicky 58l, Christian Mueringer 60c(inset), Filmfoto 60c, Michael Lane 67c/F, Denis and Yulia Pogostins 091cr/E, Pan Xunbin 099br/D, G215 099br/D, Petr Bukal 099br/D, Modfos 131tr/E, Mikepaschos 133tr, Danny Kosmayer 133br, Rune Kristoffersen 134bl, Tul Chalothonrangsee 134br, Borirak Mongkolget 136tl/A, Choo Poh Guan 136t/A, Rafcha 136tc/A, Maxpayne222 136tr/A, Joy Prescott 146bl, Dbvirago 148tr, Noppharat Manakul 153tl, Zvonko Djuric 154br, Pathiphan Nanthasarn 160tr, Ximagination 161cl, Sebastian Kaulitzki 41r**,** Viktor Shnyra 157cl, Aliaksei Marchanka 158tr, Vladislav Gajic 159tr; **Alamy Stock Photo:** Nigel Cattlin 156tr, Suzanne Long 098bl/B, Zizza Gordon - Panama Wildlife 179tl, Photo Researchers/Science History Images 180tr, Dpa Picture Alliance Archive 180cl, BJ Warnick/Newscom 180cr, Tom Uhlman 036c, Fotoknips/Mauritius images GmbH 004cl1, William Arthur 005bl, Martin Shields 007tl, Oliver Burston/Ikon Images 008b, Julian Stratenschulte/Dpa picture alliance 009tr, Voisin/Phanie 010t, US East Coast Photos 012b, Scenics & Science 013r, Birgit Reitz-Hofmann 016c/A, Photo Researchers/Science History Images 016l/A, World History Archive 016b, Scenics & Science 019bl/G, Nigel Cattlin 019bc/G, David Chapman 021bl, Blickwinkel/Meyers 025b, David Hosking 025c, Dmitry Naumov 030r, Jessie Cohen-Smithsonian's National Zoo via CNP/BJ Warnick/Newscom 033bl, Photo Researchers/Science History Images 42b, Simone Janssen 54t, Dylan Beckshot 54l, Ozgur Coskun 55c, Rick & Nora Bowers 58r, C.W. Jefferys/The Granger Collection 60t, Kevin Maskell 61c(inset), David Chapman 61c, Jim West 62t, Flpa 63c, Sorin Colac 64r, Blickwinkel/McPhoto/Pum 67t, Julian Stratenschulte/ dpa picture alliance 67r/F, Friedrich Stark 68t, Jeff Morgan 07 069t, Food Collection 069b, Dr Lr/Bsip SA 074b/C, Mike Greenslade/Australia 076b, Javier Larrea/ Age footstock 077, Sue Wilson 079c/B, Steffen Hauser/ Botanikfoto 085tc/A, Joerg Boethling 085tr/A, IanDagnall Computing 085b, Dpa picture alliance archive 088cr/B, Kevin Galvin 090cl/B, Rolf Nussbaumer Photography 092cr/C, Martin Siepmann/ ImageBROKER 093cl/F, Callista Images 093cr/G, Ruffer/ Agencja Fotograficzna Caro 094b, Custom Life Science Images 096bc/C, The Photolibrary Wales 101tr/A, Nealehaynes.com 07831659607/Buzz Pictures 101bl/C, Education & Exploration 1 103bl, Pako Mera 105bl/E, Photo Researchers/Science History Images 117tr/A, ART Collection 117l/B, David Shale/Nature Picture Library 118tr/A, BSIP SA 122tr/A, Mediscan 122cl/B, Photo Researchers/Science History Images 125cr/E, GL Archive 126tr/A, 914 collection 126cl/B, Crossrail/Amer Ghazzal/Alamy Live News 132bl, Nobumichi Tamura/ Stocktrek Images, Inc. 133bl, Fotoknips/Mauritius images GmbH 134bc, Photo Researchers/Science History Images 140tr,140cr, Mediscan 141cr. Chronicle 144cr1, Kat Woronowicz/ZUMA Press, Inc 145cr, Andrei Tkachev/Itar-Tass News Agency 148cl, Martin Shields 150bl, Nigel Cattlin 152bc, Martin Shields 155bc, Mediscan 109tr/D, Doug Perrine/Nature Picture Library 128bl, Anastasia Ika 159bl, Blickwinkel/Hartl 160cl, BJ Warnick/Newscom 168tr, Jake Lyell 168cl, Ami Vitale/ National Geographic Image Collection 169cr, See Li/ Alamy Live 171tr, Christine Whitehead 172tr, Mathew B Brady/Archive Pics 172bl, Usaid 176tr, Leo Francini 176c, Paul R. sterry/Nature Photographers Ltd 176bl, Nigel Cattlin 176bc, Andrew Woodley 181br, Pavel Chernobrivets 183tr; **Blackthorn Arable Ltd:** Martyn Cox 156cr,157tr; **Chantal Abergel:** 167bl**; Centers for Disease Control and Prevention:** 51t**,** James Gathany 166cl, Centers for Disease Control and Prevention/Public Health Image Library 117br/C; **Djibouti Nature:** Houssein Rayaleh 100cl/B; **David Good (The Good Project):** 59c, 53b; **Dr Ajanta Haldar and American Journal of Blood Research:** 143br; **DK Images:** Peter Anderson 009cl, David Murray 41b, Peter Gardner 091bl/F, Derek Hall 097c/Fa, DK Images 113cl/E, Dave King 122bl/C; **Dr. Gunther von Hagens, BODY WORLDS, Institute for Plastination:** 38tr, 38b; **Elsevier:** Andrew Wade 184cr; **Food Standards Agency/Crown Copyright:** Food Standards Agency/ Crown Copyright: Department of Health in association with the Welsh Assembly Government, the Scottish Government and the Food Standards Agency in Northern Ireland 074t; **Getty Images:** The Sydney Morning Herald/Fairfax Media 004br, Ariel Skelley/ DigitalVision 010b, VI-Images/Getty Images sports 011t, Jose Luis Pelaez Inc/DigitalVision 011b, Brain J. Skerry/National Geographic 025t, Phill Magakoe/AFP 026t, Kali9/E+ 029tl, Marwan Naamani/AFP 48t, Laurence Griffiths/Getty Images sport 52t, Pool JO SYDNEY 2000/Gamma-Rapho 52tr, Doug Pensinger/ Getty Images sport 52b, Tui De Roy/Minden Pictures 53t, George Grall/National Geographic Image Collection 59t, Tessa Bunney/Corbis 68t, Issouf Sanogo/AFP 074b/B, Sovfoto/Universal Images Group 075t, Pool JO SYDNEY 2000/Gamma-Rapho 101cl/B, William Parker/UK Press 113cr/F, Patrick Aventurier/ Gamma-Rapho 114tr/A. The Sydney Morning Herald/ Fairfax Media 115bl/E, Fred VIELCANET/Gamma-Rapho 123br, The Sydney Morning Herald/Fairfax Media 135br, John Shearer/WireImage 136bl, Vince Bucci/ Stringer/Getty Images Entertainment 143tl, Daniel Mihailescu/Afp 170br; **Home Office:** OGL 182cl; **Ireland's Revenue Customs Service:** 182cr; **IUCN:** 159tl; **Minden Pictures:** Konrad Wothe 100tr/A; **Mark Levesley:** 073br; **NASA:** 007cl, Don Davis 144tr; **NHS Blood and Transplant:** 020br/C; **Ottobock:** 48br**; Olympus Europa Holding GmbH:** Olympus Europa Holding GmBH/2013/Automated fluorescence microscope BX63 from Olympus 016r/A**; Press Association Images:** John Stillwell/PA Archive 005tr; **Pearson Education, Inc.:** Trevor Clifford 014tl/A,014tr/B,014cl/C,014cr/D,014bl/E,015tl/A,015tr/ B,015bl/C,015br/D, Image Source 102tr/A, Trevor Clifford 59b, Pearson Education, Inc 071cl,071cr, 071b, 106tr/A, Tsz-shan Kwok 084cl/B, Trevor Clifford 123tr/D, John Foxx Collection/Imagestate 149tr, Sozaijiten 161cr, Tsz-shan Kwok 084cl/B; **Reuters:** Finbarr O'Reilly 165bl, Sergio Moraes 130br, Anton Meres 072, Enrique Marcarian 173cr, Marcos Brinidicci 079tr/C, Alexandra Beier 020l/B, Reuters 53c; **Royal Zoological Society of Scotland:** Royal Zoological Society of Scotland/Edinburgh Zoo 022; **Shutterstock:** MicheleB 55b, Zuzule 55b, Alexey Goosev 55b, Wolfgang Berroth 156tr, Fleckner 112tl/A, D. Kucharski K. Kucharska 113br/G, Wael hamdan 060tr, Gail Johnson 006bl, Rob Byron 007cr, Tolmachevr 007bl, Mikeledray 012c, Sebastian Kawlitzki 013tl, Krichie 013c, Prostock-studio 013b, yd39 004tr, Rawpixel.com 004cr, Jose Luis Calvo 018tl, 018c/A, Mikeledray 018cl/A, Meoita 018bl/A, Olesia Bilkei 019c/F, Pan Xunbin 019br/G, Komsan Loonprom 020t/A,020b/A, Ulrich22 009cr, Reynardt 031b, Max Earey 032b, Gigajoe 033t, Hung Chung Chih 033br, Shutterstock 091cr/D, 021tr, Solent News 021cr, loflo69 024t, Sebastian Kaulitzki 028t, Iwaew 034b, Matka Wariatka 035b, Fauren 034tl/A, Curioso 034tr/A, Justin Black 036t, HansMusa 037tl/A, Fotokostic 37bl/A, Geoffrey Kuchera 37tr/A, Rei Imagine 37br/A, Alexander Raths 37b, Stockphoto-graf 50tr/A, Aksenova Natalya 50t1/A, Gorodenkoff 40t, Caimacanul 43b, Poznyakov 43b, Watchares Hansawek 46c, HelloRF Zcool 48bl, Jakkrit Orrasri 44t, Reha Mark 45t, Cherries 55t, Chantal de Bruijne 54c, Elnavegante 58c, Dwph 60b, Danita Delmont 61t, Feathercollector 61b(inset), Nick Pecker 61b, Robert cicchetti 62b, Ariyaphol Jiwalak 64tr, Uladzimir zgurski 64l, Shutterstock 65, Alila Medical Media 184tr, Necla bayraktar 181tr, Luiz Kagiyama 179tc, JhveePhoto 177cr, Natulrich 166br, Eileen_10 168br, Ratikova 160br, N-studio 161c, Lars Christensen 161c, Milart 161cr, Rsooll 161bl, Ajcespedes 164tr, Muddy Knees 164cl, Toey Toey 170tr, Linas T 152tr, Ethan Daniels 151br, IanRedding 146tr, Macklin Holloway 146br, Warpaint 147, Brad Thompson 144cr2, IrinaK 145tl, Eric Isselee 145tc, Kzenon 136cr, 137, PureSolution 139, Eric Isselee 130tr, Stephen Farhall 130cr, Lars Christensen 131b/F(ii), 108MotionBG 131bl/ F(i), Stefan Petru Andronache 131bl/F(iii), Milart 131bl/ F(iv), 066c, Rsooll 131bl/F(v), Bernhard Richter 133cr, lyd39 134tr, Rawpixel.com 135tr, Picturepartners 125tr/C, Damsea 119bl, Nikita G. Bernadsky 120t, Africa Studio 121tr/C, Pendakisolo 114br/C, Darkocv 116tc/A, Pavel1964 116tr/A, JonMilnes 109tl/C, Choksawatdikorn 109bl/E, Kateryna Kon 109br/E, Caimacanul 107cr/E, Bogdan Wankowicz 098tr/A, Rattiya Thongdumhyu 099cr/C, Marilyn barbone 099br/D, Madlen 099br/D, Djgis 099br/D, Roger Meerts 100bl/C, Jeannette Lambert 096br/D, Valentyn Volkov 097tc/E, Djgis 097tr/E, Brian A Jackson 097cr/Fb, Ethan Daniels 097bc/Fc, Rkakoka 092c/B, Royaltystockphoto. com 093cr/H, Artem kutsenko 090tl/A, Anna Kucherova 090tc/A, 12photography 090tr/A, Elena Masiutkina, Danny E Hooks 085c/A, Szefei 087cr/D, Samib123 089cl/E, Trekandshoot 080tr/A, You Touch Pix of EuToch 080cl/B, Brian A Jackson 084tr/A, Rigsbyphoto 080c/B, Sheila Fitzgerald 080bl1/C, Keith Homan 080bl2/C, Txking 075c, Radu Bercan 076t, Siriporn prasertsri 073cr, Food Travel Stockforlife 070cr, AnglianArt 070b, Stefan Petru Andronache 66c, Johnfoto18 66l, Eric Isselee 66r, Kuttelvaserova Stuchelova 67l/F, Pedarilhos 68b, Lebendkulturen.de 128tl/A,128tr, Evlakhov Valeriy 129bl/G(i), Johannes Kornelius 129bl/G(ii), Alexander Vasilyev 141tr; **Science Source:** Ted Kinsman 032t; **Superstock:** D. Parer & E. Parer-Cook/Minden Pictures 112tr/B; **Science Photo Library:** Alexander Tsiaras 008t, Animated Healthcare Ltd 017tr, Dr Alvin Telser/Visuals Unlimited Inc 017r/C, Herve Conge, ISM 017bc/E, Animated Healthcare Ltd 018tr, Steve Gschmeissner 47b, Dennis Kunkel Microscopy 079cl/B, Voisin/Phanie 106cl/B, Martin M. Rotker 108tr/A, St.Bartholomew's Hospital 110b, Kwangshin Kim 124cl/B, Dennis Kunkel Microscopy 132tr, A. Barrington Brown, Gonville & Caius College 140tl, 140br, Peggy Greb/US department of agriculture 142bl, Martin Bond 149bl, Power and Syred 153bl, Michael P. Gadomski 157bl, Bill Barksdale/Agstockusa 162tr, Biology Media 167br, Aj Photo 024b, Alain Gougeon/Ism 027c, Dr G. Moscoso 029c, Bernard Benoit 030l, Sheila Terry 42t, Frans Lanting/Mint Images 67(egg), Custom Medical Stock Photo 51tc, Martin Oeggerli 094c, Peggy Greb/US Department Of Agriculture 076c, Dr Keith Wheeler 097br/Fd, Medical Photo NHS Lothian 45c, Innerspace Imaging 178tr, Biophoto Associates 178cr, Steve Gschmeissner 179bc, Philippe Psaila 176cr, Martyn F. Chillmaid 177br; **University of Wisconsin:** University of Wisconsin/Mike Clayton/Plant Teaching Collection 154tr; **Visuals Unlimited, Inc.:** Carolina Biological Supply Co 090br/C, Simko 124tr/A; **Wellcome Images:** Wessex Reg. Genetics Centre 141tc.